STRATEGIC MANAGEMENT THEORY

STRATEGIC MANAGEMENT THEORY

An Integrated Approach

CHARLES W. L. HILL
University of Washington

GARETH R. JONES
Texas A & M University

HOUGHTON MIFFLIN COMPANY   **Boston**   **Toronto**
Dallas   Geneva, Illinois   Palo Alto   Princeton, New Jersey

Senior Sponsoring Editor:	Patrick Boles
Development Editor:	Julie Hogenboom
Project Editor:	Liza Martina
Assistant Design Manager:	Pat Mahtani
Cover & Interior Designer:	Sandra González
Production Coordinator:	Renée Le Verrier
Manufacturing Coordinator:	Sharon Pearson
Marketing Manager:	Mary Jo Conrad/Diane McOscar

Cover Photo: Michael Tcherevkoff/The Image Bank

Printed in the U.S.A.

Library of Congress Catalog Card Number: 91-71987

ISBN: 0-395-62135-6

CDEFGHIJ–D–98765432

For my wife Jennifer
        G.R.J.
For Alexandra, Elizabeth, and Charlotte
        C.W.L.H.

Contents

Preface

The favorable reception of the first edition of *Strategic Management Theory: An Integrated Approach* has led us to build and expand upon its principles for the second edition. We utilized feedback from users of the first edition to increase the book's value. We have maintained comprehensive and up-to-date coverage of the burgeoning strategic management literature. We have reexamined the balance between strategy formulation and strategy implementation and added to the flow of material so that a more comprehensive picture of the strategic management process is created.

Comprehensive and Up-To-Date Coverage

In many places we have added to the text to expand and improve our coverage of relevant material. From the most current research, we have created new chapters and improved existing ones. In particular, we have greatly expanded our treatment of business and corporate level strategy by writing two completely new chapters and revising three from the last edition. Some of the additional material discussed includes the following.

- New material on managerial motives, ethics, and social responsibility (Chapter 2).
- Discussion of the role of distinctive competences and barriers to imitation in building and sustaining a company's competitive advantage (Chapter 4).
- A view of the strategic implications of flexible manufacturing systems, design for manufacturing, total quality control, just-in-time inventory systems, and self-managing work teams (Chapter 4).
- Discussion of the way in which competition at the business level often revolves around how a company can pursue a cost leadership and a differentiation strategy simultaneously (Chapter 5).
- A new chapter on the relationship between business-level strategy and industry structure (Chapter 6). This outlines how the characteristics of different industry environments affect the way a firm chooses to compete. For example, we discuss how innovating companies in emerging industries can establish and exploit a first-mover advantage. We discuss how pricing strategy, capacity-expansion strategy, and strategy towards suppliers and distributors becomes a crucial competitive weapon in mature consolidated industries. And we discuss strategies for coping with industry decline.
- Due to the increased interest in global strategy, we have split our corporate-level strategy chapter into two new chapters. Chapter 7 deals with vertical integration and diversification, and Chapter 8 deals with global competition

and global strategy. In each of these chapters we offer an account of the latest research and thinking. Included are discussions of long-term contracting and strategic alliances as alternatives to vertical integration and diversification (Chapter 7), and the strategic characteristics of the transnational corporation (Chapter 8).

- New sections on joint ventures and strategic alliances as ways of securing a competitive advantage in new industry environments (Chapter 9).
- A new look at how to design structure so as to simultaneously secure a low cost and a differentiation advantage, and a new look at global strategy and the choice of the appropriate structure and control systems to implement the strategy (Chapter 12).

Balanced and Integrated Progression of Topics

We have incorporated this new material into our existing framework in a way that preserves the balance and flow of the text. As in the first edition, this book is designed so that each chapter builds upon the previous. The new chapters on business and corporate-level strategy provide students with a strong foundation for understanding the process of value creation that underlies strategic management.

In addition, we have maintained our approach of going beyond the uncritical presentation of text material, to debate at length the strengths and weaknesses of various strategic management techniques, and the advantages and disadvantages of different strategies and structures. Our objective continues to be to demonstrate to students that in the real world, strategic issues are inevitably complex, and necessarily involve a consideration of pros and cons, and a willingness to accept tradeoffs. At the same time we have made the text very accessible to students.

To achieve balance we have not allowed any one disciplinary orientation to determine the content of this text. In addition to the strategic management literature, we have drawn on the literature of economics, marketing, organizational theory, operations management, finance, and international business. The perspective of this book is truly strategic in that it integrates the contributions of these diverse disciplines into a comprehensive whole.

Instructor's Resource Manual

We have maintained and refined the format of the Instructor's Resource Manual that users found so beneficial last time. For each chapter in the book there is a **synopsis,** a list of **teaching objectives,** a **lecture outline, answers** to **discussion questions,** a comprehensive set of **true/false** and **multiple choice questions** and **answers,** and **transparency masters** for most of the figures and tables. In addition we offer sample **course outlines** for the material that we have class-tested and found to be very effective.

Teaching Aids

With the second edition of *Strategic Management Theory,* we offer an expansive support package to meet your teaching needs.

First, a package of 75 **color transparencies** accompanies the book. These include nearly all of the art found in the text. In addition, transparency masters of most of the book's figures and tables can be found in the Instructor's Resource Manual.

Second, *Policy Expert,* a **software package** for case analysis is available with the book. This software package allows students to input financial data and perform several kinds of strategic and financial analyses. These include the calculation of a wide variety of business formulas, the carrying out of "what if" scenarios, the development of strategic management models in an expert system, and other applied applications useful for case analysis and presentation.

Together, the Instructor's Resource Manual and teaching aids provide an integrated package that supports the approach we have taken throughout the book. Further details for using the support package can be found in the Instructor's Resource Manual.

Acknowledgments

This book is far more than the product of two authors. We wish to thank the Departments of Management at the University of Washington and Texas A & M University for providing the setting and atmosphere in which the book could be written, and the students of these universities who reacted to and provided input for many of our ideas. In addition, the following reviewers provided valuable suggestions for improving the manuscript from its original form to its current form.

Thomas H. Berliner
The University of Texas at Dallas

Geoffrey Brooks
Western Oregon State College

Gene R. Conaster
Golden State University

Eliezer Geisler
Northeastern Illinois University

Lynn Godkin
Lamar University

W. Grahm Irwin
Miami University

Geoffrey King
California State University—Fullerton

Robert J. Litschert
Virginia Polytechnic Institute and
State University

Lance A. Masters
California State University—
San Bernadino

Joanna Mulholland
West Chester University of
Pennsylvania

Malika Richards
Indiana University

Joseph A. Schenk
University of Dayton

Barbara Spencer
Clemson University

Robert P. Vichas
Florida Atlantic University

Bobby Vaught
Southwest Missori State

Finally, thanks are due to our families for their patience and support during the course of this revision process. We would like to thank our wives, Alexandra Hill and Jennifer George, for their ever increasing support and affection.

C.W.L.H.

G.R.J.

STRATEGIC
MANAGEMENT

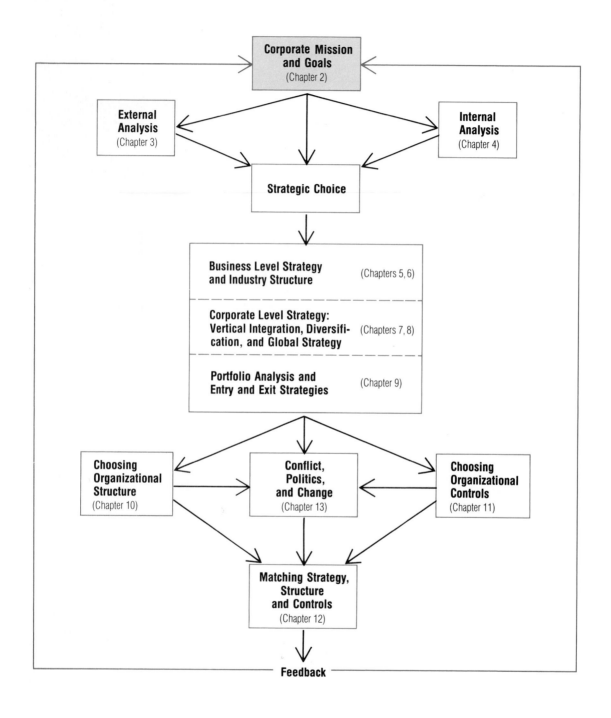

P A R T

I

INTRODUCTION

Chapter 1

THE STRATEGIC MANAGEMENT PROCESS

1.1 OPENING INCIDENT: ROYAL DUTCH/SHELL

Royal Dutch/Shell, the world's largest oil company, is well known for its addiction to strategic planning. Despite the fact that many management gurus and CEOs now consider strategic planning an anachronism, Shell is convinced that long-term strategic planning has served the company well. Part of the reason for this success is that at Shell, planning does not take the form of complex and inflexible ten-year plans generated by a team of corporate strategists far removed from operating realities. Rather, planning involves the generation of a series of "what if" scenarios whose function is to try to get general managers at all levels of the corporation to think strategically about the environment in which they do business.

The strength of Shell's scenario-based planning system was perhaps most evident during the early 1980s. At that time, the price of a barrel of oil was hovering at around $30. With exploration and development costs running at an industry average of around $11 per barrel, most oil companies were making record profits. Moreover, industry analysts were generally bullish; many were predicting that oil prices would increase to around $50 per barrel by 1990. Shell, however, was mulling over a handful of future scenarios, one of which included the possibility of a breakdown of the OPEC oil cartel's agreement to restrict supply, an oil glut, and a drop in oil prices to $15 per barrel. In 1984 Shell instructed the managers of its operating companies to indicate how they would respond to a $15 per barrel world. This "game" set off some serious work at Shell exploring the question "What will we do if it happens?"

By early 1986 the consequences of the "game" included efforts to cut exploration costs by pioneering advanced exploration technologies, massive investments in cost-efficient refining facilities, and a process of weeding out the least-profitable service stations. All this planning occurred at a time when most oil companies were busy diversifying outside the oil business rather than trying to improve the efficiency of their core operations. As it turned out, the price of oil was still $27 per barrel in early January 1986. But the failure of the OPEC cartel to set new production ceilings in 1985, new production from the North Sea and Alaska, and declining demand due to increased conservation efforts had created a growing oil glut. In late January the dam burst. By February 1 oil was priced at $17 per barrel, and by April the price was $10 per barrel.

Because Shell had already visited the $15 per

barrel world, it had gained a head start over its rivals in its cost-cutting efforts. As a result, by 1989 the company's average oil and gas exploration costs were less than $2 per barrel, compared with an industry average of $4 per barrel. Moreover, in the crucial refining and marketing sector Shell made a net return on assets of 8.4 percent in 1988, more than double the 3.8 percent average of the other oil majors: Exxon, BP, Chevron, Mobil, and Texaco.

As Shell enters the 1990s, its future scenarios depict a world of radical environmentalism, initially among private consumers, and then increasingly among nation-states. In anticipation of this trend, Shell's strategies for the 1990s stress products that are less environmentally harmful. Shell started investing in capacity to produce unleaded gasoline earlier than many of its competitors and last year sold more unleaded gasoline than any other oil company worldwide. By 1989 nearly 60 percent of the gasoline it sold was unleaded—a quarter as much again as the industry average—compared with 30 percent in 1984. Natural gas, which is less environmentally harmful than oil, is the other main part of Shell's green plan. Shell is currently investing $700 million in a synthesis plant in Malaysia that will convert natural gas into refined oil products. In addition, Shell is well down the road toward developing an economical process for converting natural gas to gasoline. The conversion will not pay unless oil prices stabilize above $20 per barrel, but Shell's future scenarios see that price level as likely by the end of the century.[1]

1.2 OVERVIEW

Why do some organizations succeed and others fail? What makes some profit-seeking organizations, such as IBM, Hewlett-Packard, Royal Dutch/Shell, and the pharmaceutical giant Merck, excellent performers year after year, while others, such as Chrysler, Navistar International Corporation, and USX, go through periods during which they struggle to survive? Why have some not-for-profit organizations, such as the United Way, been able to build up a stable constituency of charitable givers, while others, such as Farm Aid, have been unable to sustain their operations for any length of time? An answer can be found in the subject matter of this book: strategic management. We consider the advantages that accrue to organizations that think strategically. We also examine how organizations that understand both their operating environment and their own internal strengths and weaknesses can identify and exploit strategies successfully.

The techniques that we discuss are relevant to many different kinds of organizations: from large, multibusiness enterprises to small, one-person enterprises; from manufacturing enterprises to service enterprises; and from publicly held profit-seeking corporations to not-for-profit organizations. Although we tend to think of strategic management as primarily concerned with profit-seeking organizations, even a small not-for-profit organization, such as a local theater or church charity, has to make decisions about how best to generate revenues, given the environment in which it is based and the organization's own strengths and weaknesses. Such decisions are, by their very nature, strategic in form and content, involving such factors as an analysis of the "competition." For example, the local church-run charity has to compete with other charities for the limited resources that individuals are prepared to give to charitable causes. Identifying how best to do so is a strategic problem.

The objective of this book is to give you a thorough understanding of the analytical techniques and skills necessary to identify and exploit strategies successfully. The first step toward achieving this objective involves an overview of the main elements of the strategic management process, and an examination of the way in which these elements fit together. That is the function of the present chapter. In subsequent chapters we consider the individual elements of the strategic management process in greater detail.

1.3 DEFINING STRATEGY

The Traditional Approach

Reflecting the military roots of strategy, *Webster's New World Dictionary* defines *strategy* as "the science of planning and directing military operations."[2] The *planning* theme remains an important component of most management definitions of *strategy*. For example, Harvard's Alfred Chandler defined *strategy* as "the determination of the basic long-term goals and objectives of an enterprise, and the adoption of courses of action and the allocation of resources necessary for carrying out these goals."[3] Implicit in Chandler's definition is the idea that strategy involves *rational* planning. The organization is depicted as choosing its goals, identifying the courses of action (or strategies) that best enable it to fulfill its goals, and allocating resources accordingly. Similarly, James B. Quinn of Dartmouth College has defined *strategy* as "the pattern or plan that integrates an organization's major goals, policies, and action sequences into a cohesive whole."[4] And finally, along the same lines, William F. Glueck defined *strategy* as "a unified, comprehensive, and integrated plan designed to ensure that the basic objectives of the enterprise are achieved."[5]

The case of Royal Dutch/Shell, discussed in the Opening Incident, is a good example of how strategic planning works and how superior planning can result in a competitive advantage. The scenario-based planning used at Shell is designed to educate general managers about the complex and dynamic nature of the company's environment. As a result of that process, the company's general managers understood their business environment better than the competition did. Accordingly, Shell was able to anticipate the crash in oil prices that occurred during 1986. Unlike its competitors, Shell by 1986 had taken steps to ensure that it would remain profitable if this contingency came to pass. In contrast, most of Shell's competitors were operating under the comforting illusion that oil prices would remain strong during the 1980s.

A New Approach

For all their appeal, planning-based definitions of *strategy* have recently evoked criticism. As Henry Mintzberg of McGill University has pointed out, the planning approach incorrectly assumes that an organization's strategy is always the outcome of rational planning.[6] According to Mintzberg, definitions of *strategy* that stress the role of planning ignore the fact that strategies can emerge from within an organization without any formal plan. That is to say, even in the absence of intent, strategies can emerge from the grassroots of an organization. Mintzberg's point is that strategy is more than what a company intends or plans to do; it is also what it actually does. With this in mind, Mintzberg has defined *strategy* as "*a pattern in a stream of decisions or actions,*"[7] the pattern being a product of whatever *intended* (planned) strategies are actually realized and of any *emergent* (unplanned) strategies. The scheme proposed by Mintzberg is illustrated in Figure 1.1.

Mintzberg's argument is that emergent strategies are often successful and may be more appropriate than intended strategies. Richard T. Pascale of Stanford University has described how this was the case for the entry of Honda Motor Co., Ltd., into the U.S. motorcycle market.[8] When a number of Honda executives arrived in Los Angeles from Japan in 1959 to establish an American subsidiary, their original aim (intended strategy) was to focus on selling 250cc and 305cc machines to confirmed motorcycle enthusiasts, rather than 50cc Honda Cubs, which were a big hit in Japan. Their instinct told them that the Honda 50s were not suitable for the U.S. market, where everything was bigger and more luxurious than in Japan.

However, sales of the 250cc and 305cc bikes were sluggish, and the bikes themselves were plagued by mechanical failure. It looked as if Honda's strategy was going to fail. At the same time the Japanese executives were using the Honda 50s to run errands around Los Angeles, attracting a lot of attention. One day they got a call from a Sears, Roebuck buyer who wanted to sell the 50cc bikes to a

FIGURE 1.1   **Emergent and deliberate strategies**

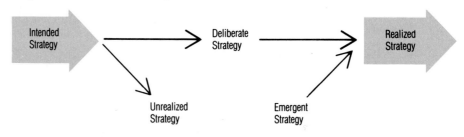

Source: Reprinted from "Strategy Formation in an Adhocracy," by James Mintzberg and Alexandra McHugh, published in *Administrative Science Quarterly*, Vol. 30, No. 2, June 1985, by permission of *Administrative Science Quarterly*. Copyright © 1985 by Administrative Science Quarterly.

broad market of Americans who were not necessarily already motorcycle enthusiasts. The Honda executives were hesitant to sell the small bikes for fear of alienating serious bikers who might then associate Honda with "wimp" machines. In the end they were pushed into doing so by the failure of the 250cc and 305cc models. The rest is history. Honda had stumbled onto a previously untouched market segment that was to prove huge: the average American who had never owned a motorbike. Honda had also found an untried channel of distribution: general retailers rather than specialty motorbike stores. By 1964 nearly one out of every two motorcycles sold in the United States was a Honda.

The conventional explanation of Honda's success is that the company redefined the U.S. motorcycle industry with a brilliantly conceived *intended* strategy.[9] The fact was that Honda's intended strategy was a near disaster. The strategy that *emerged* did so not through planning but through unplanned action taken in response to unforeseen circumstances. Nevertheless, credit should be given to the Japanese management for recognizing the strength of the emergent strategy and for pursuing it with vigor.

The critical point that emerges from the Honda example is that in contrast to the view that strategies are planned, successful strategies can emerge within an organization without prior planning. As Mintzberg has noted, strategies can take root in all kinds of strange places, virtually wherever people have the capacity to learn and the resources to support that capacity.

In sum, Mintzberg's revision of the concept of strategy suggests that strategy involves more than just planning a course of action. It also involves the recognition that successful strategies can emerge from deep within an organization. In practice, the strategies of most organizations are probably a combination of the intended and the emergent. The message for management is that it needs to recognize the process of emergence and to intervene when appropriate, killing off bad emergent strategies but nurturing potentially good ones. To make such decisions, however, managers must be able to judge the worth of emergent strategies. They must be able to think strategically.

1.4 COMPONENTS OF STRATEGIC MANAGEMENT

The strategic management process can be broken down into a number of different components. These components are illustrated in Figure 1.2, and each forms a chapter of this book. Thus you need to understand how the different components fit together. The components include selection of the corporate mission and major corporate goals, analysis of the organization's external competitive environment and internal operating environment, the selection of appropriate business- and corporate-level strategies, and the designing of organizational structures and control systems to implement the organization's chosen strategy. The task of analyzing the organization's external and internal environment and then selecting an appropriate strategy is normally referred to as **strategy formulation.** The task

FIGURE 1.2   **Components of strategic management**

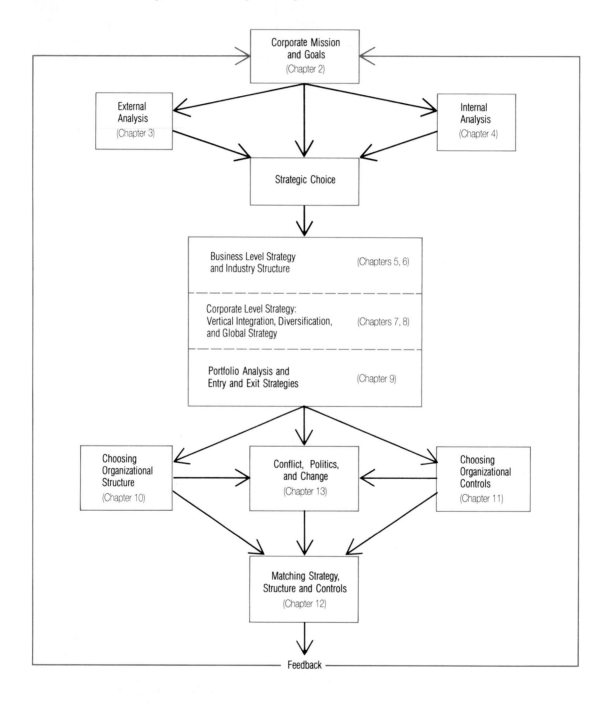

of designing appropriate organizational structures and control systems, given the organization's choice of strategy, is usually called **strategy implementation.**

The traditional approach has been to stress that each of the components illustrated in Figure 1.2 constitutes a *sequential* step in strategic management. In the traditional view, each *cycle* of the process begins with a statement of the corporate mission and major corporate goals. The mission statement is followed by environmental analysis and strategic choice, and the strategy making ends with the design of the organizational structure and control systems necessary to implement the organization's chosen strategy. In practice, however, that sequence is likely to be the case only for the formulation and implementation of *intended* strategies.

As noted earlier, emergent strategies arise from within the organization without prior planning—that is to say, without going through the steps illustrated in Figure 1.2 in a *sequential* fashion. However, top management still has to evaluate emergent strategies. Such evaluation involves comparing each emergent strategy with the organization's goals, external environmental opportunities and threats, and the organization's own internal strengths and weaknesses. The objective is to assess whether the emergent strategy fits the organization's needs and capabilities. In addition, Mintzberg stresses that an organization's capability to produce emergent strategies is a function of the kind of corporate culture fostered by the organization's structure and control systems.

In other words, the different components of the strategic management process are just as important from the perspective of emergent strategies as they are from the perspective of intended strategies. The essential differences between the strategic management process for intended and for emergent strategies are illustrated in Figure 1.3. The formulation of intended strategies is basically a top-down process, whereas the formulation of emergent strategies is a bottom-up process.

Mission and Major Goals

The first component of the strategic management process is defining the **mission** and **major goals** of the organization. This topic is covered in depth in Chapter 2. The mission and major goals of an organization provide the context within which intended strategies are formulated and the criteria against which emergent strategies are evaluated.

The mission sets out why the organization exists and what it should be doing. For example, the mission of national airline might be defined as satisfying the needs of individual and business travelers for high-speed transportation at a reasonable price to all the major population centers of North America.

Major goals specify what the organization hopes to fulfill in the medium to long term. Most profit-seeking organizations operate with a hierarchy of goals in which the maximization of stockholder wealth is placed at the top. Secondary goals are objectives judged necessary by the company if it is to maximize stockholder wealth. For example, General Electric operates with a secondary goal of

FIGURE 1.3   **The strategic management process for intended and emergent strategies**

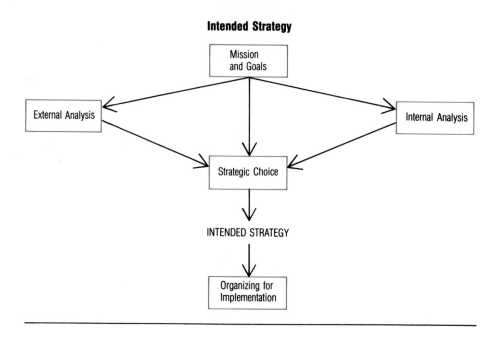

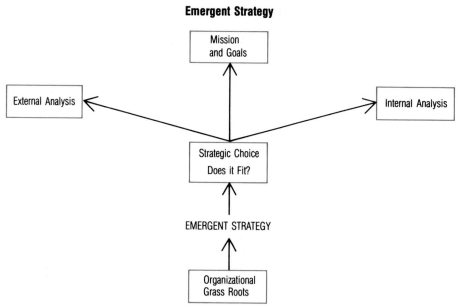

being first or second in every major market in which it competes. This secondary goal reflects the belief at General Electric that building market share is the best way to achieve the primary goal of maximizing stockholder wealth. Not-for-profit organizations typically have a more diverse set of goals. The major goal of Band Aid, for example, was to alleviate starvation in Ethiopia, whereas the goal of a performing arts theater might be to provide high-quality cultural entertainment at a reasonable cost to the general public.

External Analysis

The second component of the strategic management process is the analysis of the organization's external operating environment. This topic is covered in detail in Chapter 3. The objective of external analysis is to identify strategic **opportunities** and **threats** in the organization's operating environment. Two interrelated environments should be examined at this stage: the immediate, or industry, environment in which the organization operates and the wider macroenvironment.

Analyzing the industry environment involves an assessment of the competitive structure of the organization's industry, including the competitive position of the focal organization and its major rivals, as well as the stage of industry development. Analyzing the macro-environment consists of examining macro-economic, social, government, legal, international, and technological factors that may affect the organization. Again consider Royal Dutch/Shell. Its external opportunities included the OPEC oil cartel reaching a sustainable agreement to restrict oil production. The agreement would increase crude oil prices and hence profits for oil majors like Shell. The threats included the possibility of a continued oil glut and radical environmentalism (both of which the company had considered during its scenario planning).

Internal Analysis

The next component of the strategic management process, internal analysis, serves to pinpoint the **strengths** and **weaknesses** of the organization. Such analysis involves identifying the quantity and quality of resources available to the organization. These issues are considered in Chapter 4, where we use the concept of the value chain to examine the factors that determine the quantity and quality of an organization's resources in manufacturing, marketing, materials management, research and development, information systems, personnel, and finance. We also discuss the role of distinctive competencies (unique company strengths) in building and sustaining a company's competitive advantage.

In addition to this, for a multibusiness enterprise, identifying strengths and weaknesses also involves assessing whether the balance of different businesses in its portfolio is a strength or a weakness. For example, if a company's businesses are concentrated in highly competitive and unprofitable industries, then the balance is a weakness. Conversely, if its businesses are concentrated in very profitable industries, then the balance is a strength. Assessing the corporate portfolio is an issue that we discuss in Chapter 9.

Strategic Choice

The next component involves generating a series of strategic alternatives, given the goals of the firm, its internal strengths and weaknesses, and external opportunities and threats. This issue is covered in Chapter 14. We do not deal with the issue until this stage in the text because we must first lay out the different strategic alternatives open to the firm and describe complexities of organizational structure and control systems. Remember, however, that for strategic decision makers who know the full range of strategic options, strategic choice follows directly from an analysis of the organization's external and internal environments.

The comparison of **s**trengths, **w**eaknesses, **o**pportunities, and **t**hreats is normally referred to as a **SWOT** analysis.[10] A SWOT analysis might generate a series of strategic alternatives. To choose among the alternatives, the organization has to evaluate them against each other with respect to their ability to achieve major goals. The objective is to select the strategies that ensure the best **alignment,** or **fit,** between external environmental opportunities and threats and the internal strengths and weaknesses of the organization. For a single-business organization, the objective is to match the company's strengths to environmental opportunities in order to gain a competitive advantage and thus increase profits. For a multi-business organization, the goal is to choose for its portfolio of businesses strategies that align the strengths and weaknesses of the portfolio with environmental opportunities and threats.

Again consider Royal Dutch/Shell. The current strategy of investing in processes that convert natural gas to environmentally clean gasoline can be seen as a counter to a potential threat by building on a company strength. The potential *threat* is radical environmentalism, which may lead to strict limits on auto emissions and auto use, thereby reducing demand for gasoline. The company *strength* is that Shell currently has the largest natural gas reserves and natural gas production of any major oil company. Thus, Shell's strategy is aimed at securing the company's future by aligning a company strength with an environmental threat.

Business-Level Strategy

For the organization operating in a single competitive environment (industry), the outcome of the process of strategic choice is the identification of an appropriate business-level strategy. The different strategic alternatives are discussed in

Chapters 5 and 6. In Chapter 5 we review the pros and cons of three generic business-level strategies: a strategy of cost leadership, a strategy of differentiation, and a strategy of focusing on a particular market niche. The organization's objective when pursuing its chosen strategy should be to establish a sustainable competitive advantage. In addition, Chapter 5 examines the different investment strategies needed to *support* each of these main strategic alternatives. The argument developed in Chapter 5 is that a company must vary its investment strategy with the stage of development of its industry in order to make its business-level strategy successful.

In Chapter 6 we consider the relationship between business-level strategy and industry structure in greater depth. We are particularly concerned in this chapter with the different strategic options that confront companies in radically different industry settings. Thus, for example, we discuss the advantages and disadvantages of establishing a first-mover advantage in a newly formed or embryonic industry. We discuss the role of market signaling, price leadership, and product differentiation for sustaining a competitive advantage in mature industries. And we discuss the different strategic options that a company can choose from in a declining industry.

Corporate-Level Strategy

An organization's corporate-level strategy must answer this question: What businesses should we be in to maximize the long-run profitability of the organization? For many organizations, the answer involves focusing the organization's full attention on continuing to compete within a single business area. However, competing successfully within a single business area also often involves **vertical integration** and **global expansion.** In some segments of the electronics industry, for example, global markets are necessary to generate the sales volume to achieve full economies of scale. Establishing a low-cost position within a single industry may thus require global expansion. Similar arguments can be made regarding vertical integration. Beyond this, organizations that are successful at establishing a sustainable competitive advantage may find that they are generating resources *in excess* of their investment requirements within their primary industry. For such organizations, maximizing long-run profitability may entail **diversification** into new business areas.

The strategies of vertical integration, global expansion, and diversification fall under the rubric of corporate-level strategies. We consider the benefits and costs of vertical integration and diversification in Chapter 7. In that chapter we also consider the role of strategic alliances as an alternative to vertical integration and diversification. The benefits and costs of a strategy of global expansion are considered in detail in Chapter 8. In addition, that chapter explores the benefits and costs of global strategic alliances, the different entry modes that can be used to enter a foreign market, and the role of host-government policies in influencing a company's choice of global strategy.

Analyzing the Corporate Portfolio

Substantially diversified companies face the problem of how best to make sense out of their many different activities. General Electric, for example, has more than 100 different business units. How do the different activities fit together? What is the relative contribution of each activity to corporate profitability? What is the outlook for each activity? Portfolio analysis offers a body of techniques designed to help organizations answer such questions. In Chapter 9, we examine these techniques and consider their strengths and weaknesses.

Portfolio analysis may indicate that a company needs to leave some existing business areas or enter new ones. A number of different entry and exit strategies are available. The options for entering new businesses include acquisitions, joint ventures, and internal new venturing. The options for exiting from an existing business include harvest, divestment, and liquidation. We discuss the merits of these entry and exit strategies in Chapter 9.

Designing Organizational Structure

To make a strategy work, regardless of whether it is intended or emergent, the organization needs to adopt the correct structure. The main options here are reviewed in Chapter 10. Choosing a structure entails allocating task responsibility and decision-making authority within an organization. The issues covered include how best to divide an organization into subunits and how to distribute authority among the different levels of an organization's hierarchy. The options reviewed include whether an organization should function with a tall or a flat structure, how centralized or decentralized decision-making authority should be, and to what extent an organization should be divided up into semi-autonomous subunits (that is, divisions or departments).

Choosing Integration and Control Systems

Strategy implementation involves more than an organization's choice of structure. It also involves the selection of appropriate organizational integration and control systems. The main options here are reviewed in Chapter 11. Strategy implementation often requires collective action or coordination between semi-autonomous subunits (such as product departments) within an organization. Thus we consider integration mechanisms that foster coordination between semi-autonomous subunits. An organization must also decide how best to assess the performance and control the actions of subunits. Its options range from market and output controls to bureaucratic and clan controls, all of which we tackle in Chapter 11.

Matching Strategy, Structure, and Controls

Implementing a strategy requires the adoption of appropriate organizational structures and control systems. After reviewing various structures and control systems in Chapters 10 and 11, in Chapter 12 we consider how to achieve a *fit* among an organization's strategy, structure, and controls. Different strategies and environments place different demands on an organization and therefore require different structural responses and control systems. For example, a strategy of cost leadership demands that an organization be kept simple (so as to reduce costs) and that controls stress productive efficiency. On the other hand, a strategy of differentiating an organization's product by unique technological characteristics generates a need for integrating the activities of the organization around its technological core and for establishing control systems that reward technical creativity. The appropriate structure and control systems are very different in these two cases.

Conflict, Politics, and Change

Although in theory the strategic management process is characterized by *rational* decision making, in practice organizational politics plays a key role. Politics is endemic to organizations: Different subgroups (departments or divisions) within an organization have their own agendas. Typically, the agendas of different subgroups conflict. Thus departments may compete with each other for a bigger share of an organization's finite resources. Such conflicts may be resolved as much by the relative distribution of power between subunits as by a rational evaluation of relative need. Similarly, individual managers often engage in contests with each other over what the correct policy decisions are. Power struggles and coalition building are major consequences of such conflicts and clearly play a part in strategic management. Strategic change tends to bring such power struggles to the fore, since by definition change entails altering the established distribution of power within an organization. In Chapter 13, we analyze the sources of organizational power and conflict and consider how organizational politics influences strategic management and can inhibit strategic change. In addition, we examine how an organization can manage conflicts to fulfill its strategic mission and implement change.

Feedback

Strategic management is an ongoing process. Once a strategy is implemented, its execution must be monitored to determine the extent to which strategic objectives are actually being achieved. This information passes back to the corporate level through feedback loops. At the corporate level it is fed into the next round of strategy formulation and implementation. It serves either to reaffirm existing corporate goals and strategies or to suggest changes. For example, when put into practice, a strategic objective may prove to be too optimistic, and so the next time more conservative objectives are set. Alternatively, feedback may reveal that strategic objectives were attainable but implementation was poor. In that case, the next round in strategic management may concentrate more on implementation. Because feedback is an aspect of organizational control, it is considered in detail in Chapter 11.

1.5 STRATEGIC MANAGERS

To compete in today's complex and ever-changing environment, an organization must have somebody who is responsible for managing strategy development. The task normally falls on the shoulders of **strategic managers.** Strategic managers are individuals who bear responsibility for the overall performance of the organization or for one of its major self-contained divisions. Their overriding concern is for the health of the *total* organization under their direction. (Many textbooks refer to such individuals as *general managers.*) Strategic managers are distinct from **functional managers** within an organization. Functional managers bear responsibility for specific business functions, such as personnel, purchasing, production, sales, customer service, and accounts. Thus their sphere of authority is generally confined to one organizational activity, whereas strategic managers oversee the operation of the whole organization. This responsibility puts strategic managers in the unique position of being able to direct the total organization in a strategic sense.

Edward Wrapp of the University of Chicago has written extensively about the characteristics of successful strategic managers.[11] In Wrapp's view, five skills are especially significant. They are summarized in Table 1.1.

First, successful strategic managers keep themselves *well informed* about a wide range of operating decisions being made at different levels in the organization. They develop a network of information sources in many different parts of the organization, which enables them to remain in touch with operating realities. Second, successful strategic managers know how best to *allocate their time and*

TABLE 1.1   **Major characteristics of successful strategic managers**

Successful strategic managers are
1.   Well informed
2.   Skilled at allocating their time and energy
3.   Good politicians (consensus builders)
4.   Experts at being imprecise
5.   Able to push through programs in a piecemeal fashion

energy among different issues, decisions, or problems. They know when to delegate and when to become involved in a particular decision. Third, successful strategic managers are *good politicians*. They play the power game with skill, preferring to build consensus for their ideas, rather than using their authority to force ideas through. They act as members or leaders of a coalition rather than as dictators.

Fourth, successful strategic managers are able to satisfy the organization that it has a sense of direction without actually committing themselves publicly to precise objectives or strategies. In other words, they are experts at *being imprecise*. At first glance this skill may seem curious, since so much of the received wisdom in the management literature suggests that part of the job of strategic managers is to set precise objectives and formulate detailed strategies. However, in a world where the only constant is change, there is value in being imprecise. Strategic managers would be foolish to commit themselves to a precise objective, given the constant state of environmental flux. *Deliberate imprecision* can often give both the organization and the manager room for maneuver and an enhanced ability to adapt to environmental change. This does not mean that the organization should operate without objectives but rather that the objectives should be open-ended. Thus a strategic manager might commit the organization to becoming number one in its industry without specifying a precise timetable for reaching this goal.

Similarly, successful strategic managers often hesitate to commit themselves publicly to detailed strategic plans, since in all probability the emergence of unexpected contingencies will require adaptation. Thus a successful strategic manager might commit the organization to diversification without stating precisely how or when this will be achieved. It is also important to note that successful strategic managers often have precise private objectives and strategies that they would like to see the organization pursue. However, they recognize the futility of public commitment, given the likelihood of change and the difficulties of implementation.

The fifth skill that Wrapp claims successful strategic managers possess is the *ability to push through programs in a piecemeal fashion*. Successful strategic managers recognize the futility of trying to push total packages or strategic programs through the organization, since significant objections to at least part of such programs are likely to arise. Instead, the successful strategic manager is willing to take less than total acceptance in order to achieve modest progress toward a goal. The successful strategic manager tries to push through his or her ideas in a piecemeal fashion, so that they appear as incidentals to other ideas, though in fact they are part of a larger program or hidden agenda that moves the organization in the direction of the manager's objectives.

Wrapp's picture of the successful strategic manager is thus very different from the picture of the rational decision maker presented in much of the strategic management literature. In Wrapp's view, successful strategic managers are skilled organizational politicians who can build coalitions that get their programs pushed through with a minimum of friction. Furthermore, successful strategic managers recognize the futility of commitment to a precise course of action in a world of constant change. Rather, they keep their options open.

1.6 LEVELS OF STRATEGIC MANAGEMENT

Within a multibusiness company, strategic managers are found not just at the apex of the organization but also at different levels within its hierarchy. Essentially, a typical multibusiness company has three main levels of management: the corporate level, the business level, and the functional level (see Figure 1.4). Strategic managers are found at the first two of these levels but their roles differ, depending on their sphere of responsibility. In addition, functional managers too have a strategic role, though of a different kind. We now look at each of the three levels and the strategic roles assigned to managers within them.

Corporate Level

The corporate level of management consists of the chief executive officer (CEO), other senior executives, the board of directors, and corporate staff. These individuals occupy the apex of decision making within the organization. The CEO is the main strategic manager at this level. His or her strategic role is *to oversee*

FIGURE 1.4   **Levels of strategic management**

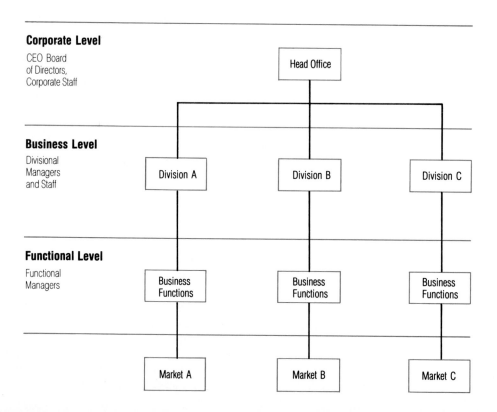

the development of strategies for the total organization. Typically, this role involves defining the mission and goals of the organization, determining what businesses it should be in, allocating resources among the different business areas, and formulating and implementing strategies that span individual businesses.

For example, consider General Electric. The company is involved in a wide range of businesses, including lighting equipment, major appliances, motor and transportation equipment, turbine generators, construction and engineering services, industrial electronics, medical systems, aerospace, and aircraft engines. The main strategic responsibilities of its CEO, Jack Welch, include setting overall strategic objectives, allocating resources among the different business areas, deciding whether the firm should divest itself of any of the businesses, and determining whether it should acquire any new ones. In other words, it is up to Welch to develop strategies that span individual businesses. He is concerned with building and managing the corporate portfolio of businesses. It is not his specific responsibility, however, to develop strategies for competing in the individual business areas, such as aerospace or major appliances. The development of such strategies is the responsibility of business-level strategic managers.

Besides overseeing resource allocation and managing the divestment and acquisition processes, corporate-level strategic managers also provide a link between the people who oversee the strategic development of a firm (strategic managers) and those who own it (stockholders). Corporate-level strategic managers, and particularly the CEO, can be viewed as the guardians of stockholder welfare. It is their responsibility to ensure that corporate strategies pursued by the company are consistent with maximizing stockholder wealth. If they are not, then ultimately the CEO is likely to be called to account by the stockholders.

Business Level

In a multibusiness company, the business level consists of the heads of individual business units within the organization and their support staff. In a single-industry company, the business and corporate levels are the same. A business unit is an organizational entity that operates in a distinct business area. Typically, it is self-contained and has its own functional departments (for example, its own finance, buying, production, and marketing departments). Within most companies, business units are referred to as *divisions*. For example, General Electric has more than 100 divisions, one for each business area that the company is active in.

The main strategic managers at the business level are the heads of the divisions. Their strategic role is to translate general statements of direction and intent from the corporate level into concrete strategies for individual businesses. Thus while corporate-level strategic managers are concerned with strategies that span individual businesses, business-level strategic managers are concerned with strategies that are specific to a particular business. As noted earlier, at General Electric the corporate level has committed itself to the objective of being first or second in every business in which the corporation competes. However, it is up to the

FIGURE 1.5   The flow of information

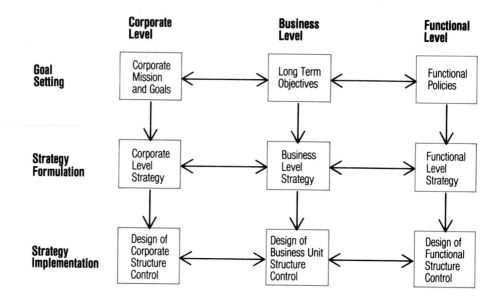

strategic managers who head each division to work out for their business the details of a strategy that is consistent with this objective.

Functional Level

By definition, there are no strategic managers at the functional level. Functional managers bear responsibility for specific business functions, such as personnel, purchasing, production, marketing, customer service, and accounts. They are not in a position to look at the big picture. Nevertheless, they have an important strategic role, for their responsibility is to develop functional strategies in production, marketing, purchasing, and so on, that help fulfill the strategic objectives set by business- and corporate-level general managers. In the case of General Electric's major appliance business, for example, manufacturing managers are responsible for developing manufacturing strategies consistent with the corporate objective of being first or second in that industry. An equally great responsibility for managers at the functional level involves strategy implementation—the execution of corporate- and business-level decisions.

1.7 STRATEGIC INFORMATION SYSTEMS

Goal setting, strategy formulation, and strategy implementation involve personnel at all levels within the organization. Communication among personnel at different levels is necessary to ensure that corporate-, business-, and functional-level strategies are *attainable* and *consistent* with each other and with corporate goals and objectives.

For example, strategic managers at the business level cannot hope to formulate realistic business-level strategies unless they receive input from functional-level managers concerning the strengths and weaknesses of each functional area. Without such input, business-level managers might decide on a strategy that the company does not have the functional resources to pursue. Similarly, corporate-level strategic managers cannot hope to formulate realistic corporate-level strategies unless they receive input from business-level managers about the strengths and weaknesses of each business unit, as well as the market opportunities and threats that each unit faces. Strategic managers also have to make certain that the strategies being pursued by different levels of the organization are consistent with overall corporate goals. The need for such information necessitates further communication among managers at the different levels.

To ensure that the strategies being pursued at each level are consistent and attainable, most organizations go to some length to establish companywide strategic information systems. Often, a committee structure within the firm is designed to facilitate communication between different levels of the hierarchy. For example, at Chrysler five- to seven-member teams are to be found at every level in the corporation from the shop floor on up. The lowest-level teams meet each quarter with their supervisors to set goals, evaluate past performance, and discuss the company's operations. The supervisor of each team is in turn a member of a higher team. The higher teams, too, meet with their supervisors on a quarterly basis. The teams continue to meet up the hierarchy until they reach the top group, which consists of the company's top executives and its CEO. This system facilitates the flow of information within the organization. It helps ensure that higher-level managers do not lose touch with operating realities and consequently pursue strategic objectives that are not attainable.

In addition to committee structures, many companies set up periodic planning conferences that are designed to bring together managers from different levels to discuss strategic problems and strategic directions. In the best-run companies, these conferences provide a forum for higher-level managers to learn about the problems confronting lower-level managers, and for lower-level managers to learn about the strategic objectives of higher-level managers. At such a conference, the merits of different strategies can be debated by all interested parties, and some kind of meaningful synthesis can be worked out.

Figure 1.5 illustrates how these information systems work, at least in theory. On the horizontal axis are the levels of corporate, business, and functional management. On the vertical axis are the three key strategic management tasks: goal setting, strategy formulation, and strategy implementation. In the boxes are the various components of strategic management just discussed. The arrows in the figure represent the way that information flows up and down the organization from level to level and from one component of strategic management to the next. Notice that the setting of corporate goals provides the context for the development of business- and functional-level objectives and vice versa. Notice too that goal setting provides, for each level, the context for strategy formulation and implementation so that a fit can be achieved in this direction as well.

1.8 STRATEGIC PLANNING IN PRACTICE

The last three sections described what might be considered a rational model of the strategic management process. In this model, a company goes through a number of well-defined steps in order to formulate *intended* strategies that align organizational strengths and weakness with environmental opportunities and threats. It is pertinent to ask whether such systems work. Do they help companies establish a sustainable competitive advantage? The answer to this question would seem to be a qualified yes. Strategic planning systems do work, but only if they are correctly designed. Moreover, as with any rational process, their efficiency is subject to the limitations of human decision makers. Even the best-designed planning system will fail to produce the desired results if corporate decision makers fail to use the information at their disposal effectively. In this section we examine common errors in the design of strategic planning systems and consider ways of guarding against the adverse effects of poor strategic decision making.

Does Strategic Planning Work?

Do companies that go through the kind of process outlined above actually generate superior performance relative to those that do not? Clearly, we would expect planning to have some positive effects; empirical evidence does indeed suggest that *on the average* companies that plan outperform those that do not. Of fourteen studies reviewed in a recent survey by Lawrence C. Rhyne, eight found varying degrees of support for the hypothesis that strategic planning improves company performance, five found no support for the hypothesis, and one reported a negative relationship between planning and performance.[12] Moreover, an empirical study by Rhyne, reported in the same article, concluded that "firms with strategic planning systems more closely resembling strategic management theory were found to exhibit superior long-term financial performance both relative to their industry and in absolute terms."[13]

In recent years, however, the use of formal planning systems has been increasingly questioned. Thomas J. Peters and Robert H. Waterman, the best-selling authors of *In Search of Excellence,* are among those who have raised doubts about the usefulness of formal planning systems.[14] Similarly, Henry Mintzberg's revision of the concept of strategy suggests that *emergent* strategies may be just as successful as the *intended* strategies that are the outcome of formal planning. Moreover, it is true that business history is filled with examples of companies that have made poor decisions on the basis of supposedly comprehensive strategic planning.[15] For example, Exxon's decisions to diversify into electrical equipment and office automation and to offset shrinking U.S. oil reserves by investing in shale oil and synthetic fuels were the product of a 1970s planning exercise that was overly pessimistic about the demand for oil-based products. Exxon foresaw ever higher prices for oil and predicted sharp falls in demand as a result. However, oil prices actually tumbled during the 1980s, invalidating one of the basic assumptions of Exxon's plan (see the Opening Incident). In addition, Exxon's diversification failed because of poor acquisitions and management problems in office automation.

Inappropriate Planning Systems

One reason for the poor reputation of strategic planning is that many executives, in their initial enthusiasm for planning techniques during the 1960s and 1970s, adopted inappropriate planning systems. As at Exxon, a common problem was that executives often assumed that it was possible to forecast the future accurately. In practice, the future is unpredictable. In the real world, the only constant is change. Even the best-laid plans can fall apart if unforeseen contingencies occur.

The recognition that in an uncertain world the future cannot be forecasted with sufficient accuracy led Royal Dutch/Shell to pioneer the scenario approach to planning discussed in the Opening Incident. Rather than try to forecast the future, Shell's planners attempt to model the company's environment and then use that model to predict a range of possible scenarios. Executives are then asked to devise strategies to cope with the different scenarios. The objective is to get managers to understand the dynamic and complex nature of their environment and to think through problems in a strategic fashion. This approach seems to work far better than the inflexible forecasting approach to planning that was popular during the 1960s and 1970s.

A further problem is that many companies have made the mistake of treating strategic planning as an exclusively corporate-level function. The result is that strategic plans are often formulated in a vacuum by planning executives who have little understanding or appreciation of operating realities. As a consequence, they formulate strategies that do more harm than good. For example, when demographic data indicated that houses and families were shrinking, planners at General Electric's appliance group concluded that smaller appliances were the wave of the future. Because the planners had little contact with homebuilders and retailers, they did not realize that kitchens and bathrooms were the two rooms that were not shrinking. Nor did they appreciate that working women wanted big refrigerators to cut down on trips to the supermarket. The result was that General Electric wasted a lot of time designing small appliances for which there was only limited demand.

The ivory-tower concept of planning also has the unfortunate effect of creating damaging tensions between corporate- and business-level personnel. The experience of General Electric's appliance group is again illuminating. Many of the planners in this group were recruited from consulting firms or from top-flight business schools. Many of the operating people believed this pattern of recruitment implied that corporate executives thought that operating managers were not smart enough to think through strategic problems for themselves. Out of this impression grew an us-versus-them state of mind that quickly escalated into out-and-out hostility. As a result, even when the planners were right, operating managers would not listen to them. In the 1970s the planners correctly recognized the importance of the globalization of the appliance market and the emerging Japanese threat. However, operating managers, who then saw Sears, Roebuck as the competition, paid them little heed.

Correcting the ivory-tower approach to planning involves recognition that if strategic planning is to be successful, it is an activity that must embrace all levels of the corporation. To some extent, this goal can be achieved by setting up the kind of strategic information systems discussed in the previous section. These systems are designed to ensure that the strategies pursued by different parts of the organization are consistent and attainable. Beyond this, however, it is important to understand that much of the best planning can and should be done by operating managers. They are the ones closest to the facts. The role of corporate-level planners should be that of facilitators who help operating managers do the planning.

Poor Strategic Decision Making

Even the best-designed strategic planning systems will fail to produce the desired results if strategic decision makers fail to use the information at their disposal in an effective manner. Poor strategic decision making most often arises from a failure to question the assumptions underlying a plan, even when readily available information shows the assumptions to be fundamentally flawed.

An interesting example of this phenomenon concerns the 1979 acquisition of Howard Johnson Co. by Britain's Imperial Group.[16] Imperial is the third largest tobacco company in the world, after British American Tobaccos and Philip Morris Companies, Inc. In the 1970s it began a diversification program designed to reduce its dependence on the declining tobacco market. Part of this program included a plan to acquire a major U.S. company. Imperial spent two years scanning the United States for a suitable acquisition opportunity. It was looking for an enterprise in a high-growth industry that had a high market share, a good track record, and good growth prospects and that could be acquired at a reasonable price. Imperial scanned more than 30 industries and 200 different companies before deciding on Howard Johnson.

When Imperial announced its plans to buy Howard Johnson for close to $500 million in 1979, the company's shareholders threatened rebellion. They were quick to point out that at $26 per share Imperial was paying double what Howard Johnson had been worth only six months previously, when share prices stood at $13. The acquisition hardly seemed to be at a reasonable price. Moreover, the motel industry was entering a low- rather than a high-growth phase, and growth prospects were poor. Besides, Howard Johnson did not have a good track record. Imperial ignored shareholder protests and bought the lodging chain. Five years later, after persistent losses, Imperial was trying to divest itself of Howard Johnson. The acquisition had been a complete failure.

What went wrong? Why, after a two-year planning exercise, did Imperial buy a company that so patently did not fit its own criteria? The answer would seem to lie not in the planning but in the quality of strategic decision making. Imperial bought Howard Johnson in spite of its planning, not because of it. What happened at Imperial was that the CEO decided independently that Howard Johnson was a good buy. A rather authoritarian figure, the CEO surrounded himself with subordinates who agreed with him. Once he had made his choice, his advisers concurred with his judgment and shared in developing rationalizations for it. No one questioned the decision itself, even though information was available to show that it was flawed. Instead, strategic planning was used to justify a decision that in practice did not conform with strategic objectives.

The Imperial example is a case of what has been referred to by social psychologist Irving L. Janis as *groupthink*.[17] Groupthink occurs when a group of decision makers embarks on a course of action without questioning underlying assumptions. Typically, a group coalesces around a person or policy. It ignores or filters out information that can be used to question the policy and develops after-the-fact rationalizations for its decision. Thus commitment is based on an emotional, rather than an objective, assessment of what is the correct course of action. The consequences can be poor decisions.

This phenomenon probably explains, at least in part, why, in spite of sophisticated strategic management, companies often make poor strategic decisions. Janis traced many historical fiascoes to defective policy making by government leaders who received social support from their in-group of advisers. In a series of case studies,[18] he suggested that the following three groups of policy advisers, like the group surrounding Imperial's CEO, were dominated by concurrence seeking or groupthink and collectively avoided information that challenged their assumptions:

1. *President Harry Truman's advisory group.* The members of this group supported the decision to escalate the war in North Korea despite firm warnings by the Chinese Communist government that U.S. entry into North Korea would be met with armed resistance from the Chinese.

2. *President John Kennedy's inner circle.* The members of this group supported the decision to launch the Bay of Pigs invasion of Cuba even though available information showed that it would be an unsuccessful venture and would damage U.S. relations with other countries.

3. *President Lyndon Johnson's close advisers.* The members of this group supported the decision to escalate the war in Vietnam despite intelligence reports and other information indicating that this action would not defeat the Vietcong

or the North Vietnamese and would entail unfavorable political consequences within the United States.

Janis observed that these groupthink-dominated groups were characterized by strong pressures toward uniformity, which inclined their members to avoid raising controversial issues, questioning weak arguments, or calling a halt to soft-headed thinking.

The groupthink phenomenon raises the problem of how to bring critical information to bear on the decision mechanism so that strategic decisions made by the company are realistic and based on thorough evaluation. Two techniques known to counteract groupthink are devil's advocacy and dialectic inquiry.

Devil's Advocacy and Dialectic Inquiry

The traditional approach to strategic decision making might be called the *expert approach*.[19] This approach involves a recommended course of action based on a set of assumptions. The generation of a single plan by a knowledgeable planner or by a planning committee whose members share assumptions is an example of the expert approach. The problem with this approach is that it is vulnerable to groupthink. In addition, the assumptions are critical. If they are incorrect, then the approach is likely to generate poor decisions.

Devil's advocacy and dialectic inquiry have been proposed as two means of guarding against the weaknesses of the expert approach.[20] Devil's advocacy involves the generation of both a plan and a critical analysis of the plan. One member of the decision-making group acts as the devil's advocate, bringing out all the reasons that might make the proposal unacceptable. In this way, decision makers can be made aware of the possible perils of recommended courses of action.

Dialectic inquiry is more complex, for it involves the generation of a plan (a thesis) and a counterplan (an antithesis). According to R. O. Mason, one of the early proponents of this method in strategic management, the plan and the counterplan should reflect plausible but conflicting courses of action.[21] Corporate decision makers consider a debate between advocates of the plan and counterplan. The purpose of the debate is to reveal problems with definitions, recommended courses of action, and assumptions. As a result, corporate decision makers and planners are able to form a new and more encompassing conceptualization of the problem, which becomes the final plan (a synthesis).

Each of the three decision-making processes is illustrated in Figure 1.6. Logic suggests that both devil's advocacy and dialectic inquiry are likely to produce better decisions than is the traditional expert approach. If either of those processes had been used in the Imperial case, it is likely that a different (and probably better) decision would have been made. However, there is considerable dispute over which of the two nontraditional methods is better.[22] Researchers have come to conflicting conclusions, and the jury is still out on this issue. From a practical

FIGURE 1.6   **Three decision-making processes**

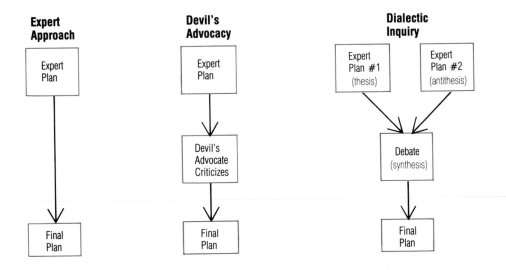

point of view, however, devil's advocacy is probably the easier method to implement because it involves less commitment in terms of time than dialectic inquiry.

1.9 SUMMARY OF CHAPTER

This chapter provides a broad overview of the strategic management process. In discussing the scope and complexity of the strategic management process, we have made the following major points:

1. The techniques of strategic management are applicable to a wide range of organizations, from large, multibusiness organizations to small, one-person businesses, from manufacturing to service organizations, and from profit-seeking to not-for-profit organizations.

2. Traditional definitions of *strategy* stress that an organization's strategy is the outcome of a rational *planning* process.

3. Mintzberg's revision of the concept of strategy suggests that strategy can *emerge* from within an organization in the absence of any prior intentions.

4. The major components of the strategic management process include defining the mission and major goals of the organization; analyzing the external and internal environments of the organization; choosing business and corporate-level strategies that align the organization's strengths and weaknesses with external environmental opportunities and threats; and adopting

organizational structures and control systems to implement the organization's chosen strategy.

5. Strategic managers are individuals who bear responsibility for the overall performance of the organization or for one of its major self-contained divisions. Their overriding concern is for the health of the *total* organization under their direction.

6. Successful strategic managers are well informed, skilled at allocating their time and energy, good politicians (consensus builders), and experts at being imprecise; they are also able to push through programs in a piecemeal fashion.

7. Strategic management embraces the whole company. Specifically, three levels of strategic management have been identified: the corporate level, the business level, and the functional level.

8. Strategic management involves communication among individuals at different levels of the organization to ensure that the strategies being pursued are attainable and consistent.

9. Strategic planning often fails because executives do not plan for uncertainty and because ivory-tower planners lose touch with operating realities.

10. In spite of systematic planning, companies may adopt poor strategies if their decision making does not question underlying assumptions and guard against the dangers of groupthink.

11. Techniques for enhancing the effectiveness of strategic decision making include devil's advocacy and dialectic inquiry.

Discussion Questions

1. What do we mean by *strategy*?

2. What are the strengths of formal strategic planning? What are its weaknesses?

3. Evaluate the 1987 Iran-Contra affair from a strategic decision-making perspective. Do you think different decisions would have been made if the Reagan administration had used a dialectic inquiry or a devil's advocacy approach when making strategic decisions? Was the sale of arms to Iran the result of an intended or an emergent strategy?

Endnotes

1. "According to Plan," *The Economist,* July 22, 1989, pp. 60–63. Arie P. de Geus, "Planning as Learning," *Harvard Business Review* (March–April 1988), 70–74. Pierre Wack, "Scenarios: Uncharted Waters Ahead," *Harvard Business*

Review (September–October 1985), 73–89. Toni Mack, "It's Time to Take Risks," *Forbes,* (October 6, 1986), pp. 125–133.

2. Definition of "strategy" from *Webster's New World Dictionary,* Third College Edition. Copyright © 1988. Used by permission of the publisher, New World Dictionaries/A division of Simon & Schuster, New York, NY.

3. Alfred Chandler, *Strategy and Structure: Chapters in the History of the American Enterprise* (Cambridge, Mass.: MIT Press, 1962).

4. James B. Quinn, *Strategies for Change: Logical Incrementalism* (Homewood, Ill.: Irwin, 1980).

5. William F. Glueck, *Business Policy and Strategic Management* (New York: McGraw-Hill, 1980).

6. Henry Mintzberg, "Patterns in Strategy Formulation," *Management Science, 24* (1978), 934–948.

7. Ibid. Italics added.

8. Richard T. Pascale, "Perspectives on Strategy: The Real Story Behind Honda's Success," *California Management Review, 26* (1984), 47–72.

9. The conventional explanation was championed by the Boston Consulting Group. See BCG, *Strategy Alternatives for the British Motorcycle Industry* (London: Her Majesty's Stationery Office, 1979).

10. K. R. Andrews, *The Concept of Corporate Strategy* (Homewood, Ill.: Dow Jones Irwin, 1971). H. I. Ansoff, *Corporate Strategy* (New York: McGraw-Hill, 1965). C. W. Hofer and D. Schendel, *Strategy Formulation: Analytical Concepts* (St. Paul, Minn.: West, 1978).

11. Edward Wrapp, "Good Managers Don't Make Policy Decisions," *Harvard Business Review* (September–October 1967), 91–99.

12. For a summary of fourteen major studies up to 1985, see Lawrence C. Rhyne, "The Relationship of Strategic Planning to Financial Performance," *Strategic Management Journal, 7* (1986), 423–436.

13. Lawrence C. Rhyne, "The Relationship of Strategic Planning to Financial Performance," *Strategic Management Journal, 7* (1986), 432.

14. Thomas J. Peters and Robert H. Waterman, *In Search of Excellence* (New York: Harper & Row, 1982).

15. For some examples, see S. Tilles, "How to Evaluate Corporate Strategy," *Harvard Business Review,* 41 (1963), 111–121. Also see "The New Breed of Strategic Planner," *Business Week,* September 17, 1984, pp. 62–68.

16. The story ran on an almost daily basis in the *Financial Times* of London during the autumn of 1979.

17. Irving L. Janis, *Victims of Groupthink,* 2nd ed. (Boston: Houghton Mifflin, 1982).

18. All these cases are discussed in detail in Janis, *Victims of Groupthink.* Further implications of the phenomenon are examined in I. L. Janis and L. Mann, *Decision Making* (New York: Free Press, 1977).

19. R. O. Mason, "A Dialectic Approach to Strategic Planning," *Management Science, 13* (1969), 403–414.

20. R. A. Cosier and J. C. Aplin, "A Critical View of Dialectic Inquiry in Strategic Planning," *Strategic Management Journal, 1* (1980), 343–356. I. I. Mintroff and R. O. Mason, "Structuring III—Structured Policy Issues: Further Explorations in a Methodology for Messy Problems," *Strategic Management Journal, 1* (1980), 331–342.

21. Mason, "A Dialectic Approach to Strategic Planning," pp. 403–414.

22. D. M. Schweiger and P. A. Finger, "The Comparative Effectiveness of Dialectic Inquiry and Devil's Advocacy," *Strategic Management Journal, 5* (1984), 335–350.

Chapter 2

CORPORATE MISSION, GOALS, AND STAKEHOLDERS

2.1 OPENING INCIDENT: ALLEGIS CORPORATION

In the early 1980s, Dick Ferris, the CEO of United Airlines, had a vision of the future in which United Airlines was one component of a "worldwide door-to-door travel service." Ferris believed that a company that provided flight, rental car, and hotel services could realize significant synergies. He spoke with zeal about a future in which travel agents around the world would sit in front of their computer screens, coordinating reservations for his airline, his hotels, and his rental cars.

Assembling the assets for this travel empire had begun in 1970 with the purchase of Westin Hotel Company. Under Ferris's leadership, United Airlines bought Hertz Company from RCA in 1985 for $587 million. In March 1987 United bought Hilton International for $980 million. At the same time United Airlines officially changed its name to Allegis Corporation in a symbolic attempt to emphasize the company's rebirth as an integrated travel operation.

The problem with this strategy was that it did not have the support of two major stake-holder groups: the company's airline pilots and stockholders. Ferris's problems with the pilots began in mid 1985 when he demanded wage and productivity concessions from the pilots union, the Air Line Pilots Association of United Airlines (ALPA), in order to compete with low-cost carriers such as People Express and Continental. He succeeded in getting the pilots to accept his demands, but only after a 29-day strike that soured management-labor relations and produced a $92 million quarterly loss. Then, in April 1985, ALPA offered to buy the airline for $4.5 billion. According to F. C. Dubinsky, ALPA chairman at United, the bid was motivated by the pilots' fear that "the airline is no longer the focus of the company. The management is a hotel management team. We want to return to our core business." The bid was refused by corporate leadership.

While these events were unfolding, a number of corporate raiders were beginning to take an interest in the company. In March 1987, Allegis's stock was trading in the $55-to-$60 range.

According to stock analysts and many institutional investors, at that price the stock was grossly undervalued. Several investment experts judged that the company would be worth at least $100 per share if its operations were sold separately. Buoyed by such estimates, real estate mogul Donald Trump was the first raider to surface. He purchased 5 percent of Allegis's stock. After issuing several statements critical of Ferris, Trump sold his stake, but not before he had "talked up" the company's stock price and made a profit of $50 million on the transaction. Then, in May 1987, Coniston Partners, an investment fund, disclosed that it had purchased 13 percent of the company's stock. Coniston's intention was to remove the board of directors and sell off the company's constituent businesses.

Ferris's reaction to the takeover bids from Coniston and ALPA was to initiate two takeover defenses. First, as part of a $15-billion jet order, Allegis provided the Boeing Company with new issue convertible notes valued at $700 million. Should a single investment entity purchase more than 40 percent of Allegis's stock, the interest rates on the notes would increase drastically, thereby severely raising the costs of any hostile takeover attempt. This tactic, however, failed to reassure the majority of Allegis's stockholders, who were becoming increasingly dissatisfied with Ferris. In response, the Allegis board suggested a massive recapitalization plan that would immediately repay stockholders $60 per share in cash and leave them with stock worth an estimated $28 per share. The problem was that this plan would add more than $3 billion to the $2.4 billion in long-term debt already on the company's balance sheet. Such a debt load would have been perilous in the competitive airline industry, and the resulting interest payments might have wiped out profits.

Ultimately the Allegis board could not countenance piling up heavy debt to salvage a master plan that shareholders disliked. Nor could it support a CEO who had so clearly alienated both Wall Street investors and many of the company's employees. Consequently, in June 1987 the board ousted Dick Ferris; repudiated his travel supermarket strategy; announced that Hertz, Westin, and Hilton International would all be sold; decided to consider selling a major stake in United Airlines to its employees; and announced plans to change the company's name back to United Airlines. In effect, after supporting Dick Ferris through two difficult years, the board reversed itself under pressure from employees and stockholders. Coniston and ALPA responded by dropping their takeover bids. In the view of both parties, the board was now proposing to do what they had wanted all along.[1]

2.2 OVERVIEW

Allegis failed to satisfy the interests of two of its major constituencies, or stakeholders: its stockholders and its employees. As a consequence, CEO Dick Ferris, the architect of Allegis's strategy, lost his job. To avoid the problems that Allegis faced, companies can and should identify and incorporate the claims of various stakeholder groups into strategic decision making. This chapter is concerned with identifying how this can be done.

The corporate mission statement is the first key indicator of how an organization views the claims of its stakeholders. The mission statement defines the business of an organization and states basic goals, characteristics, and guiding philosophies. Its purpose is to set the organizational context within which strategic decisions will be made—in other words, to give an organization strategic focus and direction. All strategic decisions flow from the mission statement. In examining how organizations formulate such statements, we concentrate on the three main components that strategy writers have recommended for inclusion in a corporate mission statement:

1. A definition of the organization's business
2. A statement of major corporate goals
3. A statement of corporate philosophy[2]

An example of a mission statement appears in Table 2.1, which shows the mission statement of NCR Corporation. The six points set out major corporate commitments to the following stakeholder groups: customers, stockholders, employees, suppliers, and the community.

After examining how to construct a mission statement, we consider a company's various **stakeholders:** individuals or groups, either within or outside the organization, that have some claim on it (see Figure 2.1). Their interests must be taken into account when a mission statement is formulated. Then we look closely

TABLE 2.1   **NCR's corporate mission statement**

NCR's mission: create value for our stakeholders

NCR is a successful, growing company dedicated to achieving superior results by assuring that its actions are aligned with stakeholder expectations. Stakeholders are all constituencies with a stake in the fortunes of the company. NCR's primary mission is to create value for our stakeholders.

We believe in conducting our business activities with integrity and respect while building mutually beneficial and enduring relationships with all of our stakeholders.

We take customer satisfaction personally: we are committed to providing superior value in our products and services on a continuing basis.

We respect the individuality of each employee and foster an environment in which employees' creativity and productivity are encouraged, recognized, valued, and rewarded.

We think of our suppliers as partners who share our goal of achieving the highest quality standards and the most consistent level of service.

We are committed to being caring and supportive corporate citizens within the worldwide communities in which we operate.

We are dedicated to creating value for our shareholders and financial communities by performing in a manner that will enhance returns on investments.

Source: Courtesy of NCR Corporation.

FIGURE 2.1   The relationship between the mission, stakeholders, and strategies

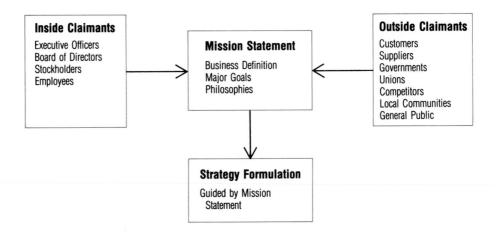

at two particularly important stakeholder groups, **stockholders** and **the general public,** analyzing how stockholders can and do influence the corporate mission, and hence corporate strategies, and considering the issue of **corporate social responsibility.**

2.3 DEFINING THE BUSINESS

The first component of a mission statement is a clear definition of the organization's business. Essentially, defining the business involves answering these questions: "What is our business? What will it be? What should it be?"[3] The answers vary, depending on whether the organization is a single-business or a diversified enterprise. A single-business enterprise is active in just one main business area. For example, U.S. Steel in the 1950s was involved just in the production of steel. By the 1980s, however, U.S. Steel had become USX, a diversified company with interests in steel, oil and gas, chemicals, real estate, transportation, and the production of energy equipment. For USX, the process of defining itself is complicated by the fact that to a large extent the concern of a multibusiness enterprise is *managing businesses.* Thus the business definition of USX involves different issues than did the definition of U.S. Steel. In this section, the problem of how to define the business of a single-business company is considered first. Discussion of the problem of how best to define the business of a diversified enterprise follows.

A Single-Business Company

To answer the question "What is our business?" Derek F. Abell has suggested that a company should define its business in terms of three dimensions: (1) Who is being satisfied (what customer groups)? (2) What is being satisfied (what customer needs)? (3) How are customer needs being satisfied (by skills or by distinctive competencies)?[4] Figure 2.2 illustrates these three dimensions.

Abell's approach stresses the need for a *consumer-oriented* rather than a *product-oriented* business definition. A product-oriented business definition focuses just on the products sold and the markets served. Abell maintains that such an approach obscures the company's function, which is to satisfy consumer needs. A product is only the physical manifestation of applying a particular skill to satisfy a particular need for a particular consumer group. In practice, there often are

FIGURE 2.2   **Abell's framework for defining the business**

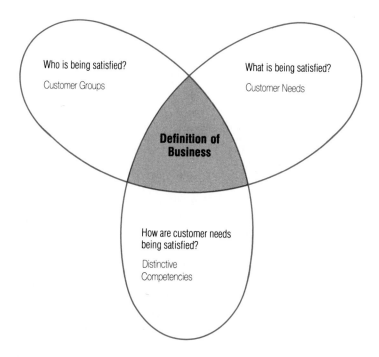

Source: Derek F. Abell, *Defining the Business: The Starting Point of Strategic Planning* (Englewood Cliffs, N.J.: Prentice-Hall, 1980), p. 17.

different ways of serving the particular need of a particular consumer group. Identifying these ways through a broad, consumer-oriented business definition can safeguard companies from being caught unawares by major shifts in demand. Indeed, by helping anticipate demand shifts, Abell's framework can assist companies in capitalizing on the changes in their environment. It can help answer the question "What will our business be?"

Unfortunately, the need to take a customer-oriented view of a company's business has often been ignored. Consequently, history is littered with the wreckage of once-great corporations that failed to define their business or that defined it incorrectly. These firms failed to see what their business would become, and ultimately they declined. Theodore Levitt described the fall of the once-mighty U.S. railroads in terms of their failure to define their business correctly:

> The railroads did not stop growing because the need for passenger and freight transportation declined. That grew. The railroads are in trouble today not because the need was filled by others (cars, trucks, airplanes, even telephones), but because it was not filled by the railroads themselves. They let others take customers away from them because they assumed themselves to be in the railroad business rather than in the transportation business. The reason they defined their industry wrong was because they were railroad oriented instead of transport oriented; they were product oriented instead of customer oriented.[5]

If the railroads had used Abell's framework, they might have anticipated the impact of technological change and decided that their business was transportation. In that case, they might have transferred their early strength in rail into dominance in today's diversified transport industry. Sadly, most railroads stuck to a product-oriented definition of their business and went bankrupt.

In contrast, IBM correctly foresaw what its business would be. Originally, IBM was a leader in the manufacture of typewriters and mechanical tabulating equipment using punch-card technology. However, IBM viewed itself as providing a means for information processing and storage, rather than as a supplier of mechanical tabulating equipment and typewriters. Given this definition, the company's subsequent moves into computers, software systems, office systems, and copiers seem logical.

The question "What should our business be?" can also be answered using Abell's framework. Recall that IBM decided that its business should be computers, word processors, and office systems—all natural extensions of its original business. Other companies do not see as much promise in their original business, perhaps because of negative and irreversible changes in consumer needs and technologies. These companies decide to switch to something different, and they diversify away from their original business. In the 1960s, many companies reduced their dependence on their original business by moving into unrelated areas. Conglomerates such as ITT Corporation, Gulf & Western Industries, and Textron are a result of this diversification movement.[6]

TABLE 2.2   Examples of business definitions

Bethlehem Steel Corp.:
Bethlehem is a large, integrated steel producer which makes and sells a wide variety of steel mill and manufactured steel products. Bethlehem is also engaged in the production and sales of coal and other raw materials, . . . in the construction and servicing of mobile offshore drilling rigs and ships, . . . in the manufacture of railroad cars and parts, . . . in the sale of equipment and supplies to the oil and gas industries, . . . and in the manufacture of home building products and custom-molded plastic products. Bethlehem also sells technology domestically and internationally.

Litton Industries, Inc.:
Litton is a technology-based company applying advanced electronics products and services to business opportunities in defense, industrial automation, and geophysical markets. Research and product engineering emphasis is on developing advanced products which the company manufactures and supplies worldwide to commercial, industrial, and government customers.

Polaroid Corp. (late 1970s definition):
Polaroid manufactures and sells photographic products based on inventions of the company in the field of one-step instant photography and light polarizing products, utilizing the company's inventions in the field of polarized light. The company considers itself to be engaged in one line of business.

Polaroid Corp. (mid 1980s definition):
Polaroid designs, manufactures, and markets worldwide a variety of products based on its inventions, primarily in the photographic field. These include instant photographic cameras and films, light polarizing filters and lenses, and diversified chemical, optical, and commercial products. The principal products of the company are used in amateur and professional photography, industry, science, medicine, and education.

Zale Corporation:
Zale's business is specialty retailing. Retailing is a people-oriented business. The corporation's business existence and continued success are dependent upon how well it meets its responsibilities to serve critically important groups of people.

Source: Adapted from company annual reports.

Table 2.2 details how a number of companies define their business. Perhaps the best example of a consumer-oriented business definition in the table is that of Zale Corporation. Given this definition, it is not surprising that Zale is one of the most successful national jewelry retailers. Yet until 1980 Zale was primarily product oriented, and that outlook endangered the company's health. According to Zale's chairman, Donald Zale, the first, foremost, and primary change has been to acquire a consumer orientation. The company makes about half of the jewelry it sells. In the past, manufacturing operations largely decided what products would be made. For a decade manufacturing ground out so-called mother's rings—rings set with children's birthstones. Zale wasn't watching the market. The business died and the company was left with a worthless inventory. This experience forced Zale to rethink its business definition.[7]

Like Zale's early definition, Polaroid's business definition until the 1980s was product oriented, stressing the company's involvement in one-step instant photography. This myopic definition has not served Polaroid well. The development of quick-turnaround photo developing and high-quality, low-cost 35mm cameras—a product that Polaroid's founder, Edwin Land, once rejected—has taken away much of Polaroid's market. At the height of its popularity in 1978, more than 8 million instant cameras were sold in the United States. Four years later the figure was closer to 5 million. Polaroid's net earnings declined from nearly $120 million in 1978 to $23.5 million in 1982. Its problem was defining its business as one-step instant photography rather than as the recording of images and memories. In other words, its business definition was guided by the products it manufactured rather than by the needs it served. Somewhat belatedly, Polaroid realized its mistake, changed its business definition, and attempted to broaden its product base—but with only limited success.[8]

Part of the reason for its difficulty in producing a turnaround is that its current business definition is still primarily product oriented. Polaroid still defines its business in terms of the products it manufactures and sells, rather than the customer needs it is seeking to satisfy.

A Diversified Company

A diversified company faces special problems when trying to define its business because it actually operates several businesses. In essence, the corporate business is often one of managing a collection of businesses. For example, USX, formerly U.S. Steel, is still known primarily for its steel interests. A consumer-oriented definition of USX's steel interests might be something like this: "USX seeks to satisfy customers' needs for a high-strength construction and fabricating material." However, USX is, in fact, a diversified company that in 1986 generated only 33 percent of its revenues from steel. The rest came from oil and gas, chemicals, real estate, transportation, and energy equipment. Clearly, the consumer-oriented definition given above applies only to the company's steel operations; it does not suffice as a definition of its *corporate* businesses.

In a diversified enterprise, the question "What is our business?" must be asked at two levels: the business level and the corporate level. At the business level, such as USX's steel operations, the focus should be on a consumer-oriented definition. But at the corporate level, management cannot simply aggregate the various business definitions, for doing so will lead to an unfocused and confusing statement. Instead, the corporate business definition should be *portfolio oriented*. In this context, **portfolio** refers to a company's collection of businesses. A portfolio-oriented definition should include the following:

1. The purpose of the company's portfolio of businesses
2. The desired scope (diversity) of the portfolio
3. The balance desired between different businesses in the portfolio

The purpose of a portfolio—the gains that a portfolio of businesses can bring a company—is discussed in more detail in Chapters 7 and 9. At this stage, it is

FIGURE 2.3   **Summary of factors important in business definitions**

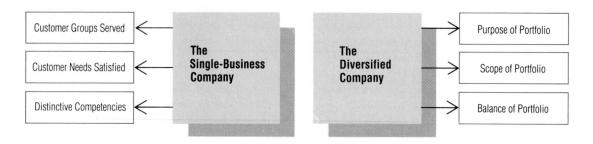

enough to note that a company should define its corporate business so that its strategic objective is clear. For example, in building its portfolio of businesses, USX wanted to become less dependent on its ailing steel operations. Unless it has a clear objective, a company runs the risk of building a portfolio without identifying the underlying industrial or financial logic behind its actions—indeed, without knowing why it is building a portfolio. This criticism has been leveled at the early U.S. conglomerates. A number of commentators claim that these companies built diversified portfolios for no reason other than to be fashionable.[9]

For similar reasons, a portfolio-oriented definition must include the desired scope of the portfolio; otherwise, the company risks pursuing portfolio diversification for its own sake. If no constraint is placed on scope, the company can diversify too widely. Finally, the company must consider the important issue of desired balance among the different businesses in its portfolio. It must decide whether it wants a balanced portfolio of activities, with each business making an equal contribution toward corporate earnings, or an unbalanced portfolio, where the size of the constituent businesses varies considerably. Most companies prefer a balanced portfolio, perhaps because an unbalanced portfolio can result in top management focusing too much attention on large businesses at the expense of the smaller ones.

A summary of factors important in the definitions of both single-business and diversified companies is given in Figure 2.3.

2.4 SETTING CORPORATE GOALS

As we indicated at the start of this chapter, the first major component of a mission statement is a definition of the company's business and the second is a statement of major corporate goals. Corporate goals spell out formally what the organization is trying to achieve; they give direction to the corporate mission statement and help guide the formulation of strategy. For example, a major corporate goal of General Electric is to be first or second in every market in which it competes.

Accordingly, General Electric's businesses typically seek market leadership rather than a secure market niche and therefore center their strategies on how to achieve market leadership. Profit-seeking organizations may operate with a variety of major corporate goals; but in theory at least, all these goals should be directed toward one end: the maximization of stockholder wealth.

Maximizing Stockholder Wealth

Stockholders provide a company with capital and in exchange expect an appropriate return on their investment. A company's stockholders are its legal owners. Consequently, the overriding goal of most corporations is to maximize stockholder wealth, which involves increasing the long-run returns earned by stockholders from owning shares in the corporation. Stockholders receive returns in two ways: (1) from dividend payments and (2) from capital appreciation in the market value of a share (that is, by increases in stock market prices).

The best way for a company to maximize stockholder wealth is to pursue strategies that maximize its own return on investment (ROI), which is a good general indicator of a company's efficiency. In short, the more efficient a company is, the better its future prospects look to stockholders and the greater is its ability to pay dividends. Furthermore, higher ROI leads to greater demand for a company's shares. Demand bids up the share price and leads to capital appreciation.

Secondary Goals

However, as management theorist Peter F. Drucker and many others have pointed out, there is danger in emphasizing only ROI.[10] An overzealous pursuit of ROI can misdirect managerial attention and encourage some of the worst management practices, such as maximizing short-run rather than long-run ROI. A short-run orientation favors such action as cutting expenditures judged to be non-essential in that span of time—for instance, expenditures for research and development, marketing, and new capital investments. Although decreasing current expenditure increases current ROI, the resulting underinvestment, lack of innovation, and poor market awareness jeopardize long-run ROI. Yet despite these negative consequences, managers do make such decisions, because the adverse effects of a short-run orientation may not materialize and become apparent to stockholders for several years. By that time, the management team responsible may have moved on, leaving others to pick up the pieces.

In a major *Harvard Business Review* article, Robert H. Hayes and William J. Abernathy argue that the widespread focus on short-run ROI has been a major factor in the long-run loss of international competitiveness by U.S. companies.[11] MIT economist Lester Thurow likewise faults the short-run orientation of many American businesses for some of their problems. He cites declining R&D expenditures and reduced innovative activity within American enterprises as evidence of this orientation.[12] The household products and drug company American

Home Products Corp., which manufactures Advil, is a case in point.[13] American Home has a history of impressive financial performance, regularly recording a return of more than 30 percent on equity. Since 1983, however, American Home has been showing signs of fatigue. Pretax income, which grew at double-digit rates for a decade, increased only 3 percent annually between 1984 and 1986.

The reason for such a decline in profit growth is the company's difficulty in coming up with new products. Its tight cost controls and focus on current profitability have stunted spending on research and development. In 1983, spending on R&D at American Home was only 3 percent of sales, compared with a drug industry average of 6.1 percent.[14] Moreover, American Home expects a new product to show profit in a year and a half rather than in three years or more, which is the norm for most companies. Thus American Home illustrates the adverse effects of short-run profit maximization.

To guard against short-run behavior, Drucker suggests that companies adopt a number of secondary goals in addition to ROI. These goals should be designed to balance short-run and long-run considerations. Drucker's list includes secondary goals relating to these areas: (1) market share, (2) innovation, (3) productivity, (4) physical and financial resources, (5) manager performance and development, (6) worker performance and attitude, and (7) social responsibility. Although such secondary goals need not be part of a mission statement, sometimes the most important ones are. Recall that General Electric stresses a market-share goal: to be first or second in every business in which it competes. Given the strong positive relationship between market share and profitability, this goal is consistent with long-run profit maximization.[15]

Even if a company does not recognize secondary goals explicitly, it must recognize them implicitly through a commitment to long-run profitability. Take Hewlett-Packard, one of the companies that Thomas J. Peters and Robert H. Waterman cite as being an "excellent" company.[16] The following quotation from Hewlett-Packard's mission statement clearly expresses the importance of an orientation toward maximizing long-run profitability and can serve as a model:

> In our economic system, the profit we generate from our operations is the ultimate source of the funds we need to prosper and grow. It is the one absolutely essential measure of our corporate performance over the long term. Only if we continue to meet our profit objective can we achieve our other corporate objectives.[17]

2.5 CORPORATE PHILOSOPHY

The third component of a mission statement is a statement of corporate philosophy, reflecting the basic beliefs, values, aspirations, and philosophical priorities that the strategic decision makers are committed to and that guide their management of the company. It tells how the company intends to do business and often

TABLE 2.3   Johnson & Johnson's credo

Our Credo

We believe our first responsibility is to the doctors, nurses and patients,
to mothers and fathers and all others who use our products and services.
In meeting their needs everything we do must be of high quality.
We must constantly strive to reduce our costs
in order to maintain reasonable prices.
Customers' orders must be serviced promptly and accurately.
Our suppliers and distributors must have an opportunity
to make a fair profit.

We are responsible to our employees,
the men and women who work with us throughout the world.
Everyone must be considered as an individual.
We must respect their dignity and recognize their merit.
They must have a sense of security in their jobs.
Compensation must be fair and adequate,
and working conditions clean, orderly and safe.
Employees must feel free to make suggestions and complaints.
There must be equal opportunity for employment, development
and advancement for those qualified.
We must provide competent management,
and their actions must be just and ethical.

We are responsible to the communities in which we live and work
and to the world community as well.
We must be good citizens—support good works and charities
and bear our fair share of taxes.
We must encourage civic improvements and better health and education.
We must maintain in good order
the property we are privileged to use,
protecting the environment and natural resources.

Our final responsibility is to our stockholders.
Business must make a sound profit.
We must experiment with new ideas.
Research must be carried on, innovative programs developed
and mistakes paid for.
New equipment must be purchased, new facilities provided
and new products launched.
Reserves must be created to provide for adverse times.
When we operate according to these principles,
the stockholders should realize a fair return.

Johnson & Johnson

Source: Courtesy of Johnson & Johnson.

reflects the company's recognition of its social responsibility (corporate social responsibility is discussed in a later section of this chapter).

Many companies establish a philosophical creed to emphasize their own distinctive outlook on business. Thus a company's creed forms the basis for establishing its corporate culture (an issue considered in Chapter 11). Take the creed of Lincoln Electric Company. It states that productivity increases should be shared primarily by customers and employees through lower prices and higher wages. This belief distinguishes Lincoln Electric from many other enterprises and, by all accounts, is acted on by the company in terms of its specific strategies, objectives, and operating policies.[18]

Another company whose philosophical beliefs are famous is health-care giant Johnson & Johnson. Johnson & Johnson summarizes its philosophy in a credo, which is reproduced in Table 2.3. The credo articulates Johnson & Johnson's belief that the company's first responsibility is to the doctors, nurses, and patients who use J&J products, followed by the employees, the communities in which Johnson & Johnson employees live and work, and finally the company's stockholders. The credo is prominently displayed in every manager's office; and according to the J&J managers, the credo guides all important decisions.

Strong evidence of the credo's influence was apparent in the company's response to the Tylenol crisis. In 1982 seven people in the Chicago area died after taking Tylenol capsules that had been laced with cyanide. Johnson & Johnson immediately withdrew all Tylenol capsules from the U.S. market at an estimated cost to the company of $100 million. At the same time the company embarked on a comprehensive communication effort involving 2,500 Johnson & Johnson employees and targeted at the pharmaceutical and medical communities. By such means, Johnson & Johnson successfully presented itself to the public as a company that was willing to do what was right, regardless of the cost. As a consequence, the Tylenol crisis enhanced rather than tarnished Johnson & Johnson's image. Indeed, because of its actions, the company was able to retain its status as a market leader in painkillers in a matter of months.[19]

2.6 CORPORATE STAKEHOLDERS

Stakeholders and the Mission Statement

Recall that stakeholders are individuals or groups that have some claim on the company. Stakeholders can be divided into internal claimants and external claimants.[20] Internal claimants are stockholders or employees, including executive officers and board members. External claimants are all other individuals and groups affected by the company's actions. Typically, they comprise customers, suppliers, governments, unions, competitors, local communities, and the general public.

All stakeholders can justifiably expect that the company will attempt to satisfy their particular demands. As John A. Pearce, a prominent strategy writer, has noted, stockholders provide the enterprise with capital and expect an appropriate return on their investment in exchange. Employees provide labor and skills and in exchange expect commensurate income and job satisfaction. Customers want value for money. Suppliers seek dependable buyers. Governments insist on adherence to legislative regulations. Unions demand benefits for their members in proportion to their contributions to the company. Rivals seek fair competition. Local communities want companies that are responsible citizens. The general public seeks some assurance that the quality of life will be improved as a result of the company's existence.

A company has to take these claims into account when formulating its strategies, or else stakeholders may withdraw their support. Stockholders may sell their shares, employees leave their jobs, and customers buy elsewhere. Suppliers are likely to seek more dependable buyers, whereas governments can prosecute the company. Unions may engage in disruptive labor disputes, and rivals may respond to unfair competition by anticompetitive moves of their own or by filing antitrust suits. Communities may oppose the company's attempts to locate its facilities in their area, and the general public may form pressure groups, demanding action against companies that impair the quality of life. Any of these reactions can have a disastrous impact on the enterprise.

A mission statement enables a company to incorporate stakeholder claims into its strategic decision making and thereby reduce the risk of losing stakeholder support. The mission statement thus becomes the company's formal commitment to a stakeholder group; it carries the message that its strategies will be formulated with the claims of those stakeholders in mind. We have already discussed how stockholder claims are incorporated into the mission statement when a company decides that its primary goal is maximizing long-run profitability. Any strategies that the company generates should reflect this major corporate goal. Similarly, the mission statement should recognize additional stakeholder claims, in terms of secondary goals or as philosophies.

Stakeholder Impact Analysis

A company cannot always satisfy the claims of all stakeholders. The claims of different groups may conflict, and in practice few organizations have the resources to manage all stakeholders. For example, union claims for higher wages can conflict with consumer demands for reasonable prices and stockholder demands for acceptable returns. Hence often the company must make choices. To do so, it must identify the most important stakeholders and give highest priority to pursuing strategies that satisfy their needs. Stakeholder impact analysis can provide such identification. Typically, stakeholder impact analysis involves the following steps:

1.   Identify stakeholders.
2.   Identify stakeholders' interests and concerns.

3. As a result, identify what claims stakeholders are likely to make on the organization.
4. Identify the most important stakeholders from the perspective of the organization.
5. Identify the resultant strategic challenges.[21]

The analysis allows the company to identify the stakeholders most critical to its continued survival and to incorporate their claims into the mission statement explicitly. From the mission statement, stakeholder claims then feed down into the rest of the strategy formulation process. For example, if community involvement is identified as a critical stakeholder claim, it must be incorporated in the mission statement, and any strategies that conflict with it must be rejected.

2.7 CORPORATE GOVERNANCE AND STRATEGY

Satisfying stockholders' demands typically receives a great deal of attention in many corporate mission statements. As providers of capital and owners of the corporation, stockholders play a unique role. Ultimately, an enterprise exists for its stockholders. In the case of most publicly held corporations, however, stockholders delegate the job of controlling the company and determining strategies to corporate managers, who become the agents, or employees, of the stockholders.[22] Accordingly, corporate managers should pursue strategies that are in the best interest of their employers, the stockholders. They should pursue strategies that maximize stockholder wealth. Managers, however, do not always act in this fashion.

Management Goals Versus Stockholder Goals

Why should managers want to pursue strategies other than those consistent with maximizing stockholder wealth? The answer depends on the personal goals of professional managers. Many writers have argued that managers are motivated by desires for status, power, job security, income, and the like.[23] A large company can satisfy such desires better than a small one. A manager gets more status, power, job security, and income as a senior manager at General Motors than as a senior manager in a small local enterprise. Consequently, managers are thought to favor the pursuit of corporate growth goals at the expense of long-run profitability. To quote Carl Icahn, one of the most renowned corporate raiders of the 1980s,

make no mistake, a strongly knit corporate aristocracy exists in America. The top man, what's more, usually finds expanding his power more important than rewarding owners (stockholders). When Mobil and USX had excess cash, did they enrich shareholders? Of course not. They bought Marcor and Marathon—disastrous investments, but major increases in the size of the manor.[24]

Thus, instead of maximizing stockholder wealth, managers may trade long-run profitability for greater growth. Figure 2.4 graphs profitability against a company's growth rate. A company that does not grow is probably missing out on some profitable opportunities.[25] A growth rate of G_0 in Figure 2.4 is not consistent with maximizing profitability ($P_1 < P_{MAX}$). A moderate growth rate of G_1, on the other hand, does allow a company to maximize profitability, producing profits equal to P_{MAX}. Past G_1, further growth involves lower profitability (that is, past G_1 the investment required to finance further growth does not produce an adequate return). Yet G_2 might be the growth rate favored by managers, for it increases their power and status. At this growth rate, profits are only equal to P_2. Because P_{MAX} is greater than P_2, a company growing at this rate is clearly not maximizing its profitability and hence the wealth of its stockholders. However, a growth rate of G_2 may be consistent with attaining managerial goals of power, status, and income.

The problem facing stockholders, therefore, is how to *govern* the corporation so that managerial desires for excessive growth or "empire building" are held in check. In addition, there is a need for mechanisms that allow stockholders to

FIGURE 2.4   **The tradeoff between profitability and growth rate**

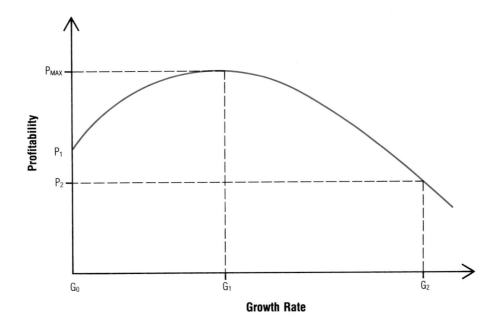

remove incompetent or ineffective managers. A number of *governance mechanisms* perform this function: shareholder meetings, the board of directors, stock-based compensation schemes, and the takeover market.

Stockholder Meetings

The constitution of most publicly held corporations specifies that companies should hold stockholder meetings at least once a year. These meetings provide a forum in which stockholders can voice their approval or discontent with management. In theory, at such meetings stockholders can propose resolutions that, if they receive a majority of stockholder votes, can shape management policy, limit the strategies management can pursue, and remove or appoint key personnel.

In practice, however, until recently stockholder meetings functioned as little more than rubber stamps for management resolutions. Stockholders must finance their own challenges and, in many cases, meet stiff regulations limiting the number of proxy votes they can solicit. Thus proposing resolutions critical of management was normally considered too expensive and difficult to be worthwhile. Rather, it was understood that stockholders could best show dissatisfaction with a company by selling their shares.

However, the recent emergence of powerful institutional investors as major stockholders is beginning to change all that. By 1987, the stock holdings of all institutional investors—pension funds, mutual funds, insurance companies, banks, brokers, and dealers—amounted to more than one-third of all corporate stock. The figure is much higher among the big companies that make up the Standard & Poor 500-stock index. For example, in 1987 the institutions held 63 percent of the stock of the Ford Motor Company, 81 percent of the stock of Digital Equipment, 79 percent of the stock of K Mart, and 72 percent of the stock of Citicorp.[26]

The significance of the growing concentration of stock in institutional hands is that institutions can no longer sell their shares without pushing down the price and taking a loss on the transaction. Jose Arau, principal investment officer for the California Public Employees Retirement System, one of the nation's largest institutional investors, has observed: "In the past you could always vote with your feet, but if you hold a thousand stocks, it's tough to do that."[27]

The lack of room to sell is putting pressure on institutions to show their dissatisfaction with management by voting proxies more aggressively. As a result, there is growing evidence that institutions are beginning to band together and put pressure on management teams that are perceived as being incompetent or pursuing strategies that are inconsistent with maximizing long-run returns.

For example, in early 1987 a group of institutional investors with major holdings in General Motors met with GM chairman Roger Smith. The institutions were angry at the $700 million "hushmail" payment made to dissident director H. Ross Perot when he quit the GM board. In addition, they criticized

Smith for GM's falling profits and market share, its weak stock price, and its poor productivity despite investments of over $40 billion in new equipment since 1979. In view of all these problems, they were also disturbed at the big bonus that GM had recently announced for its senior executives. The institutions then threatened to introduce at the next shareholder meeting a resolution that would be critical of management. In response, within a matter of weeks GM's management announced a series of major policy changes. The company stated that it would buy back stock, cut capital spending, trim production capacity, reduce excessive inventories, and replace cash bonuses for managers with a stock-based compensation plan linked to long-term performance. The institutional shareholders then withdrew their proposal.[28] Direct pressure from institutional investors had succeeded in changing critical aspects of strategy at General Motors.

The Role of the Board

Stockholder interests are looked after within the company by the board of directors. Board members are directly elected by stockholders, and under corporate law the board represents the stockholders' interests in the company. Thus the board can be held legally accountable for the company's actions. Its position at the apex of decision making within the company allows the board to monitor corporate strategy decisions and ensure that they are consistent with stockholder interests. In addition, the board has the legal authority to hire, fire, and compensate corporate employees, including, most importantly, the CEO.[29] Thus, if the board's sense is that corporate strategies are not in the best interest of stockholders, it can apply sanctions. In the case of Allegis Corporation, discussed in the Opening Incident, one factor that led to the dismissal of CEO Dick Ferris was that his strategies lost the support of the Allegis board.

The typical board comprises a mix of insiders and outsiders. Inside directors are required because they have valuable information about the company's activities. Without such information the board cannot adequately perform its monitoring function. However, since insiders are full-time employees of the company, their interests tend to be aligned with those of management. Thus, outside directors are required to bring objectivity to the monitoring and evaluation processes. Outside directors are not full-time employees of the company. Many of them are full-time professional directors who hold positions on the boards of several companies. The need to maintain a reputation as competent outside directors gives them an incentive to perform their tasks as objectively and effectively as possible.

Critics charge that inside directors may be able to dominate the outsiders on the board. Insiders can use their position within the management hierarchy to exercise control over the content of company-specific information that the board receives. Thus, they can present information in a way that puts management in a favorable light. In addition, insiders have the advantage of intimate knowledge of the company's operations. Because superior knowledge and control over information are sources of power (see Chapter 13), insiders may be better positioned to influence board-room decision making than outsiders. Hence, the board may become the captive of insiders and serve merely as a rubber stamp for management decisions, rather than as a guardian of stockholder interests. A board dominated by insiders may pursue strategies consistent with the interests of management rather than of stockholders.

Some critics even contend that most boards are dominated by the company CEO.[30] In support of this view, they point out that both inside and outside directors are often the personal nominees of the CEO. The typical inside director is subordinate to the CEO in the company's hierarchy and therefore is unlikely to criticize his or her immediate boss. In addition, since outside directors too are often the nominee of the CEO, even they can hardly be expected to evaluate the CEO objectively. Thus the loyalty of the board may be biased toward the CEO as opposed to stockholders. This problem has prompted management gurus such as Peter Drucker to comment that the one thing all boards have in common is that they do not function.

Nevertheless, there are signs that many corporate boards are moving away from merely rubber-stamping top-management decisions and are beginning to play a much more active governance role. The catalyst has been an increase in the number of lawsuits filed by stockholders against board members. The trend started in 1985 when a Delaware court ruled that the directors of Trans Union Corporation had been too quick to accept a takeover bid. The court held the directors personally liable for the difference between the offer they accepted and the price the company might have fetched in a sale. The directors then agreed to make up the $23.5 million difference. Since then, a number of major suits have been filed by stockholders against board members. These include suits directed against board members at Holly Farms, Northrop Corporation, Lincoln Savings & Loan, Lotus Development Corp., and RJR Nabisco.[31]

Spurred on by the threat of legal action, increasing numbers of boards have started to assert their independence from company management in general and from corporate CEOs in particular. For example, at ALCOA the board engineered the resignation of CEO Charles W. Parry, who had pursued an unsuccessful diversification strategy. They replaced Parry with a fellow director, Paul O'Neill, and gave him the task of refocusing the company on its core aluminum business.

It must also be said, however, that many boards still have a tendency to act as rubber stamps and seem reluctant to challenge CEOs. For example, Sunstrand CEO Evans Erikson resigned under pressure from institutional investors in 1988 after the company pleaded guilty to defense fraud. But for years, Sunstrand's lavish spending and lax financial controls went unquestioned by directors, prompting the Defense Department to take on oversight responsibility.[32] In summary, it would seem that although many board members are beginning to take their governance responsibilities more seriously, a large number of weak boards still remain.

Stock-based Compensation Schemes

To get around the problem of captive boards, stockholders have urged many companies to introduce stock-based compensation schemes for their senior executives. For example, the introduction of stock-based incentive schemes at General Motors was in response to direct pressure from institutional investors (see above). These schemes are designed to align the interests of managers with those of stockholders. In addition to their regular salary, senior executives are given stock options in the firm, so they receive a major portion of their income from dividend payments and stock price appreciations. Thus, they have a direct interest in adopting strategies consistent with maximizing stockholder wealth for, as significant stockholders themselves, they will gain from such strategies. Lee Iacocca, for example, earned $20 million in 1986 from the sale of Chrysler stock that he was given when he arrived at Chrysler in 1979 to head the company. This gain can be viewed as Iacocca's reward for adopting strategies consistent with the best interests of Chrysler's stockholders.

Recent studies have confirmed that stock-based compensation schemes for senior executives can align management and stockholder interests. For instance, one study found that managers were more likely to consider the effects of their acquisition decisions on stockholder wealth if they themselves were significant shareholders.[33] According to another study, managers who were significant stockholders were less likely to pursue diversification strategies consistent with maximizing the size of the company rather than its profitability.[34] For all their attractions, stock-based compensation schemes have yet to be universally adopted by American companies. Some critics argue that the schemes do not always have the desired effect, since stock compensation plans can harm stockholders by diluting their interests and rewarding management unjustifiably for improvements in stock prices. Critics note that stock prices often increase more because of improvements in the overall economy than because of managerial effort, and they ask why management should be rewarded for such an increase. In addition, when stock prices are falling because of factors outside the company's control, as can occur during a slump in general economic activity, then executives may see the value of their stockholdings decline rapidly. Under such circumstances, stock-based compensation schemes give managers little incentive to align their goals with those of stockholders in general.

The Takeover Constraint and
Corporate Raiders

If the board is loyal to management rather than to stockholders or if stock-based compensation schemes have not been adopted by the company, then, as suggested earlier, management may pursue strategies that maximize the company's growth rate rather than its profitability. Stockholders, however, still have some residual power, for they can always sell their shares. If they start doing so in large numbers, the price of the company's shares will decline. If the share price falls far enough, the company might be worth less on the stock market than the book value of its assets, at which point it may become a takeover target.

The risk of being bought out is known as the **takeover constraint.** The takeover constraint effectively limits the extent to which managers can pursue strategies that put their own interests above those of stockholders. If they ignore stockholder interests and the company is bought out, senior managers typically lose their independence and probably their jobs as well. So the threat of takeover can constrain management action. The experience of Allegis Corporation, presented in the Opening Incident, is one example of this process.

Increasingly, the threat of takeover is being enforced by **corporate raiders.** The corporate raider is a phenomenon that emerged in a big way during the late 1970s and early 1980s. Corporate raiders are individuals or institutions who buy up large blocks of shares in companies that they think are pursuing strategies inconsistent with maximizing stockholder wealth. They argue that if these companies pursued different strategies, they could create more wealth for stockholders. Raiders buy stock in a company either (1) to take over the business and run it more efficiently or (2) to precipitate a change in the top management, replacing the existing team with one more likely to maximize stockholder welfare.

Raiders, of course, are motivated not by altruism but by gain. If they succeed in their takeover bid, they can institute strategies that create value for stockholders—including themselves. Icahn's 1985 takeover of TWA for $400 million illustrates the process. TWA was in deep trouble when Icahn bought the company. Its high cost structure was pricing the airline out of lucrative international routes and out of business. Icahn cut costs by persuading pilots and machinists to agree to pay cuts of up to 26 percent. He broke a flight attendants' strike, replacing veterans with younger workers whose pay was up to 50 percent lower. By deciding not to renew leases for three Boeing 747 jumbo jets and selling a fourth, he also pared overhead costs. In all, TWA's cost reductions amounted to $600 million per year.[35]

Even if a takeover bid fails, raiders can still earn millions, for their stockholdings will typically be bought out by the defending company for a hefty premium. Called **greenmail,** this source of gain has stirred much controversy and debate about its benefits. The 1986 bid by international financier Sir James Goldsmith for the Goodyear Tire & Rubber Company, the largest U.S. tire manufacturer, provides a good example of some of the issues raised.[36]

During the slump of the late 1970s and early 1980s, Goodyear, like most auto-related businesses, faced severe financial constraints.[37] The recovery of the auto industry did not help much. Between 1983 and 1985, Goodyear's tire sales rose barely 2 percent and gross profits from tires fell 15 percent. However, between 1983 and 1985, its heavy depreciation policy helped Goodyear generate a strong, positive cash flow amounting to more than $2 billion.

What did Goodyear do with that money? It lacked the confidence to invest heavily in making tires; the competition was too intense. Goodyear could have returned the money to stockholders, who could then have reinvested it in more productive companies. That at least would have been consistent with maximizing stockholder wealth. Instead Goodyear chose to expand by diversifying into the oil industry—an area that it knew nothing about. In 1983 Goodyear bought Celeron Corp., an exploration and production company in the area of oil and gas, and ended up investing $1.2 billion in this business. Stockholders were not happy. Despite a bull market, by October 1986 Goodyear's stock was trading at $32 a share, just about where it had been three years before. Moreover, Goodyear's price-to-earnings ratio was a little more than half of that of the average stock.

Stockholders on their own could do little to change Goodyear's strategy. They could and did sell their shares, but since the company was not dependent on the stock market for new capital, the effect of declining share prices was minimal. Goodyear's stockholders were also too dispersed to get together and effectively pressure management to change its strategy. When Goodyear shares dropped to $32, Goldsmith saw an opportunity to make some money out of the company. He started buying shares, accumulating 12.5 million, and then offered to buy the rest for $4.7 billion. In effect, Goldsmith was saying, "I think that Goodyear is worth at least 50 percent more than the market values it—but only if I run the company myself."

Goldsmith stated his strategy for Goodyear. Specifically, he wanted the company to get back into the business it knew best, tires, and leave the business it did not know at all, oil. He also wanted Goodyear to trim back its tire operations, closing plants and reducing capacity in order to increase efficiency. Goldsmith's bid seemed likely to succeed until the insider-trader scandal concerning Ivan Boesky broke into the news. The uncertainty caused by the scandal persuaded Goldsmith to drop the bid and sell his shares back to Goodyear—for a profit of $93 million. One commentator at the time noted,

> Goodyear in effect bribed Goldsmith to take a walk. Management dipped into the corporate treasury to save its own hide. But the company also, as *The Wall Street Journal* put it, largely agreed—to carry out Sir James's ideas for the company's future. It will focus again on tires, and it will sell off businesses in which it isn't expert—presumably oil and aerospace.[38]

The Goodyear case illustrates both the bad and the good aspects of the corporate raider phenomenon. Some would argue that Goldsmith blackmailed (greenmailed) Goodyear for $93 million. The resultant debt that the company incurred will burden it for years to come. Others, however, might counter that without Goldsmith's intervention, inefficient management teams would have gone on pursuing their own desires for bigger size rather than maximizing stockholder welfare. In that context, the $93 million earned by Goldsmith can be considered a generous consulting fee rather than greenmail. Though these opposing views may never be reconciled, perhaps the most important conclusion is that a company would probably not have to deal with a takeover bid and its consequences if it were already perceived as providing stockholders with a satisfactory long-run return on their investment.

Junk Bonds, Poison Pills, and Golden Parachutes

During the 1980s, the threat of hostile takeover increased significantly, in part because of the easy availability of junk-bond financing. Popularized by the now bankrupt investment bank Drexel Burnham Lambert, junk bonds carry interest rates from 3 to 5 percent higher than the yields on government bonds of comparable maturity. The junk-bond concept is similar to that of a home mortgage. Individuals raise money to purchase their home using the house plus their down payment as collateral for the mortgage. Similarly, with junk-bond financing a corporate raider can raise the cash necessary to acquire a takeover target by using the assets and projected cash flow of the takeover target plus the raider's own equity contribution as collateral. A junk-bond issue is typically arranged for a raider by an investment bank and subscribed to by institutional investors (who are attracted by the high interest rates). Junk bonds have enabled raiders to raise large sums of money to finance takeovers without having to contribute a great deal in the way of equity. This possibility has made even the largest companies vulnerable to takeover by raiders who, in financial terms, are relatively small.

Although the growth of junk-bond financing has undoubtedly strengthened the takeover constraint, further limiting the extent to which managers can pursue strategies that put their own interests above those of stockholders, the widespread use of junk bonds has also raised serious concerns. Critics charge that the level of debt taken on in junk-bond-financed takeovers significantly increases the risk of bankruptcy and forces managers to focus on short-term profits at the expense of long-term investments in R&D and new capital equipment.[39] For example, the collapse of Campeau's Allied and Federated Department Stores, two large chains (including Bloomingdale's, Filene's, and others,) has been attributed to Campeau Corporation's high level of debt. Campeau financed both purchases with junk bonds.

On the other hand, the bankruptcy of Drexel Burnham Lambert in 1990, the main investment bank in the junk-bond market, took a lot of the steam out of junk-bond issues and will, in all probability, lead to a reduction in the number of junk-bond-financed hostile takeovers over the next few years. In particular, institutional investors appear to be far more cautious about subscribing to highly leveraged junk-bond issues than they were prior to Drexel's demise. However, as many commentators have pointed out, junk bonds themselves are here to stay. Evidence of this can be found in the rush among well-regarded investment banks, such as Merrill Lynch, Morgan Stanley, Salomon Brothers, and Goldman Sachs, to grab a share of Drexel's junk-bond business.[40]

One response by management to the threat posed by junk-bond-financed takeovers has been to create so-called *poison pills*. The purpose of a poison pill is to make it difficult for a raider to acquire a company. The poison pill devised by Household International in 1985 is typical. The Household board of directors unilaterally changed the company's constitution. In response to any takeover bid involving a premium over market value of less than $6 billion, stockholders could not sell their stock without the prior permission of the board. At that time, Household had a market value of less than $2 billion, so the constitution change effectively gave the board the ability to reject any takeover attempt that offered less than $8 billion for Household. Because no raiders in their right mind would offer $8 billion for a company valued at less than $2 billion, the tactic essentially nullified the takeover constraint with regard to Household.

The right of companies to create poison pills has been challenged on several occasions in the law courts by stockholders who object to the unilateral restrictions imposed by management on their right to sell stock to a prospective acquirer. To date the courts have tended to side with management (the right of Household's board to issue restrictions was upheld by a Delaware court). However, there are many examples of stockholders at stockholder meetings introducing resolutions that effectively limit the ability of a company to devise a poison-pill defense, so it remains to be seen just how successful and widespread this tactic is going to be.

Another response to the threat posed by junk-bond-financed takeovers has been the increasing use of *golden parachute contracts*. Golden parachutes are severance contracts that handsomely compensate top-level managers for the loss of their jobs in the event of a takeover. These contracts came into being because of fears that takeover threats were forcing managers to focus on maximizing short-term earnings in an attempt to boost the company's current stock price, thereby reducing the risk of takeover at the expense of long-run investments in R&D and new capital equipment. Managers also complained that the threat of takeover reduced their willingness to fund risky but potentially profitable investments. By reducing managers' concerns about the loss of their jobs, advocates argue, golden parachute contracts encourage managers to focus on long-run investments and to take necessary risks. In addition, because management is less concerned with possible job loss, golden parachute contracts can increase the probability that top management will review takeover proposals objectively, taking stockholder interests into account when deciding how to respond.

For these reasons, golden parachute contracts, when used properly, can be beneficial. On the other hand, some stockholders see golden parachutes as little more than an "insurance against incompetence" or as a "reward for failure," and they argue that managers should not be rewarded for losing their job.[41] One way of ensuring that this does not occur while still preserving the beneficial aspects of golden parachute contracts may be to link the payment of a golden parachute to the premium earned by stockholders in the event of a takeover bid.

The Efficacy of Corporate Governance

As we have seen, in theory managers are constrained by stockholder meetings, the board of directors, stock compensation schemes, and the threat of takeover to adopt strategies consistent with maximizing stockholder wealth. Notwithstanding recent developments, however, in practice management often dominates stockholder meetings and the board of directors. Thus these institutions have a tendency to rubber-stamp managerial decisions. Also, as noted above, stock compensation schemes are not universally adopted and do not always work as intended. In addition, critics contend that in practice the threat of takeover is an imperfect constraint on managerial action.[42] For example, research evidence suggests that only the most unprofitable companies face a greater than average chance of being acquired. Mediocre companies are apparently no more likely to be acquired than are excellent companies, even though mediocre companies are probably not using their resources to the best effect. Thus there seems to be considerable scope for managers to pursue strategies inconsistent with stockholder wealth before they face a hostile takeover bid. Moreover, the use of poison-pill contracts may nullify the takeover constraint.

For all these reasons, the governance mechanisms discussed here do not always provide complete protection for stockholder interests. In some circumstances it may be difficult for stockholders to remove incompetent managers or managers who pursue empire-building growth strategies at the expense of company profitability. Several writers have observed that although corporate governance mechanisms normally succeed in removing incompetent managers when a company is facing a financial crisis, they are not very effective at placing limits on managerial discretion in noncrisis situations. Thus, for example, the board of Diamond Shamrock Corp. supported the company's CEO, Bill Bricker, over a ten-year period, during which he pursued an aggressive but unprofitable diversification strategy designed to transform what was originally a chemical company into a big-league energy conglomerate. The board continued to support Bricker despite considerable stockholder opposition and the failure of the company to show any profit from its energy operations. Only after a loss of over $600 million, a crash in the company's stock price, and three hostile takeover bids in twelve months did the board finally withdraw its support for Bricker and ask him to resign. If the board had been functioning as theory says it should, in all probability Bricker would have been removed years earlier.[43]

Leveraged Buyouts

The imperfections in corporate governance mechanisms have been used by Harvard Business School professor Michael Jensen to explain the dramatic growth of leveraged buyouts (LBOs) in the United States.[44] The total value of the 76 LBOs undertaken in 1979 was $1.4 billion (in 1988 dollars). In comparison, the total value of the 214 LBOs undertaken in 1988 exceeded $77 billion—nearly one-third of the value of all mergers and acquisitions in the United States.

Whereas in a typical takeover a raider buys enough stock to gain control of a company, in an LBO a company's own executives are often (but not always) among the buyers. Most LBOs are financed by junk bonds. The management group undertaking an LBO typically raises cash by issuing bonds and then uses that cash to buy the company's stock. Thus, LBOs involve a swap of equity for debt. In effect, the company replaces its stockholders with creditors (bondholders), thereby transforming the corporation from a public into a private entity. However, often the same institutions that were major stockholders prior to an LBO are also major bondholders after an LBO. The difference is that as stockholders they were not guaranteed a regular dividend payment, whereas when they become bondholders they are guaranteed regular payment from the company.

Jensen's theory is that LBOs solve many of the problems created by imperfect corporate governance mechanisms. According to Jensen, a major weakness and source of waste in the public corporation is the conflict between stockholders and managers over the payout of *free cash flow*. He defines *free cash flow* as cash flow in excess of that required to fund all investment projects with positive net present values when discounted at the relevant cost of capital. Since free cash flow is by definition cash that cannot be profitably reinvested within the company, Jensen argues that it should be distributed to stockholders.

However, managers generally resist distributing surplus cash resources to stockholders. Rather, for reasons discussed earlier, they have a tendency to invest such cash in growth-maximizing or empire-building strategies. Jensen makes his point with reference to the Ford Motor Company:

> A vivid example is the Ford Motor Company which sits on nearly $15 billion in cash and marketable securities in an industry with excess capacity. Ford's management has been deliberating about acquiring financial service companies, aerospace companies, or making some other multibillion-dollar diversification move—rather than deliberating about efficiently distributing Ford's excess cash to its owners so they can decide how to re-invest it.[45]

Jensen sees a solution to this problem in LBOs. Although management does not have to pay out dividends to stockholders, it does have to make regular debt payments to bondholders or face bankruptcy. Thus, according to Jensen, the debt used to finance an LBO helps limit the waste of free cash flow by compelling managers to pay out excess cash to service debt payments, rather than spending it on empire-building projects with low or negative returns, excessive staff, indulgent perquisites, and other organizational inefficiencies. Further, Jensen sees debt as a way of motivating managers to look for greater efficiencies. The need to service high debt payments is argued to force managers to slash unsound investment programs, reduce overhead, and dispose of assets that are more valuable outside the company. The proceeds generated by these restructurings can then be used to reduce debt to more sustainable levels, creating a leaner, more efficient, and more competitive organization.

However, by no means all commentators are as enthusiastic about the potential of LBOs. Robert Reich, professor of political economy and management at Harvard's John F. Kennedy School of Government, is one of the most vocal critics of LBOs.[46] Reich sees LBOs as being driven by the desires of Wall Street's "paper entrepreneurs" to collect lucrative fees, rather than by desires to improve efficiency. For illustration, he points out that the RJR Nabisco LBO generated almost $1 billion in fees, including $153 million in advisory fees, $294 million in financing fees for investment banks, and $325 million in commercial-bank fees.

Furthermore, Reich sees two main problems with LBOs. First, he argues that the necessity of paying back large loans forces management to focus on the short term and cut back on long-term investments, particularly in R&D and new capital spending. The net effect is likely to be a decline in the competitiveness of LBOs. Second, Reich believes that the debt taken on to finance an LBO significantly increases the risk of bankruptcy. The strong economy of the 1980s may have obscured this fact. Strong demand has allowed companies to service high debt payments. But what might happen if a recession hits? Reich cites a study by the Brookings Institute, which examined the effects of a recession similar in severity to that which rocked the United States in 1974 and 1975. The Brookings computer simulation revealed that, with the levels of corporate debt prevailing in the late 1980s, 1 in 10 U.S. companies would succumb to bankruptcy.

Although it is still too early to say for sure whether Reich or Jensen is closer to the truth, it is interesting to note that the high-visibility bankruptcies of a number of junk-bond-financed LBOs during 1989 and 1990 seemed to reduce dramatically the number of new LBOs during 1990. The bankruptcies, which included Hillsborough Holdings, SCI Television, and Leaseway, were brought about by the inability of these LBOs to meet their debt payments, which is exactly the problem that Reich argues can be expected with junk-bond-financed LBOs.

2.8 CORPORATE SOCIAL RESPONSIBILITY

The Concept of Social Responsibility

Corporate responsibility refers to corporate actions that protect and improve the welfare of society along with the corporation's own interests.[47] Strategic decisions of large corporations inevitably involve social as well as economic consequences; the two cannot be separated.[48] Moreover, the social consequences of economic actions typically affect the company's outside claimants, especially local communities and the general public. For example, if a large company decides for economic reasons to close a plant employing thousands of workers in a small community, the social impact of the closing on that community is both direct and fundamental. Many steel towns in the Midwest have turned into ghost towns after such closings. Similarly, when a manufacturing enterprise builds a major plant in a rural community, it probably changes the social fabric of that community forever. Thus, when selecting a strategy on the basis of economic criteria, a company is also making a choice that will have wider social consequences.

Why Be Socially Responsible?

Should companies be socially responsible? Should they build certain social criteria or goals into their strategic decision making? Many companies do incorporate broad declarations of social intent into their mission statement. Indeed, for a number of good reasons, companies should be socially responsible.

In its purest form, social responsibility can be supported for its own sake simply because it is the noble, or right, way for a company to behave. Less pure but perhaps more practical are arguments that socially responsible behavior is in a company's self-interest. Since economic actions have social consequences affecting a company's outside claimants, if a company wants to retain the support of the claimants, it must take those social consequences into account when formulating strategies. Otherwise it may generate ill will and opposition. For example, if a community perceives a company as having an adverse impact on the local environment, it may block the company's attempts to build new facilities in the area.

Edward H. Bowman of the University of Pennsylvania's Wharton School has taken this point further, arguing that social responsibility is actually a sound investment strategy.[49] He maintains that a company's social behavior affects the price of its stock. In other words, socially responsible policy can also benefit a company's important inside claimants, the stockholders. According to Bowman, many investors view companies that are not socially responsible as riskier investments. Moreover, many institutional investors, such as churches, universities, cities, states, and mutual funds, pay attention to corporate social behavior and thus influence the market for a company's stock.

Evidence can certainly be found in favor of Bowman's arguments. The withdrawal of American assets from South Africa by companies such as IBM and General Motors in 1986, for example, can at least in part be attributed to a desire to create a favorable impression with investors. At that time, for social or political reasons, many investors were selling any stock they held in companies that maintained a substantial presence in South Africa. Similarly, Union Carbide saw its market value plunge more than 37 percent in 1985 in the aftermath of the gas leak at its Bhopal plant in India (which killed 1,757 people and left 17,000 seriously injured) and subsequent revelations concerning poor safety procedures at many Union Carbide plants. For Union Carbide, the consequence was a takeover bid from GAF Corporation (which ultimately failed), extended litigation, and a negative image problem.

Bowman has also shown that companies concerned about social responsibility tend to be more profitable.[50] To test the effect of social responsibility on profits, Bowman performed a line-by-line content analysis of the 1973 annual reports of food-processing companies in order to ascertain the amount of prose devoted to issues of corporate social responsibility. He then used this figure as a surrogate for actual company concern. He found that companies with some social responsibility prose performed better than those with none (14.7 percent return on equity against 10.2 percent return on equity over the previous five years).

On the other hand, there are those who argue that a company has no business pursuing social goals. Nobel laureate Milton Friedman, for one, insists that concepts of social responsibility should not enter the corporate strategic decision process:

> What does it mean to say that the corporate executive has a social responsibility in his capacity as a businessman? If this statement is not pure rhetoric, it must mean that he is to act in some way that is not in the interests of his employers. For example . . . that he is to make expenditures on reducing pollution beyond the amount that is in the best interests of the corporation or that is required by law in order to contribute to the social objective of improving the environment. . . . Insofar as his actions in accord with his social responsibility reduce returns to stockholders, he is spending their money. Insofar as his actions raise the price to customers, he is spending the customer's money. Insofar as the actions lower the wages of some employees, he is spending their money.[51]

Essentially, Friedman's position is that a business has only one kind of social responsibility: to use its resources for activities that increase its profits, *so long as it stays within the rules of the game,* which is to say, so long as it engages in open and free competition without deception or fraud.

Corporate Social Responsibility and Regulation

Friedman's views cannot be ignored, particularly in a country like the United States, where the rules of the game are well established. American society recognizes that businesses, if left to themselves, will not always behave in a socially responsible manner. The need to generate profit can conflict with society's desire for responsible behavior. For this reason, governments, acting in the interests of society as a whole, have enacted legislation to regulate corporate behavior. Thus there are rules to safeguard consumers from abuse by companies, rules to ensure fair competition, and rules to protect the environment (from pollution, for example).

Unfortunately, companies do not always obey these rules. In a major survey of corporate crimes from 1970 to 1980, *Fortune* magazine found plenty of evidence to this effect.[52] Of 1,043 major corporations in the study, 117, or 11 percent, were involved in at least one major delinquency during the period covered. Some companies were multiple offenders. In all, 188 citations were given by *Fortune,* covering 163 separate offenses: 98 antitrust violations; 28 cases of kickbacks, bribery, or illegal rebates; 21 cases of illegal political contributions; 11 cases of fraud; and 5 cases of tax evasion.

Bethlehem Steel illustrates the kind of cases identified here. The company pleaded guilty to criminal activity over the five-year period 1972–1976. It was operating a kickback scheme for the purpose of bribing representatives of shiplines to steer repair work to Bethlehem's seven shipyards. Another case involves Archer-Daniels-Midland Company, which was successfully prosecuted in 1976 for defrauding grain buyers by short-weighing. Still another instance of corporate crime is offered by E. I. Du Pont de Nemours's dye group. Wanting to raise prices, in late 1970 the executives of Du Pont's dye business contacted the competition and won an agreement for a follow-the-leader scheme. In January 1971, Du Pont announced a 10 percent price increase; the competition followed suit in February and March. When charged with price fixing, the nine companies involved all pleaded no contest and were fined between $35,000 and $50,000 each.

The very fact that companies do not always behave lawfully is in itself an argument for stressing social responsibility in the mission statement of an enterprise. By expressing its commitment to "free enterprise" or to "maintaining fair relationships with our customers," a company is sending a message both to its own employees and to important stakeholders that it intends to act within the bounds of the law.

The Practice of Social Responsibility

How should a company decide which social issues it will respond to and to what extent it will trade profits for social gain? The spectrum of actual corporate behavior among companies that espouse social responsibility is quite broad. It encompasses mere reaction to the strict requirements of the law, some response to direct pressure from interest groups, and commitment to incorporating wider social concerns within the corporate ethic.

Although the concept of social responsibility implies voluntary response by the company, some degree of external coercion, perhaps from government or from other pressure groups, is likely to occur in a number of situations. Such prodding may be difficult to resist. Where no pressure exists, the incentive to adopt a social policy commitment will be less. There are, however, some criteria that a company may apply to help it choose which social action to undertake. This approach is to judge both the private and the social effects of particular strategies. A company can rank them according to their profitability and their social benefits, as shown in Figure 2.5.[53]

FIGURE 2.5   **Comparing profitability and social returns from strategies**

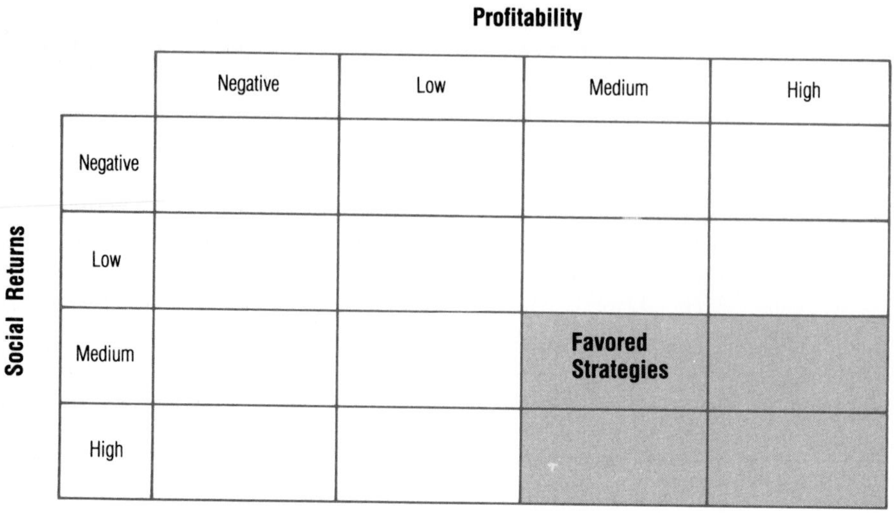

Profitability

	Negative	Low	Medium	High
Negative				
Low				
Medium			**Favored Strategies**	
High				

Social Returns (vertical axis label)

If this framework is used, strategies showing both high profitability and high social benefits would be the most likely to be adopted. Those with high profitability but negative social effects would worry a socially responsible company and probably would not be pursued. On the other hand, even the most socially concerned company would hesitate to adopt strategies with high social gains but negative or low profitability.

2.9 SUMMARY OF CHAPTER

The primary purpose of this chapter is to identify various factors that constitute the organizational context within which strategies are formulated. Normally, these factors are explicitly recognized through the corporate mission statement. The mission statement thus sets the boundaries within which strategies must be contained. Specifically, the following points are made:

1. The mission statement is the starting point of strategic management. It sets the context within which strategies are formulated.

2. The mission statement contains three broad elements: a definition of the company's business, a statement of the major goals of the corporation, and a statement of corporate philosophy.

3. For a single-business company, defining the business involves focusing on consumer groups to be served, consumer needs to be satisfied, and the technologies by which those needs can be satisfied. This amounts to a consumer-oriented business definition.

4. For a diversified company, defining the business involves focusing on the purpose behind owning a portfolio of businesses, the desired scope of the enterprise, and the desired balance between the constituent businesses in the portfolio.

5. A company's major corporate goal should reflect concern for the welfare of the company's owners—its stockholders. Maximizing long-run profits is the major goal consistent with maximizing stockholder wealth.

6. To avoid adverse short-run consequences of an overzealous focus on profitability, a company needs to adopt a number of secondary goals that balance short-run and long-run considerations.

7. A company's corporate philosophy makes clear how the company intends to do business. A statement of this philosophy reflects the company's basic values, aspirations, beliefs, and philosophical priorities.

8. Every company has its stakeholders—individuals who have some claim on the organization. They can be divided into inside and outside claimants. The company needs to recognize their claims in its mission statement, for if it does not, it may lose their support.

9. The claims of stakeholders can conflict. Frequently, a company does not have the resources to satisfy all claimants. Thus it has to identify the stakeholder groups that are most important to its continued survival and satisfy their claims first. It can uncover this information through a stakeholder impact analysis.

10. Stockholders are among a company's most important internal claimants. If stockholder wealth is not maximized, then the company runs the risk of becoming a takeover target. Companies sometimes fall into this trap because of managerial obsessions with the size of the business and the power and status that it brings. Corporate raiders have become a major means of disciplining such companies through takeover bids.

11. Satisfying a company's claimants often involves stressing corporate social responsibility. Social responsibility is important because a company's economic actions inevitably have social consequences that directly affect its claimants. Thus stressing social responsibility is in the company's best interest.

12. Deciding which social issues to respond to can prove difficult for a company. However, by comparing the social impact of strategies against their economic returns, a company can identify strategies with negative or positive social consequences.

Discussion Questions

1. Why is it important for a company to take a consumer-oriented view of its businesses? What are the possible shortcomings of such a view?

2. What are the strategic implications of a focus on short-run returns? Discuss in terms of the impact on product innovation, marketing expenditure, manufacturing, and purchasing decisions.

3. Are corporate raiders a positive or negative influence on the U.S. economy? How can companies reduce the risk of takeover?

4. Companies should always be socially responsible, whatever the cost. Discuss.

Endnotes

1. Kenneth Labich, "How Dick Ferris Blew It," *Fortune,* July 6, 1987, pp. 42–46. Jodi Klein, "The Lack of Allegiance at Allegis," *Business & Society Review* (Spring 1988), 30–33. James Ellis, "The Unraveling of an Idea," *Business Week,* June 22, 1987, pp. 42–43.

2. Derek F. Abell, *Defining the Business: The Starting Point of Strategic Planning* (Englewood Cliffs, N.J.: Prentice-Hall, 1980). K. Andrews, *The Concept of Corporate Strategy* (Homewood, Ill.: Dow Jones Irwin, 1971). John A. Pearce, "The Company Mission as a Strategic Tool," *Sloan Management Review* (Spring 1982), 15–24.

3. These three questions were first proposed by P. F. Drucker. See Drucker, *Management—Tasks, Responsibilities, Practices* (New York: Harper & Row, 1974), pp. 74–94.

4. Abell, *Defining the Business,* p. 17.

5. Theodore Levitt, "Marketing Myopia," *Harvard Business Review* (July–August 1960), 45–56.

6. F. J. Weston and S. K. Mansinghka, "Tests of the Efficiency Performance of Conglomerate Firms," *Journal of Finance,* 26 (1971), 919–935.

7. T. Mack, "Polishing the Gem," *Forbes,* January 28, 1985, p. 64.

8. For details, see "Polaroid: Turning Away from Land's One Product Strategy," *Business Week,* March 2, 1981, pp. 108–112; "Polaroid Can't Get Its Future in Focus," *Business Week,* April 4, 1983, pp. 31–32; "Polaroid Hopes to Snap Out of Sales Slump," *The Wall Street Journal,* November 11, 1985, p. 6; and "The Marketing Man Who Hopes to Reform Polaroid," *International Management* (June 1986), 35.

9. S. R. Reid, "A Reply to the Weston and Mansinghka Criticisms Dealing with Conglomerate Mergers," *Journal of Finance,* 26 (1971), 937–940.

10. Peter F. Drucker, *The Practice of Management* (New York: Harper, 1954).

11. Robert H. Hayes and William J. Abernathy, "Managing Our Way to Economic Decline," *Harvard Business Review* (July–August 1980), 67–77.

12. Lester C. Thurow, *The Zero Sum Solution* (New York: Simon and Schuster, 1985), 69–89.

13. "Too Much Penny-Pinching at American Home?" *Business Week,* December 22, 1986, pp. 64–65.

14. Figures are taken from Standard & Poor's COMPUSTAT service.

15. The evidence of the Profit Impact of Market Strategy (PIMS) data base provides strong support for this proposition, although the direction of causation has not been proven. See R. D. Buzzell, T. G. Bradley, and R. G. M. Sultan, "Market Share: A Key to Profitability," *Harvard Business Review* (January–February 1975), 97–106.

16. Thomas J. Peters and Robert H. Waterman, *In Search of Excellence* (New York: Harper & Row, 1982).

17. Excerpt from Hewlett-Packard's Mission Statement. Courtesy of Hewlett-Packard Company.

18. M. D. Richards, *Setting Strategic Goals and Objectives* (St. Paul, Minn.: West, 1986).

19. For details, see "Johnson & Johnson (A)," *Harvard Business School Case* #384-053, Harvard Business School.

20. Pearce, "The Company Mission," pp. 15–24.

21. I. C. Macmillan and P. E. Jones, *Strategy Formulation: Power and Politics* (St. Paul, Minn.: West, 1986), 66.

22. M. C. Jensen and W. H. Meckling, "Theory of the Firm: Managerial Behavior, Agency Costs and Ownership Structure," *Journal of Financial Economics,* 3, (1976), 305–360.

23. For example, see R. Marris, *The Economic Theory of Managerial Capitalism* (London: Macmillan, 1964); and J. K. Galbraith, *The New Industrial State* (Boston: Houghton-Mifflin, 1970).

24. Carl Icahn, "What Ails Corporate America—And What Should Be Done?" *Business Week,* October 27, 1986, p. 101.

25. E. T. Penrose, *The Theory of the Growth of the Firm* (London: Macmillan, 1958).

26. Bruce Nussbaum and Judith Dobrzynski, "The Battle, for Corporate Control," *Business Week,* May 18, 1987, pp. 102–109.

27. Quoted in Christopher Power and Vick Cahan, "Shareholders Aren't Just Rolling Over Anymore," *Business Week,* April 27, 1987, pp. 32–33.

28. Nussbaum and Dobrzynski, "The Battle for Corporate Control," pp. 102–109.

29. O. E. Williamson, *The Economic Institutions of Capitalism* (New York: Free Press, 1985).

30. M. L. Mace, *Directors: Myth and Reality* (Cambridge, Mass.: Harvard University Press, 1971). S. C. Vance, *Corporate Leadership: Boards of Directors and Strategy* (New York: McGraw-Hill, 1983).

31. Michele Galen, "A Seat on the Board is Getting Hotter," *Business Week,* July 3, 1989, pp. 72–73.

32. Judith Dobrzynski, Michael Schroeder, Gregory Miles, and Joseph Weber, "Taking Charge: Corporate Directors Flex Their Muscle," *Business Week,* July 3, 1989, pp. 66–71.

33. W. G. Lewellen, C. Eoderer, and A. Rosenfeld, "Merger Decisions and Executive Stock Ownership in Acquiring Firms," *Journal of Accounting and Economics,* 7 (1985), 209–231.

34. C. W. L. Hill and S. A. Snell, "External Control, Corporate Strategy, and Firm Performance," *Strategic Management Journal,* 9, (1988), pp. 577–590.

35. "Carl Icahn: Raider or Manager?" *Business Week,* October 27, 1986, pp. 98–104.

36. J. K. Glassman, "Aprés Ivan," *The New Republic,* December 15, 1986, pp. 11–13.

37. See "The Two Worlds of Jimmy Goldsmith," *Business Week,* December 1, 1986, pp. 98–102; "Goodyear May Be Acquired by Goldsmith," *The Wall Street Journal,* November 19, 1986, p. 2; and Glassman, "Aprés Ivan," p. 12.

38. Glassman, "Aprés Ivan," p. 12.

39. For an interesting discussion of the issues here, see Chapter 1 of J. C. Coffee, L. Lowebstein, and S. Rose-Ackerman, *Knights: Raiders & Targets* (Oxford: Oxford University Press, 1988). See also M. C. Jensen, "The Takeover Controversy: Analysis and Evidence," Chapter 20 in the same volume.

40. J. H. Dobrzynski, "After Drexel," *Business Week,* February 26, 1990, pp. 37–40.

41. H. Singh and F. Harianto, "Management-Board Relationships, Takeover Risk, and the Adoption of Golden Parachutes," *Academy of Management Journal,* 32 (1989), pp. 7–24.

42. A. J. Singh, *Takeovers: Their Relevance to the Stockmarket and the Theory of the Firm* (Cambridge, England: Cambridge University Press, 1971).

43. See "The Downfall of a CEO," *Business Week,* February 16, 1987, pp. 76–84.

44. See Michael C. Jensen, "Agency Costs of Free Cash Flow, Corporate Finance, and Takeovers," *American Economic Review,* (1986), 323–329; and Michael C. Jensen, "The Eclipse of the Public Corporation," *Harvard Business Review* (September–October 1989), 61–74.

45. Jensen, ibid., p. 66.

46. Robert B. Reich, "Leverage Buyouts: America Pays the Price," *The New York Times Magazine,* January 29, 1989, pp. 32–40.

47. K. Davis, W. C. Frederick, and R. L. Blomstrom, *Business and Society; Concepts and Policy Issues* (New York: McGraw-Hill, 1980).

48. Henry Mintzberg, "The Case for Corporate Social Responsibility," *Journal of Business Strategy* (December 1983), 3–15.

49. Edward H. Bowman, "Corporate Social Responsibility and the Investor," *Journal of Contemporary Business* (Winter 1973), 21–43.

50. Edward H. Bowman and M. Haire, "Strategic Posture Towards Corporate Social Responsibility," *California Management Review* (Winter 1975), 49–58.

51. Milton Friedman, "A Friedman Doctrine: The Social Responsibility of Business Is to Increase Its Profits," *The New York Times Magazine,* September 13, 1970, pp. 33.

52. I. Ross, "How Lawless Are Big Companies?" *Fortune,* December 1, 1980, pp. 56–64.

53. J. F. Pickering and T. T. Jones, "The Firm and Its Social Environment," in J. F. Pickering and T. A. J. Cockerill, Eds., *The Economic Management of the Firm* (Oxford: Philip Allan, 1984), pp. 277–323.

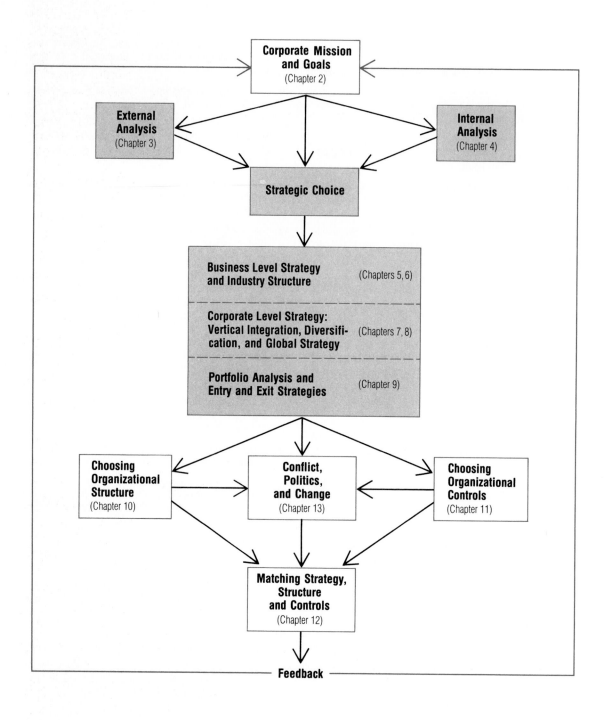

STRATEGY
FORMULATION

Chapter 3

ANALYZING THE EXTERNAL ENVIRONMENT: THE IDENTIFICATION OF OPPORTUNITIES AND THREATS

3.1 OPENING INCIDENT: USX

U.S. Steel, the forerunner of USX, was formed in the early 1900s by merging ten steel companies. For more than half a century U.S. Steel dominated the American steel industry. Into the 1960s the company accounted for as much as 55 percent of the industry's sales. By 1986, however, the market share of the steel-making arm of USX had fallen to 17 percent, and in that year steel operations posted enormous losses (estimated at $1.4 billion). The once-dominant force in a consolidated domestic industry found itself struggling to hold on to a dwindling market share in a highly competitive global industry.

Most of the decline in the company's market share occurred after the boom years of 1972–

1974, when demand for steel was at an all-time high. Since then the American steel market has been dealt a number of blows. For instance, low-cost foreign producers, utilizing state-of-the-art production facilities, captured a large share of the domestic market. In 1980, foreign steel mills held 16 percent of the domestic market; by 1985, benefiting from a strong dollar, they had captured 22 percent. In addition, new steel-making technologies, based on electric arc furnaces, have allowed domestic minimills to produce steel at a lower cost than the large, integrated operations of the steel majors, which, in some cases, are still based on the technology of the 1930s. As a result, minimills and specialty steel companies increased their share of the market from 21 percent in 1980 to around 40 percent in 1985.

Another blow to the mature industry has been the growing popularity of high-tech synthetic substitutes for steel, which are pushing out steel products in many market segments. For example, auto manufacturers increasingly prefer plastic rather than steel body panels. Moreover, the high costs of severance pay, pensions, and insurance for terminated workers and the low liquidation value of steel plants have made the shutdown of steel-making capacity expensive. In 1983, it cost USX $1.2 billion to shut down 16 percent of its capacity and shed 15,400 jobs. These high costs of exit have made it difficult for established companies to reduce their capacity in line with demand. As a direct result, 40 percent of total domestic capacity was lying idle in 1987.

Hindsight is always 20/20, so it is easy to criticize USX for failing to respond to those market threats until it was too late. Nevertheless, there is little doubt that if USX had responded to the threats as they began to emerge in the 1960s, it would not be facing problems of such magnitude today. The company could have made massive cost-reducing investments while it was making good money; it could have become a major player in the minimills and specialty steel segments; or it could have diversified into the manufacture of synthetics. However, instead of formulating strategic responses to these environmental threats, USX, along with other steel majors, continued to indulge in cozy price-leadership agreements and to lobby Washington for import controls. In short, USX continued to behave like a dominant company in a strong domestic industry, whereas it was fast becoming a high-cost manufacturer in a much larger, and rapidly changing, global industry.[1]

3.2 OVERVIEW

A company's external environment can be broken down into two parts: the industry environment that the company competes in and the macro-environment. Both environments and their relationship to the company are illustrated in Figure 3.1. A company's industry environment consists of elements that directly affect the company, such as competitors, customers, and suppliers. The macro-environment consists of the broader economic, social, demographic, political, legal, and technological setting within which the industry and the company are placed.

For a company to succeed, its strategy must be consistent with the external environment. Superior performance is the product of a good fit between strategy and environment. To achieve a good fit, managers must first understand the forces that shape competition in the external environment. This understanding enables them to identify external environmental trends and to respond by adopting appropriate strategies. In other words, they make the correct strategic choices in relation to the environment, thereby maximizing the company's profitability. In contrast, companies that fail often do so because their managers do not understand the forces that shape competition in the external environment. Consequently, they make poor strategic choices (the company's strategy does not fit the environment), and the company's profitability suffers. USX, discussed in the Opening Incident, is a company whose strategy did not fit its environment. USX

FIGURE 3.1   **The external environment**

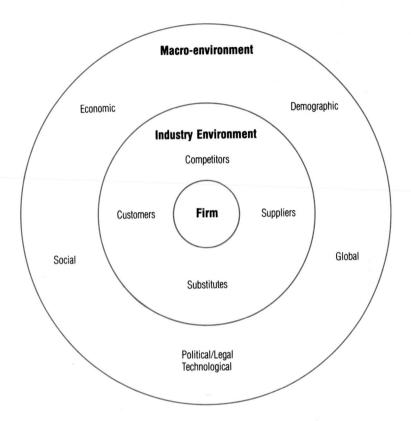

failed to anticipate the threats to its position that arose from changes in the environment of the steel industry. The strategy USX was pursuing in the early 1980s was suited to the environment of the steel industry in the 1960s but not in the 1980s, and USX's market share and profitability declined.

The objective of this chapter is to discuss a number of models that can assist strategic managers in analyzing the external environment. The models provide a framework that can be used to identify environmental *opportunities* and *threats*. Opportunities arise when environmental trends create the potential for a company to increase profits. For example, the baby boom of the 1950s and early 1960s gave Mothercare Stores, Inc., the opportunity to expand its maternity ware and child-care products business into a national operation. Threats arise when environmental trends endanger the integrity and profitability of a company's business: Trends in the steel industry threatened USX's business.

Having identified profitable opportunities, strategic managers need to formulate strategies that enable the company to exploit those opportunities and maximize its return on investment. Because external threats can squeeze profitability out of a company, strategic managers must also formulate strategies that defend a company's profitability against such threats. The different strategic alternatives that a company can adopt to maximize opportunities and counter threats are discussed in Chapters 5, 6, 7 and 8. In this chapter, we focus on the issue of identifying opportunities and threats.

We begin with a discussion of a model for analyzing the industry environment. Next we discuss the competitive implications that arise when groups of companies within an industry pursue similar strategies. We then move on to consider the nature of industry evolution. Finally, we review a number of macroenvironmental issues. By the end of this chapter, you should be familiar with the main factors that strategic managers have to take into consideration when analyzing a company's external environment for opportunities and threats.

3.3 ANALYZING THE INDUSTRY ENVIRONMENT

An *industry* can be defined as a group of companies offering products or services that are close substitutes for each other. Close substitutes are products or services that satisfy the same basic *consumer* needs. For example, the metal and plastic body panels used in automobile construction are close substitutes for each other. Despite different production technologies, auto supply companies manufacturing metal body panels are in the same basic industry as companies manufacturing plastic body panels. They are serving the same consumer need, that of auto assembly companies for body panels.

The task facing strategic managers is to analyze competitive forces in an industry environment in order to identify the opportunities and threats that confront a company. Michael E. Porter of the Harvard School of Business Administration has developed a framework that helps managers do this.[2] Porter's framework is known as the **five forces model.** It focuses on five forces that shape competition within an industry: (1) the risk of new entry by potential competitors, (2) the degree of rivalry among established companies within an industry, (3) the bargaining power of buyers, (4) the bargaining power of suppliers, and (5) the closeness of substitutes to an industry's products (see Figure 3.2).

Porter's argument is that the stronger each of these forces is, the more limited are established companies in their ability to raise prices and earn greater profits. Within Porter's framework, a strong competitive force can be regarded as a threat since it depresses profits. A weak competitive force can be regarded as an opportunity since it allows a company to earn greater profits. Because of factors beyond a company's direct control, such as industry evolution, the strength of the five forces may change through time. In such circumstances, the task facing strategic managers is to recognize opportunities and threats as they arise and to formulate appropriate strategic responses. In addition, it is possible for a company, through its choice of strategy, to alter the strength of one or more of the

FIGURE 3.2   **Porter's five forces model**

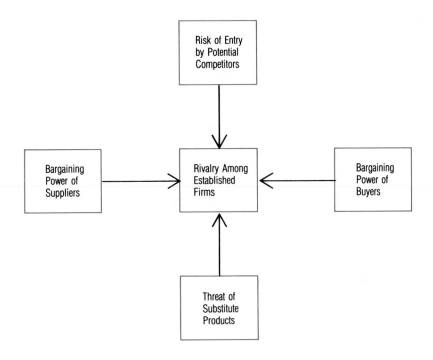

five forces to its advantage. This is part of the subject matter of the following chapters. In this chapter, we focus on understanding the impact that each of the five forces has on a company.

Potential Competitors

Potential competitors are companies that currently are not competing in an industry but have the capability to do so if they choose. The American Telephone & Telegraph Company, for example, was regarded as a potential competitor in the personal computer industry in the early 1980s, for it had the technology, sales force, and capital necessary to manufacture and sell PCs. AT&T, in fact, did enter the industry in 1985. Established companies try to discourage potential competitors from entering, since the more companies enter an industry, the more difficult it becomes for established companies to hold their share of the market and to generate profits. Thus a high risk of entry by potential competitors represents a threat to the profitability of established companies. On the other hand, if the risk of new entry is low, established companies can take advantage of this opportunity to raise prices and earn greater returns.

The strength of the competitive force of potential rivals is largely a function of the height of barriers to entry. The concept of barriers to entry implies that there are significant costs to joining an industry. The greater the costs that potential competitors must bear, the greater are the barriers to entry. High entry barriers keep potential competitors out of an industry even when industry returns are high. The classic work on barriers to entry was done by economist Joe Bain, who identified three main sources of barriers to new entry: brand loyalty, absolute cost advantages, and economies of scale.[3]

Brand loyalty   Brand loyalty is buyers' preference for the products of established companies. A company can create brand loyalty through continuous advertising of brand and company names, patent protection of products, product innovation through company research and development programs, an emphasis on high product quality, and good after-sales service. Significant brand loyalty makes it difficult for new entrants to take market share away from established companies. Thus brand loyalty reduces the threat of entry by potential competitors who may see the task of breaking down well-established consumer preferences as too costly.

Absolute cost advantages   Lower absolute costs give established companies an advantage that is difficult for potential competitors to match. Absolute cost advantages can arise from superior production techniques as a result of past experience, patents, or secret processes; control of particular inputs required for production, be they labor, materials, equipment, or management skills; or access to cheaper funds because existing companies represent lower risks than established companies. If established companies have an absolute cost advantage, then again the threat of entry is significantly reduced.

Economies of scale   Economies of scale are the cost advantages associated with large company size. Sources of scale economies include cost reductions gained through mass-producing a standardized output, discounts on bulk purchases of raw-material inputs and component parts, the spreading of fixed costs over a large volume, and scale economies in advertising.[4] If these cost advantages are significant, then a new entrant faces the dilemma of either entering on a small scale and suffering a significant cost disadvantage or taking a very large risk by entering on a large scale and bearing significant capital costs. A further risk of large-scale entry is that the increased supply of products will depress prices and result in vigorous retaliation by established companies. Thus, when established companies have scale economies, the threat of entry is reduced.

If established companies have built brand loyalty for their products, have an absolute cost advantage with respect to potential competitors, or have significant scale economies, then the risk of entry by potential competitors is significantly reduced. When this risk is low, established companies can charge higher prices and earn greater profits than otherwise would have been possible. Clearly, it is in the interest of companies to pursue strategies consistent with these aims. Indeed, empirical evidence suggests that the height of barriers to entry is *the most important* determinant of profit rates in an industry.[5] Examples of industries where entry barriers are significant include pharmaceuticals, household detergents, and aerospace. In the first two cases, product differentiation achieved through substantial expenditures for research and development and for advertising has built brand loyalty, making it difficult for new companies to enter these industries on a significant scale. So successful have the differentiation strategies of Procter & Gamble and Unilever been in household detergents that these two companies dominate the global industry.

In the aerospace industry, the barriers to entering the commercial airline market are primarily due to scale economies. Development costs alone can be staggering. For example, before McDonnell Douglas Corp. sold a single MD-11, the wide-body jetliner designed to take the company well into the twenty-first century, more than $1.5 billion was spent on development and tooling.[6] Industry analysts estimate that, just to break even on a new model like the MD-11, a company has to sell more than 200 aircraft, a figure representing 13 percent of expected industry sales of wide-body jets between 1990 and 2000. In addition, the cost disadvantages of not achieving an efficient scale of production are substantial in airplane manufacture. Companies that are able to achieve only half of the market share necessary to break even face a 20 percent unit-cost disadvantage.[7] In aerospace, the up-front capital costs, the need to achieve a significant market share to break even, and the cost disadvantages of not achieving an efficient scale of production are likely to deter all but the most determined potential competitors from entry. In spite of this, it should be noted that Airbus Industrie, a European consortium, did manage to enter successfully the commercial aerospace industry in the 1980s, although with the help of significant government backing.

Rivalry Among Established Companies

The second of Porter's five competitive forces is the extent of rivalry among established companies within an industry. If this competitive force is weak, companies have an opportunity to raise prices and earn greater profits. If this competitive force is strong, however, significant price competition, including price wars, may result from the intense rivalry among companies. Price competition limits profitability by reducing the margins that can be earned on sales. Thus intense rivalry among established companies constitutes a strong threat to profitability. The extent of rivalry among established companies within an industry is largely a function of three factors: (1) industry competitive structure, (2) demand conditions, and (3) the height of exit barriers in the industry.

Competitive structure   Competitive structure refers to the number and size distribution of companies in an industry. Different competitive structures have different implications for rivalry. Structures vary from **fragmented** to **consolidated.** A fragmented industry contains a large number of small or medium-size companies, none of which is in a position to dominate the industry. A consolidated industry is dominated by a small number of large companies or, in extreme cases, by just one company (a monopoly). Examples of fragmented industries include agriculture, video rental, health clubs, real estate brokerage, and sun-tanning parlors. Examples of consolidated industries include aerospace, automobiles, and pharmaceuticals. The most common competitive structure in the United States is a consolidated structure—what economists call an *oligopoly*.[8] The range of structures and their different characteristics are illustrated in Figure 3.3.

Many fragmented industries are characterized by low entry barriers and commodity-type products that are hard to differentiate. The combination of these characteristics tends to result in boom-and-bust cycles. Low entry barriers imply that whenever demand is strong and profits are high there will be a flood of new entrants hoping to cash in on the boom. Examples can be found in the explosion in the number of video stores, health clubs, and sun-tanning parlors during the 1980s. Often, the flood of new entrants into a booming fragmented industry creates excess capacity. Once excess capacity develops, companies start to cut prices in order to utilize their spare capacity. The difficulty companies face when trying to differentiate their products from those of competitors can worsen this tendency. The result is a price war, which will depress industry profits, force some companies out of business, and deter any more new entrants. Thus, for example, after a decade of expansion and booming profits, many health clubs are now finding that they have to offer large discounts in order to hold on to their membership. In general, the more commodity-like an industry's product, the more vicious will be the price war. This bust part of the cycle will continue until overall industry capacity is brought in line with demand (through bankruptcies), at which point prices may stabilize again.

In other words, a fragmented industry structure constitutes a threat rather than an opportunity. Most booms will be relatively short-lived because of the

FIGURE 3.3   **The continuum of industry structures**

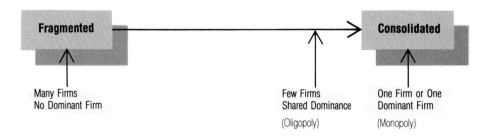

ease of new entry and will be followed by price wars and bankruptcies. Since differentiation is often difficult in these industries, the best strategy for a company to pursue in such circumstances may be one of cost minimization. It will allow a company to rack up high returns in a boom and survive any subsequent bust.

The nature and intensity of competition for consolidated industries are much more difficult to predict. The one certainty about consolidated industries is that the companies are *interdependent*. Interdependence means that the competitive actions of one company directly effect the profitability of others in the industry. For example, General Motors' introduction of cut-rate financing to sell autos in 1986 had an immediate negative impact on the sales and profits of Chrysler Corp. and Ford Motor Company, which then had to introduce similar packages in order to protect their market share.

Thus, in a consolidated industry, the competitive action of one company directly affects the market share of its rivals, forcing a response from them. The consequence can be a dangerous competitive spiral, with rival companies trying to undercut each other's prices and pushing industry profits down in the process. The fare wars that racked the airline industry during the seven years after the deregulation of 1979 provide a good illustration of what can happen when companies are highly interdependent. As a result of the fare wars, in 1982 the airline industry as a whole lost over $700 million. Braniff International Corporation and Continental Airlines Corp. were pushed into bankruptcy, and Eastern and People Express sold out to Texas Air to avoid bankruptcy.

Clearly, the interdependence of companies in consolidated industries and the possibility of a price war constitute a major threat. Companies often attempt to reduce this threat by following the price lead set by a dominant company in the industry. However, companies must be careful, for explicit price-fixing agreements are illegal, although tacit agreements are not. (A tacit agreement is one arrived at without direct communication. Instead, companies watch and interpret each other's behavior. Normally, tacit agreements involve following the price lead set by a dominant company.)[9] However, tacit price-leadership agreements are prone to breakdown under adverse economic conditions. This is essentially what is now beginning to occur in the beer industry. For most of the 1980s Anheuser-Busch was the acknowledged price leader in this industry. The resulting absence of price competition helped keep industry profits high. However, slow growth in beer consumption during the late 1980s put pressure on the earnings of all beer majors and persuaded Philip Morris' Miller Brewing division and Adolph Coors Co. to break ranks and institute a policy of deep and continuous discounting for most of their beer brands. In late 1989 market leader Anheuser-Busch announced that it would start offering similar discounts in order to protect its sales volume. Thus, following the breakdown of a tacit price-leadership agreement, the beer industry seems to be sliding toward a price war.

More generally, when price wars are a threat, companies often compete on nonprice factors such as product quality and design features. This type of competition constitutes an attempt to build brand loyalty and minimize the likelihood of a price war. The effectiveness of this strategy, however, depends on how easy it is to differentiate the industry's product. Although some products (such as autos) are relatively easy to differentiate, others (such as airline travel) are essentially commodities that are very difficult to differentiate.

Demand conditions   Industry demand conditions are another determinant of the intensity of rivalry among established companies. Growing demand tends to moderate competition by providing greater room for expansion. Demand grows when the market as a whole is growing through the addition of new consumers or when existing consumers are purchasing more of an industry's product. When demand is growing, companies can increase revenues without taking market share away from other companies. Thus growing demand gives a company a major opportunity to expand operations.

Conversely, declining demand results in more competition as companies fight to maintain revenues and market share. Demand declines when consumers are leaving the marketplace or when each consumer is buying less. When demand is declining, a company can attain growth only by taking market share away from other companies. Thus declining demand constitutes a major threat, for it increases the extent of rivalry between established companies. The issue of what determines demand conditions is discussed in more detail later in the chapter, when we consider industry evolution.

Exit barriers   Exit barriers are a serious competitive threat when industry demand is declining. Exit barriers are economic, strategic, and emotional factors that keep companies competing in an industry even when returns are low. If exit barriers are high, companies can become locked into an unfavorable industry. Excess productive capacity can result. In turn, excess capacity tends to lead to intensified price competition, with companies cutting prices in an attempt to get the orders necessary to utilize their idle capacity.

Common exit barriers include the following:

1.   Investments in plant and equipment that have no alternative uses and cannot be sold off. If the company wishes to leave the industry, it has to write off the book value of these assets.

2.   High fixed costs of exit, such as severance pay to workers who are being made redundant.

3.   Emotional attachments to an industry, such as when a company is unwilling to exit from its original industry for sentimental reasons.

4.   Strategic relationships between business units. For example, within a multi-industry company, a low-return business unit may provide vital inputs for a high-return business unit based in another industry. Thus the company may be unwilling to exit from the low-return business.

5.   Economic dependence on the industry, such as when a company is not diversified and so relies on the industry for its income.

The steel industry illustrates the adverse competitive effects of high exit barriers. A combination of declining demand and new low-cost sources of supply created overcapacity in the global steel industry during the late 1980s. American companies, with their high-cost structure, were on the sharp end of this decline. Demand for American steel fell from a 1977 peak of 160 million tons to 70 million tons in 1986. The result was excess capacity amounting to an estimated 45 million tons in 1987, or 40 percent of total productive capacity.[10] In order to try to utilize this capacity, many steel companies slashed their prices. As a consequence of the resulting price war, industry profits were low, and several of the majors, including the LTV Corp. and Bethlehem Steel, faced bankruptcy.

Since the steel industry was characterized by excess capacity for most of the 1980s, why did companies not reduce that capacity? The answer is that many tried to, but the costs of exit slowed this process and prolonged the associated price war. For example, in 1983 USX shut down 16 percent of its raw steel-making capacity at a cost of $1.2 billion. USX had to write off the book value of these assets; they could not be sold. In addition, it had to cover pensions and insurance for 15,400 terminated workers.[11] Given such high exit costs, companies such as USX have remained locked into this unprofitable industry. The effect of impeded exit has been more intense price competition than might otherwise have been the case. Thus high exit barriers, by slowing the speed with which companies leave the industry, threatens the profitability of all companies within the steel industry.

Interactions between factors   The extent of rivalry among established companies within an industry is a function of competitive structure, demand conditions, and exit barriers. Particularly within a consolidated industry, the *interaction* of these factors determines the extent of rivalry. For example, the environment

TABLE 3.1   Demand conditions and exit barriers as determinants of opportunities and threats in a consolidated industry

		Demand conditions	
		Demand decline	Demand growth
Exit barriers	High	High threat of excess capacity and price wars	Opportunities to raise prices through price leadership and to expand operations
	Low	Moderate threat of excess capacity and price wars	Opportunities to raise prices through price leadership and to expand operations

of a consolidated industry may be favorable when demand growth is high. Under such circumstances, companies might seize the opportunity to adopt price-leadership agreements. However, when demand is declining and exit barriers are high, the probable emergence of excess capacity is likely to give rise to price wars. Thus, depending on the interaction between these various factors, the *extent* of rivalry between established companies in a consolidated industry might constitute an opportunity or a threat. These issues are summarized in Table 3.1.

The Bargaining Power of Buyers

The third of Porter's five competitive forces is the bargaining power of buyers. Buyers can be viewed as a competitive threat when they force down prices or when they demand higher quality and better service (which increase operating costs). Alternatively, weak buyers give a company the opportunity to raise prices and earn greater returns. Whether buyers are able to make demands on a company depends on their *power* relative to that of the company. According to Porter, buyers are most powerful in the following circumstances:

1. When the supply industry is composed of many small companies and the buyers are few in number and large. These circumstances allow the buyers to dominate supply companies.
2. When the buyers purchase in large quantities. In such circumstances, buyers can use their purchasing power as leverage to bargain for price reductions.
3. When the supply industry depends on the buyers for a large percentage of its total orders.
4. When the buyers can switch orders between supply companies at a low cost, thereby playing off companies against each other to force down prices.
5. When it is economically feasible for the buyers to purchase the input from several companies at once.
6. When the buyers can use the threat to supply their own needs through vertical integration as a device for forcing down prices.

An example of an industry whose buyers are powerful is the auto components supply industry. Auto-component suppliers are numerous and typically small in scale. Their customers, the auto manufacturers, are large in size and few in number. Chrysler, for example, does business with close to 2,000 different component suppliers and normally contracts with a number of different companies to supply the same part. The auto majors have used their powerful position to play off suppliers against each other, forcing down the price they have to pay for component parts and demanding better quality. If a component supplier objects, then the auto major uses the threat of switching to another supplier as a bargaining tool. Additionally, both Ford and General Motors have used the threat of manufacturing a component themselves rather than buying it from auto-component suppliers as a device for keeping component prices down.

The opposite circumstances arise when a company has more power than its buyers. For example, by virtue of its patent, Xerox Corporation had a twenty-five-year monopoly in the production of photocopiers. Buyers were dependent on Xerox, which was the only source of supply. This power gave Xerox the opportunity to raise prices above those that would have been set under more competitive conditions, such as the prices currently prevailing in the industry.

④ The Bargaining Power of Suppliers

The fourth of Porter's competitive forces is the bargaining power of suppliers. Suppliers can be viewed as a threat when they are able to force up the price that a company must pay for input or reduce the quality of goods supplied, thereby depressing the company's profitability. Alternatively, weak suppliers give a company the opportunity to force down prices and demand higher quality. As with buyers, the ability of suppliers to make demands on a company depends on their *power* relative to that of the company. According to Porter, suppliers are most powerful in the following circumstances:

1. When the product that suppliers sell has few substitutes and is important to the company.

2. When the company's industry is *not* an important customer to the suppliers. In such circumstances the health of suppliers does not depend on the company's industry. Thus suppliers have little incentive to reduce prices or improve quality.

3. When suppliers' respective products are differentiated to such an extent that it is costly for a company to switch from one supplier to another. In such circumstances, the company is dependent on its suppliers and *unable* to play them off against each other.

4. When suppliers can use the threat of vertically integrating forward into the industry and competing directly with the company as a device for raising prices.

5. When buying companies are *unable* to use the threat of vertically integrating backward and supplying their own needs as a device for reducing input prices.

For a long time the airlines exemplified an industry whose suppliers were powerful. In particular, the airline pilots and aircraft mechanics unions, as suppliers of labor, were in a very strong position with respect to the airlines. The airlines depended on union labor to fly and service their aircraft. Because of labor agreements and the probability of damaging strikes, nonunion labor was not regarded as a feasible substitute. The unions used this position to raise pilots' and mechanics' wages above the level that would have prevailed in more competitive circumstances, such as those currently found in the industry. This situation persisted until the early 1980s, when the resultant high-cost structure of the airline industry was driving many airlines into bankruptcy. The airlines then used the threat of bankruptcy to break union agreements and drive down labor costs, often by as much as 50 percent.

The Threat of Substitute Products

The final element of Porter's five forces model is the competitive force of substitute products. Substitute products are the products of industries that serve similar consumer needs to those of the industry being analyzed. For example, companies in the coffee industry compete indirectly with those in the tea and soft-drinks industries. (All three industries serve consumer needs for drinks.) The prices that companies in the coffee industry can charge are limited by the existence of substitutes such as tea and soft drinks. If the price of coffee rises too much relative to that of tea or soft drinks, then coffee drinkers will switch from coffee to those substitutes. This phenomenon occurred when unusually cold weather destroyed much of the Brazilian coffee crop in 1975–1976. The price of coffee rose to record highs, reflecting the shortage, and consumers began to switch to tea in large numbers.

The existence of close substitutes constitutes a strong competitive threat, limiting the price a company can charge and thus its profitability. However, if a company's products have few close substitutes (that is, if substitutes are a weak competitive force), then, other things being equal, the company has the opportunity to raise prices and earn additional profits; and its strategies should be designed to take advantage of this fact.

3.4 IDENTIFYING GROUPS WITHIN INDUSTRIES

The Concept of Strategic Groups

So far we have had little to say about how companies in an industry might differ from each other and what implications the differences might have for the opportunities and threats that they face. In practice, companies in an industry often differ from each other with respect to factors such as distribution channels used, market segments served, product quality, technological leadership, customer service, pricing policy, advertising policy, and promotions. Within most industries, it is possible to observe groups of companies in which each member follows the same basic strategy as other companies in the group but a strategy different from the one followed by companies in other groups. These groups of companies are known as **strategic groups**.[12]

Normally, a limited number of groups captures the essence of strategic differences between companies within an industry. For example, the global auto industry contains a number of different strategic groups. First, there is a group of companies that manufacture a restricted range of cars aimed at serving market segments at the bottom, or basic transportation, end of the market. These companies compete primarily on price. Their strategy is to minimize costs through the attainment of scale economies and competitive pricing to gain market share. Members of this group include Hyundai Motor Company (of South Korea) and Yugo GV (of Yugoslavia).

Second, there is a group of companies that manufacture a restricted range of cars aimed at serving segments at the top, or luxury, end of the market. For these companies, luxury, quality, and outstanding performance, rather than cost, are the critical competitive dimensions. The strategy of these companies is to stress the uniqueness of their product, its outstanding quality and performance, and the status of owning such a car. Examples of such companies include BMW AG, Daimler-Benz AG (Mercedes-Benz), and Jaguar Cars, Inc. They command a high price for their products.

Third, there is a group of companies whose strategy is to manufacture a comprehensive model range of cars aimed at serving the majority of market segments. This strategy focuses on minimizing cost through the realization of scale economies so that the companies can compete on price in the low end of the

FIGURE 3.4   Strategic groups in the automobile industry

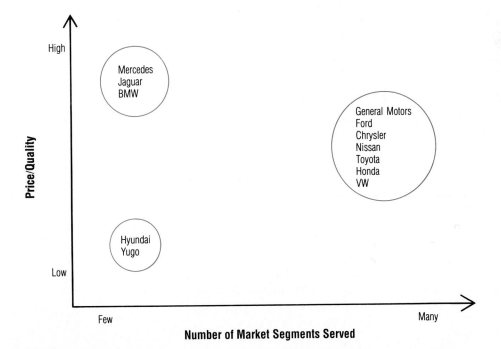

market. At the same time it stresses quality and performance so that the companies can compete at the top end of the market on quality. General Motors, Ford, Chrysler, Nissan Motor Company, Honda, Toyota Motor Corp., and Volkswagen AG are among the companies pursuing such a strategy.

As our discussion suggests, it should be possible to plot these three strategic groups along two main dimensions: price/quality and number of market segments served. This has been done in Figure 3.4. In practice, however, there are more than three strategic groups in the auto industry. We have limited our discussion to three groups for the sake of clarity. Figure 3.4 is also a simplification, since it focuses on only two strategic dimensions.

Implications of Strategic Groups

The concept of strategic groups has a number of implications for industry analysis and the identification of opportunities and threats. First, a company's immediate competitors are those in its strategic group. Since all the companies in a strategic group are pursuing similar strategies, consumers tend to view the products of such enterprises as being direct substitutes for each other. Thus a major threat to a company's profitability can come from within its own strategic group.

Second, different strategic groups can have a different standing with respect to each of Porter's five competitive forces. In other words, the risk of new entry by potential competitors, the degree of rivalry among companies within a group, the bargaining power of buyers, the bargaining power of suppliers, and the competitive force of substitute products can all vary in intensity among different strategic groups within the same industry.

For example, in the auto industry, companies in low-volume strategic groups, such as the now-defunct American Motors Company, traditionally lacked the buying power of those in high-volume strategic groups, such as General Motors. This put companies from low-volume strategic groups in a much weaker position vis-à-vis suppliers than companies in high-volume strategic groups. Thus AMC was unable to bargain down suppliers' prices in the way GM could.

Some strategic groups, then, are more desirable than others, for they have a lower level of threats and greater opportunities. Managers must evaluate whether their company would be better off competing in a different strategic group. If the environment of another strategic group is more benign, then moving into that group can be regarded as an opportunity.

Yet this opportunity is rarely without costs, mainly because of **mobility barriers** between groups. Mobility barriers are factors that inhibit the movement of companies between groups in an industry. They include the barriers to entry into a group and the barriers to exit from a company's existing group. For example, BMW would encounter mobility barriers if it attempted to enter the high-volume strategic group to which General Motors, Chrysler, and Ford belong. These mobility barriers would include the capital costs of building mass-production facilities to manufacture a comprehensive model range of cars (barriers to entry) and the probable loss of BMW's unique, or luxury, status (barriers to exit). Thus a company contemplating entry into another strategic group must evaluate the height of mobility barriers before deciding whether the move is worthwhile.

Mobility barriers also imply that companies within a given group may be protected to a greater or lesser extent from the threat of entry by companies based on other strategic groups. If mobility barriers are low, then the threat of entry from companies in other groups may be high, effectively limiting the prices companies can charge and the profits they can earn without attracting new competition. If mobility barriers are high, then the threat of entry is low, and companies within the protected group have an opportunity to raise prices and earn higher returns without attracting entry.

3.5 COMPETITIVE CHANGES DURING INDUSTRY EVOLUTION

The Industry Life-Cycle Model

Over time most industries pass through a series of well-defined stages, from initial growth, through maturity, and eventually into decline. These stages have different implications for the nature of competition. Specifically, the strength of each of Porter's five competitive forces typically changes as an industry evolves. The changes give rise to different opportunities and threats at each stage of an industry's evolution.[13] The task facing strategic managers is to *anticipate* how the strength of each force will change with the stage of industry development and to formulate strategies that take advantage of opportunities as they arise and that counter emerging threats.

The industry life-cycle model is a useful tool for analyzing the effects of industry evolution on competitive forces. The model is similar to the product life-cycle model discussed in the marketing literature.[14] Using the industry life-cycle model, we can identify five industry environments, each occurring during a distinct stage of an industry's evolution: (1) an embryonic industry environment, (2) a growth industry environment, (3) a shakeout environment, (4) a mature industry environment, and (5) a declining industry environment. Figure 3.5 illustrates them.

An *embryonic* industry is one that is just beginning to develop (for example, the hand-held calculator industry in the late 1960s). Typically, growth at this stage is slow because of such factors as buyers' unfamiliarity with the industry's product, high prices due to the inability of companies to reap any significant scale economies, and poorly developed distribution channels.

Once demand for the industry's product begins to take off, the industry develops the characteristics of a growth industry. In *growth* industry, first-time demand is expanding rapidly as many new consumers enter the market. Typically, industry growth takes off when consumers become familiar with the product,

FIGURE 3.5   **Stages of the industry life cycle**

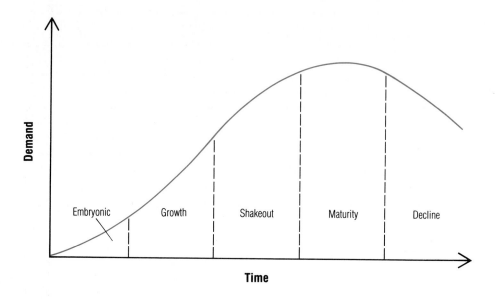

when prices fall because of the attainment of experience and scale economies, and as distribution channels develop. The personal computer industry was at this stage of development between 1981 and 1984. In the United States, 55,000 PCs were sold in 1981. By 1984 the figure had risen to 7.5 million—a 136-fold increase in just three years.[15]

Explosive growth of the type experienced by the PC industry in the early 1980s cannot be maintained indefinitely. Sooner or later the rate of growth slows, and the industry enters the shakeout stage. In the *shakeout* stage, demand approaches saturation levels. In a saturated market, there are few potential first-time buyers left. Most of the demand is limited to replacement demand. A dramatic example of a shakeout occurred in the PC industry during 1984–1986. The average annual growth rate of demand between 1984 and 1986 was 3.3 percent, compared with an average annual growth rate of 3,000 percent between 1981 and 1984.

The shakeout stage ends when the industry enters its *mature* stage. In a mature industry, the market is totally saturated and demand is limited to replacement demand. During this stage, growth is low or zero. What little growth there is comes from population expansion bringing new consumers into the market.

Eventually, most industries enter a decline stage. In the *decline* stage, growth becomes negative for a variety of reasons, including technological substitution (for example, air travel for rail travel), social changes (greater health consciousness hitting tobacco sales), demographics (the declining birthrate hurting the market for baby and child products), and international competition (low-cost foreign competition pushing the American steel industry into decline).

Finally, it is important to remember that the industry life-cycle model is a generalization. In practice, industry life cycles do not always follow the pattern illustrated in Figure 3.5. In some cases, growth is so rapid that the embryonic stage is skipped altogether, as happened in the personal computer industry. In other instances, industries fail to get past the embryonic stage, as occurred with the ill-fated laser disk. Industry growth can be revitalized after long periods of decline, either through innovations or through social changes. For example, the health boom brought the bicycle industry back to life after a long period of decline. The time span of the different stages can also vary significantly from industry to industry. Some industries can stay in maturity almost indefinitely if their products become basic necessities of life, as is the case for the automobile industry. Others skip the mature stage altogether and go straight into decline. That is essentially what occurred in the vacuum-tube industry. Vacuum tubes were replaced by transistors as a major component in electronic products while the industry was still in its growth stage. Still other industries may go through not one but several shakeouts before they enter full maturity.

Implications of Industry Evolution

For strategic managers, the most important aspect of industry evolution concerns its impact on Porter's five competitive forces and, through them, on opportunities and threats. Industry evolution has major implications for two of the five competitive forces—potential competitors and rivalry among established companies—and less substantial implications for the competitive forces of buyers, suppliers, and substitutes. We discuss each in turn.

Potential competitors and industry evolution   The ways in which entry barriers change with industry evolution are summarized in Table 3.2. In an embryonic industry and in the early stages of a growth industry, entry barriers are usually based on the control of technological knowledge.[16] Consequently, at those stages the threat of entry by potential competitors tends to be relatively low. This gives industry incumbents what is commonly known as a *first-mover advantage*. However, the importance of technological knowledge as a barrier to entry is typically short-lived. Sooner or later potential rivals manage to work out the technological requirements for competing in an industry, and technological barriers to entry decline in importance.

The best thing for a company to do when technological entry barriers are high is to take advantage of the relative lack of new competition to build up market share and brand loyalty. For example, in the embryonic stage of the PC industry, Apple Computer had a virtual monopoly of the relevant knowledge (that is, Apple had a first-mover advantage). This technological advantage allowed Apple to become the market leader. Thus, when technological entry

TABLE 3.2   **How barriers to entry change with industry evolution**

		Stage of industry evolution				
		Embryonic	Growth	Shakeout	Maturity	Decline
Entry barriers	Technology	High to medium	Medium to low	Low	Low	Low
	Scale economies	Low	Low to medium	Medium to high	Medium to high	Medium to high
	Brand loyalty	Low	Low to medium	Medium to high	Medium to high	Medium to high

barriers were eroded by imitators such as IBM, Apple had already established a degree of brand loyalty for its products. This enabled Apple to survive in the industry when competitive pressures increased.

Normally, the importance of control over technological knowledge as a barrier to entry declines significantly by the time an industry enters its growth stage. In addition, because few companies have yet achieved significant scale economies or differentiated their product sufficiently to guarantee brand loyalty, other barriers to entry tend to be low at this stage. Given the low entry barriers, the threat from potential competitors is normally highest at this point. However, paradoxically, high growth usually means that new entrants can be absorbed into an industry without a marked increase in competitive pressure.

As an industry goes through the shakeout stage and enters maturity, barriers to entry increase and the threat of entry from potential competitors decreases. As growth slows during the shakeout, companies can no longer maintain historic growth rates merely by holding on to their market share. Competition for market share develops, driving down prices. Often the result is a price war, as happened in the airline industry during the 1980–1986 shakeout. To survive the shakeout, companies begin to focus both on costs minimization and on building brand loyalty. The airlines, for example, tried to cut operating costs by hiring nonunion labor and to build brand loyalty by introducing frequent-flyer programs. By the time an industry matures, the surviving companies are those that have brand loyalty and low-cost operations. Because both of these factors constitute a significant barrier to entry, the threat of entry by potential competitors is greatly diminished. High entry barriers in mature industries give companies the opportunity to increase prices and profits.

Finally, as an industry enters the decline stage, entry barriers remain high and the threat of entry is low. Economies of scale and brand loyalties are by now well established. In addition, the low profitability characteristic of this stage makes the industry less attractive to potential competitors.

Rivalry among established companies and industry evolution   The extent and character of rivalry among established companies also change as an industry evolves, presenting a company with new opportunities and threats. These are summarized in Table 3.3. In an embryonic industry, rivalry normally focuses on perfecting product design and educating consumers. This rivalry can be intense, as in the race to develop superconductors, and the company that is the first to solve design problems often has the opportunity to develop a significant market position. An embryonic industry may also be the creation of one company's innovative efforts, as happened with personal computers (Apple) or vacuum cleaners (the Hoover Company). In such circumstances, the company has a major opportunity to capitalize on the lack of rivalry and build up a strong hold on the market.

During an industry's growth stage, rivalry tends to be low. Rapid growth in demand enables companies to expand their revenues and profits without taking market share away from competitors. A company has the opportunity to expand its operations. In addition, a strategically aware company takes advantage of the relatively benign environment of the growth stage to prepare itself for the intense competition of the coming industry shakeout.

As an industry enters the shakeout stage, rivalry between companies becomes intense. What typically happens is that companies that have become accustomed to rapid growth during an industry's growth phase continue to add capacity at rates consistent with past growth. Managers use historic growth rates

TABLE 3.3   **How rivalry among established firms changes with industry evolution**

		Stage of industry evolution				
		Embryonic	Growth	Shakeout	Maturity	Decline
Competitive features	Price competition	Low	Low	High	Normally low-medium, can be high	High
	Brand loyalty	Low	Low	Medium to high	High	High
	Overall rivalry	Low	Low	High	Medium, can be high	High

to forecast future growth rates, and they plan expansions in productive capacity accordingly. As an industry approaches maturity, however, demand no longer grows at historic rates. The consequence is the emergence of excess productive capacity. This is illustrated in Figure 3.6, where the solid line indicates the growth in demand over time and the dotted line indicates the growth in productive capacity over time. As can be seen, past point t_1, the growth in demand slows as the industry becomes mature. However, capacity continues to grow until time t_2. The gap between the solid and dotted lines signifies excess capacity. In an attempt to utilize this capacity, companies often cut prices. The result can be an intense price war that drives many of the most inefficient companies into bankruptcy.

A good example of this phenomenon recently occurred in the semiconductor industry. In 1983, there were twenty plants in operation worldwide producing dynamic random-access memories (DRAMs). Propelled by strong market growth and optimistic predictions, by early 1985 the number of plants had more than doubled. By mid 1985, however, there was a significant unanticipated slowdown in the growth rate of the market. As a consequence, by the end of 1985 from 30 to 40 percent of industry DRAM capacity was standing idle. Overcapacity triggered fierce price cutting and the withdrawal of several incumbent pro-

FIGURE 3.6   **Growth in demand and capacity**

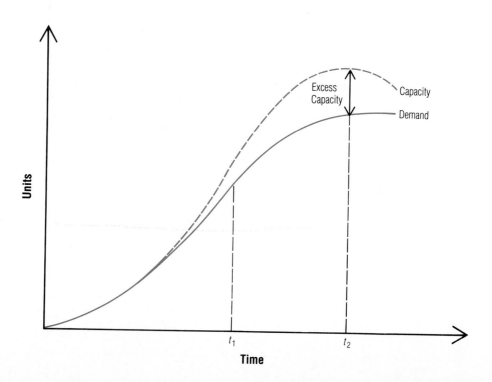

ducers. As a result, by 1987 the number of plants producing DRAMs had fallen 30 percent from the 1985 high.

As a result of the shakeout, most industries by maturity have consolidated and become oligopolies. In the airline industry, for example, as a consequence of the shakeout, the top five companies controlled 85 percent of the industry in 1990, up from only 50 percent of 1984.[17] In mature industries, companies tend to recognize their interdependence and try to avoid price wars. Stable demand gives them the opportunity to enter into price-leadership agreements. The net effect is to reduce the threat of intense rivalry among established companies, thereby allowing greater profitability. However, as noted earlier, the stability of a mature industry is always threatened by further price wars. A general slump in economic activity can depress industry demand. As companies fight to maintain their revenues in the face of declining demand, price-leadership agreements break down, rivalry increases, and prices and profits fall.

The periodic price wars that occur in the gasoline market illustrate this situation. During periods of strong demand for oil, most producers followed the price lead set by OPEC. As demand for oil weakened in the mid 1980s, however, the price lead set by OPEC broke down and severe price competition developed. Mature industries thus are characterized by long periods of price stability, when rivalry is relatively mild, interspersed with periods of intense rivalry and price wars, brought on by a general worsening of macroeconomic conditions. The threat of a price war never disappears. Given this factor, companies should look for opportunities to reduce the sensitivity of their product to price changes.

Finally, within a declining industry, the degree of rivalry among established companies usually increases. Depending on the speed of the decline and the height of exit barriers, competitive pressures can become as fierce as in the shakeout stage.[18] The main problem in a declining industry is that falling demand leads to the emergence of excess capacity. In an attempt to utilize this capacity, companies begin to cut prices, thus sparking a price war. As noted earlier, the American steel industry has experienced these problems because of the attempt of steel companies to utilize their excess capacity (40 percent of the steel industry's total productive capacity was classified as excess in 1986).[19] Exit barriers play a part in adjusting excess capacity. The greater the exit barriers, the harder it is for companies to reduce capacity and the greater is the threat of severe price competition.

Buyers, suppliers, and industry evolution   Industry evolution can change the nature of the relationships between an industry and its buyers and suppliers. As an industry evolves toward maturity, it becomes both larger and more consolidated. These changes enhance the bargaining power of companies in the industry vis-à-vis suppliers and buyers in a number of ways. First, the larger a company is, the more important it is to suppliers as a customer for their products and the greater its bargaining power. Second, the more consolidated an industry is, the less suppliers are able to play off companies against each other in an attempt to increase prices. Third, the more consolidated an industry is, the less buyers are able to play off companies against each other in an attempt to drive down prices.

Hence, as an industry moves toward maturity, the competitive power of buyers and suppliers shrinks.

Substitute products and industry evolution   The competitive force of substitute products depends to some extent on the ability of companies in an industry to build brand loyalty for their own products. Other things being equal, the greater the brand loyalty for an industry's products, the less likely are consumers to switch to the products of substitute industries. Generally, as an industry evolves toward maturity, companies within it begin to expend more effort on differentiating their products to create brand loyalty. This gives a company some protection not only from companies in its own industry, but also from those in substitute industries. Thus, as it moves toward maturity, an industry begins to develop a greater degree of protection against the competitive force of substitute products. However, the emergence of significant new substitutes may push a mature industry into decline, as synthetic materials have done in the steel industry.

Summary: Industry Evolution

The discussion of the effects of industry evolution on competition suggests that the strength of Porter's five competitive forces varies across an industry's life cycle. Rapid expansion makes for weak competitive forces in growth industries. Opportunities for expansion and capturing market share are greatest during this stage. Competitive threats then increase sharply during the shakeout period. The threat of price competition is one of the most important problems that strategic managers have to deal with at this stage. As an industry enters maturity, competitive threats tend to decline and the opportunity exists to limit price competition through price-leadership agreements. Thus, mature industries tend to be characterized by relatively high profitability.[20] Nonprice competition may often play a greater role at this stage, so it is important for a company to capitalize on opportunities to differentiate its product. This situation changes again when an industry enters the decline stage. Competitive intensity increases, particularly when exit barriers are high, profits fall, and the threat of price wars once more becomes substantial.

3.6 ANALYZING THE MACRO-ENVIRONMENT

Macro-environmental factors are factors external to an industry that influence the level of demand within it, directly affecting company profits. Many of these factors are constantly changing, and the change process itself gives rise to new opportunities and threats. Strategic managers must understand the significance of macro-environmental factors and be able to assess the impact of changes in the macro-environment on their company and on the opportunities and threats it faces. Seven elements of the macro-environment are of particular importance here: the macroeconomic environment, the technological environment, the social environment, the demographic environment, the political and legal environment, and the global environment.

The Macro-Economic Environment

The state of the macroeconomic environment determines the general health and well-being of the economy. This, in turn, affects companies' ability to earn an adequate rate of return. The four most important macroeconomic indicators in this context are the growth rate of the economy, the interest rates, currency exchange rates, and inflation rates.

Economic growth   The rate of growth in the economy has a direct impact on the level of opportunities and threats that companies face. Because it leads to an expansion in consumer expenditure, economic growth tends to produce a general easing of competitive pressures within an industry. This gives companies the opportunity to expand their operations. Because economic decline leads to a reduction in consumer expenditure, it increases competitive pressures and constitutes a major threat to profitability. Economic decline frequently causes price wars in mature industries. This happened in the heavy construction equipment industry during the recession of 1979, when many of the major companies, such as International Harvester, came close to bankruptcy.

Although the precise level of economic growth is notoriously difficult to predict, strategic managers need to be aware of the outlook for the economy. For example, it would make little sense to embark on an ambitious expansion strategy if most forecasters are expecting a sharp economic downturn. Conversely, if the economy is currently in poor shape but a general upturn in activity is forecasted, companies might be well advised to take up an expansion strategy.

Interest rates   The level of interest rates can determine the level of demand for a company's products. Interest rates are important whenever consumers routinely borrow money to finance their purchase of these products. The most obvious example is the housing market, where the mortgage rate directly affects demand, but interest rates also have an impact on the sale of autos, appliances, and capital equipment, to give just a few examples. For companies in such industries, rising interest rates are a threat and falling rates an opportunity.

Interest rates also determine the cost of capital for a company. This cost can be a major factor in deciding whether a given strategy is feasible. For instance, a company may finance an ambitious expansion strategy with borrowed money. This course of action may make good sense if interest rates are low and are predicted to stay at that level, but it would be folly if forecasts predict that interest rates will rise to record levels.

Currency exchange rates   Currency exchange rates define the value of the dollar relative to the value of the currencies of other countries. Movement in currency exchange rates has a direct impact on the competitiveness of a company's products in the global marketplace. When the value of the dollar is low compared with the value of other currencies, products made in the United States are relatively inexpensive and products made overseas are relatively expensive. A low or declining dollar reduces the threat from foreign competitors while creating opportunities for increased sales overseas. For example, the 45 percent fall in the value of the dollar against the Japanese yen between 1985 and 1987 sharply increased the price of imported Japanese cars, giving American manufacturers some degree of protection against the Japanese threat. (Actually, the subsequent decline in Japanese auto imports was offset by the increase in U.S.-based production by Japanese companies.) However, when the value of the dollar is high, as it was during the 1984–1985 period, then imports become relatively cheap and the threat from foreign producers increases. A high dollar also limits opportunities for overseas sales because of the relatively high price of goods manufactured in the United States.

Inflation rates   Inflation can destabilize the economy, producing slower economic growth, higher interest rates, and volatile currency movements. If inflation keeps increasing, investment planning becomes a hazardous business. The key characteristic of inflation is that it makes the future less predictable. In an inflationary environment, it may be impossible to predict with any accuracy the real value of returns that can be earned from a project five years hence. Such uncertainty makes companies less willing to invest. Their holding back, in turn, depresses economic activity and ultimately pushes the economy into a slump. Thus high inflation is a threat to companies.

The Technological Environment

Since World War II, the pace of technological change has accelerated, unleashing a process that has been called a "perennial gale of creative destruction."[21] Technological change can make established products obsolete overnight. At the same time it can create a host of new product possibilities. Thus it is both creative and destructive—both an opportunity and a threat. Since accelerating technological change also shortens the average product life cycle, organizations need to anticipate the changes that new technologies bring with them: They need to analyze their environment strategically.[22]

Witness recent changes in the electronics industry. For forty years, until the early 1960s, vacuum tubes were a major component in radios and then in record players and early computers. The advent of transistors destroyed the market for vacuum tubes but at the same time created new opportunities connected with transistors. Transistors took up far less space than vacuum tubes, encouraging a trend toward miniaturization that continues.

The transistor held its position as the major component in the electronics industry for just a decade. In the 1970s microprocessors were developed, and the market for transistors declined rapidly. At the same time, however, the microprocessor created yet another set of new product opportunities—hand-held calculators (which destroyed the market for slide rules), compact disk players, and personal computers, to name just a few. Strategically aware electronics companies, by anticipating the effects of change, benefited from the progression of new technologies. Unaware companies went out of business.

New technologies also give rise to new ways of manufacturing established products. In turn, these new processes give rise to opportunities and threats. Robotics, especially as applied to the automation of vehicle assembly plants, is one example of a new process technology. Another is the steel industry's development of minimills using new electric arc smelting techniques. This particular technology took away from large, integrated steel operations, such as U.S. Steel and Bethlehem Steel, the considerable advantage they once enjoyed because of economies of scale. Thus minimills have emerged as a major threat to established American steel manufacturers. Many minimills can now turn out steel at a lower cost than can large, integrated plants that use thirty-year-old technology. Indeed, by 1985 minimills and specialty steel mills held 40 percent of the U.S. market, and domestic integrated companies had a 38 to 40 percent market share, down from close to 70 percent ten years earlier.[23]

The Social Environment

Like technological change, social change creates opportunities and threats. One of the major social movements of the 1970s and 1980s was the trend toward greater health consciousness. Its impact has been immense, and companies that recognized the opportunities early have often reaped significant gains. Philip Morris, for example, capitalized on the growing health trend when it acquired Miller Brewing Company and then redefined competition in the beer industry with its introduction of low-calorie beer (Miller Lite). Similarly, PepsiCo was able to gain market share from its archrival, Coca-Cola Company, by introducing diet colas and fruit-based soft drinks first. The health trend has also given rise to booming sales of mineral waters, with a market growth of 15 percent per year during the mid 1980s. In an attempt to capitalize on this opportunity, many of the country's largest beverage companies are currently expanding into this fragmented industry. At the same time the health trend has created a threat for many industries. The tobacco industry, for example, is now in decline as a direct result of greater consumer awareness of the health implications of smoking. Similarly, the sugar industry has seen sales decline as consumers have decided to switch to artificial sweeteners.

The Demographic Environment

The changing composition of the population is another factor that can create both opportunities and threats. For example, as the baby-boom generation of the 1960s has moved through the population, it has created a host of opportunities and threats. Currently, baby boomers are getting married and creating an upsurge in demand for the consumer appliances normally bought by couples marrying for the first time. Thus companies such as Whirlpool Corporation and General Electric are looking to capitalize on the predicted upsurge in demand for washing machines, dishwashers, spin dryers, and the like. The other side of the coin is that industries oriented toward the young, such as the toy industry, have seen their consumer base decline in recent years.

The Political and Legal Environment

Political and legal factors also have a major effect on the level of opportunities and threats in the environment. One of the most significant trends in recent years has been the move toward deregulation. By eliminating many legal restrictions, deregulation has opened a number of industries to intense competition. The deregulation of the airline industry in 1979, for example, created the opportunity to establish low-fare carriers—an opportunity that Texas Air, People Express, and others tried to capitalize on. At the same time, the increased intensity of competition created many threats, including, most notably, the threat of prolonged fare wars, which have repeatedly thrown the airline industry into turmoil during the last decade.

Deregulation apart, companies also face serious legal constraints, which limit their potential strategic options. Antitrust laws, for example, can prevent companies from trying to achieve a dominant market position through acquisitions. In 1986, both PepsiCo and Coca-Cola attempted to buy up smaller soft-drink manufacturers, Pepsi bidding for the Seven-Up Company and Coca-Cola for Dr. Pepper Co. Both acquisitions were forbidden by the Federal Trade Commission on the grounds that if they went through, Pepsi and Coca-Cola between them would control more than 80 percent of the soft-drink market. Seven-Up subsequently merged with Dr. Pepper, a move that has created the possible threat (to Pepsi and Coca-Cola) of a third major company emerging in the industry.

For the future, fears about the destruction of the ozone layer, acid rain, and global warming may be near the top of the political agenda in the 1990s. Given these concerns, governments seem increasingly likely to enact tough environmental regulations to limit air pollution. Rather than resisting this trend, companies should try to take advantage of it. For example, back in 1974, when ozone depletion was still a theory, E. I. Du Pont de Nemours & Company decided to start research into substitutes for ozone-damaging chlorofluorcarbons (CFCs), widely used in aerosols, air conditioners, and refrigeration equipment. At the same time, Du Pont made a pledge to phase out production of CFCs if they were shown to be a threat to public health. In March 1988, in response to NASA data, Du Pont honored that commitment and promised to phase out production of CFCs within ten years. Although Du Pont stands to lose $600 million per year from the sales of CFCs, since the mid 1970s the company's research has yielded three viable alternatives to CFCs, each of which is now produced commercially. Thus, by anticipating regulations and undertaking appropriate action, Du Pont is now well positioned to take a large share of the market for CFC substitutes if, as seems increasingly likely, CFCs are banned.

The Global Environment

Changes in the global environment can create both opportunities for market expansion and serious threats to a company's domestic and international market share. As the world enters the 1990s, developments are occurring that may have great significance for the future of American enterprise. The first is the emergence of the European Community as a free-trade block containing a single market that is half again as large as the United States. After the removal of trade barriers between Community members in 1992, the European Community could have the fastest growing and potentially most wealthy economy in the industrialized world. American business would be well advised to take advantage of this growth and to recognize the threat posed by major European companies. European companies may use their strong domestic economy as a springboard from which to invade U.S. markets, much as the Japanese did in the 1970s. American companies need to anticipate these developments rather than ignore them as was all too often the case with the Japanese.

A second development is in Eastern Europe, where the collapse of state communism and the rapid shift toward free-market economies by several Eastern European countries has created potentially enormous growth opportunities. The challenge facing American enterprise is to capitalize on these opportunities before Western European and Asian competitors do. A third development concerns the continuing emergence of "Asian tigers." In particular, Thailand looks set to join a list of major Asian competitors that already includes Japan, South Korea, and Taiwan. As a group, these countries will pose a significant competitive threat for the foreseeable future. At the same time, their markets represent largely untapped growth opportunity.

3.7 SUMMARY OF CHAPTER

This chapter details a framework that strategic managers can use to analyze the external environment of their company, enabling them to identify opportunities and threats. The following major points are made in the chapter:

1. Superior performance is the result of a fit between strategy and the environment. In order to achieve such a fit, strategic managers must be able to identify environmental opportunities and threats.

2. The main technique used to analyze competition in the industry environment is the five forces model. The five forces are (a) the risk of new entry by potential competitors, (b) the extent of rivalry among established firms, (c) the bargaining power of buyers, (d) the bargaining power of suppliers, and (e) the threat of substitute products. The stronger each of these forces is, the more competitive is an industry and the lower is the rate of return that can be earned in that industry.

3. The risk of entry by potential competitors is a function of the height of barriers to entry. The higher the barriers to entry are, the lower is the risk of entry and the greater are the profits that can be earned in the industry.

4. The extent of rivalry among established companies is a function of an industry's competitive structure, demand conditions, and barriers to exit. Strong demand conditions moderate the competition among established companies and create opportunities for expansion. When demand is weak, intensive competition can develop, particularly in consolidated industries with high exit barriers.

5. Buyers are most powerful when a company depends on them for business but they themselves are not dependent on the company. In such circumstances, buyers are a threat.

6. Suppliers are most powerful when a company depends on them for business but they themselves are not dependent on the company. In such circumstances, suppliers are a threat.

7. Substitute products are the products of companies based in industries serving consumer needs similar to the needs served by the industry being analyzed. The more similar the substitute products are to each other, the lower is the price that companies can charge without losing customers to the substitutes.

8. Most industries are composed of strategic groups. Strategic groups are groups of companies pursuing the same or a similar strategy. Companies in different strategic groups pursue different strategies.

9. The members of a company's strategic group constitute its immediate competitors. Since different strategic groups are characterized by different opportunities and threats, it may pay a company to switch strategic groups. The feasibility of doing so is a function of the height of mobility barriers.

10. Industries go through a well-defined life cycle, from an embryonic stage, through growth, shakeout, and maturity, and eventually into decline. Each stage has different implications for the competitive structure of the industry, and each stage gives rise to its own set of opportunities and threats.

11. Important components of the macro-environment include the macroeconomic environment, the technological environment, the social environment, the demographic environment the political and legal environment, and the global environment. Although largely outside of the company's direct control, macro-environmental trends can profoundly affect the magnitude of opportunities and threats facing a company.

Discussion Questions

1. Under what environmental conditions are price wars most likely to occur in an industry? What are the implications of price wars for a company? How should a company try to deal with the threat of a price war?

2. Discuss Porter's five forces model with reference to what you know about the airline industry. What does the model tell you about the level of competition in this industry?

3. Identify a growth industry, a mature industry, and a declining industry. For each industry, identify the following: (a) the number and size distribution of companies, (b) the nature of barriers to entry, (c) the height of barriers to entry, and (d) the extent of product differentiation. What do these factors tell you about the nature of competition in each industry? What are the implications for the company in terms of opportunities and threats?

4. Assess the impact of macro-environmental factors on the likely level of enrollment at your university over the next decade. What are the implications of these factors for the job security and salary level of your professors?

Endnotes

1. Sources include "It's USX vs. Everybody," *Business Week,* October 6, 1986, pp. 26–27; Organization for Economic Cooperation and Development, *Steel in the 80s* (Paris: OECD, 1980); "Better 'X' Than Steel," *Industry Kbek,* July 21, 1986, p 23; and Frank Koelble, "Strategies for Restructuring the U.S. Steel Industry," *33 Metal Producing* (December 1986), 28–33.

2. Michael E. Porter, *Competitive Strategy—Techniques for Analyzing Industries and Competitors* (New York: Free Press, 1980). See also Porter, *Competitive Advantage: Creating and Sustaining Superior Performance* (New York: Free Press, 1985).

3. Joe S. Bain, *Barriers to New Competition* (Cambridge, Mass.: Harvard University Press, 1956).

4. For a more complete discussion of the sources of scale economies, see Chapter 4.

5. Most of this information on barriers to entry can be found in the industrial organization economics literature. See especially the following works: Bain, *Barriers to New Competition;* M. Mann, "Seller Concentration, Barriers to Entry and Rates of Return in 30 Industries," *Review of Economics and Statistics,* 48 (1966), 296–307; and W. S. Comanor and T. A. Wilson, "Advertising, Market Structure and Performance," *Review of Economics and Statistics,* 49 (1967), 423–440.

6. S. Greenhouse, "Dicey Days at McDonnell Douglas," *The New York Times,* February 22, 1987, p. 4.

7. C. F. Pratten, *Economies of Scale in Manufacturing Industry* (London: Cambridge University Press, 1971).

8. F. M. Scherer, *Industrial Market Structure and Economic Performance* (Chicago: Rand McNally, 1981).

9. For a discussion of tacit agreements, see I. C. Schelling, *The Strategy of Conflict* (Cambridge, Mass.: Harvard University Press, 1960).

10. Koelble, "Strategies," pp. 28–33.

11. "It's USX vs. Everybody," pp. 26–27.

12. The development of strategic-group theory has been a strong theme in the strategy literature during recent years. Important contributions include the following: R. E. Caves and Michael E. Porter, "From Entry Barriers to Mobility Barriers," *Quarterly Journal of Economics* (May 1977), 241–262; K. R. Harrigan, "An Application of Clustering for Strategic Group Analysis," *Strategic Management Journal*, 6 (1985), 55–73; K. J. Hatten and D. E. Schendel, "Heterogeneity Within an Industry: Firm Conduct in the U.S. Brewing Industry, 1952–71," *Journal of Industrial Economics*, 26 (1977), 97–113; and Michael E. Porter, "The Structure Within Industries and Companies' Performance," *The Review of Economics and Statistics*, 61 (1979), 214–227.

13. Indeed, Charles W. Hofer has argued that life-cycle considerations may be the most important contingency when formulating business strategy. See Charles W. Hofer, "Towards a Contingency Theory of Business Strategy," *Academy of Management Journal*, 18 (1975), 784–810. There is also empirical evidence to support this view. See C. R. Anderson and C. P. Zeithaml, "Stages of the Product Life Cycle, Business Strategy, and Business Performance," *Academy of Management Journal*, 27 (1984), 5–24; and D. C. Hambrick and D. Lei, "Towards an Empirical Prioritization of Contingency Variables for Business Strategy," *Academy of Management Journal*, 28 (1985), 763–788.

14. The difference is that individual products can have their own life cycle within the broader context of an industry life cycle.

15. "The PC Wars: IBM vs. the Clones," *Business Week*, July 28, 1986, pp. 62–68.

16. Porter, *Competitive Strategy*, pp. 215–236.

17. "Nice Going, Frank, But Will It Fly?" *Business Week*, September 29, 1986, pp. 34–35.

18. The characteristics of declining industries have been summarized by K. R. Harrigan, "Strategy Formulation in Declining Industries," *Academy of Management Review*, 5 (1980), 599–604.

19. J. J. Innace, "Slippery Footing and the Fall of the Axe," *33 Metal Producing* (December 1986), 25–27.

20. The evidence of the effect of industrial organization economics on the relationship between profitability and market structure would seem to support the idea that mature industries are characterized by high profitability. For a review, see D. A. Hay and D. J. Morris, *Industrial Economics: Theory and Evidence* (Oxford: Oxford University Press, 1979).

21. The phrase was originally coined by J. Schumpeter, *Capitalism, Socialism and Democracy* (London: Macmillan, 1950), p. 68.

22. See M. Gort and J. Klepper, "Time Paths in the Diffusion of Product Innovations," *Economic Journal* (September 1982), 630–653. Looking at the history of forty-six different products, Gort and Klepper found that the length of time before other companies entered the markets created by a few inventive companies declined from an average of 14.4 years for products introduced before 1930 to 4.9 years for those introduced after 1949.

23. Innace, "Slippery Footing," pp. 25–27.

Chapter 4

INTERNAL ANALYSIS: STRENGTHS, WEAKNESSES, AND DISTINCTIVE COMPETENCIES

4.1 OPENING INCIDENT: CATERPILLAR TRACTOR CO.

Caterpillar Tractor's first half-century was one of remarkable success. To quote one commentator, "Caterpillar has combined lowest-cost manufacturing with higher cost but truly outstanding distribution and after-market support to differentiate its line of construction equipment. As a result, Caterpillar, ranking as the 24th largest and 39th most profitable company in the United States, is well ahead of its competitors and most of the Fortune 500 glamor companies."[1] In essence, Caterpillar had capitalized on distinctive competencies in two of its major functional areas, manufacturing and marketing, to build a strong competitive position.

In 1982, however, things suddenly went bad for Caterpillar. The company reported its first loss in forty-eight years. A dramatic slump in world demand for heavy earth-moving and construction equipment, a strong dollar that increased the costs of Caterpillar's exports, and intense new low-cost competition from Komatsu of Japan combined to make 1982 the worst year in the company's history. Caterpillar's response to these threats was to re-examine the basis of its former competitive advantage. It found that although it still had by far the best dealer network in the industry, it had lost its cost advantage to Komatsu. Instead of having distinctive competencies in two major areas, Caterpillar now had them in only one—and that was not enough.

To re-establish its former cost advantage, Caterpillar embarked on an aggressive new manufacturing strategy, involving a $1-billion plant modernization program called PWAF

(Plant with a Future). New high-tech machine tools (including robots) were purchased and grouped with existing machines in work areas called *cells*. Each cell is a self-contained work unit that undertakes a major amount of assembly on an individual product. In an operation such as Caterpillar's PWAF, a large number of cells work in parallel. The use of cells improved product quality, lowered inventory requirements, and strengthened employee morale; it also decreased operating costs. In addition, Caterpillar installed sophisticated computer-controlled just-in-time inventory systems in its PWAF, reducing the need to hold expensive inventories of parts and equipment.

The result of Caterpillar's attempts to regain its low-cost position was impressive. Between 1982 and the end of 1986 Caterpillar cut operating costs by 22 percent and aimed to reduce costs by a further 15 to 20 percent by 1990. Although Caterpillar has a long way to go, its manufacturing strategy is having a positive effect on performance. After three years of losses, in 1985 and 1986 Caterpillar netted profits while continuing to hold on to its 35 to 40 percent share of the U.S. market.[2]

4.2 OVERVIEW

In Chapter 3, we reviewed the elements of the external environment that determine the opportunities and threats facing a company. In this chapter, we focus on identifying a company's *strengths* and *weaknesses* and examine functional-level strategies that can build and exploit the strengths and correct the weaknesses. For example, historically, Caterpillar's low-cost manufacturing position was one of its strengths. When Caterpillar lost this advantage to Komatsu of Japan, its manufacturing function turned into a weakness. The company's manufacturing strategy in the 1980s was designed to correct this weakness and to build a new distinctive competence for Caterpillar in manufacturing by the 1990s.

The term **distinctive competence** refers to company strengths that competitors cannot easily match or imitate. Distinctive competencies represent the *unique* strengths of a company. Building a competitive advantage involves the strategic exploitation of distinctive competencies; they form the bedrock of a company's strategy. For example, Caterpillar has always exploited its distinctive competence in distribution and after-sales service to maintain buyer loyalty and protect its market share. This distinctive competence has allowed the company to charge higher prices and earn greater profits than its competitors. Similarly, the 3M Company has been able to exploit its distinctive competence in research and development to produce a wide range of product innovations that have allowed 3M to earn high profits.

We begin this chapter by considering the source of distinctive competencies. Next, we look at the **value chain** concept and consider the way in which distinctive competencies help a company maximize value created through its value chain. The objective is to show how the different functional areas of a firm—such as manufacturing, marketing, materials management, and R&D—are related to each other. Third, we review each functional area in depth. The objective here is to identify both the sources of company-level strengths and weaknesses and the basic **functional strategies** that can be used to build strengths and correct weaknesses. Functional strategies are simply the strategies pursued by the individual functional areas of a company. Thus, we talk about manufacturing strategy, marketing strategy, R&D strategy, human-resources strategy, and the like.

Bear in mind that functional-level strategies are formulated not in a vacuum but in the context set by business-level strategies. Furthermore, strategy formulation is not a top-down process (see Chapter 1). Distinctive competencies help determine the set of feasible business-level strategies. In other words, an examination of a company's strengths and weaknesses at the functional level tells management what the company *can* and *cannot* do at the business level. Thus strategy formulation is an interactive process, and functional-level strategies and considerations are an integral part of it.

4.3 DISTINCTIVE COMPETENCIES

Strategically, the importance of a company's distinctive competencies is that they enable the company to outperform competitors and earn greater profits. Competitors are motivated to try to imitate these distinctive competencies, and if successful, they ultimately eliminate the company's competitive advantage. Many personal computer companies, for example, are trying to imitate the image-oriented graphics that constitute a major distinctive competence of Apple Computer. The more difficult it is for competitors to imitate a company's distinctive competencies, the more *sustainable* is the company's competitive advantage.

Source of Distinctive Competencies

Distinctive competencies arise from two complementary sources: a company's *resources* and its *capabilities*. Resources are the financial, physical, human, technological, and organizational assets of the firm. They can be divided into *tangible resources* (land, buildings, plant, and equipment) and *intangible resources* (brand names, reputation, patents, and technological or marketing know-how). To give rise to a distinctive competence, a company's resources must be both *unique* and *valuable*. A unique resource is one that no other company has. For example, Polaroid's distinctive competence in instant photography was based on a unique intangible resource: the technological know-how involved in instant film processing. This know-how was protected from imitation by a thicket of patents. A resource is valuable if it in some way helps create strong demand for the company's products. Thus, Polaroid's technological know-how was valuable because it created strong demand for Polaroid's photographic products.

Capabilities are a company's skills at coordinating its resources and putting them to productive use. These skills reside in an organization's routines—that is, in the way a company makes decisions and manages its internal processes to achieve organizational objectives. More generally, a company's capabilities are the product of its organizational structure and control systems. These systems specify how and where decisions are made within a company, the kind of behaviors that will be rewarded by the company, and the cultural norms and values of the company. (We discuss how organizational structure and control systems help a company obtain capabilities in Chapters 10 and 11.) It is important to keep in mind that capabilities are, by definition, intangible. They reside not so much in individuals as in the way individuals interact, cooperate, and make decisions within the context of an organization.[3]

The distinction between resources and capabilities is of the utmost importance in understanding the source of a distinctive competence. A company may have unique and valuable resources; but unless it has the capability to use those resources effectively, it may not be able to create or sustain a distinctive competence. For illustration, consider the case of EMI Ltd. and the CAT scanner. The CAT scanner is the greatest advance in radiology since the discovery of X-rays in 1895. CAT scanners generate cross-sectional views of the human body. They were invented by Godfrey Hounsfield, a senior research engineer at EMI, who subsequently won a Nobel Prize for his achievement. As a result of Hounsfield's work, EMI initially had sole possession of a unique and valuable intangible resource: the technological know-how necessary to make CAT scanners. However, EMI lacked the capability to exploit that resource successfully in the marketplace. It lacked the marketing skills required to educate potential consumers about the benefits of the product, and it lacked the after-sales service and support skills necessary to market such a technologically complex product successfully. As a result, eight years after introducing the CAT scanner, EMI was no longer in the CAT scanner business and an imitator, General Electric, had become the market leader. In other words, despite possessing a unique and valuable intangible resource (technological know-how) EMI was unable to establish a distinctive competence and generate high profits because of its lack of capability to exploit that resource.

It is also important to recognize that a company may not need unique and valuable resources to establish a distinctive competence as long as it has capabilities that no competitor possesses. For example, the steel minimill operator Nucor is widely acknowledged to be the most cost-efficient steel maker in the United States. Nucor's distinctive competence in low-cost steel making, however, does not come from any unique and valuable resources. Nucor has the same resources (plant, equipment, skilled employees, know-how) as many other minimill operators. What is different about Nucor is the company's unique capability to manage its resources in a highly productive manner. Nucor's structure, control systems, and culture promote efficiency-seeking at all levels within the company.

In sum, for a company to have a distinctive competence, it (like Polaroid) must at a minimum possess a unique and valuable resource and the capabilities (skills) necessary to exploit that resource, or it (like Nucor) must have some unique capability to manage common resources. A company's distinctive competence is strongest when the company possesses *both* unique and valuable resources *and* unique capabilities to manage those resources.

Barriers to Imitation

Since distinctive competencies allow companies to earn superior profits, competitors want to imitate them. However, the greater the barriers to imitation, the more difficult imitation is and, therefore, the more sustainable a company's competitive advantage is. It is important to note at the outset, however, that ultimately almost any distinctive competence can be imitated by a competitor. The critical issue is the *time* that competitors take to do this. The more time competitors need to imitate a distinctive competence, the greater is the opportunity for the company to build both a strong market position and a *reputation* with consumers that is subsequently difficult for competitors to attack. Moreover, the longer it takes competitors to imitate a company's distinctive competence, the greater is the opportunity for the company to improve on that competence or build other competencies, thereby staying one step ahead of the competition.

Imitating resources   The easiest distinctive competencies for competitors to imitate tend to be based on possession of unique and valuable *tangible* resources such as buildings, plant, and equipment. Such resources are visible to competitors and can often be purchased on the open market. For example, if a company's competitive advantage is based on sole possession of efficient-scale manufacturing facilities, competitors may move fairly quickly to establish similar facilities. Thus, although Ford gained a competitive advantage over General Motors in the 1920s by virtue of being the first to adopt an assembly-line manufacturing technology to produce automobiles, General Motors quickly imitated that innovation and competed away Ford's distinctive competence.

Intangible resources can be more difficult to imitate. This is particularly true of brand names, which are important because they symbolize a company's reputation. In the computer industry, for example, the IBM brand name is synonymous with high quality and superior after-sales service and support. Similarly, the Christian Dior brand name stands for exclusive *haute couture* clothing. Customers often display a preference for the products of such companies, primarily because *the brand name is an important guarantee of high quality.* Although competitors might like to imitate well-established brand names, the law prohibits them from doing so.

Marketing and technological know-how are also important intangible resources. However, unlike brand names, company-specific marketing and technological know-how can be relatively easy to imitate. The movement of skilled marketing personnel between companies may facilitate the general diffusion of know-how. For example, in the 1970s Ford was generally acknowledged to be the best marketer among the big three U.S. auto companies. In 1979 Ford lost a lot of its marketing know-how to Chrysler when Ford's most successful marketer,

Lee Iacocca, joined Chrysler after being fired by Henry Ford III following "personal disagreements." Iacocca subsequently hired many of Ford's top marketing people to work with him at Chrysler. More generally, successful marketing strategies are relatively easy to imitate because they are so visible to competitors. Thus, Coca-Cola quickly imitated PepsiCo's Diet Pepsi brand with the introduction of its own brand, Diet Coke.

In theory, the patent system should make technological know-how relatively immune to imitation. Patents give the inventor of a new product a seventeen-year exclusive production agreement. Thus, for example, pharmaceutical giant Merck recently patented a cholesterol-reducing drug that is marketed under the brand name of Mevacor. Approved by the FDA in August 1987, Mevacor generated sales of $430 million in 1988 and is targeted to generate annual sales of $1 billion by 1992. It is relatively easy to use the patent system to protect a chemical compound from imitation; however, many other inventions are not so easily protected. In electrical and computer engineering, it is often possible to "invent around" patents. Although EMI took out patents on the CAT scanner, General Electric was able to use reverse engineering skills to figure out how the CAT scanner worked. It then developed a product that though not identical to EMI's CAT scanner (and thus not in violation of EMI's patent) was very similar and performed the same basic function. A study found that 60 percent of patented innovations were successfully invented around in four years.[4] The study suggests that, in general, distinctive competencies based on technological know-how can be relatively short-lived.

Imitating capabilities   Imitation of a company's capabilities tends to be more difficult than imitation of its tangible and intangible resources. A principal reason is that a company's capabilities are often *invisible* to outsiders. Remember that capabilities are based on the way in which decisions are made and processes are managed deep within a company. It is difficult for outsiders to discern the nature of a company's internal operations. Thus, for example, it may be difficult for outsiders to identify with precision why 3M is so successful at developing new products or why Nucor is such an efficient steel producer.

On its own, the invisible nature of capabilities would not be sufficient to halt imitation. In theory, competitors could still gain insights into how a company operates by hiring people away from that company. However, a company's capabilities rarely reside in a single individual. Rather, they are the product of how numerous individuals interact within a unique organizational setting. Thus it is possible that no one individual within a company may be familiar with the totality of a company's internal operating routines and procedures. When this is the case, hiring people away from a successful company may not be sufficient to imitate key capabilities.

Consider the way in which a football team works. The success of a team is not the product of any one individual. Rather, it is the product of how individuals work together *as a team;* it is the product of an unwritten or tacit understanding between the players of the team. Thus the transfer of a star player from a winning team to a losing team may not be sufficient to improve the performance of the losing team.

Summary: The Durability of Distinctive Competencies

We have seen how distinctive competencies arise from a company's resources and capabilities. For a company to have a distinctive competence, at a minimum it must possess a unique and valuable resource and the capabilities (skills) necessary to exploit that resource or it must possess unique and valuable capabilities. We have also seen how resources are easier to imitate than capabilities. Thus, a distinctive competence that is based on a company's unique capabilities is probably more durable (less imitable) than one based on its resources.

At this juncture two other factors regarding the durability of a distinctive competence also need to be noted. First, the time that it takes competitors to imitate a company's distinctive competence is a major determinant of durability. The slower competitors are to respond, the greater is the competitive advantage and reputation that a company can build, and the more difficult it will be to attack the company's position later. For example, the failure of U.S. auto manufacturers to react quickly to the distinctive competence of Japanese auto companies in the manufacture of compact, low-cost, high-quality motor cars gave the Japanese companies time to build a strong market position and reputation that is now proving difficult to attack.

Second, durability is also dependent on the stability of the environment. Resources and capabilities that are suited to one environmental state may not be suited to another. Thus, although the resources and capabilities of U.S. Steel gave the company a distinctive competence in the steel industry of the 1950s and 1960s, this was no longer true by the 1970s and 1980s (see the Opening Incident of Chapter 3). What had changed in the intervening period was not so much U.S. Steel as the environment of the global steel industry. As a result, U.S. Steel's resources and capabilities no longer constituted a distinctive competence.

As a general point, it should be noted that the increasing pace of technological change in recent years has reduced the life span of many resources—particularly those related to plant, equipment, and technological know-how. Proprietary technology, for example, is increasingly subject to a high risk of obsolescence due to competitors' discoveries.

4.4 THE VALUE CHAIN

The value a company creates is measured by the amount that buyers are willing to pay for a product or service.[5] A company is profitable if the value it creates exceeds the cost of performing value-creation functions, such as procurement, manufacturing, and marketing. To gain a competitive advantage, a company must either perform value-creation functions at a lower cost than its rivals or perform them in a way that leads to differentiation and a premium price. To do either, it must have a distinctive competence in one or more of its value-creation functions. If it has significant weaknesses in any of these functions, it will be at a competitive disadvantage.

Value creation can be illustrated with reference to a concept called the value chain, which has been popularized by Professor Michael E. Porter of the Harvard School of Business Administration.[6] The form of the value chain is given in Figure 4.1. The value chain is divided between *primary* activities and *support* activities. Each activity adds value to a product.

Primary activities have to do with the physical creation of a product, its marketing and delivery to buyers, and its support and after-sales service. In this chapter, we consider the activities involved in the physical creation of a product to be *manufacturing* and those involved in marketing, delivery, and after-sales service to be *marketing*. Thus establishing distinctive competencies in primary value-creation activities means establishing them in manufacturing and marketing.

Support activities provide the inputs that allow the primary activities of manufacturing and marketing to take place. The *materials-management function* controls the transmission of physical materials through the value chain, from procurement through operations and into distribution. The efficiency with which

FIGURE 4.1   The value chain

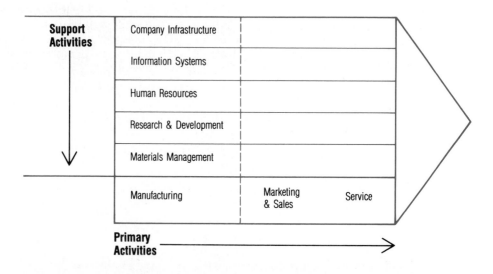

Source: Adapted with permission of The Free Press, a Division of Macmillan, Inc. from *Competitive Advantage: Creating and Sustaining Superior Performance* by Michael E. Porter. Copyright © 1985 by The Free Press, a division of Macmillan Publishing Company, Inc.

this movement is carried out can significantly lower the cost of value creation. In addition, effective materials management can monitor the quality of inputs to manufacturing, thereby increasing the quality of a company's outputs and facilitating premium pricing. The *R&D function* develops new product and process technologies. Technological developments can lower manufacturing costs and result in the creation of more attractive products that demand a premium price. Thus R&D can affect primary manufacturing and marketing activities and, through them, value creation. The *human-resources function* ensures that the company has the right mix of people to perform its primary manufacturing and marketing activities and that it meets the staffing requirements of other support activities. The *information-systems function* makes certain that management has the information to maximize the efficiency of its value chain and to exploit information-based competitive advantages in the marketplace. Finally, *company infrastructure* consists of a number of activities, including general management, planning, finance, and legal and government affairs. The infrastructure embraces all other activities of the company and can be viewed as setting the context within which they take place. As with primary activities, establishing a distinctive competence in support activities can give the company a competitive advantage.

If a company can gain a distinctive competence in a primary or a support value-creation function, its profit margin will increase. On the other hand, when those functions are weak, the company's value creation will lead to higher cost or to an output that is valued less by consumers. In either case, its profit margin will be squeezed.

4.5 MANUFACTURING

With the rise of low-cost overseas competition, American companies have come to recognize the importance of manufacturing strategy. The objective of a company's manufacturing strategy should be to produce cost-competitive goods that are sufficiently high in quality. If a company can achieve this objective, its manufacturing function can be classified as a strength. If not, manufacturing must be regarded as a weakness. Three factors warrant particular attention in a consideration of manufacturing strategy and manufacturing strengths and weaknesses: the experience curve, the product-process life cycle, and the recent emergence of flexible manufacturing technologies.

The Experience Curve

The concept of the experience curve was popularized by management consultants at the Boston Consulting Group (BCG) in the 1970s, although the basic idea had been around for at least thirty years before that.[7] The experience curve refers to systematic manufacturing-cost reductions that occur over the life of a product.

FIGURE 4.2   **A typical experience curve**

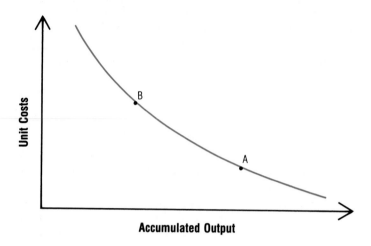

The BCG has noted that manufacturing costs for a product typically decline by some characteristic amount each time *accumulated* output is doubled. The relationship was first observed in the aircraft industry, where it was found that each time accumulated output of airframes was doubled, unit costs typically declined to 80 percent of their previous level.[8] Thus, the fourth airframe typically cost only 80 percent of the second airframe to produce, the eighth airframe only 80 percent of the fourth, the sixteenth only 80 percent of the eighth, and so on. The outcome of this process is a relationship between unit manufacturing costs and accumulated output similar to that illustrated in Figure 4.2.

The strategic significance of the experience curve is clear. It suggests that increasing a company's product volume and market share will also bring cost advantages over the competition. Thus because company A in Figure 4.2 is farther down the experience curve than company B, it has a clear cost advantage over company B. Manufacturing is a strength for company A but a weakness for company B. Two reasons explain the cost reductions that underlie the experience curve: learning effects and plant-level economies of scale.

Learning effects   Learning effects refer to cost savings that come from learning by doing. Labor learns by repetition how best to carry out a task such as assembling airframes. In other words, labor productivity increases over time as individuals learn the most efficient way to perform a particular task. Equally important, it has been observed that in new manufacturing facilities, management typically learns how best to run the new operation. Hence production costs eventually decline because of increasing labor productivity and management efficiency.

Learning effects tend to be most significant in situations where a technologically complex task is repeated, since there is more to learn. Thus learning effects are more significant in an assembly process involving 1,000 complex steps than in an assembly process involving 100 simple steps. No matter how complex a task, however, learning effects typically die out after a limited period of time. Indeed, it has been suggested that they are really important only during the start-up period of a new process and cease after two or three years.[9] Any decline in the experience curve after such a point, therefore, is due to economies of scale.

Economies of scale   Economies of scale at the plant level refer to unit-cost reductions achieved through mass-production techniques. The classic example of such economies is Ford's Model T automobile. The world's first mass-produced car, the Model T Ford was introduced in 1923. Until then it had cost Ford approximately $3,000 (in 1958 dollars) to build and assemble an automobile. By introducing mass-production techniques, the company achieved greater division of labor (that is, splitting assembly into small, repeatable tasks) and specialization and reduced the cost of manufacturing cars to less than $900 per unit (in 1958 dollars) at large output volumes.[10]

As in the Model T case, so in many other situations plant-level scale economies lower costs. Du Pont, for example, was able to reduce the cost of rayon fiber from 53 cents per pound to 17 cents per pound in less than two decades, mainly through plant-level scale economies. But these economies do not continue indefinitely. Indeed, most experts agree that after a certain **minimum efficient scale (MES)** is reached, there are few, if any, plant-level scale economies to be had from expanding volume.[11] Minimum efficient scale refers to the minimum plant size necessary to gain significant economies of scale. In other words, as shown in Figure 4.3, the long-run unit-cost curve of a company is L-shaped. At outputs beyond MES in Figure 4.3, additional cost reductions are hard to achieve.

FIGURE 4.3   **A typical long-run unit-cost curve**

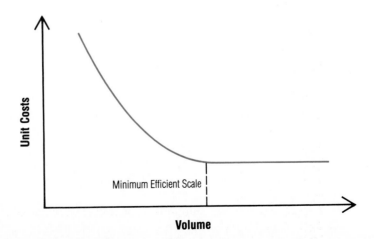

Minimum Efficient Scale

Unit Costs

Volume

Strategic implications   The experience-curve concept is clearly important. If a company wishes to attain a low-cost position, it must try to ride down the experience curve as quickly as possible. This involves constructing efficient-scale manufacturing facilities, even before the company has the demand, and aggressively pursuing cost reductions from learning effects. The company probably also needs to pursue an aggressive marketing strategy, cutting prices to the bone and stressing heavy sales promotions in order to build up cumulative volume as quickly as possible. Once down the experience curve, the company is likely to have a significant cost advantage vis-à-vis its competitors, for it will have gained a distinctive competence in low-cost manufacturing.

However, the company farthest down the experience curve must not become complacent about its cost advantage—for three reasons. First, since neither learning effects nor economies of scale go on forever, the experience curve is likely to bottom out at some point, and further cost reductions will be hard to achieve. Thus in time other companies can catch up with the cost leader. Once this happens, a number of low-cost companies can have cost parity with each other. In such circumstances, establishing a sustainable competitive advantage must involve strategic factors in addition to the minimization of production costs.

Second, cost advantages gained from experience effects can be made obsolete by the development of new technologies. For example, the price of television picture tubes followed the experience-curve pattern from the introduction of television in the late 1940s until 1963. The average unit price dropped from $34 to $8 (in 1958 dollars) in that time. The advent of color television interrupted the experience curve. Manufacturing picture tubes for color TVs required a new manufacturing technology, and the price for color TV tubes shot up to $51 by 1966. Then the experience curve reasserted itself. The price dropped to $48 in 1968, $37 in 1970, and $36 in 1972.[12] In short, technological change can alter the rules of the game, requiring former low-cost companies to take steps to reestablish their competitive edge.

A final reason for avoiding complacency is that high volume does not necessarily give a company a cost advantage. Some technologies have different cost functions. For example, the steel industry has two alternative manufacturing technologies: an integrated technology based on the basic oxygen furnace and a minimill technology based on the electric arc furnace. As illustrated in Figure 4.4, the electric arc furnace is cost efficient at relatively low volumes, whereas the basic oxygen furnace is most efficient at high volumes. Even when both operations are producing at their most efficient output levels, steel companies with basic oxygen furnaces do *not* have a cost advantage over minimills. Consequently, the pursuit of experience economies by an integrated company using basic oxygen technology may not bring the kind of cost advantages that a naive reading of the experience-curve phenomenon would lead the company to expect. Indeed, in recent years integrated companies have not been able to get enough orders to run at optimum capacity. Hence their production costs have been considerably higher than those of minimills.[13] More generally, as we shall discuss shortly, in

FIGURE 4.4   **Unit production costs in an integrated steel mill and a minimill**

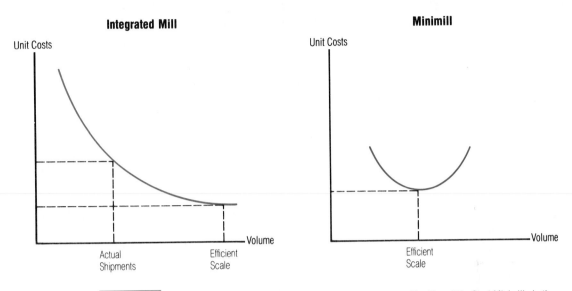

Source: Adapted from D. F. Barnett and R. W. Crandall, *Up From the Ashes: The Rise of the Steel Minimills in the United States* (Washington, D.C.: Brookings Institute, 1986), p. 40. Reprinted by permission.

many industries new flexible manufacturing technologies hold out the promise of allowing small manufacturers to produce at unit costs comparable to those of large assembly-line operations.

The Product-Process Life Cycle

A second concept that has played a role in the development of manufacturing strategy and the identification of manufacturing strengths and weaknesses is the product-process life cycle, originally developed by former Harvard Business School professors Robert H. Hayes and Steven G. Wheelwright.[14] The process-product life cycle suggests that manufacturing efficiency is optimized when a company matches its manufacturing process with its product structure.

Product-process framework   A version of Hayes and Wheelwright's framework appears in Figure 4.5. The horizontal axis summarizes a company's product structure; the vertical axis summarizes different process technologies (process structure). Hayes and Wheelwright suggest that in the first instance manufacturing efficiency is optimized for companies on the diagonal of this matrix.

For example, typical of a company positioned in the upper left-hand corner of the matrix is a commercial printer. In such a company, each job is unique, and

FIGURE 4.5   **Product and process structure**

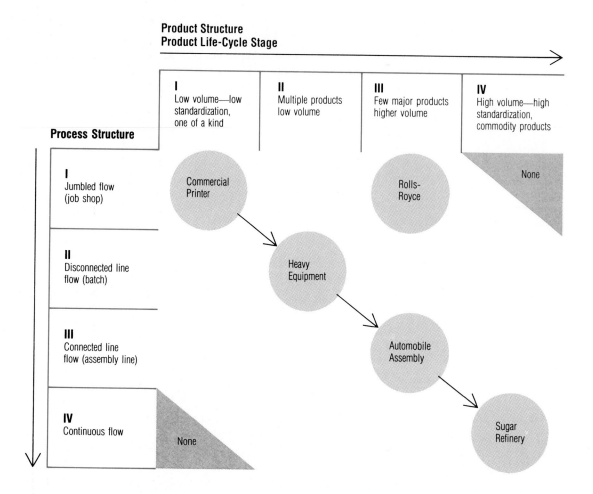

a jumbled flow (or job-shop processing) is usually selected as most effective in meeting product requirements. The characteristics of the product require a flexible, job-shop type of technology. Farther down the diagonal, we find a manufacturer of heavy equipment, such as Caterpillar or Navistar. These companies produce a range of different products, some of which may be customized. The fact that each item is not unique allows the company to attain some economies of scale by moving from a job-shop technology to a disconnected line flow (or batch processing), where batches of a given model proceed irregularly through a series of work stations.

Still farther down the diagonal are mass-production operations such as high-volume auto assembly. The company's product structure is characterized by a limited range of high-volume products. By adopting a connected line flow (or full assembly-line technology), the company can realize significant economies of scale (as in the classic example of the Model T Ford). Finally, in the right-hand corner of the matrix are refinery operations, such as sugar refining and petroleum refining. These operations use continuous-flow technology to manufacture high volumes of a standardized, commodity-type product.

In Figure 4.5, the two shaded corners of the matrix are void of individual companies. The upper right-hand corner characterizes a commodity product produced by a job-shop process. Such an arrangement would be uneconomical, if not impractical. The lower left-hand corner represents a one-of-a-kind product that is made by a continuous-flow process. Again, such an arrangement would not be practical; continuous-flow processes do not have the flexibility to manufacture one-of-a-kind products.

Strategic implications   Hayes and Wheelwright's framework has both static and dynamic implications. From a static perspective, it suggests that matching product structure with process structure is the best way to minimize manufacturing costs. Companies off the diagonal are unlikely to be able to minimize unit costs. For example, the framework suggests that it is not cost efficient for a company to attempt to produce a few high-volume products utilizing a disconnected line flow. Thus, from the perspective of manufacturing costs, a match of product and process structure might be considered a company strength, and a mismatch might be considered a weakness.

However, Hayes and Wheelwright also recognize that under certain conditions it may be profitable for a company to seek a position off the diagonal. For example, Rolls-Royce Motors, Ltd., makes a limited product line of automobiles using a process that is more like a job shop than an assembly line (see Figure 4.5). As a result, Rolls-Royce's manufacturing costs are considerably above those of an automobile company on the diagonal, such as Ford or Chrysler. Nevertheless, because of its reputation for high quality and luxury stemming from its job-shop process, Rolls-Royce can charge a price high enough to cover its high manufacturing costs. In other words, Rolls-Royce carries out its value-creation activities in a way that leads to differentiation and a premium price. It pays Rolls-Royce to be off the diagonal because the company competes primarily on the basis of quality and image rather than cost. A company like Ford, however, has to remain on the diagonal if it is to compete effectively, because Ford competes on the basis of cost (price).

From a dynamic perspective, the main implications of the product-process framework stem from the fact that for some industries at least, industry evolution takes place down the diagonal of the matrix. The first three stages of the product-structure dimension, for example, roughly correspond to the kind of product structures found within companies in the embryonic, growth, and maturity phases of an industry's evolution. The implication is that *companies competing on cost* need to match their process structure with the requirements of industry evolution. Thus in embryonic industries a jumbled flow may be most appropriate, whereas in mature industries a connected line flow may work best. However, these relationships are not inevitable. The heavy-equipment industry, for example, has reached maturity, and yet most companies still produce a low volume of multiple products—because that is what the market demands. Nevertheless, from a dynamic perspective, the framework is of some use in predicting how a company should change its process structure to match the stage of industry evolution.

Flexible Manufacturing Technology

Implicit in the product-process life-cycle approach to manufacturing strategy is the idea that a tradeoff exists between cost and quality. In order to achieve greater quality, the product-process life cycle suggests that a penalty has to be accepted in the form of greater costs. Recent advances in manufacturing technology are beginning to make this view outdated. In particular, the rise of flexible manufacturing technologies may allow companies to achieve both low costs and high quality simultaneously. The term *flexible manufacturing technology* refers to a collection of computer-based technologies that are designed to (1) increase the utilization of individual machines through better scheduling, (2) reduce set-up times, and (3) improve quality control at all stages of the manufacturing process.

Because of those features, Patricia Nemetz of Eastern Washington University, and Louis Fry, have argued that flexible manufacturing technologies allow companies to be highly responsive to unique customer demands, yet also able to compete on the basis of cost, while maintaining superior quality and dependability.[15] A company using flexible manufacturing technology may be able to produce many small batches of products for different groups of consumers at a cost that at one time could be achieved only through mass production of a highly standardized output. As a result, the age-old tradeoff between cost and quality may be disappearing.[16]

Flexible manufacturing technologies vary in their sophistication and complexity. The two most common technologies are **flexible machine cells** and **flexible manufacturing systems.**[17]

A flexible machine cell is a grouping of various types of machinery, a common materials handler, and a centralized cell controller (computer). Each cell normally contains from four to six machines capable of performing a variety of operations. The typical cell is dedicated to the production of a family of parts or products. The settings on machines are controlled by computer. This type of control allows each cell to switch quickly between the production of different parts or products.

Improved capacity utilization and reductions in work-in-progress and in waste are major benefits of flexible machine cells. Improved capacity utilization results from the reduction in set-up times and from the computer-controlled coordination of production flow between machines (which eliminates bottlenecks). The tight coordination between machines also reduces work-in-progress (for example, stockpiles of partly finished products). Reductions in waste result from the ability of computer-controlled machinery to identify how to transform inputs into outputs while producing a minimum of unusable waste material. As a consequence of all these factors, a free-standing machine might be in use 50 percent of the time, but the same machines when grouped into a cell can be used more than 80 percent of the time and produce the same end product with half the waste. Increases in productivity and lower costs are the results.

Flexible manufacturing systems are more complex than cells. A flexible manufacturing system achieves centralized coordination between a number of independent cells by utilizing a sophisticated centralized computer—that is, a computer responsible for coordinating the activities of all the cells in a work place. Flexible manufacturing systems are designed to be efficient for the production of small batches of products or parts. The enhanced coordination of production flow between cells allows for improved logistics in materials handling over that which can be achieved by each cell individually. In addition, by using several cells operating in parallel to perform the same function, the production process does not come to a halt if a single cell breaks down. The results include further reductions in work-in-progress and increases in capacity utilization and productivity. The net effect is to reduce costs. At the same time, the centrally controlled materials-handling system allows for the introduction of superior statistical quality-control procedures.

The benefits of installing flexible manufacturing systems can be dramatic. For example, after the introduction of a flexible manufacturing system, General Electric's locomotive operations reduced the time needed to produce locomotive motor frames from sixteen days to sixteen hours. IBM's flexible manufacturing plant in Austin, Texas, can turn out a lap-top computer in less than six minutes, with 75 percent greater efficiency than a conventional plant. Caterpillar Tractor cut its unit costs by 22 percent between 1982 and 1986 after the introduction of cell-based flexible manufacturing technologies. Similarly, after introducing a flexible manufacturing system, Fireplace Manufacturers Inc., one of the country's largest fireplace businesses, reduced scrap left over from the manufacturing process by 60 percent, increased inventory turnover threefold, and increased labor productivity by more than 30 percent.[18]

Nevertheless, reported implementation difficulties have resulted in a failure to realize the potential benefits inherent in flexible manufacturing systems. The difficulties seem to arise from a failure to understand the full benefits of flexible manufacturing technologies and a lack of integration of the manufacturing function with other functions of the firm.[19] If flexible manufacturing technologies are to realize their promise, they need to be closely integrated with other functions. For example, integration with R&D allows engineers to design products for efficient manufacturing. In addition, integration with materials management allows for the efficient implementation of just-in-time inventory systems, which are necessary for improved logistics. Both of these issues are discussed in subsequent sections of this chapter.

4.6 MARKETING

In recent years there has been an increasing tendency to view marketing (as well as manufacturing) from a strategic perspective.[20] Three key decision areas are central to strategic marketing management and the development of marketing competencies: (1) the selection of target market segments that determine *where* the company will compete; (2) the design of the marketing mix (price, promotion, product, place) that determines *how* the company will compete in these target markets; and (3) positioning strategy. A company that performs each of these tasks well can create a differential advantage for itself in the marketplace. The marketing function is a strength for such a company. If a company fails to create a differential advantage, its marketing function must be regarded as a weakness.

Selection of Target Market Segments

Markets are rarely homogeneous (except in the cases of certain commodities). The typical market is made up of different types of buyers with diverse wants regarding such critical factors as product characteristics, price, distribution channels, and service. A market segment is a group of buyers with similar purchasing characteristics. For example, the auto market might be divided into a compact segment, a status segment, a sports vehicle segment, and so on.

The critical strategic choice that a company faces is how to position itself vis-à-vis different market segments. It has three basic alternatives (see Figure 4.6). In **undifferentiated marketing,** a single marketing mix is offered to the entire market. This strategy rarely succeeds, given the different demands of different segments. In **differentiated marketing,** a different marketing mix is offered to each segment served. In **focused marketing,** the company competes in just one segment and develops the most effective marketing mix to serve that segment.

The classic example showing why undifferentiated marketing is normally a major weakness is the strategy that Ford adopted for the Model T in the 1920s. To minimize production costs, Henry Ford proclaimed that consumers could have any car "as long as it is black." This strategy worked fine until Alfred Sloan of General Motors realized the potential for adopting a differentiated marketing strategy, offering different cars to different segments. Even though differentiation meant that GM spent more than Ford to produce a car, the strategy worked because it recognized the diversity of consumer needs and wants.

FIGURE 4.6   **Market segmentation and marketing strategy**

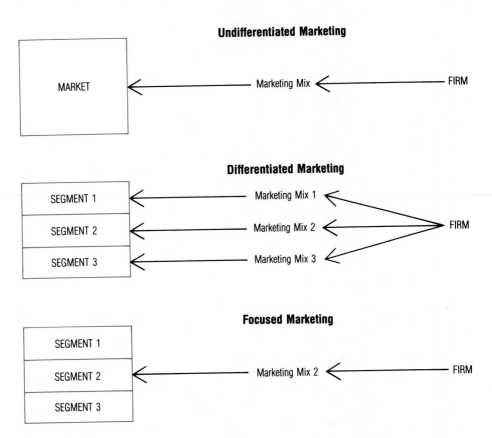

An example of a focused strategy is that pursued by Rolls-Royce. By focusing on the needs of status-conscious high-income consumers, Rolls-Royce has established a profitable niche for itself in the auto industry (and has eliminated the need for the company to adopt a low-cost manufacturing position).

One of the most difficult choices faced by many companies is the choice between a focused and a differentiated marketing strategy. A differentiated marketing strategy lets a company capture customers from many different market segments, thus permitting greater growth. Its drawback is that a broadened customer base may cause the company to lose the unique appeal generated by focusing on just one segment. Rolls-Royce, for example, would probably lose much of its prestige appeal if it began to manufacture compact cars. Making such a choice involves business-level strategy considerations, and we take up this dilemma in the next chapter.

Designing the Marketing Mix

The marketing mix is the set of choices that determine a company's offer to its target market(s). The marketing mix is normally defined in terms of the four P's of marketing: product, price, promotion, and place. Table 4.1 summarizes these main components. A company alters its marketing mix to discriminate among different segments. For example, the market for personal computers consists of a number of segments, including a segment of scientific users, an office segment, an educational segment, and a home-user segment. Each segment is likely to desire different product characteristics (the scientific segment, for example, might require specialist features that other segments do not need). The distribution channels utilized will also vary, as will advertising, promotional, and pricing strategies. Zenith Data Systems Corp., for example, has done well in the educational segment by offering 40 percent price discounts to colleges that buy its PC-compatible machines and by giving away free software to academic and student users as a promotional tool. IBM has excelled in the business segment by capitalizing on its reputation and using its substantial sales force to sell PCs directly to businesses. Hewlett-Packard has done well in the scientific segment by designing its machines to suit the specific requirements of engineers and research scientists.

A company's objective when designing a marketing mix is to try to create a **differential advantage** or to exploit any differential advantage it already has. A differential advantage enables a company to distinguish its offer from that of its competitors in the segments in which it competes. In other words, a differential advantage helps the company establish a distinctive competence, or strength, in marketing. It may be obtained through any element of the marketing mix: creation of a superior product or a more attractive design, better after-sales service, better advertising, more persuasive point-of-sales promotions, and so on. For example, much of IBM's differential advantage stems from name recognition. Caterpillar's comes from its dealer network, spare-parts availability, and reputation for turning out a high-quality product. Anheuser-Busch derives its differential advantage from name recognition of its Budweiser brand beer, as well as

TABLE 4.1   Components of the marketing mix

Product	Price	Promotion	Place
Quality	List price	Advertising	Distributors
Features	Discounts	Sales promotions	Direct selling
Name/reputation	Allowances	Packaging	Retailers
	Credit		Locations
			Inventory
			Transport

from its competitive pricing and promotional skills. In most industries, only by creating a differential advantage can a company ordinarily obtain high profits. Thus companies lacking any differential advantage must view their marketing function as a major weakness.

Positioning

As the final element of marketing strategy, positioning draws on the two earlier principles of marketing strategy: (1) the choice of target market segments that a company decides to focus on and (2) the design of the marketing mix to create a differential advantage that defines how the company will compete with rivals in each segment. For example, Porsche is positioned in the prestige segment of the auto market with a differential advantage based on technical performance. Similarly, Rolls-Royce is positioned in the prestige segment of the auto market with a differential advantage based on status, quality, and luxury. In contrast, Chrysler has positioned itself in a number of different segments of the auto market, including the compact segment, midsize-family-car segment, and high-performance-car segment. A company's success in positioning its products generally determines whether the company has a distinctive competence in marketing or not.

4.7 MATERIALS MANAGEMENT

The role of materials management is to oversee purchasing, production planning and control, and distribution.[21] Sometimes referred to as *logistics management*, materials management is becoming an increasingly important function in many companies because it can help a company both to lower its costs and to boost product quality.

Cost Reductions

For the average U.S. manufacturing enterprise, materials and transport costs account for nearly 60 percent of sales revenues. Minimizing these costs leads to more value. In addition, according to the *Census of Manufactures*, U.S. manufacturing companies annually reinvest four or five times more capital in inventories than in new plant and equipment.[22] Efficient materials management can reduce the amount of cash a company has tied up in inventories, freeing money for investment in plant and equipment.

One technique specifically designed to reduce materials-management costs is the just-in-time (JIT) inventory system. Under a JIT system, inputs are shipped from suppliers to manufacturers at the last possible moment. JIT requires that a company enter into a close relationship with its suppliers. This relationship includes the establishment of computer links between suppliers and the company to facilitate coordination and scheduling. The major cost saving comes from increasing inventory turnover, which reduces inventory-holding costs, such as warehousing and storage costs. For example, Ford's switch to JIT systems in the early 1980s reportedly brought the company a huge one-time saving of $3 billion. At Ford, minimal inventory now turns over nine times a year instead of the former, six, and carrying costs have been reduced by a third.

JIT systems have also helped improve the competitive position of many service companies. For example, Kroger, a nationwide grocery, drug, and convenience store, grades its suppliers on the timing of delivery. Goods that are sent too soon increase the space needed to store inventory, slow the turnover, and create the probability that goods will have to be paid for before they are resold. Kroger's grading system allows the company to track suppliers and know which are the most reliable and the fastest.

The drawback of JIT systems is that they leave a company without a buffer stock of inventory. Although inventory stockpiles are inefficient and expensive, they can help tide a company over shortages of inputs brought on by labor disputes among suppliers or other unforeseen disruptions. However, in general, the advantages far outweigh the risks.

In addition to setting up JIT systems with suppliers, effective materials management can assist with internal logistics—that is, with optimizing the flow of materials through the company's manufacturing process and out to buyers. To a large degree, flexible manufacturing systems attempt to replicate JIT principles *within* a company's manufacturing process. Thus, each work cell in a flexible manufacturing cell system is served by a common materials handler that delivers the right parts to the right machines "just in time," thereby further reducing work-in-progress. The function of materials management is to oversee these internal logistics and to coordinate them with external logistics (such as relationships with suppliers) so that the whole system runs smoothly.

Quality Control

Materials management also has an important responsibility for quality control. Utilizing sophisticated statistical quality-control procedures in conjunction with JIT systems, the materials-management function can monitor the quality of inputs from suppliers. By rejecting substandard parts before they enter the manufacturing process, materials management can significantly reduce the number of defects in finished products. In addition, along with manufacturing, materials management should be responsible for monitoring the quality of component parts as they go through the manufacturing process. This monitoring can be done by applying stringent quality-testing procedures to products as they pass from work station to work station. The ultimate objective is to eradicate all defects from finished products.

The long-run results of increased quality control are illustrated in Figure 4.7a. Increased quality control improves the performance reliability of a compa-

FIGURE 4.7a   **The effect of quality on market share**

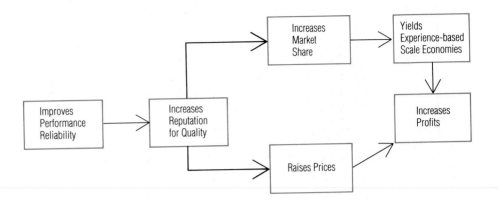

FIGURE 4.7b   **The effect of quality on costs**

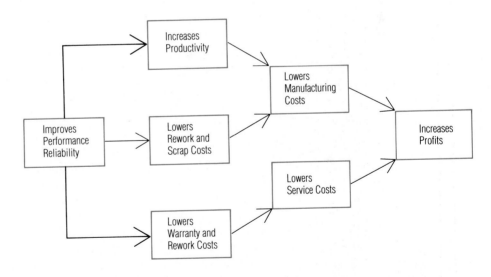

Source: Adapted from "What Does Product Quality Really Mean?" by David A. Garvin, *Sloan Management Review,* 26, Fall 1984, Fig. 1, pp. 37, by permission of the publisher. Copyright © 1984 by the Sloan Management Review Association. All rights reserved.

ny's end product (there are fewer defects). In turn, this increases a company's reputation for quality and may enable a company to charge a premium price for its product. In addition, a reputation for quality may result in an increase in market share, which can help the company realize experience-based scale economies. The overall effect is to increase company profitability.

There is an important relationship between quality control and cost savings.[23] It is illustrated in Figure 4.7b, which shows that increased performance reliability of a company's end products reduces costs from three sources. First, productivity increases because labor time is not wasted assembling poor-quality products that cannot be sold. This saving leads to a direct reduction in unit costs. Second, increased reliability means lower rework and scrap costs. Third, greater product reliability means lower warranty and rework costs. The net effect is to increase value-added by reducing both manufacturing and service costs.

Materials-Management Organization

According to materials-management specialists Jeffrey G. Miller and Peter Gilmour of Harvard Business School, the concept of a materials-management function reflects the fact that purchasing, production, and distribution are not separate activities but three aspects of one basic task: controlling the flow of materials and products from sources of supply through manufacturing and channels of distribution and into the hands of customers—in other words, through the value chain.[24] Tight coordination and control of the flow of materials allow a company to take advantage of cost savings, inventory reductions, and performance improvement opportunities unavailable without a materials-management function.

Despite the cost and quality-control advantages of a materials-management function, according to Miller and Gilmour, only about half of U.S. companies actually operate with such a function. Those that do not include many companies in which purchasing costs, inventories, and customer service levels are important and interdependent aspects of establishing a competitive advantage. Such companies typically operate with a traditional organization structured along the lines illustrated in Figure 4.8a. In such an organization, purchasing, planning and control, and distribution are not integrated. Indeed, planning and control are part of the manufacturing function, and distribution is seen as part of the marketing function. Such companies are unable to establish materials management as a major strength and consequently may face higher production costs. Figure 4.8b shows what a typical materials-management organization looks like. Its purchasing, planning and control, and distribution are all integrated within a single materials-management function. This arrangement allows the company to transform materials management into an important strength, or distinctive competence.

4.8 RESEARCH AND DEVELOPMENT

Investment in research and development often produces spectacular results. Examples include Xerox's twenty-five-year domination of the photocopier market

FIGURE 4.8a   Traditional reporting relationships

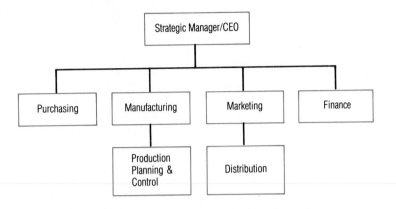

FIGURE 4.8b   Materials-management organization

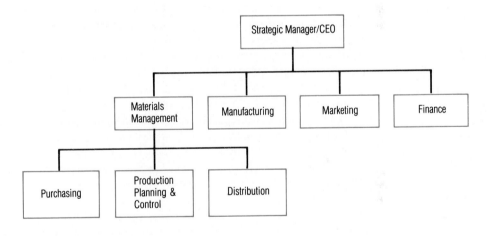

after the company's initial development of the invention; Du Pont's steady stream of inventions such as Cellophane, nylon, Freon (used in all air conditioners), and Teflon (nonstick pans); Sony's development of the Walkman; and Bausch & Lomb's development of contact lenses. However, research and development also involves great risks of failure: Only about 12 to 20 percent of R&D-based projects actually generate profit when they get to the marketplace.[25] The remaining 80 to 88 percent fail. Two well-publicized recent failures were AT&T's losses on its venture into the computer industry (which amounted to a staggering $1.25 billion in 1986) and Sony's development of Betamax video players, which have lost out to VHS systems (in 1986 Betamax had only a 5 percent share of the video player market).[26]

The High Failure Rate of New Products

Four main reasons have been advanced to explain why 80 to 88 percent of new products fail to generate an economic return. The first reason is uncertainty. Developing new products is a risky business. No one can really predict what the demand for a new product will be. Although good market research can reduce the risks of failure, it cannot eradicate them altogether.

Poor commercialization is often cited as a second reason for failure. This occurs when there is an intrinsic demand for a new technology but the technology is not well adapted to consumer needs. One reason many of the early personal computers failed to sell, for example, is that you needed to be a computer programmer to be able to use them. It took Steve Jobs at Apple Computer to understand that if the technology could be made "user friendly" there would be an enormous market for it. Thus, the original personal computers marketed by Apple incorporated little in the way of radical new technology, but they did succeed in making existing technology accessible to the average person.

A third reason for failure is that companies often make the mistake of marketing a technology for which there is not enough demand. One of the best examples is the Anglo-French supersonic jetliner, Concorde. A miracle of high technology, Concorde can carry 140 passengers at twice the speed of sound, reducing the trans-Atlantic flight time by 60 or 70 percent. However, only eight Concordes were ever sold. The reason was simple: At the price that it cost to produce the aircraft, there was never any demand for it. Thus the whole venture was a costly mistake.

A fourth reason for failure is that many companies are slow to get their products to market. The longer the time between initial development and final marketing, the more likely it is that someone else will beat you to market and gain a first-mover advantage.

Nevertheless, despite the high failure rate of new products, a number of companies have managed to establish an undisputed distinctive competence in R&D. These include 3M, Du Pont, Merck, and (despite Betamax) Sony. Such competence can be achieved by formulating an R&D strategy that stresses a close relationship with R&D skills—that is, the risk of failure can be reduced by matching R&D strategy to R&D skills.

R&D Strategy and R&D Skills

A company's R&D strategy can be broken down into three types: (1) strategies of product innovation, aimed at developing entirely new products ahead of competitors; (2) strategies of product development, aimed at improving the quality or features of existing products; and (3) strategies of process innovation, aimed at improving manufacturing to reduce costs and increase quality.[27] The basic R&D skills necessary to support each strategy vary along the lines illustrated in Figure 4.9. They include skills (1) in basic scientific and technological research, (2) in exploiting new scientific and technological knowledge, (3) in project management, (4) in prototype design and development, (5) in integrating R&D with manufacturing, and (6) in integrating R&D with marketing. Possession of these skills constitutes a strength in R&D.

The first two skills require the employment of research scientists and engineers and the establishment of a work environment that fosters creativity. A number of top companies try to achieve this by setting up university-style research facilities where scientists and engineers are given time to work on their own research projects in addition to projects that are linked directly to ongoing company research. At Hewlett-Packard, for example, the company labs are open to engineers around the clock. In addition, Hewlett-Packard encourages its corporate researchers to devote 10 percent of company time to exploring their own ideas—and does not penalize them if they fail. Similarly, at 3M there is the "15 percent

FIGURE 4.9   Strategy and R&D skills

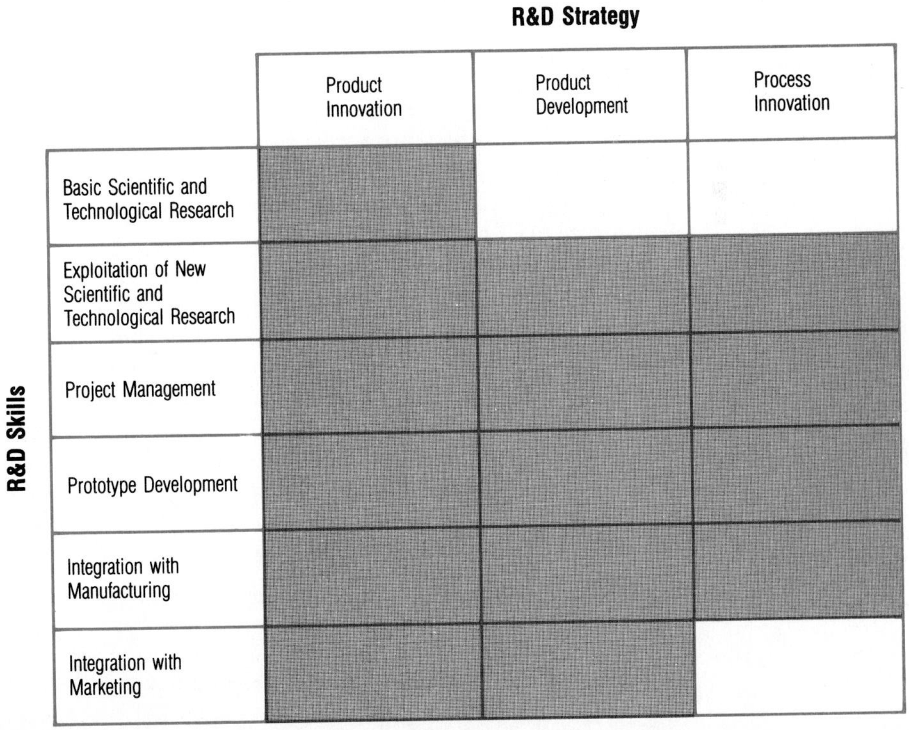

rule," which allows researchers to spend 15 percent of the workweek researching any topic that they want to investigate, as long as there is the potential of a payoff for the company. The most famous outcome of this policy is the ubiquitous yellow Post-it Notes. The idea for them evolved from a researcher's desire to find a way to keep the bookmark from falling out of his hymn book. Post-its are now a major 3M consumer business, with 1988 revenues of around $300 million.

Project management requires two important skills. The first is the ability to select among competing projects at an early stage of development so that the most promising receive funding and potential costly failures are killed off. The second, which is often overlooked, is the ability to take a new product from its inception to the marketplace in as short a time as possible. This skill is absolutely essential when several companies are racing to get competing products to the market so that they can gain a first-mover advantage. For example, after Intel Corporation's introduction of its powerful 386 microprocessor in 1986, a number of companies, including IBM and Compaq, were racing to be the first to introduce a 386-based personal computer. Compaq beat IBM by six months and gained a major share of the high-power market as a result.

A major reason for Compaq's success is that it utilizes a team approach to project management. The project-management team includes engineers and marketing, manufacturing, and finance people. Each function works in parallel rather than sequentially. While engineers are designing the product, manufacturing people are setting up the manufacturing facilities, marketing people are working on distribution and are planning marketing campaigns, and finance people are working on project funding. The net effect of this approach can be to reduce the time it takes to get a product from the drawing board to the marketplace by over 50 percent when compared with sequential development.

Skills in prototype design and development are particularly important for technologically complex products or processes where major bugs may have to be worked out before the product or process is ready for the market. Prototypes of commercial jetliners, for example, must undergo extensive testing and refinement before mass production can begin.

Skills in integrating R&D with manufacturing are perhaps the most overlooked and yet among the most critical skills of all. The essence of these skills is the ability to design products that are easy to manufacture. The easier products are to manufacture, the lower manufacturing costs are and the less room there is for making mistakes. Designing for manufacturing can lower costs and increase product quality. For example, after Texas Instruments redesigned an infrared sighting mechanism that it supplies to the Pentagon, the company found that it had reduced the number of parts from 47 to 12, reduced the number of assembly steps from 56 to 13, reduced the time spent fabricating metal from 757 minutes per unit to 219 minutes per unit, and reduced unit assembly time from 129 minutes to 20 minutes. The result was a dramatic decline in manufacturing costs and product defects.

Finally, skills in integrating R&D and marketing are crucial if a new product is to be properly commercialized. Without integration with marketing, a company runs the risk of developing products for which there is little or no demand, such as the Concorde.

Product innovation   As Figure 4.9 shows, product innovation requires the most skills. The company must be able to carry out basic research, exploit the results of that research to develop new products, screen new products to select only those that have the greatest probability of success, ensure that it has the ability to manufacture these products, and make certain that there is a market for them and that they meet market requirements.

Given the cost of establishing all these skills, only the largest companies in an industry tend to pursue a new product innovation strategy *on a continual basis* (although it is not unusual for small companies to generate important one-time innovations). Only companies such as AT&T, Du Pont, 3M, Hewlett-Packard, and IBM have the requisite funds to support basic research laboratories, and only they can afford to bear the risks. AT&T and IBM, for example, have spent millions of dollars during the last few years in an attempt to develop superconducting materials. Yet despite spectacular advances, both companies predict that another twenty years may pass before they develop marketable products.[28] Clearly, most small and medium-size companies cannot support research efforts on that scale.

Product development   As Figure 4.9 shows, a product development strategy typically involves lower risks than does product innovation. The company is not introducing a totally new product but rather is refining an existing one with a known demand. It does not have to undertake basic research, nor need it develop skills to exploit *new* scientific knowledge and technologies. Instead, the company takes on existing technology and refines or extends the products associated with it. Such companies are often classified as imitators. In the Japanese electronics industry, for example, Sony has been the traditional innovator, and Matsushita Electric Industrial Co., Ltd., with its Panasonic brand, and Sharp Electronics Corporation have been major followers or imitators.

Product development, however, need not mean imitation. One of the most notable developers of products has been Apple Computer. The original founders of Apple took computer technology that had originally been worked out by Intel, Texas Instruments, and NASA and used that technology to develop a dramatic extension of existing computer products—the first personal computer.

Many companies undertake product development on a regular basis to upgrade their own product line continually. Nowhere is this more evident than in the automobile industry: Its annual model changes involve incremental product developments. Leadership in product design, rather than the creation of new markets or the imitation of market innovators, is the distinctive competence being sought. Thus auto companies tend to stress prototype development and integration of R&D with marketing to ensure that new models appeal to consumers. The failure of General Motors to do this in recent years reduced the company's sales and market share at the end of the 1980s.

Process innovation   The motive for process innovation differs from the motive for product innovation and development strategies. In the latter cases, market expansion is normally the primary goal. In the former, the strategic aim is cost reduction and an increase in product quality. Although process innovation does not usually require basic technological and scientific research, it does demand skills to exploit new scientific and technological know-how. Because the goal is related to manufacturing efficiency, close integration between manufacturing and R&D is also called for. Caterpillar's PWAF project, cited in the Opening Incident, is one example of a cost-motivated process innovation. IBM's development of a low-cost assembly line to turn out its PS/2 personal computers is another.

Industry Life-Cycle Factors

Industry life-cycle factors affect the propensity of companies to pursue different R&D strategies.[29] Figure 4.10 illustrates the implications of life-cycle factors for R&D strategies. The rate of new product innovation is greatest in the embryonic

FIGURE 4.10   **R&D strategy over the industry life cycle**

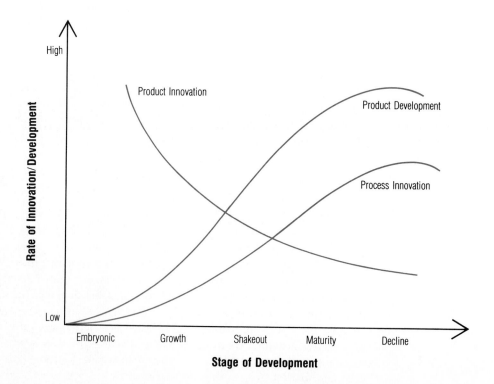

and early growth stages of an industry, falling off thereafter. At those stages, an innovating company has the chance to set the technological context for industry development. That was Sony's thrust when it introduced the Betamax video player. Its innovation lost out to the rival VHS system; however, had Sony succeeded in establishing Betamax as the industry standard, the company would have reaped substantial rewards.

As an industry matures, basic product characteristics become more standardized, and the significance of innovations declines. Complementing this trend, product development strategies become more important. Detroit's obsession with annual model changes is an example of how the phenomenon manifests itself in the auto industry. At maturity, company R&D tends to be oriented less toward basic research and more toward product development and design. A similar trend can be observed with respect to process innovations. Early in an industry's development, rapid growth permits companies with efficient and inefficient manufacturing processes to coexist, but as growth slows and competitive intensity increases, manufacturing efficiency becomes an important precondition for survival. At this stage, companies devote more attention to cost-reducing process innovations. Caterpillar's Plant with a Future and IBM's high-tech personal computer assembly line can be seen as natural responses to the increase in competitive pressure as an industry enters a shakeout.

4.9 HUMAN RESOURCES

"Our people are our greatest resource" is one of the statements most commonly found in corporate annual reports; it is also one of the most important. Without the right people in the right positions, no strategy, however well formulated in other respects, is likely to succeed. This recognition has led to the recent development of strategic human-resource management.[30] Strategic human-resource management has two important objectives: (1) to manage the human resources of a company so as to achieve the highest possible employee commitment and productivity; (2) to match people with a company's short-run and long-run strategic requirements. To achieve the first objective, companies are increasing employee participation in the work process. To achieve the second, companies are adopting work-force planning.

Employee Participation

Poor productivity is the scourge of American industry. Low labor productivity increases the costs of value creation. Low productivity growth relative to our major competitors has contributed to the relative decline in U.S. competitiveness. For example, between 1977 and 1982 U.S. manufacturing productivity grew at a sluggish 0.6 percent per year compared with 2.1 percent in West Germany, 2.7 percent in the United Kingdom, and 3.4 percent in Japan.[31] In response to this problem, many U.S. companies are turning to employee participation to boost productivity and product quality. Quality circles and self-managing teams are perhaps the most significant approaches to participation.

Quality circles   Quality circles were introduced in the United States as long ago as the 1920s. However, they fell into disuse until they were picked up by the Japanese after World War II. Since the late 1970s they have been adopted by an increasingly large number of U.S. businesses. The typical quality circle consists of from five to twelve volunteers drawn from different areas of a function. They meet one or two hours a week to discuss ways of improving quality, efficiency, and the work environment. Quality circles can generate ideas that reduce costs and improve product quality; however, they do not organize work more efficiently or force managers to adopt a participatory style. As a result, they tend to fade away after a few years.

Self-managing teams   Self-managing teams are a relatively recent phenomenon in American industry. Few companies used them until the mid 1980s, but since then they have spread rapidly. The growth of flexible manufacturing cells, which group workers into teams, has undoubtedly facilitated the spread of self-managing teams. The typical team consists of from five to fifteen employees who produce an entire product instead of subunits. Team members learn all tasks and rotate from job to job. A more flexible work force is one result. Team members can fill in for absent coworkers and respond quickly to changes in models and production runs. Teams also take over managerial duties such as work and vacation scheduling, ordering materials, and hiring new members. The greater responsibility that is thrust on team members is seen as a motivator. People generally respond well to being given greater autonomy and responsibility. In addition, performance bonuses linked to team production and quality targets work as a further motivator.

The net effect of these changes is reportedly an increase in productivity of 30 percent or more and a substantial increase in product quality. Further cost savings arise from eliminating supervisors and creating a flatter organizational hierarchy. Perhaps the most potent combination is that of self-managing teams and flexible manufacturing cells. The two seem to be designed for each other. For example, following the introduction of flexible manufacturing technology and work practices based on self-managing teams in 1988, a General Electric plant in Salisbury, North Carolina, increased productivity by a remarkable 250 percent compared with GE plants that produced that same products in 1985.[32] By the same token, however, it must be remembered that teams are no panacea. Unless they are integrated with flexible manufacturing technology, self-managing teams in all probability will fail to live up to their potential.

Work-Force Planning

The aim of a work-force plan is to match people with a company's strategic requirements, both in the short run and in the long run. The critical elements of a work-force plan are (1) forecasts that estimate the company's labor needs, (2) an inventory that establishes whether there is a match between the company's current human resources and future needs, (3) an analysis of the supply and demand for human resources, and (4) the formulation of alternative approaches to head off human-resource imbalances.[33]

4.10 INFORMATION SYSTEMS

We live in an information age. The sharp reduction in the cost of information-systems (IS) technology has allowed computer systems to move from back-office support applications to applications offering a significant competitive advantage.[34] The applications of IS technology are many and embrace all the primary and support activities of the value chain. Table 4.2 offers examples of applications and shows that IS technology enhances a company's control over its costs and helps create a differential advantage.

TABLE 4.2   Examples of information systems applications

Activities	Applications	Implications
Manufacturing	Computer-controlled manufacturing systems	Lower costs/better quality control
Marketing	Telemarketing	Increased orders/differential advantage
	Remote terminals for salespersons	Increased orders/differential advantage
	Electronic market research	Increased orders/differential advantage
Materials management	Automated warehousing/just-in-time inventory systems	Lower costs
	Automated order processing	Lower costs
	Computer-scheduled distribution	Lower costs
Research and development	Computer-aided design	Lower costs/differential advantage
Human resources	Automated personnel scheduling	Lower costs

Specific examples of the strengths of IS technology come from a range of companies: Caterpillar applied IS technology in its PWAF project to manage just-in-time inventory systems and manufacturing cells. Major airlines depend on computer-controlled reservation systems to create a differential advantage and capture customers. Auto manufacturers rely on computer-aided design systems to make fuel-efficient automobiles and speed up product development (thereby lowering costs). Salespeople count on remote computer terminals to help them increase the scope and speed of price quotes. In addition, IS technology has fostered the growth of new products, such as credit cards. It has also enabled companies to change their competitive scope. For example, Dow Jones & Co., Inc., publisher of *The Wall Street Journal,* pioneered a page transmission technology that links seventeen U.S. printing plants to produce a truly national newspaper. Using the same technology, Dow Jones has also started *The Asian Wall Street Journal* and *The Wall Street Journal Europe;* it can maintain control over much of the editorial content while printing the paper in plants all over the world.

According to Michael E. Porter and V. E. Millar, creating a distinctive competence in information systems and exploiting information-based competitive advantages require the following steps[35]:

1. *Assess information intensity.* The first task is to evaluate the existing and potential information intensity of the company's processes and products. An information-intensive manufacturing process is one that involves many complex assembly steps. Assembling an automobile, for instance, requires the bringing together of as many as 7,500 different parts. Clearly, the scope for IS technology to reduce costs through better manufacturing coordination and control is much greater in such a case than in an assembly process involving 20 parts. An information-intensive product is one that has a high information content, such as Dun & Bradstreet's service for corporate analysts.

2. *Identify how IS technology might create a competitive advantage.* Managers need to evaluate in a systematic way how IS technology can create a competitive advantage. This evaluation requires assessing the impact of IS technology on the value chain and on industry competition (that is, on the five competitive forces discussed in Chapter 3), for the stronger the impact of IS technology on the value chain, the greater is the potential change in industry competition. Through investments in IS technology, many companies have succeeded in altering the basis of competition in their favor and have created an IS-based distinctive competence. Citibank N.A. did so in the early 1970s with its introduction of automated teller machines, and American Airlines did so in the 1960s with the introduction of the first computerized reservation system.

3. *Develop a plan for taking advantage of IS technology.* To create or exploit a distinctive competence in IS technology, a systematic IS plan must be worked out. This plan should rank the strategic investments needed in hardware and software, as well as in new product development activities that are necessary

to establish a distinctive competence. Organizational changes reflecting the role that IS technology can play both within functional activities and in linking functional activities need to be recognized. In essence, the IS function needs to be closely integrated with other functions to exploit information-based competitive advantages to their full extent.

If those steps are followed, a company may place itself in a position where it has a distinctive competence in information systems. This support function helps it establish distinctive competencies in other areas, thus contributing toward overall value creation in a number of different ways. By the same token, however, a company that does not develop a distinctive competence in information systems will find its ability to establish distinctive competencies in other areas limited. Low-cost manufacturing and materials management, for example, are difficult to achieve without mastery of IS technologies. Thus strengths in information systems are becoming increasingly important. A company whose information system skills are weak will almost certainly find itself at a competitive disadvantage.

4.11 COMPANY INFRASTRUCTURE

Company infrastructure is the last support function in the value chain. It consists of the activities that set the organizational context within which other support and primary functions take place. Strategic management, planning, finance, accounting, legal affairs, and government relations are all part of the infrastructure. These activities are often viewed as overhead—a somewhat unjust view, since they can be an important source of competitive advantage.[36] By helping a company identify its strengths, weaknesses, opportunities, and threats, planning skills are often a major strength. Many strategic mangers, such as Chrysler's Lee Iacocca, can be considered a company strength. Financial and accounting skills are perhaps among the most important company strengths. The ability of Texas Air to keep on growing by acquisitions in the airline industry, despite depressed profits, can largely be attributed to the company's skills in raising finance and keeping lines of credit open. In addition, legal skills and skills in government relations can also be an important source of competitive advantage, particularly for companies that depend on government contracts for business (such as defense contractors) or for companies that must negotiate with regulatory bodies on a regular basis (such as telephone companies).

More generally, and perhaps more importantly, a company's culture, organizational structure, and internal control systems can all be viewed as part of the infrastructure within which other value-creation activities take place. Organizational structure, control systems, and culture all help define where decisions are made and how processes are managed. They help define the organizational routines or *capabilities* of a company. In turn, as noted early in this chapter, a company's capabilities are major determinants of whether the company has a distinctive competence in one or more of its value-creation activities. Thus, in a very real sense, a company's ability to create value depends on the nature of its infrastructure.

A company's organizational structure and control systems (its capabilities) also help achieve coordination between the different activities of the value chain. Establishing a competitive advantage often requires close coordination between different value-creation activities. We have already observed how coordination between (1) R&D and marketing, (2) R&D and manufacturing, and (3) manufacturing and materials management are all-important preconditions for establishing distinctive competencies. More generally, meeting consumer needs almost always involves coordination among the different activities of the value chain. The role of a company's capabilities in achieving coordination is of the utmost importance.

Given the importance of the company infrastructure—and in particular organization structure, controls, and culture—in establishing capabilities and achieving coordination within the value chain, we shall return to discuss these issues in greater depth in the implementation chapters in Part III.

4.12 FINANCIAL RESOURCES

As already noted, a company's financial position can constitute either a strength or a weakness. Indeed, it can seriously affect the company's ability to build distinctive competencies in other areas, given that doing so often requires substantial investments. The critical considerations here are cash flow, credit position, and liquidity.

Cash Flow

Cash flow—perhaps the most important financial consideration for a company—refers to the surplus of internally generated funds over expenditures. A positive cash flow enables a company to fund new investments without borrowing money from bankers or investors. This ability is obviously a strength, since the company avoids paying interest or dividends. If current operations cannot generate a positive cash flow, the company is in a relatively weak financial position.

A company's cash-flow position often depends on the industry life cycle. In the embryonic and early growth stages of an industry, most companies reinvest all their cash in operations. Companies in such industries are cash hungry. They have to construct manufacturing capacity to meet demand, undertake research to perfect basic product design, and bear marketing expenditures to expand demand for the product. Later in an industry's development, the necessary production facilities will have been built and basic product design features perfected. Consequently, demands for cash tend to be less substantial as an industry matures, enabling companies to generate a strong positive cash flow. Thus cash flow may move from being a weakness to a strength as the company's industry matures.

Credit Position

Even if cash flow is a weakness, a company can still establish a reasonably secure overall financial standing if it has a good credit position. A good credit position can enable a company to expand by using borrowed money. To establish good credit, a company must (1) have a low level of current debt or (2) be viewed by bankers and investors as having good prospects. Many bio-technological companies, for example, have a negative cash flow but a strong overall financial position—because investors are willing to underwrite short-term losses in anticipation of big profit gains from innovations in genetic engineering.

To a large extent, a company's ability to establish a good credit position depends on how the company projects itself to bankers and investors. Companies based in embryonic or high-growth industries have an advantage, since the outlook for their business is generally more positive than for companies based in mature or declining industries. However, even a troubled company based in a highly competitive mature industry can establish good lines of credit if it is able to build up the confidence of investors. This is exactly what Lee Iacocca did in 1979 when he persuaded the U.S. government to underwrite a $1.5-billion loan for Chrysler.

Liquidity

A company is said to be *liquid* when its current assets exceed its current liabilities. Liquidity takes the form of idle working capital, such as marketable securities, or funding in reserve, such as unused lines of credit. A company's liquidity is a measure of its ability to meet unexpected contingencies—for instance, a sudden dip in demand or a price war. Companies that lack liquidity are in a weak financial position because they may be unable to meet these contingencies. Companies with major investments in fixed assets, such as steel mills or auto plants, tend to be less liquid than companies with a lower level of fixed assets. The reason is that fixed assets cannot be easily translated into cash and often require major fixed costs, which place heavy demands on the company's cash reserves in times of trouble.

4.13 SUMMARY OF CHAPTER

This chapter shows how distinctive competencies arise out of the unique strengths found within a company's individual functions, or value-creation activities. These competencies enable a company to establish a sustainable competitive advantage, whereas their lack places a company at a considerable competitive disadvantage. The pursuit of functional strategies can help a company (1) exploit existing distinctive competencies and (2) establish new distinctive competencies. The main points made in this chapter can be summarized as follows:

1. Distinctive competencies derive from unique company-level strengths. They are the bedrock of a company's strategic advantage. They are based on a company's resources and capabilities. The life span of a competence depends on its durability and imitability.

2. To gain a competitive advantage, a company must either perform value-creation activities at a lower cost than its rivals or perform them in a way that leads to differentiation and a premium price. To do either, a company must have a distinctive competence in one or more of its value-creation functions.

3. Strengths in manufacturing enable a company to minimize manufacturing costs for a given level of product quality. Establishing a distinctive competence in manufacturing involves exploiting experience-curve economies and matching process structure with product structure. A company that attains both of these objectives will find that its manufacturing costs are at least as low as, if not lower than, those of its nearest rivals. In addition, flexible manufacturing systems can give companies a manufacturing-based competitive advantage.

4. Strengths in marketing enable a company to differentiate its product. Establishing a distinctive competence in marketing involves appropriate market segmentation and the design of a marketing mix that enables the company to establish a differential advantage. A company that achieves this will be able to increase volume sold or charge a higher price than a company that does not.

5. Strengths in materials management enable a company to minimize the costs of logistics functions and improve product quality. Establishing a distinctive competence in materials management involves creating a materials-management function that oversees purchasing, production planning, and distribution activities. A company that achieves this will be able to minimize costs in each of these areas and enhance product quality.

6. Strengths in R&D enable a company to create new market opportunities through product innovation, differentiate its product through product development, or minimize product costs for a given quality through process innovation. Establishing a distinctive competence in R&D involves matching R&D skills to the requirement of an R&D strategy. Companies that lack appropriate skills will not be able to build an R&D-based competitive advantage.

7. Strengths in human-resource management enable a company to motivate its work force and to match people to strategic labor requirements. Motivating the work force requires the introduction of team-based approaches to production. Establishing a distinctive competence in human resources also involves planning to acquire individuals with the requisite mix of skills and experience.

8. Strengths in information systems enable a company to exploit information-based competitive advantages in other business functions, from manufacturing to human-resource management. Establishing a distinctive competence in information systems involves assessing the information intensity of company products and processes, identifying ways in which information systems can lead to a competitive advantage, and developing a company-wide plan for taking advantage of information systems.

9. A company's infrastructure consists of activities that set the organizational context within which other support and primary functions take place. These activities include general management, planning, finance, accounting, legal affairs, and government relations. A distinctive competence in any of these areas can assist a company in obtaining a sustainable competitive advantage.

10. The most critical components of a company's financial resources are its cash flow, credit, and liquidity positions. A positive cash flow, good credit, and high liquidity constitute strengths, whereas a negative cash flow, poor credit (high debt), and low liquidity are weaknesses.

Discussion Questions

1. What is the purpose of the value chain? How can it assist strategic managers in identifying a company's strengths and weaknesses with respect to (a) operating costs and (b) differentiation?

2. What functional strategies might a company pursue for each of the value-creation activities to minimize its overall operating costs?

3. What functional strategies might a company pursue for each of the value-creation activities to maximize the uniqueness of its product?

4. To what extent are the strategies you listed in response to Question 2 incompatible with the strategies you listed in response to Question 3?

Endnotes

1. W. K. Hall, "Survival Strategies in a Hostile Environment," *Harvard Business Review* (September–October 1980), 75–85.

2. "Caterpillar Is Betting on Pint-sized Machines," *Business Week,* November 25, 1985, p. 41. "For Caterpillar the Metamorphosis Isn't Over," *Business Week,* August 31, 1987,

pp. 72–74. "Where to Find the Top 100s," *Forbes,* July 13, 1987, p. 164.

3. Among others, the source of organizational capabilities has been discussed by the following: Jay Barney, "Organizational Culture: Can It Be a Source of Competitive Advantage?" *Academy of Management Review,* 11 (1986), 656–665; S. A. Lipperman and R. P. Rumelt, "Uncertain Imitability: An Analysis of Inter-Firm Differences Under Competition," *Bell Journal of Economics,* 23 (1982), 418–438; and Richard R. Nelson and Sidney G. Winter, *An Evolutionary Theory of Economic Change* (Cambridge, Mass.: Belknap, 1982).

4. See Edwin Mansfield, "How Economists See R&D," *Harvard Business Review* (November–December 1981), 98–106.

5. Michael E. Porter, *Competitive Advantage: Creating and Sustaining Superior Performance* (New York: Free Press, 1985).

6. Ibid.

7. See W. J. Abernathy and K. Wayne, "Limits of the Learning Curve," *Harvard Business Review* (September–October 1974), 109–119; Boston Consulting Group, *Perspectives on Experience* (Boston: Boston Consulting Group, 1972); G. Hall and S. Howell, "The Experience Curve from an Economist's Perspective," *Strategic Management Journal,* 6 (1985), 197–212; and W. B. Hirschmann, "Profit from the Learning Curve," *Harvard Business Review* (January–February 1964), 125–139.

8. A. A. Alchian, "Reliability of Progress Curves in Airframe Production," *Econometrica,* 31 (1963), 679–693.

9. Hall and Howell, "The Experience Curve," pp. 197–212.

10. Abernathy and Wayne, "Limits of the Learning Curve," pp. 109–119.

11. For example, see F. M. Scherer, A. Beckenstein, E. Kaufer, and R. D. Murphy, *The Economies of Multiplant Operations* (Cambridge, Mass.: Harvard University Press, 1975).

12. Abernathy and Wayne, "Limits of the Learning Curve," pp. 109–119.

13. D. F. Barnett and R. W. Crandall, *Up from the Ashes: The Rise of the Steel Minimill in the United States* (Washington, D.C.: Brookings Institute, 1986).

14. For example, see these three articles by Robert H. Hayes and Steven G. Wheelwright: "Link Manufacturing Process and Product Life Cycles," *Harvard Business Review* (January–February 1979), 133–153; "The Dynamics of Process-Product Life Cycles," *Harvard Business Review* (March–April 1979), 127–136; and "Competing Through Manufacturing," *Harvard Business Review* (January–February 1985), 99–109.

15. Patricia Nemetz and Louis Fry, "Flexible Manufacturing Organizations: Implications for Strategy Formulation and Organization," *Academy of Management Review,* 13(4) (1988), 627–638.

16. For further details see Nigel Greenwood, *Implementing Flexible Manufacturing Systems* (New York: Halstead Press, 1986); and Richard Schonberger, *Japanese Manufacturing: Nine Hidden Lessons in Simplicity* (London: Free Press, 1986).

17. This description is based on Patricia Nemetz, "Flexible Manufacturing Strategies, Technologies, and Structures: A Contingency Based Empirical Analysis" (Ph.D. diss. University of Washington, 1990).

18. "Factories That Turn Nuts into Bolts," *U.S. News and World Report,* July 14, 1986, pp. 44–45. Joel Kotkin, "The Great American Revival," *Inc.* (February 1988), 52–63.

19. This was a finding of Nemetz, "Flexible Manufacturing Strategies."

20. For example, see J. M. Hulbert and N. E. Toy, "A Strategic Framework for Marketing Control," *Journal of Marketing,* 41 (1977), 12–20; R. M. Johnson, "Market Segmentation: A Strategic Management Tool," *Journal of Marketing Research,* 8 (1971), 15–23.

21. D. Ammer, "Materials Management as a Profit Center," *Harvard Business Review* (January–February 1969), 49–60. Jeffrey G. Miller and Peter Gilmour, "Materials Managers: Who Needs Them?" *Harvard Business Review* (July–August 1979), 57.

22. Miller and Gilmour, "Materials Managers," p. 57.

23. David Garvin, "What Does Product Quality Really Mean?" *Sloan Management Review,* 26 (1984), 25–44.

24. Miller and Gilmour, "Materials Managers," p. 57.

25. These figures are averages taken from research by Edwin Mansfield and his associates. For example, see Edwin Mansfield, "How Economists see R&D," *Harvard Business Review* (November–December 1981), 98–106; and Edwin Mansfield, J. Rapoport, J. Schnee, S. Wagner, and M. Ham-

burger, *Research and Innovation in the Modern Corporation* (New York: Norton, 1971).

26. For details, see P. Petre, "AT&T's Epic Push into Computers," *Fortune,* May 25, 1987, pp. 42–50.

27. V. Scarpello, W. R. Boulton, and C. W. Hofer, "Reintegrating R&D into Business Strategy," *Journal of Business Strategy,* 6 (Spring 1986), 49–56.

28. See "Our Life Has Changed," *Business Week,* April 6, 1987, pp. 94–100.

29. W. J. Abernathy and J. M. Utterback, "Patterns of Industrial Innovation," *Technology Review,* 80 (1978), 1–9.

30. C. Fomrun, N. Tichy, and M. A. Devanna, *Strategic Human Resource Management* (New York: Wiley, 1983).

31. See Charles W. L. Hill, Michael Hitt, and Robert Hoskisson, "Declining U.S. Competitiveness: Reflections on a Crisis," *Academy of Management Executive,* 2 (1988), 51–60.

32. John Hoerr, "The Payoff from Teamwork," *Business Week,* July 10, 1989, pp. 56–62.

33. J. Sweet, "How Manpower Development Can Support Your Strategic Plan," *Journal of Business Strategy,* 2 (Summer 1981), 78–81.

34. See F. W. McFarland, "Information Technology Changes the Way You Compete," *Harvard Business Review* (May–June 1984), 98 103; and Michael E. Porter and V. E. Millar, "How Information Gives You a Competitive Advantage," *Harvard Business Review* (July–August 1985), 149–160.

35. Porter and Millar, ibid.

36. Porter, *Competitive Advantage,* p. 43.

Chapter 5

BUSINESS-LEVEL
STRATEGY

5.1 OPENING INCIDENT: HOLIDAY INNS INC.

The history of the Holiday Inns Inc. motel chain is one of the great success stories in American business. Its founder, Kemmons Wilson, vacationing in the early 1950s, found existing motels to be small, expensive, and of unpredictable quality. This discovery, along with the prospect of unprecedented highway travel that would come with the new interstate highway program, triggered a realization: There was an unmet customer need, a gap in the market for quality accommodations. Holiday Inns was to meet that need.

From the beginning, Holiday Inns set the standard for motel features like air conditioning and ice makers, while keeping room rates reasonable.[1] These amenities enhanced the motels' popularity, and a Wilson invention, motel franchising, made rapid expansion possible. By 1960 Holiday Inns motels dotted America's landscape; they could be found in virtually every city and on every major highway. Before the 1960s ended, more than 1,000 of them were in full operation, and occupancy rates averaged 80 percent. The concept of mass accommodation had arrived.

By the 1970s, however, the motel chain was in trouble. The service offered by Holiday Inns appealed to the average traveler, who wanted a standardized product (a room) at an average price. In essence, Holiday Inns had been target-ing the middle of the hotel-room market. But travelers were beginning to make different demands on hotels and motels. Some wanted luxury and were willing to pay higher prices for better accommodations and service. Others sought low prices and accepted rock-bottom quality and service in exchange. Although the market had fragmented into different groups of customers with different needs, Holiday Inns was still offering an undifferentiated, average-cost, average-quality product.[2]

Holiday Inns missed the change in the market and thus failed to respond appropriately to it, but the competition did not. Companies like Hyatt Corp. siphoned off the top end of the market, where quality and service sold rooms. Chains like Motel 6 and Days Inn captured the basic-quality, low-price end of the market. In between were many specialty chains that appealed to business travelers, families, or self-caterers—people who want to be able to cook in their hotel rooms. Holiday Inns' position was attacked from all sides. The company's earnings declined as occupancy rates dropped drastically, and marginal Holiday Inns motels began to close as competition increased.

Wounded but not dead, Holiday Inns is counterattacking. The original chain has been upgraded to suit quality-oriented travelers. At the same time, to meet the needs of different

142

kinds of travelers, the company has created new hotel and motel chains, including the luxury Holiday Inn Crowne Plazas; the Hampton Inns, which serve the low-price end of the market; and the all-suite Embassy Suites. Holiday Inns has attempted to meet the demands of the many niches, or segments, in today's hotel market. However, although it is still the biggest motel operator, it has lost its leading role in the industry. Now it is simply one company in a mature and overcrowded market.[3]

5.2 OVERVIEW

As the Holiday Inns example suggests, this chapter examines *how a company can compete effectively in a business or industry* and scrutinizes the various strategies that a company can adopt to maximize its competitive advantage and profitability. Chapter 3, on the industry environment, provided concepts for analyzing industry opportunities and threats. Chapter 4 discussed how a company can develop distinctive competencies at the functional level in order to gain a competitive edge. The purpose of Chapter 5 is to consider the business-level strategies that a company can use to compete effectively in the marketplace.

We begin by examining the basis of all business-level strategy: the process of deciding what products to offer, what markets to compete in, and what distinctive competencies to pursue. Second, we discuss three **generic competitive business-level strategies:** cost leadership, differentiation, and focus. The discussion centers on how to organize and combine decisions about product, market, and distinctive competencies so that a company can follow one of the generic strategies. We then look at how the industry lifecycle affects the choice of a generic strategy. Third, we examine the various **investment strategies** that a company may adopt at the business level to match its generic competitive strategies. Two factors are important in the choice of investment strategy: (1) a company's relative competitive strength in the industry and (2) a company's stage in the industry life cycle. By the end of the chapter, you will understand how the successful choice of business-level strategy is a product of matching environmental opportunities and threats (discussed in Chapter 3) to a company's strengths and weaknesses (discussed in Chapter 4). Then in Chapter 6 we extend this analysis and discuss how a company should tailor its business-level strategy to the industry structure in which it competes.

5.3 FOUNDATIONS OF BUSINESS-LEVEL STRATEGY

In Chapter 2, on defining the business, we discussed how Derek F. Abell saw the process of business definition as one involving decisions about (1) customer needs, or what is to be satisfied, (2) customer groups, or who is to be satisfied, and (3) distinctive competencies, or how customer needs are to be satisfied.[4]

These three decisions are at the heart of business-level strategy choice because they provide the sources of a company's competitive advantage over its rivals and determine how the company will compete in a business or industry. Consequently, we need to look at the ways in which companies can gain a competitive advantage at the business level.

Customer Needs and Product Differentiation

Customer needs are anything that can be satisfied by means of the characteristics of a product or service. *Product differentiation* is the process of creating a competitive advantage by designing product characteristics to satisfy customer needs. All companies must differentiate their products to a certain degree in order to satisfy some minimal level of customer needs. However, some differentiate their products to a much greater degree than others, and this difference can give them a competitive edge.

Some companies offer the customer a low-price product without engaging in much product differentiation.[5] Others seek to create something unique about their products so that they satisfy customer needs in ways that other products cannot. The uniqueness may relate to the physical characteristics of the product, such as quality or reliability, or it may lie in the product's appeal to customers' psychological needs, such as need for prestige or status.[6] Thus a Japanese auto may be differentiated by its reputation for reliability, and a Corvette or a Porsche may be differentiated by its ability to satisfy customers' status needs. Alternatively, product differentiation may be achieved by the number or diversity of models offered by the company. For example, in a recent catalogue, Sony offered twenty-four different 19-inch color television sets aimed at the top end of the market. Similarly, Baskin-Robbins provides at least thirty-one flavors of ice cream aimed at ice-cream lovers, and Foot Locker stocks the largest selection of athletic shoes available to appeal to the greatest number of buyers. Another way to differentiate a product is through a company's distinctive competence, as we discuss below. In practice, the kind of product differentiation that a company pursues is closely linked to the customer groups it serves.

Customer Groups and Market Segmentation

Market segmentation may be defined as the way a company decides to group customers, based on important differences in their needs or preferences, in order to gain a competitive advantage.[7] In general, a company can adopt three alternative strategies toward market segmentation.[8] First, it may choose not to recognize that different groups of customers have different needs and may adopt the approach of serving the average customer. Holiday Inns did this for much of its history. Second, a company may choose to segment its market into different constituencies and develop a product to suit the needs of each group. This approach matches that of Holiday Inns after it lost market share. Third, a company can choose to recognize that the market is segmented but concentrate on servicing only one market segment, or niche.

Why would a company want to make complex product/market choices and create a different product tailored to each market segment rather than create a single product for the whole market? The answer is that the decision to provide many products for many market niches allows a company to satisfy customer needs better. As a result, customer demand for the company's products rises and generates more revenue than would be the case if the company offered just one product for the whole market.[9] The contest between Ford and General Motors back in the 1920s illustrates this point.

Ford produced more motor cars in the 1920s than any other company. It was also the lowest-cost producer, for Henry Ford believed that one product would satisfy the entire market. The strategy worked well until GM's Alfred Sloan recognized the potential of segmenting the market and offering differentiated products.[10] Sloan developed five car divisions—Chevrolet, Pontiac, Oldsmobile, Cadillac, and Buick—each producing a wide range of different kinds of cars. Although this approach cost more, GM could recoup the costs with a differentiated pricing policy: Different car models were directed at different socioeconomic market segments. Because the product policy satisfied different customer needs, it was wildly successful. GM passed Ford in market share and profit and stayed ahead until 1986. Essentially, *Ford and GM made different decisions about which customer groups and customer needs to satisfy, and as a result they obtained different competitive advantages.* Holiday Inns made the same mistake that Ford made in the 1920s. It failed to realize that a company has to respond to customer groups and needs if it is to maximize profitability.

Sometimes, however, the nature of the product or the nature of the industry does not allow much differentiation—for example, bulk chemicals or cement.[11] In these cases, there is little opportunity for obtaining a competitive advantage through product differentiation and market segmentation because there is little opportunity for serving customer needs and customer groups in different ways. Instead, price is the main criterion used by customers to evaluate the product, and the competitive advantage lies with the company providing the lowest-priced product.

Deciding on Distinctive Competencies

The third issue in business-level strategy is to decide what distinctive competence to pursue in order to satisfy customer needs and groups.[12] Here we define *distinctive competence* as the means by which a company attempts to satisfy customer needs and groups in order to obtain a competitive advantage. Thus, for example, some companies use their production technology to develop a distinctive competence in manufacturing as a way of satisfying customer needs. The company tries to ride down the experience curve to provide customers with lower-cost products. Other companies may choose to concentrate on research and development to build a distinctive competence in technology and satisfy customer needs through the design and performance characteristics of their products. Still others may decide to satisfy customer needs by the quality of their service and the responsiveness of service personnel—that is, they may focus on developing competence in sales and marketing. The point is that, in making business strategy choices, a company must decide how to *organize and combine* its distinctive competencies in order to gain a competitive advantage. The source of these distinctive competencies is discussed at length in Chapter 4.

In sum, a product/market/distinctive-competence perspective provides a framework for understanding the foundations of competitive business-level strategy. Each of the generic competitive strategies discussed below is the result of different product/market/distinctive-competence decisions made to obtain a competitive advantage over industry rivals.

5.4 CHOOSING A GENERIC COMPETITIVE STRATEGY AT THE BUSINESS LEVEL

In this section, we examine the strategies that enable companies to compete effectively in a business or industry. Companies pursue a business-level strategy to gain a competitive advantage that allows them to outperform rivals and achieve above-average returns. They can choose from three generic competitive ap-

TABLE 5.1   **Product/market/distinctive-competence choices and generic competitive strategies**

	Cost leadership	Differentiation	Focus
Product differentiation	Low (principally by price)	High (principally by uniqueness)	Low to high (price or uniqueness)
Market segmentation	Low (mass market)	High (many market segments)	Low (one or a few segments)
Distinctive competence	Manufacturing and materials management	Research and development, sales and marketing	Any kind of distinctive competence

proaches: **cost leadership, differentiation,** and **focus.**[13] These strategies are called *generic* because all businesses or industries can pursue them regardless of whether they are manufacturing, service, or not-for-profit enterprises. Each of the generic strategies results from a company's making consistent choices on product, market, and distinctive competencies—choices that reinforce each other. Table 5.1 summarizes the choices appropriate for each generic strategy.

Cost-Leadership Strategy

A company's goal in pursuing a cost-leadership or low-cost strategy is to outperform competitors by producing goods or services at a cost lower than theirs. Two advantages accrue from this strategy. First, because of its lower costs, the cost leader is able to charge a lower price than its competitors yet make the same level of profit as they do. If companies in the industry charge similar prices for their products, the cost leader makes a higher profit than its competitors because of its lower costs. Second, if price wars develop and companies start to compete on price as the industry matures, the cost leader will be able to withstand competition better than the other companies because of its lower costs. For both these reasons, cost leaders are likely to earn above-average returns. But how does a company become the cost leader? It achieves this position by means of the product/market/distinctive-competence choices that it makes to gain a low-cost competitive advantage. Table 5.1 outlines these strategic choices.

Strategic choices   The cost leader chooses a low level of product differentiation. Differentiation is expensive, and if the company produces a wide range of products or expends resources to make its products unique, then its costs rise.[14] The cost leader aims for a level of differentiation not markedly inferior to that of the differentiator (a company that competes by spending resources on product development) but a level obtainable at low cost.[15] The cost leader does not try to be the industry leader in differentiation; it waits until customers want a feature or service before providing it. For example, a cost leader does not introduce stereo sound in television sets. It adds stereo sound only when it is obvious that consumers want it.

The cost leader also normally ignores the different market segments and aims for the average customer, again for the sake of lowest cost. Thus, in product/market terms, the company seeks a level of product differentiation that appeals to the average customer. Even though no customer may be totally happy with the product, the fact that *the company normally charges a lower price than its competitors* puts the product within a customer's range of choices.

The development of a distinctive competence in manufacturing is most important to a low-cost company, which attempts to ride down the experience curve so that it can lower its manufacturing costs. Since the company charges less for its products, it can attract the extra sales volume that allows it to obtain these experience-curve effects (that is, costs go down as production output increases). Besides, cost minimization means matching product and process structures and adopting efficient materials–management techniques. Consequently, the manufacturing and materials–management functions are the center of attention in the cost-leadership company, and the other functions shape their distinctive competencies to meet the needs of manufacturing.[16] For example, the sales function develops the competence of capturing large, stable sets of customer orders that allow manufacturing to make longer production runs and so reduce costs. The research and development function specializes in process improvements to lower the costs of manufacture, as well as product improvements to make production easier. Chrysler, for example, reduced the number of parts involved in manufacturing a car from 75,000 to 40,000 in order to decrease costs.

In short, the cost leader gears all its strategic product/market/distinctive-competence choices to the single goal of squeezing out every cent of production costs to provide a competitive advantage. A company like Heinz is an excellent example of a cost leader. Beans and canned vegetables do not permit much of a markup. The profit comes from the large volume of cans sold (each can having only a small markup). Therefore the H. J. Heinz Company goes to extraordinary lengths to try to reduce costs—by even 1/20th of a cent per can—because this will lead to large cost savings and thus bigger profits over the long run. As you will see in the chapters in Part III on strategy implementation, the other source of cost savings in pursuing cost leadership is the design of the organization structure to match this strategy, since structure is a major source of a company's costs. As we discuss in Chapter 12, a low-cost strategy implies tight production controls and rigorous use of budgets to control the production process.

Advantages and disadvantages   The advantages of each generic strategy are best discussed in terms of Porter's five forces model introduced in Chapter 3.[17] The five forces involve threats from competitors, from powerful suppliers, from powerful buyers, from substitute products, and from new entrants. The cost leader is protected from *prospective competitors* by its cost advantage. Its lower costs also mean that it will be less affected than its competitors by increases in the price of inputs if there are *powerful suppliers* and less affected by a fall in the price it can charge for its products if there are *powerful buyers*. Moreover, since cost leadership usually requires a big market share, the cost leader purchases in relatively large quantities, increasing bargaining power vis-à-vis suppliers. If *substitute products* start to come into the market, the cost leader can reduce its price to compete with them and retain its market share. Finally, the leader's cost advantage constitutes a *barrier to entry,* since other companies are unable to enter the industry and match the leader's costs or prices. The cost leader is therefore relatively safe as long as it can maintain its cost advantage.

The principal dangers of the cost-leadership approach lurk in competitors' ability to find ways of producing at lower cost and beat the cost leader at its own game. For instance, if technological change makes experience-curve economies obsolete, new companies may apply lower-cost technologies that give them a cost advantage over the cost leader. The specialty steel mills discussed in Chapter

3 gained this advantage. Competitors may also draw a cost advantage from labor-cost savings. Foreign competitors in Third World countries have very low labor costs; for example, wage costs in the United States are on the order of 600 or so percent more than in South Korea or Mexico. Many American companies now assemble their products abroad as part of their low-cost strategy; many are forced to do so simply to compete.

Competitors' ability to easily *imitate* the cost leader's methods is another threat to the cost-leadership strategy. For example, the ability of IBM-clone manufacturers to produce IBM-compatible products at costs similar to IBM's (but, of course, sell them at a much lower price) is a major worry for IBM. Finally, the cost-leadership strategy carries a risk that the cost leader, in the single-minded desire to reduce costs, may lose sight of changes in customer tastes. Thus a company may make decisions that reduce costs but drastically affect demand for the product. Holiday Inns experienced that problem. Similarly, the Joseph Schlitz Brewing Co. reduced the quality of its beer's ingredients, substituting inferior grains to reduce costs. Consumers immediately caught on; demand for the product dropped dramatically; and the company was eventually absorbed into the Stroh Brewing Co. As mentioned earlier, the cost leader cannot abandon product differentiation, and even low-priced products, such as Timex watches, cannot be too inferior to the more expensive Seikos if the low-cost/low-price policy is to succeed.

Although all companies try to contain their costs, the cost leader takes an extreme position in this regard and makes all its product/market/distinctive-competence choices with cost minimization in mind. Its ability to charge a lower price is the competitive advantage that allows it to be the industry price setter. However, given the huge growth in low-cost competition from abroad, it appears that cost leadership may become increasingly difficult to pursue in many industries. Even Japanese countries are now experiencing this problem. Their cost edge has been eroded by companies in Taiwan and Korea, such as Gold Star and Samsung, which are now the cost leaders. Japanese companies are increasingly looking to differentiation as a competitive strategy. Honda, for example, began building Acura to compete in the luxury car market, and Toyota and Nissan quickly responded with Lexus and Infiniti, respectively.

Differentiation Strategy

The objective of the generic strategy of differentiation is to achieve a competitive advantage by creating a product or service that is *perceived* by customers to be unique in some important way. The differentiated company's ability to satisfy a customer need in a way that its competitors cannot means that it can charge a **premium price.** The ability to increase revenues by charging premium prices (rather than by reducing costs like the cost leader) allows the differentiator to outperform its competitors and make above-average returns. The premium price is usually substantially above the price charged by the cost leader, and customers pay it because they believe the product's differentiated qualities to be worth the difference. Consequently, the product is priced on the basis of what the market will bear.[18] Thus Mercedes-Benz autos are much more expensive in the United States than in Europe because they confer more status here. Similarly, a basic BMW is not a lot more expensive to produce than an Oldsmobile, but its price is determined by customers who perceive that the prestige of owning a BMW is something worth paying for. Similarly, Rolex watches do not cost much to produce; their design has not changed very much for years; and their gold content is only a fraction of the watch price. Customers, however, buy the Rolex because of the unique quality they perceive in it: its ability to confer status on its wearer. In stereos, the name Bang & Olufsen of Denmark stands out, in jewelry Tiffany & Company, in airplanes Lear jets. All these products command premium prices because of their differentiated qualities.

Strategic choices   As Table 5.1 shows, a differentiator chooses a high level of product differentiation. As noted earlier, product differentiation can be achieved in a wide variety of ways. Procter & Gamble claims that its product quality is high and that Ivory soap is 99.44 percent pure. The Maytag Co. stresses reliability and the best repair record of any washer on the market. Sony emphasizes the quality of its television sets. In technologically complex products, technological features are the source of differentiation, and many people pay a premium price for the items. Differentiation can also be based on *service,* the ability of the company to offer comprehensive after-sales service and product repair—an especially important consideration when one buys complex products such as autos and domestic appliances, which are likely to break down periodically. Companies like IBM and Federal Express have excelled in service and reliability. In service organizations, quality of service attributes are also very important. Why can Neiman-Marcus and Nordstrom charge premium prices? They offer an exceptionally high level of service. Similarly, firms of lawyers or accountants stress the service aspects of their operations to clients: their knowledge, professionalism, and reputation.

Finally, a product's appeal to customers' psychological desires can become a source of differentiation. The appeal can be to prestige or status, as it is with BMWs and Rolex watches; to patriotism, as with buying a Chevrolet; to safety of home and family, as with Prudential Insurance; or to value for money, as with Sears, Roebuck and J. C. Penney. Differentiation can also be tailored to age groups as well as to socioeconomic groups. Indeed, the bases of differentiation are endless.

A company that pursues a differentiation strategy attempts to differentiate itself along as many dimensions as possible. The less it resembles its rivals, the more it is protected from competition and the wider its market appeal. Thus BMWs are not just prestige cars; they also offer technological sophistication, luxury, and reliability, as well as good, although very expensive, repair service. All these bases of differentiation help increase sales.

Generally, a differentiator chooses to segment its market into many niches. Now and then a company offers a product designed for each market niche and chooses to be a **broad differentiator,** but a company might choose to serve just those niches where it has a specific differentiation advantage. For example, Sony produces twenty-four models of television, filling all the niches from midpriced to high-priced sets. However, its lowest-priced model is always priced about $100 above that of its competitors, bringing into play the premium price factor. You have to pay extra for a Sony. Similarly, although Mercedes-Benz has recently filled niches below its old high-priced models with its 190 and 290 series, nobody would claim that Mercedes is going for every market segment. As we mentioned earlier, GM was the first company that tried to fill most of the niches, from the cheapest Chevrolet to the highest-priced Cadillac and Corvette.

Finally, in choosing which distinctive competence to pursue, a differentiated company concentrates on the organization function that provides the sources of its differentiation advantage. Differentiation on the basis of technological competence depends on the research and development function. Attempts to increase market segments are aided by the marketing function. A focus on a specific function does not mean, however, that manufacturing and the control of production costs are unimportant. A differentiator does not want to increase costs unnecessarily and tries to keep them somewhere near those of the cost leader. However, since developing the distinctive competencies needed to provide a differentiation advantage is expensive, a differentiator usually has higher costs than the cost leader. Still, it must control those costs so that the price of the product does not exceed what customers are willing to pay. The cost of producing some differentiated products, such as Rolex watches, is relatively low and the markup is relatively high; in such cases, companies can manipulate the price to match the market segments they serve. Nevertheless, since bigger profits are earned by controlling costs, as well as by maximizing revenues, it pays to control production costs, though not to minimize them to the point of losing the source of differentiation.[19]

Advantages and disadvantages   The advantages of the differentiation strategy can now be discussed in the context of the five forces model. Differentiation safeguards a company against *competitors* to the degree that customers develop **brand loyalty** for its products. Brand loyalty is a very valuable asset because it protects the company on all fronts. For example, *powerful suppliers* are rarely a problem because the differentiated company's strategy is geared more toward the price it can charge than toward the costs of production. Thus a differentiator can tolerate moderate increases in the prices of its inputs better than the cost leader can. Differentiators are unlikely to experience problems with *powerful buyers* because buyers are at their mercy. Only they can supply the product, and they command brand loyalty. Differentiators can pass on price increases to customers because customers are willing to pay the premium price. Differentiation and brand loyalty also create an *entry barrier* for other companies seeking to enter the industry. New companies are forced to develop their own distinctive competence to be able to compete, and doing so is very expensive. Finally, the threat of *substitute products* depends on the ability of competitors' products to meet the same customer needs as the differentiator's products and to break customers' brand loyalty. This can happen, as when IBM-clone manufacturers captured a large share of the home-computer market, but many people are still willing to pay the price for an IBM even though there are many IBM clones about. The issue is how much of a premium price a company can charge for uniqueness before customers switch products.

The main problems with the differentiation strategy center on the company's long-term ability to maintain its perceived uniqueness in customers' eyes. We have seen in the last ten years how quickly competitors move to *imitate and copy* successful differentiators. This has happened in many industries, such as computers, autos, and home electronics. Patents and first-mover advantages—the advantages of being the first to market a product or service—last only so long, and as the overall quality of products goes up, brand loyalty declines. Furthermore, the increasing use of consumer magazines that objectively compare the quality of competing products has helped consumers to become more knowledgeable in the marketplace. The result is that differentiators always have to be one step ahead of their imitators; otherwise, they will get left behind. No longer are consumers afraid of taking a risk. If the price is right and the features are minimally suitable, consumers will switch products, giving the cost leader an advantage over the differentiator.

One final threat to the differentiator is that the source of a company's uniqueness may be overridden by changes in consumer tastes and demands. The Opening Incident describes how Holiday Inns lost its competitive advantage because the market had segmented into complex niches while the company was still serving the needs of the average customer. A company must be constantly on the lookout for ways to match its unique strengths to changing product/market opportunities and threats. Otherwise it will be outperformed by its competitors. Clothing manufacturers know this well, and they change their clothes' styles every year to keep up with consumers' changing tastes.

Thus the disadvantages of this strategy are the ease with which competitors can imitate a differentiator's product and the difficulty of maintaining a premium price.[20] When differentiation stems from the design or physical features of the product, differentiators are at great risk because imitation is easy. The risk is that over time products like VCRs or stereos become *commodity-like* products for which the importance of differentiation diminishes as the price starts to fall. When differentiation stems from service quality or reliability or from any *intangible source,* like the Federal Express guarantee or the prestige of a Rolex, a company is much more secure. It is difficult to imitate intangibles, and the differentiator can reap the benefits of this strategy for the long run.

In summary, strategy of differentiation requires the firm to develop a competitive advantage by making product/market/distinctive-competence choices that reinforce one another and together increase the value of a product or service in the eyes of consumers. When a product has uniqueness in customers' eyes, differentiators can charge a premium price. However, they must watch out for imitators and be careful that they do not charge a price higher than the market will bear. Assessing the price they can charge for the uniqueness of a product is a crucial part of this strategy because the accuracy of the assessment is what determines the long-run profitability of differentiation.

Both Cost Leadership and Differentiation

Recently, changes in production technique—in particular, the development of flexible manufacturing technologies (discussed in Chapter 4)—have made the choice between cost-leadership and differentiation strategies less clear-cut. Because of technological developments it has become increasingly possible for a company to take advantage of the benefits of both. The reason is that the new flexible technologies allow firms to pursue a differentiation strategy at a low cost.

Traditionally, differentiation was obtainable only at high cost because the necessity of producing different models for different market segments meant that firms had to have short production runs, which raise manufacturing costs. In addition, the differentiated firm had to bear higher marketing costs than the cost leader because it was servicing many market segments. As a result, differentiators had higher costs than cost leaders that could produce large batches of standardized products. However, flexible manufacturing may enable a firm pursuing differentiation to manufacture a range of products at a cost comparable to those of the cost leader. The use of robots and flexible manufacturing cells reduces the costs of retooling the production line and the costs associated with small production runs. Indeed, a factor promoting the current trend toward market fragmentation and niche marketing in many consumer goods industries is the substantial reduction of the costs of differentiation by flexible manufacturing.

Another way that a differentiated producer may be able to realize significant scale economies is by standardizing many of the component parts used in its end products. For example, in the mid 1980s Chrysler began to offer twelve different models of cars to different segments of the auto market. However, despite different appearances, all twelve models were based on a common platform, known as the K-car platform. Very different models of K-cars used many of the same components, including axles, drive units, suspensions, and gear boxes. As a result, Chrysler was able to realize significant scale economies in the manufacture and bulk purchase of standardized component parts.

Another way that a firm can reduce both production and marketing costs is by limiting the number of models in the product line by offering packages of options rather than letting consumers decide exactly what options they require. It is increasingly common for auto manufacturers, for example, to offer an economy auto package, a luxury package, and a sports package to appeal to the principal market segments. Package offerings substantially reduce manufacturing costs because long production runs of the various packages are possible. At the same time, the firm is able to focus its advertising and marketing efforts on particular segments so that these costs are also reduced. Once again the firm is getting gains from differentiation and from low cost at the same time.

Just-in-time inventory systems can also help reduce costs and improve the quality and reliability of a company's products. This is important to differentiated firms where quality and reliability are essential ingredients of the product's appeal. Rolls-Royces, for example, are never supposed to break down. Improved quality control enhances a company's reputation and thus allows it to charge a premium price.

Taking advantage of the new production and marketing developments, some firms are managing to reap the gains from cost-leadership and differentiation strategies simultaneously. Since they can charge a premium price for their products compared with the price charged by the pure cost leader, and since they have lower costs than the pure differentiator, they are obtaining at least an equal, and probably a higher, level of profit than firms pursuing only one of the generic strategies. Hence the combined strategy is the most profitable to pursue, and companies are quickly moving to take advantage of the new production, materials-management, and marketing techniques. Indeed, American companies must take advantage of them if they are to regain a competitive advantage, for the Japanese pioneered many of these new developments. This explains why firms like Toyota and Sony are currently much more profitable than their U.S. counterparts, General Motors and Zenith. However, American firms like McDonald's, Apple Computer, and Intel are currently pursuing both strategies simultaneously.

Focus Strategy

The third pure generic competitive strategy, the focus strategy, differs from the other two chiefly because it is directed toward serving the needs of a *limited customer group or segment*. A focused company concentrates on serving a particular market niche, which may be defined geographically, by type of customer, or by segment of the product line.[21] For example, a geographical niche may be defined by region or even by locality. Selecting a niche by type of customer might mean serving only the very rich or the very young or the very adventurous. Concentrating only on a segment of the product line means focusing only on vegetarian foods or on very fast motor cars or on designer clothes. In following a focus strategy, a company is *specializing* in some way.

Having chosen its market segment, a company may pursue a focus strategy through either a differentiation or a low-cost approach. In essence, a focused company is a specialized differentiator or cost leader. Few focus firms are able to pursue both cost leadership and differentiation together because of their small size. If a focus firm uses a low-cost approach, it competes against the cost leader in the market segments where it has no cost disadvantage. For example, in local lumber or cement markets, the focuser has lower transportation costs than the low-cost national company. The focuser may also have a cost advantage because it is producing complex or custom-built products that do not lend themselves easily to economies of scale in production and therefore offer few experience-curve advantages. With a focus strategy, a company concentrates on small-volume custom products, where it has a cost advantage, and leaves the large-volume standardized market to the cost leader.

If a focuser pursues a differentiation approach, then all the means of differentiation that are open to the differentiator are available to the focused company. The point is that the focused company competes with the differentiator in only one or in just a few segments. For example, Porsche, a focused company, competes against General Motors in the sports car segment of the car market but not in other market segments. Focused companies are likely to develop differentiated product qualities successfully because of their knowledge of a small customer set (such as sports car buyers) or knowledge of a region. Furthermore, concentration on a small range of products sometimes allows a focuser to develop innovations faster than a large differentiator. However, the focuser does not attempt to serve all market segments because doing so would bring it into direct competition with the differentiator. Instead, a focused company concentrates on building market share in one market segment and, if successful, may begin to serve more and more market segments and chip away at the differentiator's competitive advantage.

Strategic choices   Table 5.1 shows the specific product/market/distinctive-competence choices made by a focused company. Differentiation can be high or low because the company can pursue a low-cost or a differentiation approach. As for customer groups, a focused company chooses specific niches in which to compete, rather than going for whole market, like the cost leader, or filling a large number of niches, like a broad differentiator. A focuser may pursue any distinctive competence because it can pursue any kind of differentiation or low-cost advantage. Thus it might seek a cost advantage and develop a low-cost manufacturing competence within a region. Or it could develop a service competence based on its ability to serve the needs of regional customers in ways that a national differentiator would find very expensive.

The many avenues that a focused company can take to develop a competitive advantage explain why there are so many small companies in relation to large ones. A company has enormous opportunity to develop its own niche and compete against low-cost and differentiated enterprises, which tend to be larger. A focus strategy provides an opportunity for an entrepreneur to find and then exploit a gap in the market by developing a product that customers cannot do without.[22] The small specialty mills discussed in the preceding chapter are a good example of how focused companies that specialize in one market can grow so efficient that they become the cost leaders. Many large companies started with a focus strategy, and, of course, one means by which companies can expand is to take over other focused companies. For example, Saatchi & Saatchi DFS Compton Inc., a specialist marketing company, grew by taking over several companies that were also specialists in their own market, such as Hay Associates, Inc., the management consultants.

Advantages and disadvantages   A focused company's competitive advantages stem from its distinctive competence. It is protected from *rivals* to the extent that it can provide a product or service that they cannot provide. This ability also gives the focuser power over its *buyers,* because they cannot get the same thing from anyone else. With regard to *powerful suppliers,* however, a focused company is at a disadvantage, because it buys in small volumes and thus is in the suppliers' power. But as long as it can pass on price increases to loyal customers, this disadvantage may not be a significant problem. *Potential entrants* have to overcome the customer loyalty that the focuser has generated; and, in turn, the development of customer loyalty reduces the threat from *substitute products.* This protection from the five forces allows the focuser to earn above-average returns on its investment. Another advantage of the focus strategy is that it permits a company to stay close to its customers and to respond to their changing needs. The problem that a large differentiator sometimes experiences in managing a large number of market segments is not an issue for a focuser.

Since a focuser produces at a small volume, its production costs often exceed those of a low-cost company. Higher costs can also reduce profitability if a focuser is forced to invest heavily in developing a distinctive competence—such as expensive product innovation—in order to compete with a differentiated firm. However, once again flexible manufacturing systems are opening up new opportunities for focused firms: Small production runs become possible at a lower cost. Increasingly, small specialized firms are competing with large companies in specific market segments where their cost disadvantage is much reduced.

A second problem is that the focuser's niche can suddenly disappear because of technological change or changes in consumer tastes. Unlike the more generalist differentiator, a focuser cannot move easily to new niches, given its concentration of resources and competence in one or a few niches. For example, a clothing manufacturer focusing on heavy-metal enthusiasts will find it difficult to shift to other segments if heavy-metal loses its appeal. The disappearance of niches is one reason that so many small companies fail.

Finally, there is the prospect that differentiators will compete for a focuser's niche by offering a product that can satisfy the demands of the focuser's customers; for example, GM's new top-of-the-line models are aimed at BMW and Mercedes-Benz. The cost leader may compete by providing a product whose low price may lure customers into switching; for example, IBM reduced its price to gain market share from the clone manufacturers. A focuser is vulnerable to attack and therefore has to constantly defend its niche.

Being Stuck in the Middle

Each generic strategy requires a company to make consistent product/market/distinctive-competence choices to establish a competitive advantage. In other words, a company must achieve a fit among the three components of business-level strategy. Thus, for example, a low-cost company cannot go for a high level of market segmentation like a differentiator or provide a wide range of products because doing so would raise production costs too much and the company would lose its low-cost advantage. Similarly, a differentiator with a technological competence that tries to reduce its expenditures on research and development or one that specializes in comprehensive after-sales service and tries to economize on its sales force to reduce costs is asking for trouble because it will lose its competitive advantage as its distinctive competence disappears.

Successful business-level strategy choice involves serious attention to all elements of the competitive plan. There are many examples of companies that, through ignorance or through mistakes, did not do the planning necessary for success in their chosen strategy. Such companies are said to be **stuck in the middle** because they have made product/market choices in such a way that they have been unable to obtain or sustain a competitive advantage.[23] As a result, they have below-average performance and suffer when industry competition intensifies.

Some stuck-in-the-middle companies started out pursuing one of the three generic strategies but made wrong decisions or were subject to environmental changes. Losing control of a generic strategy is very easy unless management keeps close track of the business and its environment, constantly adjusting product/market choices to suit changing industry conditions. We saw in the Opening Incident how this can happen. There are many paths to being stuck in the middle. Sometimes a low-cost company may decide to use some of its profits to diversify into product markets where it has little expertise or to invest in research and development that management thinks may bolster the prestige of the organization. Such actions are expensive and have no guarantee of success. Bad strategic decisions can quickly erode the cost leader's above-average profitability.

Quite commonly, a focuser can get stuck in the middle when it becomes overconfident and starts to act like a broad differentiator. People Express is a good example of a company in this situation. It started out as a specialized carrier serving a narrow market niche: low-priced travel on the Eastern Seaboard. In pursuing this focus strategy based on cost leadership, it was very successful; but when it tried to expand to other geographical regions and began taking over other airlines to increase its number of planes, it lost its niche. People Express became one more carrier in an increasingly competitive market, where it had no special competitive advantage against the other national carriers. The result was financial troubles. People Express was swallowed up by Texas Air and incorporated into Continental Airlines.

Differentiators, too, can fail in the market and end up stuck in the middle if competitors attack their markets with more specialized or low-cost products that blunt their competitive edge. This happened to IBM in the large-frame computer market. The increasing movement toward flexible manufacturing systems will increase the problems faced by cost leaders and differentiators. Many large firms will become stuck in the middle unless they make the investment needed to pursue both strategies simultaneously. No company is safe in the jungle of competition, and each must be constantly on the lookout to exploit competitive advantages as they arise and to defend the advantages it already has.

In sum, successful management of a generic competitive strategy requires strategic managers to attend to two main things. First, they need to ensure that the product/market/distinctive-competence decisions they make are oriented toward one specific competitive strategy. Second, they need to monitor the environment so that they can keep the firm's strengths and weaknesses in tune with changing opportunities and threats.

Generic Strategies and the Industry Life Cycle

In Chapter 3, on analyzing the industry environment, Table 3.3 summarizes how the basis of rivalry among companies changes as their industry ages during the life cycle. The table shows that competition by price and by product differentiation becomes increasingly pronounced at later stages of the industry life cycle. We discuss the effect of these changes on business-level strategy in detail in the next chapter; however, the industry life cycle has several implications for companies pursuing a specific generic strategy. First, it implies that pursuing a cost-leadership strategy is least important at early stages in the life cycle because companies can sell all they can produce. Thus, although low costs help increase profit margins, at the embryonic stage most companies are trying to differentiate their products in order to develop customers' tastes for them.

By the growth stage, however, companies must choose which competitive strategy to follow, because the growth stage is succeeded by the shakeout, where only the strongest survive. Some companies attempt to become the *cost leaders;* others strive to become *differentiators;* still others *focus* their efforts on their chosen niche. Some will be better in making their product/market choices than others, so that by the shakeout stage the companies *stuck in the middle* will be the ones to exit the industry first.

By the maturity stage, an industry is composed of a *collection of companies pursuing each of the generic strategies.* This is where the strategic group concept, discussed in Chapter 3, becomes important. Essentially, all the companies pursuing a low-cost strategy can be viewed as composing one strategic group, and all those pursuing differentiation constitute another; the focusers form a third group.[24] The *mobility barrier* surrounding each group is based on the generic business-level strategy pursued by companies in the group. That is, once a company has made an investment in one generic strategy, changing to another is very expensive, and the expense restricts intra-industry competition. For example, if a company invests resources to develop a distinctive competence in cost leadership, it will find entering the differentiator group very difficult because it lacks the extensive sales force or advanced technological competence necessary to compete with the differentiator. Similarly, differentiators cannot enter the low-cost group unless they have the capacity to reduce their costs to the level of companies in that group because they *have* made an investment in the necessary sales force or technology. Thus, when strategic groups are based on different generic competitive strategies, there is likely to be a stable pattern of industry competition over time.

This is why the development of a cohesive set of product/market/distinctive-competence choices to pursue a generic strategy is so important early on. The strategy sets the scene for profitability in later stages of the industry life cycle because the emergence of strategic groups defined by strategy type simultaneously protects companies from potential industry entrants and limits the degree to which companies pursuing different strategies can compete against each other.

The advent of companies pursuing both a cost-leadership and a differentiation strategy further complicates this picture. As this trend continues, the implication is that these companies will have little trouble attacking the strategic groups presently made up of pure differentiators or pure cost leaders because they possess the competencies of companies already in these groups. Companies pursuing both strategies simultaneously will become the dominant competitors in an industry—that is, the ones who set industry pricing and output decisions. Increasingly, it appears that firms will be confronting other firms in head-on competition, and the battle for competitive advantage will become more acute in the industry setting. We discuss the relationship between business-level strategy and the industry structure environment in considerable detail in the next chapter. There we examine how the gains from a generic competitive strategy also depend on the structure of industry competition and competitive relations between companies in the industry.

Summary: Three Generic Strategies

The three generic strategies represent the principal ways in which organizations can compete in an industry. They protect companies from the five forces of competition and ultimately, for the companies that survive the shakeout stage, provide protection by means of mobility barriers. However, many companies do fail along the way. Sometimes companies do not continue to develop the functional competencies necessary to sustain their dominance. Sometimes they lose their product differentiation advantage to a competitor. Sometimes the market changes, and the niches or segments they were filling disappear. It is therefore not enough just to choose a generic competitive strategy. If above-average returns are to be consistently obtained, as many resources must be devoted to maintaining a competitive strategy as to establishing it. Consequently, if a company is to pursue a generic competitive strategy or develop two strategies simultaneously, it must evaluate the potential returns from the strategy against the cost of the resources that have to be invested in order to develop it. This is the issue to which we now turn.

5.5 CHOOSING AN INVESTMENT STRATEGY AT THE BUSINESS LEVEL

We have been discussing business-level strategy in terms of making product/market/distinctive-competence choices to gain a competitive advantage. However, there is a second major choice to be made at the business level: the choice of which type of investment strategy to pursue in support of the competitive strategy.[25] An *investment strategy* refers to the amount and type of resources—both human and financial—that must be invested to gain a competitive advantage. Generic competitive strategies provide competitive advantages, but they are expensive to develop and maintain. Differentiation is the most expensive of the three because it requires that a company invest resources in many functions, such as research and development and sales and marketing, to develop distinctive competencies. Cost leadership is less expensive to maintain once the initial investment in a manufacturing plant and equipment has been made. It does not require such sophisticated research and development or marketing efforts. The focus strategy is cheapest because fewer resources are needed to serve one market segment than to serve the whole market.

In deciding on an investment strategy, a company must evaluate the potential returns from investing in a generic competitive strategy against the cost of developing the strategy. In this way, it can determine whether a strategy is likely to be profitable to pursue and how profitability will change as industry competition changes. Two factors are crucial in choosing an investment strategy: the strength of a company's position in an industry relative to its competitors and the stage of the industry life cycle in which the company is competing.[26]

Competitive Position

Two attributes can be used to determine the strength of a company's relative competitive position. First, the larger a company's *market share,* the stronger is its competitive position and the greater are the potential returns from future investment. This is because a large market share provides experience-curve economies and suggests that the company has developed brand loyalty. The strength and uniqueness of a company's *distinctive competencies* are the second measure of competitive position. If it is difficult to imitate a company's research and development expertise, its manufacturing or marketing skills, its knowledge of particular customer segments, or its reputation or brand-name capital, the company's relative competitive position is strong and its returns from the generic strategy increase.

In general, the companies with the largest market share and strongest distinctive competence are in the best position.

These two attributes obviously reinforce one another and explain why some companies get stronger and stronger over time. A unique competence leads to increased demand for the company's products, and then, as a result of larger market share, the company has more resources to invest in developing its distinctive competence. Companies with a smaller market share and little potential for developing a distinctive competence are in a weaker competitive position.[27] Thus they are less attractive sources for investment.

Life-Cycle Effects

The second main factor influencing the investment attractiveness of a generic strategy is the *stage of the industry life cycle*. Each life cycle stage is accompanied by a particular industry environment, presenting different opportunities and threats. Each stage, therefore, has different implications for the investment of resources needed to obtain a competitive advantage. For example, competition is strongest in the shakeout stage of the life cycle and least important in the embryonic stage, so the risks of pursuing a strategy change over time. The difference in risk explains why the potential returns from investing in a competitive strategy depend on the life-cycle stage. Table 5.2 summarizes the relationship among the stage of the life cycle, competitive position, and investment strategy at the business level.

TABLE 5.2   **Choosing an investment strategy at the business level**

		Strong competitive position	Weak competitive position
Stage of industry life cycle	Embryonic	Share building	Share building
	Growth	Growth	Market concentration
	Shakeout	Share increasing	Market concentration or harvest/liquidation
	Maturity	Hold-and-maintain or profit	Harvest or liquidation/divestiture
	Decline	Market concentration, harvest, or asset reduction	Turnaround, liquidation, or divestiture

Choosing an Investment Strategy

Embryonic strategy   In the embryonic stage, all companies, weak and strong, emphasize the development of a distinctive competence and a product/market policy. During this stage, investment needs are great because a company has to establish a competitive advantage. Many fledgling companies in the industry are seeking resources to develop a distinctive competence. Thus the appropriate business-level investment strategy is a **share-building strategy.** The aim is to build market share by developing a stable and unique competitive advantage to attract customers who have no knowledge of the company's products.

Companies require large amounts of capital to build research and development competencies or sales and service competencies. They cannot generate much of this capital internally. Thus a company's success depends on its ability to demonstrate a unique competence to attract outside investors, or venture capitalists. If a company gains the resources to develop a distinctive competence, it will be in a relatively stronger competitive position. If it fails, its only option may be to exit the industry. In fact, companies in weak competitive positions at all stages in the life cycle may choose to exit the industry to cut their losses.

Growth strategies   At the growth stage, the task facing a company is to consolidate its position and provide the base it needs to survive the coming shakeout. Thus the appropriate investment strategy is the **growth strategy.** The goal is to maintain a company's relative competitive position in a rapidly expanding market and, if possible, to increase it—in other words, to grow with the expanding market. However, other companies are entering the market and catching up with the industry innovators. As a result, companies require successive waves of capital infusion to maintain the momentum generated by their success in the embryonic stage. For example, differentiators are engaging in massive research and development, and cost leaders are investing in plant to obtain experience-curve economies. All this investment is very expensive.

The growth stage is also the time when companies attempt to consolidate existing market niches and enter new ones so that they can increase their market share. Increasing the level of market segmentation is also expensive. A company has to invest resources to develop a new sales and marketing competence. Consequently, at the growth stage companies fine-tune their competitive strategy and make business-level investment decisions about the relative advantages of a differentiation, low-cost, or focus strategy, given financial needs and relative competitive position. For example, if one company has emerged as the cost leader, the other companies in the industry may decide not to compete head-on with it. Instead, they pursue a growth strategy using a differentiation or focus approach and invest resources in developing unique competencies. Because companies spend a lot of money just to keep up with growth in the market, finding additional resources to develop new skills and competencies is a difficult task for strategic managers.

Companies in a weak competitive position at this stage engage in a **market concentration strategy** to consolidate their position. They move to specialize in some way and adopt a focus strategy in order to reduce their investment needs. If very weak, they may also choose to exit the industry.

Shakeout strategies   By the shakeout stage, demand is increasing slowly and competition by price or product characteristics has become intense. Thus companies in strong competitive positions need resources to invest in a **share-increasing strategy** to attract customers from weak companies that are exiting the market. In other words, companies attempt to maintain and increase market share despite fierce competition. The way companies invest their resources depends on their generic strategy.

For cost leaders, because of the price wars that can occur, investment in cost control is crucial if they are to survive the shakeout stage. Differentiators in a strong competitive position choose to forge ahead and become broad differentiators. Their investment is likely to be oriented toward marketing, and they are likely to develop a sophisticated after-sales service network. They also widen the product range to match the range of customer needs. Differentiators in a weak position reduce their investment burden by withdrawing to a focused strategy—the market concentration strategy—in order to specialize in a particular niche or product. Weak companies exiting the industry engage in a harvest or liquidation strategy, both of which are discussed below.

Maturity strategies   By the maturity stage, a strategic group structure has emerged in the industry, and companies have learned how their competitors will react to their competitive moves. At this point companies want to reap the rewards of their previous investments in developing a generic strategy. Until now profits have been reinvested in the business, and dividends have been small. Investors in strong companies have obtained their rewards through capital appreciation because the company has reinvested most of its capital to maintain and increase market share. As market growth slows in the maturity stage, a company's investment strategy depends on the level of competition in the industry and the source of the company's competitive advantage.

In environments where competition is high because technological change is occurring or where barriers to entry are low, companies need to defend their competitive position. Strategic managers need to continue to invest heavily in maintaining the company's competitive advantage. Both low-cost companies and differentiators adopt a **hold-and-maintain** strategy to support their generic strategies. They expend resources to develop their distinctive competencies so as to remain the market leaders. For example, differentiated companies may invest in improved after-sales service, and low-cost companies may invest in the latest production technologies, such as robotics. Doing so is expensive but is warranted by the revenues that will accrue from maintaining a strong competitive position.

Additionally, companies move to develop both a low-cost and a differentiation strategy simultaneously. Differentiators take advantage of their strong position to develop flexible manufacturing systems in order to reduce their production costs. Cost leaders move to start differentiating their products to expand their market share by serving more market segments. For example, Gallo moved into the premium wine and wine cooler market segments to take advantage of low production costs.

However, when a company is protected from industry competition, it may decide to exploit its competitive advantage to the full by engaging in a **profit strategy.** A company pursuing this strategy attempts to maximize the present returns from its previous investments. Typically, it reinvests proportionally less in its business and increases returns to shareholders. The strategy works well as long as competitive forces remain relatively *constant,* so that the company can maintain the profit margins developed by its competitive strategy. However, the company must constantly remain alert for threats from the environment and must take care not to become complacent and unresponsive to changes in the competitive environment.

All too often market leaders fail to exercise such vigilance, imagining that they are impregnable to competition. For example, General Motors felt secure against foreign car manufacturers until changes in oil prices precipitated a crisis. Kodak, which had profited for so long from its strengths in film processing, was slow to respond to the threat of electronic imaging techniques. Paradoxically, the most successful companies often fail to sense changes in the market. For example, Holiday Inns' failure to perceive changes in customer needs was to some extent the result of its single-minded efforts to develop its existing motel chain. Developing two chains side by side would have required more resources, but that was what the market demanded. A company's ability to raise capital becomes very important in such situations; otherwise, its distinctive competence may disappear.

Companies in a weak competitive position at the maturity stage use the decline strategies discussed below.

Decline strategies   The decline stage of the industry life cycle begins when demand for the industry's product starts to fall. There are many possible reasons for decline, including foreign competition and product substitution. A company may lose its distinctive competence as its rivals enter with new or more efficient technologies. Thus it must decide what investment strategy to adopt in order to deal with new industry circumstances. Table 5.2 lists the strategies that companies can resort to when their competitive position is declining.[28]

The initial strategies that companies can adopt are market concentration and asset reduction.[29] With a **market concentration strategy,** a company attempts to consolidate its product and market choices. It narrows its product range and exits marginal niches in an attempt to redeploy its investments more efficiently and improve its competitive position. Reducing customer needs and the customer groups served may allow the company to pursue a focus strategy in order to survive the decline stage. (As noted earlier, weak companies in the growth stage tend to adopt this strategy.) That is what International Harvester did as the demand for farm machinery fell. It now produces only medium-size trucks under the name Navistar.

An **asset reduction strategy** requires a company to limit or reduce its investment in a business and to extract, or milk, the investment as much as it can. This approach is sometimes called a **harvest strategy** because the company reduces to a minimum the assets it employs in the business and foregoes investment for the sake of immediate profits.[30] A market concentration strategy generally indicates that a company is trying to turn around its business so that it can survive in the long run. A harvest strategy implies that a company will exit the industry once it has harvested all the returns it can. Low-cost companies are more likely to pursue a harvest strategy simply because a smaller market share means higher costs and they are unable to move to a focus strategy. Differentiators, in contrast, have a competitive advantage in this stage if they can move to a focus strategy.

At any stage of the life cycle, companies that are in weak competitive positions may apply **turnaround strategies.**[31] The question that a company has to answer is whether there is a viable way to compete in the industry and how much will such competition cost. If a company is stuck in the middle, then it must assess the investment costs of developing a generic competitive strategy. Perhaps a company pursuing a low-cost strategy has not made the right product or market choices, or a differentiator has been missing niche opportunities. In such cases, the company can redeploy resources and change its competitive strategy.

Sometimes a company's loss of competitiveness may be due to poor strategy implementation. If so, the company must move to change its structure and control systems rather than its strategy. For example, Dan Schendel, a prominent management researcher, found that 74 percent of the turnaround situations he and his colleagues studied were due to inefficient strategy implementation. The strategy-structure fit at the business level is thus very important in determining competitive strength.[32] We discuss it in detail in Chapter 12.

If a company decides that turnaround is not possible, either for competitive or for life-cycle reasons, then the two remaining investment alternatives are **liquidation** and **divestiture.** As the terms imply, the company moves to exit the industry either by liquidating its assets or by selling the whole business. Both can be regarded as radical forms of harvesting strategy because the company is seeking to get back as much as it can from its investment in the business. Often, however, it can only exit at a loss and take a tax write-off. Timing is important, because the earlier a company senses that divestiture is necessary, the more it can get for its assets. There are many stories about companies that buy weak or declining companies, thinking that they can turn them around, and then realize their mistake as the new acquisitions become a drain on their resources. Often the acquired companies have lost their competitive advantage, and the cost of regaining it is too great. However, there have also been spectacular successes, like that achieved by Lee Iacocca, who engaged in a low-cost strategy involving the firing of more than 45 percent of Chrysler's work force.

5.6 SUMMARY OF CHAPTER

The purpose of this chapter is to discuss the factors that must be considered if a company is to develop a business-level strategy that allows it to compete effectively in the marketplace. The formulation of business-level strategy involves matching the opportunities and threats in the environment to the company's strengths and weaknesses by making choices about products, markets, technologies, and the investments necessary to pursue the choices. All companies, from one-person operations to the strategic business units of large corporations, must develop a business strategy if they are to compete effectively and maximize their long-term profitability. The chapter makes the following main points:

1. Selecting a business-level strategy involves two main decisions: (a) choosing a generic competitive strategy and (b) choosing an investment strategy.

2. At the heart of generic competitive strategy are choices concerning product differentiation, market segmentation, and distinctive competence.

3. The combination of those three choices results in the specific form of generic competitive strategy employed by a company.

4. The three generic competitive strategies are cost leadership, differentiation, and focus. Each has advantages and disadvantages. A company must constantly manage its strategy; otherwise, it risks being stuck in the middle.

5. Increasingly, developments in manufacturing technology are allowing firms to pursue both a cost-leadership and a differentiation strategy and thus obtain the economic benefits of both strategies simultaneously. Technical developments also allow small firms to compete with large firms on equal footing in particular market segments and hence increase the number of firms pursuing a focus strategy.

6. The choice of generic competitive strategy is affected by the stage of the industry life cycle.

7. The second choice facing a company is an investment strategy for supporting the competitive strategy. The choice of investment strategy depends on two main factors: (a) the strength of a company's competitive position in the industry and (b) the stage of the industry life cycle.

8. The main types of investment strategy are share building, growth, share increasing, hold-and-maintain, profit, market concentration, asset reduction, harvest, turnaround, liquidation, and divestiture.

Discussion Questions

1. Why does each generic competitive strategy require a different set of product/market/dis- tinctive-competence choices? Give examples of pairs of companies in the (a) computer industry

and (b) auto industry that pursue different competitive strategies.

2. How can companies pursuing a cost-leadership, differentiation, or focus strategy become stuck in the middle? In what ways can they regain their competitive advantage?

3. Over the industry life cycle, what investment strategy choices should be made by (a) differentiators in a strong competitive position and (b) differentiators in a weak competitive position?

4. How do technical developments affect the generic strategies pursued by firms in an industry? How might they do so in the future?

Endnotes

1. "The Holiday Inns Trip: A Breeze for Decades, Bumpy Ride in the '80s," *The Wall Street Journal,* February 11, 1987, p. 1.

2. Holiday Inns, *Annual Report,* 1985.

3. Bureau of Labor Statistics, *U.S. Industrial Outlook* (Washington, D.C., 1986).

4. Derek F. Abell, *Defining the Business: The Starting Point of Strategic Planning* (Englewood Cliffs, N.J.: Prentice-Hall, 1980), p. 169.

5. Michael E. Porter, *Competitive Strategy: Techniques for Analyzing Industries and Competitors* (New York: Free Press, 1980).

6. R. Kotler, *Marketing Management,* 5th ed. (Englewood Cliffs, N.J.: Prentice-Hall, 1984). M. R. Darby and E. Karni, "Free Competition and the Optimal Amount of Fraud," *Journal of Law and Economics,* 16 (1973), 67–86.

7. Abell, *Defining the Business,* p. 8.

8. Michael E. Porter, *Competitive Advantage: Creating and Sustaining Superior Performance* (New York: Free Press, 1985).

9. R. D. Buzzell and F. D. Wiersema, "Successful Share Building Strategies," *Harvard Business Review,* 59 (1981), 135–144. L. W. Phillips, D. R. Chang, and R. D. Buzzell, "Product Quality, Cost Position, and Business Performance: A Test of Some Key Hypotheses," *Journal of Marketing,* 47 (1983), 26–43.

10. Alfred R. Sloan, *My Years at General Motors* (New York: Doubleday, 1972).

11. Porter, *Competitive Strategy,* p. 45.

12. Abell, *Defining the Business,* p. 15.

13. Although many other authors have discussed cost leadership and differentiation as basic competitive approaches (e.g., F. Scherer, *Industrial Market Structure and Economic Performance,* 2nd ed. [Boston: Houghton Mifflin, 1980]), Porter's model (Porter, *Competitive Strategy*) has become the dominant approach. Consequently, this model is the one developed below, and the discussion draws heavily on his definitions. The basic cost-leadership/differentiation dimension has received substantial empirical support (e.g., D. C. Hambrick, "High Profit Strategies in Mature Capital Goods Industries: A Contingency Approach," *Academy of Management Journal,* 26 [1983], 687–707).

14. Porter, *Competitive Advantage,* p. 37.

15. Porter, *Competitive Advantage,* pp. 13–14.

16. D. Miller, "Configurations of Strategy and Structure: Towards a Synthesis," *Strategic Management Journal,* 7 (1986), 217–231.

17. Porter, *Competitive Advantage,* pp. 44–46.

18. Charles W. Hofer and D. Schendel, *Strategy Formulation: Analytical Concepts* (St. Paul, Minn.: West, 1978).

19. W. K. Hall, "Survival Strategies in a Hostile Environment," *Harvard Business Review,* 58(5) (1980), 75–85. Hambrick, "High Profit Strategies in Mature Capital Goods Industries," pp. 687–707.

20. Porter, *Competitive Strategy,* p. 46.

21. Ibid., p. 38.

22. Peter F. Drucker, *The Practice of Management* (New York: Harper, 1954).

23. Porter, *Competitive Strategy,* p. 43.

24. G. Dess and R. Davies, "Porter's (1980) Generic Strategies as Determinants of Strategic Group Membership and Organizational Performance," *Academy of Management Journal,* 27 (1984), 467–488.

25. Hofer and Schendel, *Strategy Formulation,* pp. 102–104.

26. Our discussion of the investment, or posturing, component of business-level strategy draws heavily on Hofer and Schendel's discussion in *Strategy Formulation,* especially Chapter 6.

27. Hofer and Schendel, *Strategy Formulation,* pp. 75–77.

28. K. R. Harrigan, "Strategy Formulation in Declining Industries," *Academy of Management Review,* 5 (1980), 599–604.

29. Hofer and Schendel, *Strategy Formulation,* pp. 169–172.

30. L. R. Feldman and A. L. Page, "Harvesting: The Misunderstood Market Exit Strategy," *Journal of Business Strategy,* 4 (1985), 79–85.

31. C. W. Hofer, "Turnaround Strategies," *Journal of Business Strategy,* 1 (1980), 19–31.

32. Hofer and Schendel, *Strategy Formulation,* p. 172.

Chapter 6

BUSINESS-LEVEL STRATEGY AND INDUSTRY STRUCTURE

6.1 OPENING INCIDENT: THE AIRLINE INDUSTRY

Before deregulation in 1978, competition over fares and ticket prices was not permitted in the airline industry, and the airlines had to find other ways to compete for customers. Their response was to attract customers by offering more frequent flights and better service. However, since they all imitated one another, no airline was able to get a competitive advantage over its rivals, and each airline's costs rose dramatically because of the cost of extra flights, improved meals, and so on. To cover their higher costs, the airlines continuously applied for fare increases. As a result, customers paid higher and higher fares to compensate for the airlines' inefficiency. In an attempt to cure this problem, Congress decided to deregulate the industry and allow competition over ticket prices and free entry into the industry. Although the airlines did not want deregulation (Why should they? They were receiving a nice profit as a protected industry.), deregulation took place in 1979. The result was chaos.

Deregulation destroyed the old competitive rules of the game. Before deregulation, the ma-

jor airlines knew how they could compete and were able to signal their intentions to one another so they understood each other's competitive moves. In the new world of price competition, entry into the industry was easy, and a host of small airlines entered to compete with the majors. During regulation each airline had not had to develop a generic strategy. There had been no incentive to keep costs low because cost increases could be passed on to consumers; and all firms had used the same means to differentiate themselves, so no airline had a competitive advantage in being unique. With no rules to tell them how to compete and no experience of free competition, the result was a price war as new, low-cost entrants like People Express and Southwest Air sought to gain market share from the majors.

For several years, price competition remained the principal competitive behavior in the airline industry, and the result was a low level of industry profitability. Most airlines lost money. However, by 1988, the airline industry had gone through a shakeout. Many of the new entrants that had precipitated the crisis had either gone bankrupt because of the price wars or had been swallowed up by the majors. Also, the majors had developed sophisticated business-level strategies based on the development of hub-and-spoke networks, which allowed them to build national route structures at low cost. These networks also made it difficult for new firms to enter the industry because the majors held all the available gates at large airports. Through all these means the majors had created new barriers to entry and therefore reduced the threat of new entrants. They were thus in a position to develop new competitive rules of the game to stabilize industry competition and prevent price competition.

Inside the industry, the majors also adopted competitive techniques to reduce the level of competitive rivalry. Very quickly, the airlines imitated one another's pricing policies. On most route segments the prices charged by the airlines diverged by less than 5 percent, and the airlines used market signaling to communicate their intention of making changes such as raising prices. By 1990 they exercised their new market power to start a policy of issuing nonrefundable tickets to reduce their costs and transfer risk to the consumer. Airline profits rocketed. By stabilizing industry competition by means of new competitive rules, they restored industry profitability and set the scene for competition in the 1990s. However, by 1991 the Gulf War had totally altered the industry environment in which the airlines operated, and a new competitive situation arose where not only the profitability but the very survival of many airlines was at stake.

6.2 OVERVIEW

As the Opening Incident suggests, even when companies have developed successful generic competitive strategies and have supported these strategies with appropriate investment strategies, they still face a crucial problem: how to respond to the actions of industry competitors, each of which is seeking to maximize its own competitive advantage and profitability. The purpose of this chapter is to discuss this crucial element of business-level strategy: the management of competitive relations in dynamic industry environments where companies are interdependent—that is, where the outcome of one company's actions depends on the responses of its rivals. Our intention is to show how the success of a company's business-level strategy also depends on the way the company manages the competitive industry environment.

In Chapter 5, we examined how the stages of the industry life cycle affect the choice of generic competitive strategy and investment strategy. The industry life cycle also determines the level and type of competition present in the industry environment, that is, its **industry structure.** Using the concepts developed in Chapter 3 on the industry environment, we start by analyzing the factors that create competition or rivalry in industry relations. Then we turn to the competitive problems that companies encounter in different industry structures and discuss how companies should manage their interactions with other companies in these contexts to maximize their competitive advantage. Different industry structures require different responses by companies if companies individually and the industry as a whole are to be highly profitable. First, we focus on how companies in *fragmented industries* try to develop competitive strategies that support their generic strategies to manage industry relations. Second, we look at the problems of developing and sustaining a first-mover advantage to exploit the potential of a generic competitive strategy in *embryonic and growth industries.* Third, we consider the nature of competitive relations in *mature industries.* Here, we focus on how a set of companies that have been pursuing successful generic competitive strategies can use a variety of competitive techniques to manage the high level of competitive interdependency found in such industries. Finally, we look at the problems of managing a company's generic competitive strategy in *stagnant* or *declining industries* where industry rivalry is high because market demand is slowing or falling. By the end of the chapter, you will understand how the successful pursuit of a generic strategy depends on the selection of the right competitive moves to deal with the actions of industry competitors.

6.3 FACTORS AFFECTING THE LEVEL OF INDUSTRY COMPETITION

Industry competition refers to the manner in which companies in an industry act to obtain a competitive advantage over their rivals. As discussed in Chapter 3, a principal factor affecting the level of industry competition is the nature of an industry's structure. Some industries are fragmented, or have many small companies. Others are consolidated, or have a few large companies. In general, industry competition is highest when there are a few large companies in the market, because the companies are highly interdependent and thus the actions of one company impinge directly on the actions of another. In consolidated industries, companies' cost, pricing, and output decisions—decisions that are the consequence of generic competitive strategy—are *interdependent,* so the potential profitability of any one company can be calculated only if the actions of other companies are taken into account. By contrast, in fragmented industries, companies are small and can be treated as if they are acting in isolation. Thus each company can make its own cost, pricing, and output decisions independent of its competitors. Emerging industries are fragmented because firms are small and are just developing generic strategies.

A second determinant of industry competition is market demand. We have already seen how market demand changes over the industry life cycle and how growing or declining demand affects the level of industry competition. Since market demand is the source of company revenue and industry profits, companies compete for their share of market demand, or market share, at all stages of the life cycle. The different ways in which companies compete when demand is growing, stable, or declining lead to different forms of competitive relations in different industry structures. Once again, companies' pricing and output decisions are crucially affected by the nature of market demand.

Finally, since the profitability of a generic strategy is, in part, a function of the value-added that a company puts into the strategy as a result of investing in its value-creation functions, the cost of developing functional competencies is very important for a company. Consequently, a third factor affecting industry competition is competition for the scarce resources—inputs of all kinds, technological, human, financial—that affect the costs at which value creation takes place and that all companies in an industry are in competition to obtain at the lowest price. Here, we are interested in company strategies toward buyers and suppliers to reduce costs or obtain a differentiation advantage. Some of these strategies are covered in this chapter and some in the next chapter, where we consider vertical integration.

To understand business-level strategy in different industry structures, we have to understand how companies seek to realize the benefits from their generic strategies by formulating these strategies to deal with interdependencies with their rivals, customers, and buyers and suppliers. This is the issue to which we now turn.

6.4 STRATEGY IN FRAGMENTED INDUSTRIES

A fragmented industry is one composed of a large number of small and medium-size companies among whom competitive interdependence is at a minimum. No company by itself is in a strong enough position to influence industry pricing and output decisions, so each company seeks its own best competitive strategy. An industry may consist of many small companies rather than a few large ones for several reasons.[1] If there are few economics of scale to be achieved, entry barriers may be low. Furthermore, customer needs may differ from region to region so that each particular market segment is small. These factors make it hard to obtain a cost advantage, and they make differentiation very difficult. In addition, customer needs may be so specialized that only small job lots of products are required, and thus there is no room for a large mass-production operation to satisfy the market. Finally, if transportation costs are high, regional production may be the only efficient way to satisfy customer needs.

For some fragmented industries, these factors dictate the competitive strategy to pursue, and the focus strategy stands out as a principal choice. Companies may specialize by customer group, customer need, or geographical region, so that a proliferation of small specialty companies operates in local or regional market segments. All kinds of custom-made products—furniture, clothing, rifles, and so on—fall into this category, as do all small service operations that cater to particular customer needs, such as laundries, restaurants, health clubs, and rental stores. Indeed, service companies make up a large proportion of the enterprises in fragmented industries because they provide personalized service to clients and therefore need to be close to clients.

However, if a company can overcome the limitations of a fragmented market, it can often reap the benefits of a cost-leadership or differentiation strategy. Entrepreneurs are eager to gain the cost advantages of pursuing a low-cost strategy or the sales-revenue-enhancing advantages of differentiation by circumventing the problems of a fragmented industry. The returns from consolidating a fragmented industry are often huge. And, of course, during the last twenty-five years many companies have overcome industry structure problems and consolidated many fragmented industries. These companies are large retailers like Wal-Mart Stores, Inc., Sears, and J. C. Penney, fast-food chains like McDonald's and Burger King, as well as chains of health clubs, repair shops, and even lawyers and consultants. What business strategies are these companies using to grow and become the industry leaders?

Chaining

Companies like Wal-Mart Stores and Midas International Corporation are pursuing a *chaining* strategy in order to obtain the advantages of a cost-leadership strategy. They establish networks of linked merchandising outlets that are so interconnected that they function as one large business entity. The amazing buying power that these companies possess through their nationwide store chains allows them to negotiate large price reductions with their suppliers and promotes their competitive advantage. These companies overcome the barrier of high transportation costs by establishing sophisticated regional distribution centers that can economize on inventory costs and maximize responsiveness to the needs of stores and customers (this is Wal-Mart's specialty). Last but not least, they realize economies of scale from the sharing of managerial skills across the chain and from nationwide rather than local advertising.

Franchising

For differentiated companies in fragmented industries, such as McDonald's or Century 21 Real Estate Corporation, the competitive advantage comes from the business strategy of *franchising*. With franchising, a local store operation is both owned and managed by the same person. When the owner is also the manager, he or she is strongly motivated to control the business closely and make sure quality and standards are consistently high so that customer needs are always satisfied. Such motivation is particularly critical in a strategy of differentiation, where it is important for a company to maintain its uniqueness. One reason that industries fragment is the difficulty of maintaining control over, and the uniqueness of, the many small outlets that must be operated. Franchising avoids this problem. In addition, franchising lessens the financial burden of swift expansion, allowing rapid growth of the company. Finally, a differentiator can also reap the advantages of large-scale advertising as well as the purchasing, managerial, and distribution economies of a large company, as McDonald's does very efficiently. Indeed, McDonald's is able to pursue cost leadership and differentiation simultaneously only because franchising allows costs to be controlled locally and differentiation can be achieved by marketing on a national level.

Horizontal Merger

Companies like Dillard's and Texas Air have been choosing a business-level strategy of *horizontal merger* to consolidate their respective industries. Such companies have essentially arranged for the merger of small companies in an industry to create a few large companies. For example, Dillard's arranged for the merger of regional store chains to create a national company; Texas Air bought Eastern and People Express to add to Continental to reduce the number of companies in the airline industry. By pursuing horizontal merger, companies are able to obtain economies of scale or secure a national market for their product. As a result they are able to pursue a cost-leadership or a differentiation strategy.

In fragmented industries, companies can pursue all three business-level strategies: focus, cost leadership, and differentiation. The challenge is to choose the most appropriate means—franchising, chaining, or horizontal merger—of overcoming a fragmented market and thus allowing the advantages of the generic strategy to be realized. The huge increase in franchising and the emergence of chain stores and restaurants in manufacturing and service industries have had a great impact on consumers in the last twenty-five years. Their effect on America has been startling. Identical fast-food chains and stores in every shopping mall are now part of the American scene. It is difficult to think of any major service activities—from consulting and accounting firms to businesses satisfying the smallest consumer need, such as beauty parlors and car-repair shops—that have not been merged and consolidated into chains.

6.5 STRATEGY IN EMBRYONIC AND GROWTH INDUSTRIES

Because economic forces prevent entrepreneurs from consolidating an industry, fragmented industries usually contain a large number of small companies. Embryonic industries often consist of large numbers of small companies because companies are newly formed or created and competitive pressures are still low. Rivalry with competitors, for example, is low for two reasons. First, the rules of the competitive game have yet to be worked out. Second, companies are not yet competing for one another's customers; they are preoccupied with developing their technical competencies. Each company can make competitive moves in relative isolation because there are two main sources of uncertainty: (1) *technological uncertainty* about what product is likely to emerge as the industry norm or leader, about what unique characteristics the product ultimately will possess, and about how it will be manufactured; (2) *strategic uncertainty* about the distinctive competencies and generic competitive strategies that will be the most profitable to pursue in order to satisfy customer needs or groups. In essence, in an embryonic industry several newly formed companies are simultaneously formulating new product/market strategies and are seeking to develop the distinctive competencies that lead to a successful generic competitive strategy.

In this competitive situation, all companies are trying to develop technological innovations that allow them to earn profits higher than their competitors'. The profits may come from product innovations that allow companies to charge a premium price for their products or from process innovations that lower the costs of value creation and increase the quality of output so companies can charge a premium price. However, over time, as the paths to technological success in the new industry environment become established—for example, as dominant product designs emerge from competing technologies—the best ways to compete in the industry become apparent. Furthermore, the high profits earned by the industry innovators act as market signals to potential competitors that want to enter the industry to try to imitate the innovation. As a result, as more and more companies compete to be first with the next round of technical improvements, companies are brought into direct competition and begin to compete for the customers of their rivals.

In this new competitive environment, the innovators who pioneered the development of new products and processes often lose their competitive advantage to the new imitators. Examples are such companies as Royal Crown, which pioneered diet cola only to lose its advantage to Coca-Cola and PepsiCo; EMI, which developed the CAT scanner but lost out to General Electric in the development race; and Bowman, which invented the pocket calculator only to see Texas Instruments reap the long-run rewards of the innovation. Embryonic industry environments present difficult competitive challenges for companies seeking to maintain their competitive advantage into the growth stage of the industry and avoid being also-rans. Why do innovators lose out to the new competitors, and how can they maximize their chances of remaining industry leaders into the growth stage and beyond? These are the issues we now discuss.

Managing First-Mover Advantages to Profit from Innovation

The key to profiting from innovation in embryonic and growth environments is to create, exploit, and sustain a first-mover advantage over industry rivals. A first-mover advantage is the competitive advantage that accrues when a company is first into the market with a new product. This advantage confers on a company a *cost-leadership or a differentiation advantage,* which allows the company to develop a successful generic competitive strategy.

Identifying first-mover advantages   There are four principal first-mover advantages. First, being first into the market may confer a *reputation effect,* which leads to a differentiation advantage. A first mover may be able to build brand loyalty simply by being the pioneer. For example, in England, Hoover was the first company to bring vacuum cleaners to the market, and even today vacuum cleaners are known there as "Hoovers." Similarly, ball-point pens are known as "Bics" after the company that developed them. In computers, Apple Computer obtained a massive reputation effect by being the first to bring a personal computer to market; Microsoft obtained a similar effect from its innovative software.

Second, being the pioneer can confer on a company an experience-curve effect that leads to a low-cost advantage. The first mover may be able to move down the experience curve rapidly, thereby achieving a cost advantage and creating a barrier to entry. For example, Du Pont's development of titanium oxide gave Du Pont a cost advantage that imitators have been unable to match. Third, being first allows a company to pre-empt and take control of scarce assets, thus raising the costs of potential imitators. For example, Alcoa's control of the lowest-cost deposits of bauxite gave it long-term control over aluminum smelting, and Wal-Mart's policy of locating stores in small southern towns that competitors had ignored pre-empted the ability of rivals to target this market segment.

Finally, by being first to the market, a company can tie up customers by making it either very difficult or very expensive for them to switch to the products of competitors—that is, customers incur *switching costs* if they move to a competitor's product. For example, in changing from one particular software package to another, a consumer incurs the costs of learning a new operating system. Similarly, someone who replaces an Apple computer with an IBM model incurs the costs of learning how to operate the IBM hardware.

Exploiting first-mover advantages   To exploit first-mover advantages, a company must try to improve product design and quality in order to build and strengthen reputation effects. It also must invest resources to support the aggressive pricing and marketing efforts required to build brand loyalty and exploit experience-curve effects in the growth stage—that is, it has to invest in developing its generic competitive strategy. If it fails to do either of these things, it is opening the way for existing or potential competitors to overtake it. Kodak, for example, put an early emphasis on product quality and in the 1920s developed sophisticated distribution and after-sales service to protect product quality and build brand loyalty. In contrast, DeHavilland, the early leader in airline manufacturing, experienced increasing technical problems with its jet aircraft that allowed Boeing to capture market share. Similarly, Texas Instruments was able to enter the pocket-calculator industry because Bowman lacked the resources to exploit production and marketing first-mover advantages. The inability to exploit first-mover advantages is the primary reason that innovators fail in the race for industry dominance.

Creating barriers to imitation   The creation of barriers to imitation also prevents competitors from imitating an innovation and protects the first-mover advantage. Barriers slow competitors' responses, allowing the first mover to remain one step ahead in the development process. Even though competitors may copy the first innovation, a company will always be one step ahead of its competition if it can create barriers that allow it to consolidate a first-mover advantage.

Barriers to imitation include patents and secret processes. In some industries, patents are a powerful device for controlling entry into the market. In the chemical and drug industries, patents provide a company with control of the market for many years. In industries such as electronics and aerospace, however, patents often provide only weak protection because they are easy to invent around. Edwin Mansfield of the Wharton Business School found that 60 percent of patented innovations were invented around within four years.[2] Thus secret processes are often better than patents. If a key process can be kept secret, imitation may be difficult and companies should not patent their techniques and hence reveal their methods. For example, Coca-Cola has never patented the formula for Coke.

First-Mover Disadvantages

There are strong advantages to be obtained from being a first mover, and the first-mover advantage is the source of many companies' industry dominance—for example, Xerox, Apple, and McDonald's. Nevertheless, several factors can turn a first-mover advantage into a weakness and make it better to be late, rather than early, into the market.

Resolution of technological uncertainty   Sometimes late movers benefit from the resolution of uncertainty about the technological processes or standards that will become the industry norm. The first mover can become locked into a technology that is rapidly replaced; rapid technological changes can make early investments obsolete. For example, Philco, an early industry leader in semiconductors, invested in a state-of-the-art manufacturing process that was quickly superseded by one developed by Texas Instruments, which became the industry leader. Similarly, Sony, the early leader in video with its Betamax system, failed to convince competitors to make Betamax the industry standard. When VHS became the dominant system, Sony's competitive advantage was eroded.

Resolution of strategic uncertainty   Sometimes late movers can benefit from the resolution of uncertainty about the basis of future competition in an industry. The basis of competition may change as a market develops, and the distinctive competencies that give a company a competitive advantage in the embryonic stage may not be the competencies that will work in the growth stage and beyond. Consequently, a first mover might invest all its resources in developing the wrong strategic capabilities; such a mistake can cause the company to lose its competitive advantage. For example, Apple initially lost out to IBM in personal computers because Apple's strategy emphasized retail distribution and educational use while IBM's emphasized a direct sales force and business use—and business users were the most rapidly growing market segment.

Free-rider effect   Late movers may be able to take advantage of a free ride on a first mover's investments in research and development, buyer education, and the development of the industry's infrastructure, including its purchasing and distribution channels. The first mover bears the costs of educating new customers and creating the market for companies that enter later. IBM is a classic example of a company that waited until the potential for the personal computer was proven before entering the market and rapidly developing a machine to take advantage of its brand name. Apple bore all the up-front costs of proving that the market existed.

Complementary assets   A number of factors can work to a first mover's disadvantage and give late movers a competitive edge. These disadvantages, however, can be overcome by a company that recognizes the need to change with the market and does not rest on its early innovations. The competitive advantage of the brand name achieved from being the first mover can be set against these disadvantages. As long as a company is open to the need to respond to technological and strategic changes, it will be able to handle the challenge by late movers successfully, as Apple has done with IBM. However, the success of a first mover's strategy in the industry growth stage is affected by its ability to develop *complementary assets,* and the existence of barriers to imitation.

Complementary assets are the assets required to exploit core technological know-how and maintain a first-mover advantage. They include (1) competitive manufacturing facilities capable of handling rapid market growth; (2) marketing know-how, a trained sales force, and access to industry distribution systems; (3) after-sales service and support networks; and (4) complementary technology—for example, software to support computer hardware. In essence, a first mover has to develop its value-creation functions and not rely purely on its technological expertise; otherwise, competitors will find it easy to attack the first mover's position as the industry develops.

Developing these competencies is expensive, and companies pursing growth and share-increasing strategies need large infusions of capital. It is for this reason that first movers often lose out to late movers that are large successful companies, established in other industries, that have the resources to develop quickly a presence in the new industry. Moving into an industry that is related to a company's principal industry by technological similarities is an example of pursuing the strategy of related diversification (discussed in the next chapter). A company like 3M is a good example of a company that moves quickly to capitalize on the opportunities presented by the opening of new product markets like those in compact disks and floppy disks. 3M is a late mover to be feared.

Choosing the Right Strategy

Given the advantages and disadvantages of being a first mover in the growth stages of an industry, a company must decide what is the best way to exploit the potential profits from an innovation. In general, the three strategic choices facing a company are (1) to develop and market the technology itself; (2) to develop and market jointly with other companies through a strategic alliance or joint venture; (3) to license the technology to others and let them develop the market. These three strategies and the two factors, complementary assets and barriers to imitation, that affect a company's choice of strategy are summarized in Table 6.1.

In general in a solo venture a first mover prefers to develop and market the technology itself when the company has or can obtain the needed complementary assets quickly *and* can erect high barriers to imitation. Usually, a company must be large to pull this off—that is, the firm must be an established company; however, there are exceptions, such as Apple Computer.

Developing and marketing the technology jointly is the preferred option when a company controls the technology but lacks the resources to build one or more of the complementary assets needed to gain a competitive advantage—that is, the company cannot fund a share-building or a growth strategy. In that situation, a small company will join a large company to capitalize on the potential profits. However, it may be possible to attract venture capitalists to fund the company, although they will demand a large share of the profits. By joining forces with venture capitalists, the company reduces the risk that a large company in a joint alliance will steal the technology and expropriate know-how.

Finally, if barriers to imitation are likely to be hard to develop and maintain because they can be invented around, *and* a company lacks the resources to develop the necessary complementary assets, the best strategy may be to sell or license the technology. The company will collect royalty payments from would-be imitators but faces the risk that they will quickly invent around the technology

TABLE 6.1   **Choosing a competitive strategy in embryonic and growth industries**

Means of developing and marketing technology	Does innovator have complementary assets?	Likely barriers to imitation
Firm in solo venture	Yes	High
Jointly by strategic alliance	No	High
Licensing established firms	No	Low

so that the royalties will soon dry up. RCA had this experience after licensing its color television technology to the Japanese. They quickly superseded RCA's technology and became the market leaders.

Summary: Embryonic and Growth Strategies

In embryonic and growth industries, there are complex industry dynamics to be dealt with if companies are to survive and prosper into the shakeout stage. During the embryonic and growth stages companies must exploit a technological advantage successfully in order to exploit a product market and develop a sustainable generic competitive strategy. Product and process innovation allows companies to charge a premium price for their product or lowers the costs of value creation. The way a company makes its choices in the growth stage determines its future profitability and its ability to cope with the dynamics of industry competition in the mature, consolidated industry setting.

6.6 STRATEGY IN MATURE INDUSTRIES

As a result of fierce competition in the shakeout stage, an industry often becomes consolidated, and so a mature industry is often one composed of a small number of large companies. This is not to suggest that a mature industry does not contain either medium-size companies or a host of small specialized ones. The large companies, however, determine the structure of industry competition because they can influence the five competitive forces. Indeed, these are the companies that developed the most successful generic competitive strategies to deal with the industry environment.

By the end of the shakeout stage, strategic groups composed of companies pursuing similar generic competitive strategies have emerged in the industry. Companies have learned to analyze each other's strategies, and they know that their competitive actions will stimulate a competitive response from rivals in their strategic group and from companies in other groups that may be threatened by their actions. For example, a differentiator that starts to lower prices because it has adopted a more efficient technology not only threatens other differentiators in its group but also threatens low-cost companies that see their competitive edge being eroded away. Hence, by the mature stage of the industry life cycle, *companies have learned the meaning of competitive interdependence.*

In mature industries, companies choose competitive moves and techniques to maximize their competitive advantage *within the structure of industry competition.* Indeed, to understand business-level strategy in mature industries, one must understand how large companies try to collectively, although indirectly (since explicit collusion among companies violates antitrust law), help stabilize industry competition to prevent entry, industry overcapacity, or cutthroat price competition that would hurt all companies. In Chapter 5 we assumed that companies in an industry can pursue a generic strategy successfully, regardless of what other companies are doing. In practice, the issue is more complicated than this because the strategy pursued by one company directly affects other companies. Because each company is trying to make maximum profits, it is bound to come into conflict with its competitors. How, therefore, can companies manage industry competition so as to *simultaneously* protect their individual competitive advantage and maintain industry rules that preserve industry profitability? (Remember that no generic strategy will generate above-average profits if competitive forces are so strong that companies are at the mercy of each other, powerful suppliers, and powerful customers.) The answer is by using competitive moves and techniques to reduce the threat of each competitive force.

In the discussion that follows, we consider the various price and nonprice methods that companies can use to simultaneously build barriers to entry and reduce industry rivalry. We then discuss methods by which firms can manage relationships with suppliers and buyers and ways to counter the threat of substitute products. In general, competitive moves involve product/market decisions concerning *differentiation, pricing, and output*. Differentiation decisions are important because differentiation is expensive and raises a company's costs. Building barriers to entry or managing rivalry through differentiation therefore raises a company's costs. Similarly, pricing decisions are important because lower product prices mean less company and industry profit. If firms are forced to lower prices to deter entry or to compete in the market, profits will be reduced. Finally, output decisions are important because the higher the level of output produced by the industry as a whole, the lower is the price that can be obtained for each unit of output and the lower are revenues. Collectively, companies want to have rules about product/market decisions to deter entry and protect industry profitability. However, at the same time companies individually want to be able to exploit their distinctive competencies by making pricing and output decisions to maximize their competitive advantage. A number of competitive techniques can help accomplish both of these goals.

Market Signaling

All industries start out fragmented, with small companies battling for market share. Then, over time, the leading players emerge, and companies start to interpret each other's competitive moves. *Market signaling* is the first means by which companies attempt to structure industry competition in order to deter entry and control rivalry.[3] Market signaling is the process by which companies convey their intentions to potential entrants and to existing competitors about product/market strategy and how they will compete in the future or how they will react to the competitive moves of their rivals. Market signaling can benefit product/market strategy in several ways.

First, companies may use market signaling to announce that they will respond vigorously to hostile competitive moves that threaten them. For example, companies may signal that if one company starts to cut prices aggressively, they will respond in kind. Or companies may signal that if one company makes a differentiation move—for instance, extends car warranties, as GM did—then all other companies will follow, to maintain the status quo and prevent any company from gaining a competitive advantage. Similarly, companies may signal to potential entrants that if the latter do enter the market, they will fight back by reducing prices or by other aggressive competitive moves. Market signaling *protects* the existing structure of competitive advantages by deterring potential imitators who wish to copy other companies' generic strategies.

Second, market signaling can be used to pre-empt competitors. One company may inform the others that it is proceeding with new product innovations or with investment in new industry production capacity that will provide a competitive advantage that the others will be unable to imitate effectively because their entry into the market will be too late. For example, software companies like Microsoft often announce new operating systems years in advance. The purposes of such an announcement are to deter prospective competitors from making the huge investments necessary to compete with the industry leaders and to let customers know that a company still has the competitive edge so important to retaining consumer loyalty. However, pre-emptive signaling can backfire, as IBM found out when it announced that its new PS/2 operating system would not be compatible with the operating systems presently standard in the industry. Other companies in the industry collectively signaled to IBM and to IBM's customers that they would band together to protect the existing operating systems, thus preserving industry standards and preventing IBM from obtaining a competitive advantage from its new technology. IBM subsequently backed down. A pre-emptive move, therefore, has to be *credible:* Competitors must believe that a company will respond as it signals and stick to its position. If a threat is not credible, the signaling company weakens its position because it cried "wolf."

A third purpose of market signaling is to allow companies to coordinate their actions indirectly and avoid costly competitive moves that lead to a breakdown in industry product policy. One company may signal that it intends to lower prices because it wishes to attract customers who are switching to the products of another industry, not because it wishes to stimulate a price war. On the other hand, signaling can be used to improve industry profitability. The airline industry is a good example of the power of market signaling. In the 1980s signals of lower prices set off price wars. In the 1990s the airlines have used market signaling to obtain uniform price increases. Similarly, the introduction of nonrefundable tickets was a market signal by one company that was quickly copied by all other companies in the industry. In sum, market signaling allows companies to give to one another information that enables them to understand each other's competitive product/market strategy and make coordinated competitive moves.

Price Leadership

Price leadership, where one company takes the responsibility for setting industry prices, is a second way of enhancing the profitability of product/market policy among companies in a mature industry.[4] By setting prices, the industry leader implicitly creates the price standards that other companies will follow. The price leader is generally the strongest company in the industry, the one with the best ability to threaten other companies that might cut prices or increase their output to seize more market share. For example, vast oil reserves made Saudi Arabia the price leader in the oil industry and allowed the Saudis to threaten that if other countries raised their output, so would Saudi Arabia, even though the price of oil would decline. Similarly, De Beers controls the price of diamonds because it controls the worldwide distribution of diamonds.

Formal price leadership, or price setting by companies jointly, is illegal under antitrust laws, so the process of price leadership is often very subtle. In the auto industry, for example, auto prices are set by imitation. The price set by the weakest company—that is, the company with the highest costs—is often used as the basis for competitors' pricing. Thus U.S. automakers set their prices, and Japanese automakers then set theirs with reference to the U.S. prices. The Japanese are happy to do this because they have lower costs than U.S. companies and are making many times the profit of the U.S. automakers without competing with them by price. Pricing is often done by market segment. The prices of different auto models in the model range indicate the customer segments that the companies are aiming for and the price range they believe the market segment can tolerate. Each manufacturer prices a model in the segment with reference to the prices charged by its competitors, not by reference to competitors' costs. Price leadership thus helps differentiators charge a premium price, and it helps low-cost companies by increasing their margins. Obviously, it makes a combined cost-leadership/differentiation strategy very profitable.

Price leadership can stabilize industry relations by preventing head-to-head competition, and it raises the level of industry profitability to allow companies funds for future investments and profitable returns to shareholders. However, the dangers of price leadership are worth noting. Price leadership helps companies with high costs; it allows them to survive without becoming more productive or more efficient. This means that they may become complacent and hide behind their own pricing policy, extracting profits that they do not reinvest to improve their productivity. In other words, they follow a profit strategy, as discussed in the Chapter 5. This practice has the long-term effect of making them vulnerable to new entrants who have lower costs because they have developed new productive techniques. This of course is what happened to U.S. automakers and in the electronics industry when the Japanese entered the market. After years of tacit price fixing with General Motors as the leader, the automakers were subject to growing low-cost Japanese competition to which they were unable to respond. Only because the Japanese automakers were foreign companies are many U.S.

auto companies surviving today in the new competitive environment. If they had been new U.S. entrants, there would be no Chrysler, and both Ford and General Motors would be much smaller and wiser companies.

Competitive Product Differentiation

An important element of product/market strategy in consolidated industries is the use of product differentiation not as a means of creating uniqueness and protecting a company's generic competitive strategy but as a way of preventing competitors from obtaining access to a company's customers and attacking its market share. Product differentiation can be used to deter potential entrants and manage industry rivalry. Product differentiation also allows companies to compete for market share by using *nonprice competitive* methods, such as offering products with different or superior features or applying different marketing techniques. Those methods minimize the risk that companies will use price competition, which hurts everyone because it reduces industry profitability.

To understand how product differentiation can be used competitively, it is useful to analyze the ways in which companies can use differentiation in a consolidated industry to achieve different goals. Table 6.2 uses two dimensions—products and market segments—to identify four product/market strategies that capitalize on the use of competitive product differentiation (notice that in this model we are considering new market segments, not new markets).

Market penetration   When a company concentrates on expanding market share in its existing product markets, it is engaging in a strategy of *market penetration*.[5] Market penetration involves using advertising to promote and build product differentiation. In a consolidated industry, advertising is used to influence consumers' brand choice and create a *brand-name reputation* for the company and

TABLE 6.2   **Four product differentiation strategies**

		Products	
		Existing	New
Market Segments	Existing	Market penetration	Product development
	New	Market development	Product proliferation

its products. In this way, a company can increase its market share by attracting the customers of its rivals. Because brand-name products often command premium prices, building market share in this situation is a very profitable business.

In some mature industries—for example, the soap and detergent, disposable diapers, and brewing industries—a market penetration strategy often becomes a way of life.[6] In these industries all companies engage in intensive advertising and battle for market share, and each company is afraid not to advertise for fear it will lose market share to rivals. As a result, in the soap and detergent industry, for example, over 10 percent of sales revenues is used for advertising to maintain and perhaps build market share. These huge advertising outlays constitute a barrier to entry for prospective entrants. Furthermore, since advertising is a form of nonprice competition, companies are competing primarily through the perceived quality of their products and not by price and are thus reducing harmful competition.

Product development   Product development is the creation of new or improved products to replace existing ones.[7] The wet shaving industry exemplifies an industry based on product replacement to create successive waves of consumer demand that, in turn, create new sources of revenue for industry companies. In 1989, Gillette came out with its new Sensor shaving system, which gave a massive boost to its market share. In turn, Wilkinson Sword responded with its version of the product.

Product development is important for maintaining product differentiation and building market share. For example, the laundry detergent Tide has gone through over fifty different changes in formulation over the past forty years to improve its performance. Tide is what is advertised, but Tide is a different product each year. The battle over diet colas is another example of the use of competitive product differentiation by product development. Royal Crown developed Diet Rite, the first diet cola. However, Coca-Cola and Pepsi-Co responded quickly with their versions of the soft drink and by massive advertising soon took over the market. Refining and improving products is an important element of defending a company's generic competitive strategy in a consolidated industry. This kind of competition can be as vicious as a price war.

Market development   Market development involves finding new market segments in which to exploit a company's products. A company pursuing this strategy wishes to capitalize on the brand name it has developed in one market segment by finding new market segments in which to compete. In this way, it is able to exploit the product differentiation advantages of its brand name. The Japanese auto manufacturers offer an interesting example of the use of market development. With their initial entry, each Japanese manufacturer offered cars aimed at the economy segments of the auto market. Thus, for example, the Toyota Corolla was aimed at the small economy car segment of the market as was the Honda Accord. However, over time, the Japanese upgraded each car, and now each is directed at more expensive market segments. The Accord is now a leading contender in the mid-size luxury sedan segment, and the Corolla fills the small-car segment that used to be occupied by the Celica, which is now aimed at a sportier market segment. By redefining their product offerings, Japanese manufacturers have profitably developed their market segments and successfully attacked their industry rivals, wresting market share from these companies. Although the Japanese used to compete as low-cost producers, market development has allowed them to become differentiators as well.

Product proliferation   Companies seldom produce just one product. Most commonly, companies produce a range of products aimed at different market segments so that they have broad product lines. Sometimes, to reduce the threat of entry, companies tailor their range of products to fill a wide array of niches because doing so increases the difficulty of entry by potential competitors.[8] The strategy of pursuing a broad product line to deter entry is known as *product proliferation*.

Because the large U.S. automakers were slow to fill the small-car market niches, they were vulnerable to the entry of the Japanese into these market segments in the United States. They really had no excuse for this situation, for in their European operations they had a long history of small-car manufacturing. They should have seen the opening and filled it ten years earlier, but in their view small cars meant small profits. Similarly, in the breakfast cereal industry, competition is based on the production of new kinds of cereal to satisfy or create new consumer desires; thus the number of breakfast cereals proliferates. This proliferation makes it very difficult for prospective entrants to attack a new market segment.

As an example of the use of product proliferation to deter entry consider Figure 6.1. It depicts product space in the restaurant industry along two dimensions: (1) atmosphere, which ranges from "fast food" to "candlelight dining," and (2) quality of food, which ranges from average to gourmet. The circles represent product spaces filled by restaurants located along the two dimensions. Thus McDonald's is situated in the average-quality/fast-food area. A gap in the product space gives a potential entrant or an existing rival an opportunity to enter the market and make inroads. The shaded unoccupied product space represents areas where new restaurants can enter the market. However, filling all the product spaces makes it very difficult for an entrant to gain a foothold in the market and differentiate itself.

The strategy of product proliferation usually means that all large companies in an industry have a product in each market segment or niche and compete head-to-head for customers. If a new niche develops, like convertibles or oat bran cereals, then the leader gets a first-mover advantage; but soon all the other companies catch up, and once again competition is stabilized and industry rivalry is reduced. Product proliferation not only deters entry, it also allows stable industry competition based on product differentiation not price—that is, it allows nonprice competition based on the development of new products. The battle is over a product's perceived quality and uniqueness, not its price.

FIGURE 6.1   **Product proliferation in the restaurant industry**

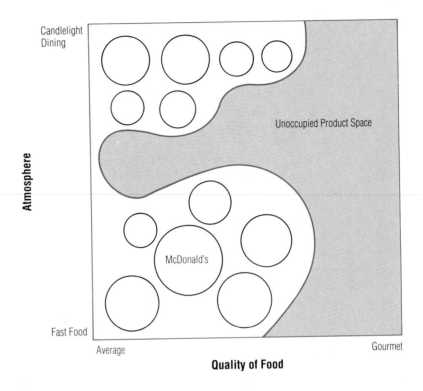

Competitive Pricing

So far, we have been discussing forms of nonprice competition in consolidated industries and techniques used by companies to avoid cutthroat competition, which reduces both company and industry levels of profitability. However, in some industries, price competition periodically breaks out, most commonly when there is industry overcapacity—that is, when companies collectively produce so much output that reducing price is the only way to dispose of it. If one company starts to cut prices, the others quickly follow because they fear the price cutter will be able to sell all its inventory and they will be left with unwanted goods. Since price wars drastically hurt each company's profits, price reductions are never the preferred form of competitive move except, perhaps, in the short run by companies that have a cost advantage.

However, in some situations strategies involving price cutting can be used to deter entry by other companies, thus protecting the profit margins of companies already in an industry. These strategies are called *limit pricing strategies*.[9] Suppose an industry has emerged where profitability is high and existing companies are earning high profit margins. Normally, new companies are attracted to this market because of the prospect of high returns. Companies enter the industry, establish productive capacity, and increase the industry's output. The result is that profit margins fall. Existing companies, however, know that high short-term prices will attract new entrants and lead to low profits. Thus one possible strategy for existing companies is to cut or hold down prices to a level where they earn an above-normal level of profit—but profit that is not high enough to signal to competitors the real potential profitability of the market. The purpose of this strategy, which is called *limit pricing,* is to encourage potential competitors to believe that prices (and hence profits) are relatively low now and will be low in the future, so it is not worthwhile for competitors to make the investments necessary to establish a generic strategy and enter the industry. Essentially, existing companies are trying to bluff potential competitors by keeping prices below the level the market will bear.

Whether limit pricing can be pursued in many industry contexts is debatable. Imitation occurs more and more quickly in today's competitive environment, and the norm these days is for cheap imitations to flood the market, rapidly bringing down prices until some kind of shakeout has occurred and stability is reestablished. It may be extremely risky for companies to depart from the normal competitive pricing practice, which is to charge a high short-term price to exploit an innovation and then to successively reduce prices as new companies enter the market in order to maintain and build market share. Sacrificing short-term high profits for the prospect of uncertain long-run returns from limit pricing is a risky strategy.

Given these problems, a second competitive pricing strategy becomes a possibility: to initially charge a high price for a product and seize short-term profits but then to aggressively cut prices in order to simultaneously build market share *and* deter potential entrants.[10] The incumbent companies signal to potential entrants that if they do enter the industry, the incumbents will use their competitive advantage to drive price down to a level where new companies will be unable to cover their costs.[11] Thus incumbents are able to pursue a market penetration strategy and build an industry reputation while deterring entry. This strategy of pricing for market penetration also allows a company to *ride down the experience curve and obtain substantial economies of scale.* Hence, even though prices are falling, so are costs so profit margins may still be maintained.

Although this strategy may work with a weak competitor and deter entry, it is unlikely to work with an established company that is trying to find profitable investment opportunities in other industries. For example, it is difficult to imagine a 3M being afraid to enter an industry because companies already there are threatening to drive down prices. 3M has the resources to withstand any short-term losses. Thus it may be in the interests of incumbent companies to accept new entry gracefully and give up market share gradually to new entrants to prevent price wars from developing.

At each stage of the industry life cycle, a company is maximizing the price it can obtain for its product given current competitive conditions. Which pricing strategy incumbent companies choose depends on their forecasts about the likely returns from their generic competitive strategies given their cost and differentiation advantages. *Companies should always be concerned to make pricing decisions that maximize the stream of profits in the long run.* Short-term profit maximization may lead to this goal, or the goal may be achieved with long-term price restraint or successive waves of price cutting to reduce costs and build market share. In general, it will depend on the industry context.

Most evidence suggests that companies first skim the market and charge high prices during the growth stage, maximizing short-run profits.[12] Then they move to a market penetration strategy and charge a lower price to rapidly expand the market and develop a reputation and obtain economies of scale, driving down costs and preventing entry. As competitors enter, they reduce prices to retard entry and give up market share to create a stable industry context where they can use nonprice competitive methods to maximize long-run profits. At that point, competitive product differentiation becomes the main basis of industry competition and prices are quite likely to rise as competition stabilizes. Competitive price and non-price decisions are therefore linked and determined by the way a company manages its generic strategy to maximize profits when companies are highly interdependent.

Capacity Control Strategies

A final competitive technique that allows companies to simultaneously deter entry and manage industry rivalry is capacity control strategies. As noted above, excess industry capacity can be a major factor influencing the level of competition in an industry because it leads to price cutting and reduced industry profitability. Excess capacity may result from a shortfall in demand, as when a recession lowers the demand for automobiles and causes companies to give customers price incentives. In this case companies can do nothing except wait for better times. However, in many cases excess capacity results because industry companies *simultaneously* respond to favorable conditions by investing in new plant in order to be able to take advantage of a predicted upsurge in demand. Paradoxically, each individual company's attempt to outperform the others results in companies' collectively producing an industry capacity problem that hurts them all. This situation is illustrated in Figure 6.2. Although demand is increasing, the result of each company's decision to increase capacity is a surge in industry capacity, which will drive down prices.

To prevent the emergence of costly excess capacity, companies in consolidated industries must devise strategies that allow them to control or at least benefit from capacity expansion programs. Before we look at these strategies, however, we need to explore in more detail the factors that cause excess capacity.[13]

Factors causing excess capacity   Capacity problems are often the result of technological factors. The introduction of new, low-cost technology sometimes causes a problem because, to prevent being left behind, all companies introduce it simultaneously. A capacity problem occurs because the old technology is still

FIGURE 6.2   **Changes in industry capacity and demand**

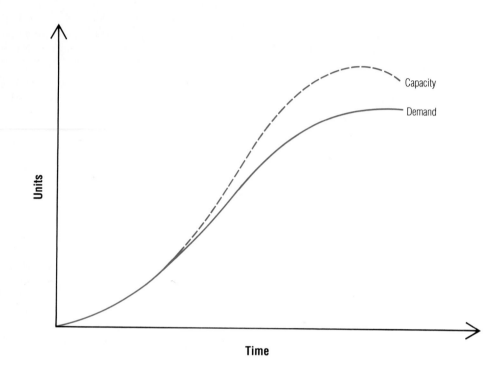

being used to produce output. In addition, new technology is often introduced in large increments that generate overcapacity. For example, an airline that needs more seats on a route must add another plane, thereby adding hundreds of seats even though only fifty may be needed. Similarly, a new chemical process may operate efficiently only at the rate of a 1,000 gallons a day, whereas the previous process was efficient at 500 gallons a day. If all industry companies change technologies, industry capacity doubles and enormous problems result.

Industry competitive factors also cause overcapacity. Obviously, entry into an industry is a major factor causing excess capacity. Japan's entry into the semiconductor industry caused massive overcapacity and price declines in microchips. Similarly, the collapse of OPEC was due to the entry of new countries able to produce oil at competitive prices. Sometimes the age of a company's plant can cause a problem. For example, in the hotel industry, given the rapidity with which the quality of hotel furnishings declines, customers are always attracted to new hotels. The building of new hotel chains next to old chains, however, can cause excess capacity. Often, companies are simply making simultaneous competitive moves based on industry trends, but those moves eventually lead to head-to-head competition. Most fast-food chains, for example, establish new outlets whenever demographic data show population increases. However, they seem to forget that all chains use such data. Thus a locality that has no fast-food outlets may suddenly see several being built simultaneously. Whether all can survive depends on the growth rate of demand relative to the growth rate of the fast-food chains.

Choosing a capacity control strategy   Given the variety of ways in which capacity can expand, it is obvious that companies need to find some means of controlling it. Companies will be unable to recoup the investments in their generic strategies if they are always plagued by price cutting and price wars, and low industry profitability produced by overcapacity causes the exit not just of the weakest companies but sometimes of major industry players as well. In general, the strategic choices are for each company individually to try to *pre-empt its rivals* and seize the initiative or for companies collectively to find indirect means of *coordinating with other companies* so that companies become aware of the mutual effects of their actions.

Pre-emptive strategy   To pre-empt rivals, a company must forecast a large increase in demand in the product market and then move rapidly to establish large-scale operations that will be able to satisfy the forecasted demand. Achieving a first-mover advantage may deter other companies from entering the market because the implication is that the pre-empter will be able to move down the experience curve, reduce its costs, and hence reduce prices and threaten a price war if necessary.

This strategy, however, is extremely risky because it involves the investment of resources in a generic strategy before the extent and profitability of the future market are clear. Wal-Mart, with its strategy of locating in small rural towns to tap an underexploited market for discount goods, has pre-empted Sears and K Mart. Wal-Mart has been able to engage in market penetration and market expansion with the secure base established in its rural strongholds.

A pre-emptive strategy is also risky if competitors are not deterred from entry but decide to enter the market. If they have a stronger generic strategy or more resources, like an AT&T or IBM, they can make the pre-empter suffer greatly. Thus, for the strategy to be successful, the pre-empter generally must be a credible company with enough resources to withstand a possible price war.

Coordination strategy   Although collusion over the timing of new investments is illegal under antitrust law, tacit coordination is found in many industries as companies attempt to understand and forecast the competitive moves of their rivals. Generally, companies use market signaling to secure coordination. They make announcements about their future investment decisions in trade journals and newspapers. In addition, they share information about their production levels and their forecasts of industry demand so as to bring industry supply and demand into equilibrium. Thus a coordination strategy reduces the risks associated with investment in the industry. The principal danger to companies comes from potential entrants that may disrupt the stability of the industry. In the U.S. car market, for example, the relative market shares and outputs of General Motors, Chrysler, and Ford were stable for many years until Japanese automakers showed them the meaning of overcapacity. Thus the avoidance of socially wasteful losses from simultaneous investments in industry capacity should not come at the expense of inefficiency or from lack of attention to maintaining a viable generic competitive strategy.

Supply and Distribution Strategy

As we saw in Chapter 3, as an industry becomes consolidated and composed of a few large companies, it becomes stronger vis-à-vis its suppliers and customers. Suppliers become dependent on the industry for buying their inputs, customers for obtaining industry outputs. By the mature stage, in order to protect market share and improve product quality, many companies are interested in taking over more of the distribution of their products and in controlling the source of inputs crucial to the production process. When they seek to own supply or distribution operations, they are pursuing a strategy of *vertical integration,* which is considered in detail in the next chapter. Here, we discuss how the choice of a means of controlling the relationships between a company and its suppliers and distributors is an important determinant of the way in which a company supports its generic strategy and develops a competitive advantage.

One important reason to control supplier/distributor relationships is that a company that can ensure its ability to dispose of its outputs or acquire inputs in a timely, reliable manner is able to reduce costs and improve product quality. A good way to analyze the issues involved in choosing a distribution/supplier strategy is to contrast the situation that exists between a company and its suppliers and distributors in Japan with the situations that exist in the United States. In this country, it is normal for a company and its suppliers to have an antagonistic relationship. Each tries to drive the best bargain to make the most profit. Moreover, the relationship between a company's buyers and suppliers tends to be superficial and anonymous because purchasing and distribution personnel are routinely rotated to prevent kickbacks. In contrast, in Japan, the relationship between a company and its suppliers and distributors is based on long-term personal relationships and trust. Suppliers in Japan are responsive to the needs of the company, respond quickly to changes in the specification of inputs, and adjust supply to meet the needs of a company's just-in-time inventory system. The results of this close relationship are lower costs and the ability to respond to unexpected changes in customers' demand. The close supplier/distributor relationship supports Japanese companies' generic strategy. Clearly, it pays a company to develop a long-term strategy toward its suppliers and distributors.

A company has many options to choose from in deciding on the appropriate way to distribute its products to gain a competitive advantage. A company may distribute its products to an independent distributor, who in turn distributes to retailers. Or a company might distribute directly to retailers or even to customers. In general, the complexity of a product and the amount of information needed about its operation and maintenance determine the distribution strategy chosen. For example, automakers typically use franchisees to control the distribution of their autos rather than a general car dealership. The reason is the high level of after-sales service and support necessary to satisfy customers. Automakers are able to penalize franchisees by withholding cars from a dealership if customer complaints rise; thus they have effective control over franchisee behavior. Also by controlling the franchisees, they can tailor price and nonprice competition to industry conditions, and this allows the large automakers to coordinate their actions by controlling the thousands of separate dealerships across the country effectively.

On the other hand, the large electronics manufacturers and the producers of consumer durables like appliances generally prefer to use a network of distributors to control distribution. To enhance market share and control the way products are sold and serviced, manufacturers choose five or six large distributors per state to control distribution. The distributors are required to carry the full line of a company's products and invest in after-sales service facilities. The result is that the manufacturer receives good feedback on how its products are selling, and the distributor becomes knowledgeable about a company's products and thus helps the company maintain and increase its control over the market. The company is able to discipline its distributors if they start to discount prices or otherwise threaten the company's reputation or generic strategy.

Large manufacturers like Johnson & Johnson, Procter and Gamble, and General Foods typically sell directly to a retailer and avoid giving profits to a distributor or wholesaler. In part, they do this because they have lower profit margins than do the makers of electronic equipment and consumer durables. However, this strategy also allows them to influence a retailer's behavior directly. For example, they can refuse to supply a particular product that a retailer wants unless the retailer stocks the entire range of the company's products. Also, the companies can ensure shelf space for new products. Coca-Cola and PepsiCo are two companies that are able to influence retailers to exclude or reduce the shelf space given to competing products. They can do so because soft drinks have the highest profit margins of any product sold in supermarkets. Gallo is one of the few wine makers that control the distribution and retailing of their own products. This is one reason Gallo is so consistently profitable.

In sum, devising the appropriate strategy for acquiring inputs and disposing of outputs is a crucial part of competitive strategy in mature industry environments. Companies can gain a competitive advantage through the way they choose to control their relationships with distributors and suppliers. By choosing the right strategy, they are able to control their costs, their price and nonprice strategies, and their reputation and product quality. These are crucial issues in mature industries.

Summary: Mature Strategies

Business-level strategy in mature industries involves the development of the means by which companies can pursue the hold-and-maintain or profit strategies discussed in Chapter 5. To maximize profitability, companies rationalize their product/market choices to reduce costs and increase revenues, and they develop means to stabilize industry competition to increase the industry's level of profitability. Controlling the five forces of industry competition—in particular, developing competitive techniques to deter entry and manage industry rivalry—is the crucial part of this process. The principal means of achieving these goals are market signaling; price leadership; the development of competitive price, differentiation, and capacity control strategies; and the selection of a strategy for dealing with suppliers and distributors. Business-level strategy involves developing rules of the game to manage relationships with competitors and with suppliers and customers. Conditions in the macro-environment, such as changes in technology or in foreign competition or in consumer tastes, sometimes change the basis of industry interdependence, alter the sources of competitive success, and reduce the ability of companies collectively to coordinate their actions. That is why periods of stability in an industry are followed by unrest and intense competition as companies jockey for position in the changed industry environment. Managing such change is the goal of business-level strategy in mature industry environments.

6.7 STRATEGY IN DECLINING INDUSTRIES

In a mature industry, demand slows and is often limited to replacement demand. Thus there is increased competition between companies for market share. Once demand starts to fall, an industry is said to be in decline, and competitive pressures become even more intense. Since declining industries are often consolidated, we need to consider how a reduction or fall in market growth affects industry competition and how it presents a new set of problems for companies to deal with.

In general, companies in declining industries still have to manage all the various aspects of competitive strategy identified in the last section—for example, price and nonprice competition. However, new options become important.

Falling market demand means that companies individually need to fine-tune their generic competitive strategies to face the new competitive situation, and collectively they need to coordinate their behavior to head off vicious price wars. Falling demand means lower industry revenues, so it becomes especially important for companies to streamline their cost structures and find the best way to invest their resources in value creation in order to maximize value-added. Since price competition reduces total industry revenues, it puts all companies at risk.

Manipulating Product/
Market Strategies

Companies manipulate their competitive product/market strategies in several ways to match a new situation.[14] Since increased competition often emerges over product quality, cost, and price, companies need to take a hard look at their product offerings to make sure they are offering the appropriate range of products and the right mix of product attributes to attract the most buyers at the least cost. Product proliferation, for example, may have gone too far, and now the sheer number of products sold is starting to raise costs with no compensating increase in demand. If this is the case, the company should concentrate more on product and market development to find new uses for its products or new products that better fit customer needs. Since all companies will be increasing their attempts at market penetration, it is important for the company to keep its advertising in line with them or risk losing market share. In terms of price policy, companies should pay particular attention to price changes by competitors; and if prices start to fall, they should keep in line with competitors.

In this situation, the benefits of pursuing a combined cost-leadership and differentiation strategy become clear. If a company can maintain its differentiation advantage, then it may be able to maintain its premium price even as prices come down. Even if some price discounts are forced by the situation, pursuing a dual strategy keeps the company the most profitable company. Thus, even if industry profitability falls, the low-cost differentiator is unlikely to suffer. Moreover, this company will be at the forefront of process innovation, so it will be the first to take advantage of new technical developments. Such a company is able to reap first-mover advantages at all stages of the industry.

Weaker companies experience competitive problems most forcefully. Thus they attempt to initiate coordinated moves and signal their willingness to follow a price leader as price cuts occur. Whether such attempts at coordination work depends on the severity of competition. As we saw in the Opening Incident, in very uncertain and competitive environments preventing price wars can be particularly difficult because all companies are acting purely in their own interests. However, if companies have forecasted slowing demand early enough, they may be able to signal their willingness to find ways of avoiding a price war. For example, they may signal their willingness to reduce industry capacity, thereby removing the dangers of excess capacity. Reducing capacity may also allow them to reduce their costs because their oldest and most inefficient plants can be liquidated first. Additionally, they may signal their intention to retreat from some market segments and consolidate in others, so they increasingly specialize only in the segments of the product line where they have a competitive advantage. In this way they can also reduce competition.

Finally, companies can move to increase industry consolidation by purchasing smaller and weaker competitors. Such purchases increase their market share and make it more difficult for potential competitors to enter the industry. The beer industry is a good example of a mature industry where in the last twenty years the big players have absorbed most of the small players (that is, the regional brewers) to create a stable industry situation in which nonprice brand-name competition and the development of new products have been the main forms of competition. The large brewers have used business-level strategy to create a highly profitable industry.

In sum, in a situation of declining demand, companies must manipulate their generic competitive strategy to reap the most returns from the changed industry environment. They must decide how to compete based on their distinctive competencies, and they should invest resources where they will have maximum effect—for example, in value-chain activities that result in lower costs or in a differentiation advantage, or in purchasing smaller competitors to reduce excess industry capacity and to increase market share. Companies must be careful not to make decisions that result in their being *stuck in the middle*. If a company fails to recognize the implications of the changed environment, or if it fails to make the right competitive moves, it may be the one purchased by its competitors and liquidated.

Market Concentration and Asset Reduction

The competitive moves discussed above are most applicable in industries where demand is falling slowly and competitive pressures are least intense. When demand is falling rapidly, more radical competitive moves become necessary. To some extent we have already discussed this issue in Chapter 5, where we noted how companies can pursue market concentration and asset reduction investment strategies in their attempt to maximize the profits associated with a declining market.

With market concentration, companies are increasing their investments in certain industry segments so as to be able to dominate the industry and obtain a competitive advantage over their rivals. In essence, they are seeking to pre-empt their rivals by seeking a *leadership position,* which will give them a first-mover advantage in the competitive battle to come.[15] This position will also allow them to become the price leader and determine the competitive rules of the declining situation. To the extent that they are focusing their investments in only one or in a few segments, they may be said to be following a *niche strategy*. Here, they are content to defend one market segment as, for example, International Harvester did when it became Navistar and only produced trucks.

On the other hand, if a company does not perceive that the returns from investing in the industry are warranted, it may choose an asset reduction strategy. Here, it may try to divest the business quickly, try to milk its investments and harvest the business to maximize cash flow, or move to liquidate the investment and exit the industry quickly. In Chapter 9, we present a model showing how a company chooses among these three strategies.

6.8 SUMMARY OF CHAPTER

The purpose of this chapter is to discuss how the structure of the industry in which companies compete affects the level of company and industry profitability. Developing a generic competitive strategy and an investment strategy is only the first part, albeit a crucial part, of business-level strategy. Tailoring that generic strategy to the industry structure by choosing industry-appropriate competitive moves and product/market strategies is the second part of successful strategy formulation at the business level. The chapter makes the following main points:

1. The main factors affecting the level of industry competition are the number and relative size of the companies in an industry, the level of market demand and whether it is growing or declining, and the availability of the resources necessary for reducing the costs of value creation.

2. In fragmented industries composed of a large number of small companies, the principal forms of competitive strategy are chaining, franchising, and horizontal merger.

3. In embryonic and growth industries, managing first-mover advantages to profit from technical innovations is a crucial aspect of competitive strategy. Companies must learn how to exploit these advantages while avoiding the disadvantages of being first in the market.

4. They can do so by choosing the right strategy to exploit the innovation. The three choices are for the company to develop and market the technology itself, to do so jointly with another company, or to license the technology to existing companies.

5. Mature industries are composed of a few large companies whose actions are so highly interdependent that the success of one company's strategy depends on the responses of its rivals.

6. The principal competitive moves and strategies used by companies in mature industries are market signaling, price leadership, competitive product differentiation, competitive pricing, capacity control, and supply and distribution strategy.

7. These strategies are interdependent and must be matched to a company's generic competitive strategy.

8. In declining industries where market demand has leveled off, companies must tailor their price and nonprice strategies to the new competitive environment. They also need to manage industry capacity to prevent the emergence of capacity expansion problems. When demand is falling, companies can adopt leadership or niche strategies to exploit the potential of a declining market; or, if prospects are poor, they can employ divestment and liquidation strategies to exit the market quickly.

Discussion Questions

1. Why are industries fragmented? What are the main ways in which companies can turn a fragmented industry into a consolidated one?

2. What are the key problems involved in maintaining a competitive advantage in a growth industry environment? What are the dangers associated with being the leader?

3. Discuss how companies can use (a) product differentiation and (b) capacity control strategies to manage rivalry and increase industry profitability.

Endnotes

1. This discussion draws heavily on Michael E. Porter, *Competitive Strategy: Techniques for Analyzing Industries and Competitors* (New York: Free Press, 1980), pp. 191–200.

2. Edwin Mansfield, "How Economists see R&D," *Harvard Business Review* (November–December 1981), 98–106.

3. Porter, *Competitive Strategy*, pp. 76–86.

4. F. M. Scherer, *Industrial Market Structure and Economic Performance*, 2nd ed. (Boston: Houghton Mifflin, 1980), Ch. 6.

5. H. Igor Ansoff, *Corporate Strategy* (London: Penguin Books, 1984), pp. 97–100.

6. Robert D. Buzzell, Bradley T. Gale, and Ralph G. M. Sultan, "Market Share—A Key to Profitability," *Harvard Business Review* (January–February 1975), 97–103. Robert Jacobson and David A. Aaker, "Is Market Share All That It's Cracked Up to Be?" *Journal of Marketing,* 49 (Fall 1985), 11–22.

7. Ansoff, *Corporate Strategy*, pp. 98–99.

8. J. Brander and J. Eaton, "Product Line Rivalry," *American Economic Review,* (June 1984), (74), 323–334.

9. Scherer, *Industrial Market Structure and Economic Performance,* Ch. 8.

10. P. Milgrom and J. Roberts, "Predation, Reputation, and Entry Deterrence," *Journal of Economic Theory,* 27 (1982), 280–312.

11. Sharon M. Oster, *Modern Competitive Analysis* (New York: Oxford University Press, 1990), pp. 262–264.

12. Donald A. Hay and Derek J. Morris, *Industrial Economics: Theory and Evidence* (New York: Oxford University Press, 1979), pp. 192–193.

13. The next section draws heavily on Marvin B. Lieberman, "Strategies for Capacity Expansion," *Sloan Management Review,* (8) (Summer 1987), 19–27; and Porter, *Competitive Strategy*, pp. 324–338.

14. Michael E. Porter, *Competitive Advantage: Creating and Sustaining Superior Performance* (New York: Free Press, 1985), pp. 254–274.

15. Kathryn Rudie Harrigan and Michael E. Porter, "End-Game Strategies for Declining Industries," *Harvard Business Review* (July–August 1983), 111–120.

Chapter 7

CORPORATE-LEVEL STRATEGY: VERTICAL INTEGRATION AND DIVERSIFICATION

7.1 OPENING INCIDENT: HANSON INDUSTRIES

In 1973 Gordon White, cofounder of British conglomerate Hanson Trust PLC, arrived in the United States to start the North American arm of Hanson Trust. Thirteen years later the company he set up, Hanson Industries, was ranked ninety-seventh among the Fortune 500 Industrials. Hanson Industries' achievement in joining the elite of U.S. companies capped a twenty-two-year period during which Hanson Trust's pretax profits had grown at an average rate of 45 percent a year. This phenomenal growth was based on a carefully thought-out corporate strategy of diversification by acquisition into many unrelated industries. Between 1984 and 1986 alone Hanson Industries bought three major U.S. companies: U.S. Industries, a building and industrial products company; SCM Corporation, a typewriter and chemicals conglomerate; and Kaiser Cement Corporation.

The basis of the company's diversification strategy has been to acquire businesses cheaply, often against the existing management's will, liquidate surplus assets, and manage what is left in such a way as to increase earnings and generate cash for the next acquisition. When seeking companies to acquire, Hanson looks for cyclical businesses that earn good returns over the long run but may be suffering from a short-term setback. It also looks for companies in which a weak division or two have depressed overall performance, as well as for once-weak companies whose stock prices do not yet reflect recent turnarounds. All these factors keep down the price of the acquisition. In addition, Hanson seeks businesses in mature industries, where demand is predictable and new capital requirements are likely to be minimal. The company deliberately steers clear of high-tech industries, where capital requirements are large and technological change makes the future uncertain.

Once Hanson acquires a company, it economizes further by selling headquarters buildings and eliminating staff jobs or pushing them down into operations. Underperforming divisions are either turned around quickly or sold. The divisions that remain are given substantial operating autonomy but are held accountable for their performance through a system of tight financial controls. Strong profit incentives are introduced to encourage divisional executives to focus on the bottom line. Hanson's objective is to markedly improve the profitability of the companies it acquires.

The working out of all these factors can produce remarkable results. For example, Hanson Industries paid $930 million for SCM in January 1986, after a bitterly contested takeover battle. By September 1986 it had sold off a number of SCM subsidiaries for more than $1 billion. Hanson held on to the typewriter and chemicals businesses, which in effect cost nothing and

which earned record pretax profits of $165 million in 1987. Since 1987, the chemicals and typewriter businesses acquired with SCM have shown a further significant improvement in performance.

Consider Smith-Corona, SCM's typewriter business. Under Hanson, Smith-Corona reduced the number of parts in its leading products from 1,400 to 400 and the required time for assembly from 8 hours to 1.5 hours. In addition, employment was cut from 5,200 workers in 1985 to 3,100 by 1988. By such moves, Smith-Corona has been able to establish a cost advantage over its major Japanese competitors. As a consequence, by 1989 Smith-Corona had regained its hold on more than 50 percent of the American typewriter market, after seeing its share sink as low as 32 percent in 1986.[1]

7.2 OVERVIEW

Corporate-level strategy is concerned with answering this question: How should we manage the growth and development of the company to maximize long-run profitability? Answering it involves choosing (1) the *businesses* and (2) the *markets* that a company is going to compete in. With regard to different businesses, the company may decide to (a) concentrate on a single business, (b) vertically integrate into adjacent businesses, or (c) diversify into new business areas. With regard to markets, the company may decide to (a) compete just within its domestic marketplace or (b) expand globally and compete in the international arena. Table 7.1 illustrates this range of choices.

In this chapter, we review in depth the decisions to concentrate on a single business, vertically integrate, and diversify into new businesses. In the next chapter we look at the issue of global expansion and discuss the different ways in which multinational companies can create value. Throughout both chapters we emphasize that to succeed, corporate strategies should *add value* to the corporation. To understand what this means, we have to go back to the concept of the value chain, introduced in Chapter 4. *To add value, a corporate strategy should enable a company, or one or more of its business units, to perform one or more of the value-creation functions at a lower cost, or perform one or more of the value-creation functions in a way that allows for differentiation and a premium price.* Thus a company's *corporate* strategy should help in the process of establishing a distinctive competence *at the business level.*

TABLE 7.1   **Corporate-level strategy options**

		Businesses		
		Single business	Vertical integration	Diversification
Markets	Domestic	e.g., Domino's Pizza, Inc.	e.g., Nucor Corporation	e.g., Southland Corporation
	Global	e.g., Holiday Inns Inc.	e.g., Exxon Corporation	e.g., Hanson Trust

For example, Hanson Trust's restructuring of SCM, discussed in the Opening Incident, reduced the operating costs of SCM's typewriter and chemicals businesses, thereby increasing the *value added* by each of these businesses. Because Hanson eliminated excess staff, reduced corporate overhead, and encouraged divisional heads to focus on the bottom line, the value-creation functions of the businesses acquired from SCM could be performed at a lower cost.

We must emphasize at the outset that companies frequently make mistakes when pursuing corporate-level strategies and may end up reducing rather than adding value. Consequently, at the end of this chapter, we discuss strategic retrenchment and turnaround as a response to failed corporate strategies.

7.3 CORPORATE GROWTH AND DEVELOPMENT

Stages of Corporate Development

Most companies begin as single-business enterprises competing within the confines of their domestic market. For such companies, maximizing long-run profitability means identifying how best to compete within their market. As you saw in Chapter 5, this process requires management to consider differentiation, cost leadership, and focus. However, it may also involve vertical integration, either backward, to gain a strategic advantage from owning supply sources, or forward, to gain a strategic advantage from owning distribution outlets. In addition, as we see in the next chapter, in today's marketplace, a company often needs a global presence in order to compete successfully. For example, global electronics manufacturers, such as Sony, have a cost advantage over domestic companies, such as Zenith and RCA Consumer Electronics Division, that comes from their huge global volume and the resulting scale economies.

Beyond these considerations, a company that manages to establish a sustainable competitive advantage in its original industry may find itself generating financial resources *in excess* of those required to maintain its position. It must then decide how to invest the excess resources in order to maximize its long-run profitability. One option may be to return the excess to stockholders in the form of higher dividends or stock buybacks. Another option is to diversify into new business areas. Diversification can take several forms but, to be viable, must *add value* to the corporation. In the case of Hanson Trust, value is added by restructuring acquired companies to reduce costs and generate extra profits. Diversification can also create value through resource sharing between businesses, by transferring skills from one business to another, and by operating an internal capital market.

Thus the growth and development of a typical modern enterprise can be divided into three main stages. At stage 1, a company operates as a single business within the confines of a single national market. At stage 2, vertical integration and global expansion strengthen the competitive position of the company's core activity; vertical integration and global expansion *support* a company's business-level strategy. Stage 3 begins when a company is generating resources *in excess* of those necessary to maintain a competitive advantage in its core activity. Typically, at this stage a company looks for diversification opportunities outside its core business to generate value from the investment of excess resources. Figure 7.1 summarizes these stages.

The model proposed in Figure 7.1 differs from that offered by Alfred Chandler of Harvard University.[2] On the basis of historical research, Chandler suggested that most U.S. companies first grew as single businesses, then vertically integrated, then diversified into related businesses, and only at that point expanded globally. Historical analogies, however, are a poor guide to

FIGURE 7.1   **Stages of corporate growth and development**

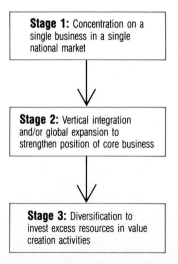

modern conditions because the emergence of truly global markets and global competition is a phenomenon of the late twentieth century. Today the imperatives of global competition often force companies to become global before they diversify.

Limits to Growth

Vertical integration, diversification, and global expansion can all create value for a company.[3] However, past some point, the value created by these strategies is also subject to the basic economic "law" of *diminishing returns*. All that this means is that in general the value added by each successive expansion move is likely to be less than the value added by the previous move. For example, a company might pursue its most promising diversification opportunity first, its next most promising diversification move second, and its next most promising move third. Although each successive diversification move may add value, each adds less value than the previous move.

Of course, in practice things do not happen quite like this. For example, a company may not know which is its most promising diversification opportunity, so it pursues its least promising opportunity first. Similarly, at least initially, successive expansions overseas tend to generate *increasing returns* as the company realizes experience-based scale economies from global volume. Nevertheless, the basic point holds: *Past some point*, extensive diversification, vertical integration, or international expansion tends to be associated with a decline in value added at the margin. The decline occurs because the most profitable opportunities have already been exploited by the company and only less profitable opportunities exist. The notion of diminishing returns to vertical integration, diversification, or global expansion implies that the *marginal value-added* associated with each successive expansion move tends to decline. (The term *marginal value-added* simply refers to the value created by each additional expansion move.)

The decline is illustrated for diversification in Figure 7.2 The extent of diversification is measured on the horizontal axis, and dollars are measured on the vertical axis (the horizontal axis could just as well measure the extent of vertical integration or global expansion). The marginal-value-added curve, *MVA,* is shown to decline, signifying that each successive diversification move adds less value than the previous move.

In addition, the bureaucratic costs of managing successive expansion moves tend to increase. This means that as a company becomes ever more vertically integrated, diversified, or global in its scope, the task of managing ever greater complexity gives rise to increasingly difficult problems of coordination and control. For example, consider the problems associated with managing an organization that has the size and complexity of General Motors. General Motors is vertically integrated (it manufactures 70 percent of all component parts used in its auto assembly operation); it is diversified with operations in autos, aerospace, data systems, and finance; and it is global in scope with assembly operations on four continents. Managing such a complex organization composed of so many

FIGURE 7.2   **Marginal value-added and costs of expansion**

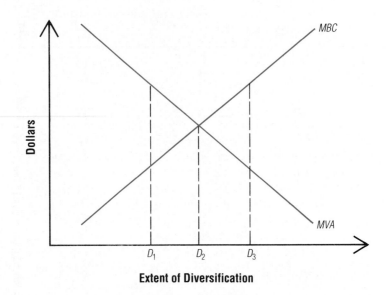

interdependent parts can be a bureaucratic nightmare. We consider the source of these problems in more detail later in this chapter and the next. In addition, we consider bureaucratic costs more closely in the section on strategy implementation when we look at how companies should design their structures and control systems to match their strategy. For now it is enough to note that ultimately, this phenomenon can result in control loss and declining economic performance.

The implication is that the *marginal bureaucratic costs* associated with each successive expansion move will tend to increase (the term *marginal bureaucratic costs* simply refers to the costs of managing each additional expansion move). This is illustrated in Figure 7.2 by the upward-sloping marginal-bureaucratic-cost curve (*MBC*).

If we now consider both the marginal value-added and the marginal bureaucratic costs associated with expansion, the implication of this discussion is that *there is a definite limit to the profitable expansion of any company*. In Figure 7.2 this limit is at the point where the two curves intersect—that is, where $MVA = MBC$. The logic is as follows: For a company that has diversified up to D_1 on the horizontal axis, the marginal value-added of diversification, although declining, still exceeds the marginal bureaucratic costs of managing that additional diversification ($MVA > MBC$). Thus it pays to pursue further diversification because the company can still create additional value by doing so. For a company that has pursued diversification up to D_3 on the horizontal axis, however, the marginal value-added exceeds the marginal bureaucratic costs ($MVA < MBC$). In this case, it pays to reduce diversification because the last (or marginal) diversification move gave rise to more bureaucratic costs than to value-added. Thus, the optimal level of diversification for this company is at D_2, where $MVA = MBC$.

In practice, of course, it is difficult to identify the optimal level of diversification, vertical integration, or global expansion. However, this does not invalidate the analysis given above. We can surmise from observation that companies often continue to pursue a strategy beyond the point at which it is profitable to do so. For example, many of the go-go conglomerates of the 1960s and 1970s, such as Esmark Corporation, General Electric, ITT, Textron, Tenneco, and United Technologies, clearly diversified beyond the point at which it was profitable to do so. As a result, all of these companies suffered a decline in profitability and subsequently spent most of the 1980s restructuring themselves, selling off many of their diversified activities, and refocusing on their strategic core.[4]

A final point is that the MVA and MBC curves depicted in Figure 7.2 are not fixed for all time; they can shift. For example, administrative innovations can reduce the bureaucratic costs of managing organizational complexity. Thus Alfred Chandler has observed how the development of the multidivisional structure at General Motors and Du Pont during the 1920s and 1930s enabled those companies to solve the problem of how to manage a moderate degree of diversification.[5] Similarly, current advances in information technology, by enabling top managers to call up detailed data about an operation at the push of a button, may have reduced the bureaucratic costs of managing large complex organizations and made greater size possible.

The effect of such administrative innovations is illustrated in Figure 7.3. Following an administrative innovation that lowers the bureaucratic costs of managing a complex organization, the marginal-bureaucratic-cost curve declines from MBC_1 to MBC_2. As a result, the optimum level of diversification for the company increases from D_1 to D_2. Put another way, because of administrative

FIGURE 7.3   **The effect of an administrative innovation**

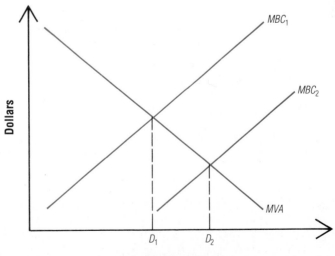

innovation the company can now profitably manage a greater degree of diversification than was previously the case.

Now that we have considered in a general sense the factors that determine the limits to profitable growth, we move on to look at each of the various corporate-level strategies in turn. We start by considering the advantages and disadvantages of concentrating on a single business before moving on to consider vertical integration and diversification.

7.4 CONCENTRATION ON A SINGLE BUSINESS

All companies begin by concentrating on a single business within the confines of their domestic market. For such companies, corporate- and business-level strategy are synonymous. To maximize profitability, they must pursue cost-leadership, differentiation, or focus strategies. Even when a company has established a sustainable competitive advantage, however, it can still benefit from continuing to serve a single business.

Advantages

By concentrating on one operation, a single-business company can focus the total human, physical, and financial resources of the organization toward competing successfully within its market. This can be important in growth industries, where demands on the company's resources are likely to be substantial but the long-term profits from establishing a competitive advantage are also substantial.

Besides, the top managers of a single business in a single national market are likely to have an intimate knowledge of the business the company is involved in, whereas in multibusiness and multinational enterprises, top managers may have to struggle just to keep abreast of the different operations of the individual subsidiary companies. Such knowledge is a major asset when a company's business is based in an intensely competitive and technologically dynamic industry that requires quick and informed top-management decision making.

Disadvantages

Concentrating on just one business has significant disadvantages as well. A company may be able to increase value-added by vertically integrating or diversifying. Vertical integration may be necessary to establish a sustainable competitive advantage within an industry. For example, even in a young, technologically dynamic, high-growth industry such as the personal computer industry, IBM's strategy for establishing a competitive advantage involves backward integration into the manufacture of proprietary components that are difficult for competitors to copy.

Beyond this, companies that concentrate on just one line of business face two other major constraints in trying to maximize profitability, and both of these constraints push profit-seeking companies toward corporate diversification. First, single-business enterprises that are based in mature industries may find opportunities for profitable growth limited by a lack of investment opportunities within their core industry. At this stage, concentrating on a single business may not represent the best use of the company's resources—especially if the company has established a competitive advantage and is now generating financial resources *in excess* of those needed to maintain that advantage. To make better use of such excess resources, companies often begin to diversify into new business areas. For example, Philip Morris, finding its growth limited by a mature tobacco industry but nevertheless generating strong cash flows from its dominant position in tobacco, diversified into the brewing industry with the acquisition of Miller Brewing Company and into the food industry with the acquisition of General Foods and Kraft.

Companies that concentrate on a single business also risk missing out on profitable opportunities stemming from the application of a company's distinctive competencies to other industries. Thus, had Philip Morris not acquired Miller Brewing, it would have missed out on the opportunity to apply its distinctive competence in marketing one consumer product (cigarettes) to marketing another (beer).

7.5 VERTICAL INTEGRATION

Vertical integration means that a company is producing its own inputs (backward integration) or is disposing of its own outputs (forward integration). A steel company that supplies its iron ore needs from company-owned iron ore mines exemplifies backward integration. An auto manufacturer that sells its cars through company-owned distribution outlets illustrates forward integration. Figure 7.4 illustrates five main stages in a typical raw-material-to-consumer production chain. For a company based in the assembly stage, backward integration involves moving into intermediate manufacturing and raw-material production. Forward integration involves movement into distribution and retail.

In addition to forward and backward integration, it is also possible to distinguish between **full integration** and **taper integration** (see Figure 7.5).[6] A

FIGURE 7.4   Different stages in the raw-material-to-consumer production chain

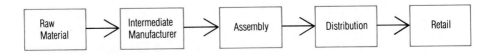

FIGURE 7.5   **Full and taper integration**

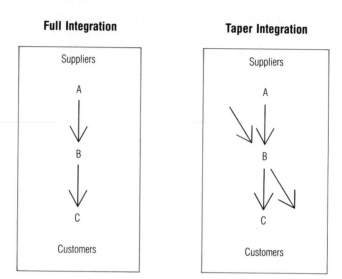

company achieves full integration when it produces all of a particular input needed for its processes or when it disposes of *all* of its output through its own operations. Taper integration occurs when a company buys from independent suppliers in addition to company-owned suppliers or when it disposes of its output through independent outlets in addition to company-owned outlets. The advantages of taper integration over full integration are discussed later in this chapter.

Creating Value Through Vertical Integration

A company pursuing vertical integration is normally motivated by a desire to strengthen the competitive position of its original, or core, business.[7] Through this strategy, the company can add value from the following sources: (1) production cost savings, (2) avoidance of market costs, (3) improved quality control, and (4) protection of proprietary technology. At the very least, these sources of additional value allow the company either to reduce its overall cost position in its core business or to charge a premium price for its product. Vertical integration, then, is consistent with a company's attempt to establish itself as the cost leader or as a differentiated player in its core business.

Reducing production costs   When vertical integration permits technologically complementary processes to be carried out in quick succession, a company can save on production costs. For example, the ability to roll steel when hot from refining offers an advantage to steel refineries with their own rolling mills. The newly refined steel does not have to be reheated to make it malleable. Similarly, the ability to turn wood pulp into newsprint without drying and reconstituting it—as would have to be done if the pulp were to be delivered to a different organization for further processing—gives an advantage to integrated pulp and paper mills.

Further production cost savings arise from the easier planning, coordination, and scheduling of adjacent processes made possible in vertically integrated organizations. For example, in the 1920s Ford profited from the tight coordination and scheduling that are possible with backward vertical integration. Ford integrated backward into steel foundries, iron ore shipping, and iron ore mining. Deliveries at Ford were coordinated to such an extent that iron ore landed at Ford's steel foundries on the Great Lakes was turned into engine blocks within twenty-four hours. Thus Ford substantially reduced its production costs by eliminating the need to hold excessive inventories.

Avoiding market costs   If a company buys its inputs or sells its outputs on the open market, it often has to bear buying and selling costs. Many of these costs, such as advertising, maintaining a sales force, and running a procurement department, can be reduced or even eliminated through vertical integration. Moreover, vertical integration can also dispose of the need to pay profits to market middlemen (commodity brokers, warehouse operators, transport companies, and the like). Since it avoids market costs, a company may find it easier to become the cost leader in its core business.

Further costs of using the market arise when a company depends on a limited number of powerful suppliers for important inputs. The suppliers may take advantage of such a situation to raise prices above those that would be found in more competitive circumstances. The company ends up having to pay exorbitantly high prices for its inputs. These prices are the costs of using the market. If the company would integrate backward and supply its own inputs, it could avoid these costs. The same arguments apply when a company sells to a limited number of powerful buyers. Recognizing the company's dependence on them for orders, the buyers can squeeze down prices, costing the company potential profit. By integrating forward, the company can circumvent powerful buyers and earn greater returns on its final sales.[8]

Protection of product quality   By protecting product quality, vertical integration enables a company to become a differentiated player in its core business. The banana industry illustrates this situation. Historically, a problem with the banana industry has been the variable quality of delivered bananas, which often arrived on the shelves of American stores either too ripe or not ripe enough. To correct this problem, major American food companies, such as General Foods, have integrated backward to gain control over supply sources. Consequently, they have been able to distribute bananas of a standard quality at the optimal time for consumption to American consumers. Knowing that they can rely on the quality of these brands, consumers are willing to pay more for them. Thus by integrating backward into plantation ownership, the banana companies have built consumer confidence, which enables them in turn to charge a premium price for their product. Similarly, when McDonald's decided to open up its first restaurant in Moscow, it found, much to its initial dismay, that in order to serve food and drink indistinguishable from that served in McDonald's restaurants elsewhere, it had to vertically integrate backward and supply its own needs. The quality of Russian-grown potatoes and meat was simply too poor. Thus, to protect the quality of its product, McDonald's set up its own dairy farms, cattle ranches, vegetable plots, and food-processing plant within the Soviet Union.

The same kind of considerations can result in forward integration. Ownership of distribution outlets may be necessary if the required standards of after-sales service with complex products are to be provided. For example, in the 1920s Kodak owned retail outlets for distributing photographic equipment. The company felt that few established retail outlets had the skills necessary to sell and service its photographic equipment. By the 1930s, however, Kodak decided that it no longer needed to own its retail outlets because other retailers had begun to provide satisfactory distribution and service for Kodak products. The company then withdrew from retailing.

Protection of proprietary technology   Proprietary technology is technology that is unique to a company and can give it an advantage over competitors. Proprietary technology can allow a company to establish more efficient production processes, thus reducing manufacturing costs, or it can be embodied in the design of a company's product, permitting the company to charge a premium price. Vertical integration makes good sense when a company needs to prevent its competitors from knowing too much about its technology. When proprietary technology involves an innovative process, vertical integration helps a company to protect its know-how and to establish itself as a cost leader in its core operation. When proprietary technology relates to a product innovation, vertical integration assists the company in establishing itself as a differentiated player in its core operation.

Recently, IBM integrated backward into the manufacture of microcircuits to protect the innovations incorporated in its new PS/2 personal computer system from being duplicated by competitors. The information pathways and graphics of the PS/2 machines are created by proprietary chips, manufactured by IBM itself, that will be difficult for competitors to decipher. By taking this step, IBM hopes to avoid the widespread copying of its machines that occurred in the case of the company's original PC system—that is, it hopes to differentiate itself.[9]

Disadvantages of Vertical Integration

Vertical integration has its disadvantages, however. Most important among them are (1) cost disadvantages, (2) disadvantages that arise when technology is changing fast, and (3) disadvantages that arise when demand is unpredictable. These disadvantages can give rise to bureaucratic costs, making the benefits of vertical integration not always as substantial as they might seem initially. When deciding whether to integrate, strategic managers need to weigh the value created by vertical integration against the bureaucratic costs of implementing the strategy. In many cases, the bureaucratic costs are such that vertical integration may reduce rather than increase value.

Cost disadvantages   Although often undertaken to gain a cost advantage, vertical integration can bring higher costs if a company becomes committed to purchasing inputs from company-owned suppliers when low-cost external sources of supply exist. For example, currently General Motors is at a cost disadvantage in relation to Chrysler because it makes 70 percent of its own components, whereas Chrysler makes only 30 percent. GM has to pay United Auto Workers wages to workers in its own component supply operations, and these wages are generally $2 more per hour than the wages paid by independent component suppliers. Thus, as General Motors exemplifies, vertical integration can be a disadvantage when a company's own sources of supply have higher operating costs than those of independent suppliers.

Company-owned suppliers might have high operating costs, relative to independent suppliers, because company-owned suppliers know that they can always sell their output to other parts of the company. The fact that they do not have to compete for orders with other suppliers reduces their incentive to minimize operating costs. Indeed, the managers of the supply operation may be tempted to pass on any cost increases to other parts of the company in the form of higher transfer prices, rather than looking for ways to reduce those costs. In essence, this lack of incentive to reduce costs can give rise to substantial *bureaucratic costs*. The problem may be less serious, however, when the company pursues taper, rather than full, integration, since the need to compete with independent suppliers can produce a downward pressure on the cost structure of company-owned suppliers.

Technological change   When technology is changing fast, vertical integration poses the hazard of tying a company to an obsolescent technology.[10] Consider a radio manufacturer who in the 1950s integrated backward and acquired a manufacturer of vacuum tubes. When in the 1960s transistors replaced vacuum tubes as a major component in radios, this company found itself tied to a technologically obsolescent business. Switching to transistors would have meant writing off its investment in vacuum tubes. Thus the company was reluctant to change and instead continued to use vacuum tubes in its radios while its nonintegrated competitors were rapidly switching to the new technology. Since it kept making an outdated product, the company rapidly lost market share. Thus vertical integration can inhibit a company's ability to change its suppliers or its distribution systems to match the requirements of changing technology.

Demand uncertainty   Vertical integration can also be risky in unstable or unpredictable demand conditions. When demand is stable, higher degrees of vertical integration might be managed with relative ease. Stable demand allows better scheduling and coordination of production flows among different activities. When demand conditions are unstable or unpredictable, achieving close coordination among vertically integrated activities may be difficult. The resulting inefficiencies can give rise to significant bureaucratic costs.

The problem involves balancing capacity among different stages of a process. For example, an auto manufacturer might vertically integrate backward to acquire a supplier of carburetors that has a capacity exactly matching the auto manufacturer's needs. However, if demand for autos subsequently falls, the automaker will find itself locked into a business that is running below capacity. Clearly, this would be uneconomical. The auto manufacturers could avoid this situation by continuing to buy carburetors on the open market rather than making them itself.

If demand conditions are unpredictable, taper integration might be somewhat less risky than full integration. When a company provides only part of its total input requirements from company-owned suppliers, in times of low demand it can keep its in-house suppliers running at full capacity by ordering exclusively from them.

Summary: Vertical Integration

Although vertical integration can create value, it may also result in substantial costs. These costs arise from the lack of incentive that company-owned suppliers have to reduce their operating costs and from a possible lack of strategic flexibility in the face of changing technology or uncertain demand conditions. Together, these costs form a major component of the bureaucratic costs of vertical integration. Their existence places a limit on the amount of vertical integration that can be profitably pursued.

However, the pursuit of taper integration rather than full integration may reduce the bureaucratic costs of vertical integration. In terms of the framework introduced earlier, taper integration can be viewed as lowering the marginal-bureaucratic-cost curve. In turn, this allows a company to profitably pursue more extensive vertical integration. This is illustrated in Figure 7.6, where MBC_F is the marginal-bureaucratic-cost curve for a company pursuing full integration and MBC_T is the marginal-bureaucratic-cost curve for a company pursuing taper integration. With full integration it pays a company to pursue vertical integration up to V_1 on the horizontal axis. Taper integration, however, creates an incentive for in-house suppliers to reduce their operating costs and increases the company's ability to respond to changing demand conditions. Thus a switch from full to taper integration reduces the marginal-bureaucratic-cost curve from MBC_F to MBC_T and allows the company to vertically integrate up to V_2 on the horizontal axis. In other words, a company that pursues taper integration can profitably

FIGURE 7.6   **Comparing the marginal bureaucratic costs of taper and full integration**

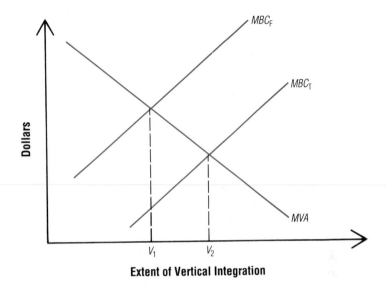

manage greater levels of vertical integration than can a company that pursues full integration. Ultimately, however, although the pursuit of taper integration may reduce bureaucratic costs, it cannot eliminate them altogether. Thus there is a very real limit to extent of vertical integration that a company can profitably manage.

7.6 ALTERNATIVE TO VERTICAL INTEGRATION: LONG-TERM CONTRACTING

The Benefits of Long-Term Contracting

One strategy that companies can adopt in order to capture some if not all of the benefits of vertical integration, without having to deal with many of the bureaucratic costs that accompany vertical integration (whether taper or full integration), is to enter into long-term contracts with suppliers or buyers. Long-term contracts are long-term cooperative relationships between two companies. One agrees to supply the other; the other agrees to continue purchasing from that supplier; and both commit themselves to working together to look for ways of lowering the costs or raising the quality of inputs into the downstream company's value-creation process. If attainable, such a stable long-term relationship allows the participating companies to share the value that might be created by vertical integration while avoiding many of the bureaucratic costs associated with ownership of an adjacent stage in the raw-material-to-consumer production chain. Thus long-term contracts can be a substitute for vertical integration.

For example, as noted in Chapter 6, many of the Japanese auto companies have cooperative relationships with their component-parts suppliers that go back decades. These relationships involve the auto companies and their suppliers in getting together and working out ways to increase value-added through, for example, the implementation of just-in-time inventory systems, or by cooperating on component-part designs for improving quality and lowering assembly costs. Thus the Japanese auto majors have been able to capture many of the benefits from vertical integration, particularly those arising from production cost savings and the protection of product quality, without having to bear the bureaucratic costs associated with formal vertical integration. The component-parts suppliers also benefit from these relationships, since they grow with the company they supply and share in its success.

In stark contrast, U.S. auto companies have tended to pursue formal vertical integration to a much greater degree than their Japanese counterparts. General Motors manufactures 70 percent of its own component parts, Ford 50 percent, and Chrysler 30 percent, compared with less than 20 percent among most Japanese auto companies.[11] The increased bureaucratic costs of managing extensive vertical integration have lowered the profits of the U.S. companies relative to their Japanese counterparts.

Moreover, when the U.S. auto companies decide not to vertically integrate, instead of entering into cooperative long-term relationships with independent component suppliers, they have tended to use their powerful position to play their component suppliers off against each other, frequently dictating terms to them. For example, in 1986 Chrysler instructed its part suppliers to cut their prices by 5 percent, regardless of prior pricing agreements. Chrysler used the threat to weed out suppliers that did not obey as a means of forcing through the policy. Such action may yield short-term benefits for an auto major, but there is a long-term cost to be born in the form of lack of trust and hostility between the company and its suppliers. This may inhibit the introduction of just-in-time inventory systems, make it difficult for suppliers and manufacturers to work together on component-part designs for lowering costs and improving quality, and generally make component suppliers hesitant to commit themselves to cost-reducing investments that make them too dependent on the business of any one auto major.

As a consequence of their inability to establish cooperative long-term relationships with their suppliers, the U.S. auto majors tend to have higher-cost and lower-quality inputs. For example, according to industry estimates, in 1985 for comparable $6,000 small cars U.S. manufacturers spent an average of $3,350 on parts, materials, and services, whereas the average Japanese company spent $2,750—a cost saving of $600 achieved largely through more efficient handling of relationships with suppliers. Long-term contracting as practiced by the Japanese was apparently associated with the lowest cost of material inputs, while *both* vertical integration *and* the lack of long-term cooperative relationships between auto majors and independent suppliers, as is typical in the United States, appear to have raised the costs and lowered the quality of inputs.[12] All this suggests that in many ways, a cooperative long-term relationship between supplier and buyer is better than formal vertical integration.

Impediments to Long-Term Contracting

Given the obvious benefits of long-term contracting, why is it not more widely practiced? The main problem seems to be a lack of trust, which makes companies hesitant to enter into long-term relationships. Lack of trust is particularly likely when one of the companies has to make substantial capital investments in *specialized assets* in order to enter into the relationship. A specialized asset is one that has few if any alternative uses. For example, an aluminum smelter is a specialized asset because it can be used to smelt only aluminum and not any other metal. An investment in specialized assets can be viewed as a sunk cost. Once made, it cannot be recovered.

Lack of trust between companies might arise from a fear that once a company has incurred sunk costs, its partner might use the expenditure as a lever to seek more favorable terms. For example, consider the case of an aluminum company trying to decide where to locate a $500-million aluminum smelter. Smelting aluminum is an energy-intensive process, so energy costs are likely to be a prime determinant of the location decision. Imagine that the aluminum company decides to site its smelter next door to a power station, after having agreed to buy power at a previously agreed-to price. The danger is that once the aluminum company incurs the $500-million investment associated with establishing its operations (that is, once the company incurs sunk costs), the power company might break its prior agreement and raise energy prices. It can do this secure in the knowledge that having committed $500 million to the new smelter, the aluminum company is in no position to close its operations and set up elsewhere.

However, there are ways of designing long-term cooperative relationships to build trust and reduce the hazards associated with making investments in specialized assets. We consider these in the next section.

Establishing Long-Term Agreements

One way of designing long-term cooperative relationships to build trust and reduce the possibility of a company reneging on an agreement is for the company making investments in specialized assets to demand a *hostage* from its partner. Another is by establishing a *credible commitment* on the part of both parties to build a trusting long-term relationship.[13]

Hostage taking   The idea behind hostage taking is that when a company makes investments in specialized assets in order to enter into a long-term relationship with a partner, it seeks a hostage from its partner that can be used as a guarantee that its partner will not subsequently renege on any agreement between the two. Thus the aluminum-smelting company discussed above, before investing any money, might demand that the power company invest in a bond that is held in trust by a third party and transferred to the aluminum company if the power company raises prices above previously agreed-to levels. The bond is the hostage used to ensure that the power company does not renege on pricing agreements.

For an example of a hostage-taking situation, consider the cooperative relationship between Boeing and Northrop. Northrop is a major subcontractor for Boeing's commercial airline division, providing many component parts for the 747 and 767 aircraft. In order to serve the special needs of Boeing, Northrop has had to make substantial investments in specialized assets. In theory, because of the sunk costs associated with such investments, Northrop is dependent on Boeing and Boeing is thus in a position to renege on previous agreements and use the threat to switch orders to other suppliers as a way of driving down prices. However, in practice Boeing is unlikely to do this since the company is also a major supplier to Northrop's defense division, providing many parts for the Stealth bomber. Boeing has had to make substantial investments in specialized assets in order to serve the needs of Northrop. Thus both companies are *mutually dependent* on each other. Boeing, therefore, is unlikely to renege on any pricing agreements with Northrop, since it knows that Northrop could respond in kind. In other words, each company holds a hostage that can be used as insurance against the other company's unilaterally reneging on prior pricing agreements.

Credible commitments   A credible commitment is a believable commitment to support the development of a long-term relationship between companies. To understand the concept of credibility in this context, consider the relationship between General Electric and IBM. GE is one of the major suppliers of advanced semiconductor chips to IBM, and many of the chips are customized to IBM's own requirements. In order to meet IBM's specific needs, GE has had to make substantial investments in specialized assets that have little other value. As a consequence, GE is dependent on IBM and faces a risk that IBM will take advantage of this dependence to demand lower prices. In theory IBM could back up its demand with the threat to switch to another supplier. However, GE reduced the risk of this occurring by getting IBM to enter into a contractual agreement that committed IBM to purchase chips from GE until the end of the 1990s. In addition, IBM agreed to share in the costs of developing the customized chips, thereby reducing GE's investments in specialized assets. Thus, by publicly committing itself to a long-term contract, and by putting some money into the development of the customized chips, IBM has essentially made a *credible commitment* to continue purchasing those chips from GE.

Summary   By establishing credible commitments or by taking hostages, companies may be able to use long-term contracts to realize much of the value associated with vertical integration, without having to bear the bureaucratic costs of formal vertical integration. As a general point, it should be noted that the growing importance of just-in-time inventory systems as a way of reducing costs and enhancing quality is increasing the pressure for companies to enter into long-term agreements in a wide range of industries. Thus we might reasonably expect to see a growth in the popularity of such agreements in the future. However, it is not always possible to reach such agreements, in which case formal vertical integration may be called for.

7.7 DIVERSIFICATION

There are two major types of diversification: *related diversification* and *unrelated diversification*. Related diversification is diversification into a new activity that is linked to a company's existing activity by commonality between one or more components of each activity's value chain. Normally, these linkages are based on manufacturing, marketing, materials management, and technological commonalities. The diversification of Philip Morris into the brewing industry with the acquisition of Miller Brewing is an example of related diversification because there are marketing commonalities between the brewing and tobacco business (both are consumer product businesses in which competitive success depends on brand-positioning skills). Unrelated diversification is diversification into a new activity that has no obvious commonalities with any of the company's existing activities. The acquisitions made by Hanson Trust, considered in the Opening Incident, are an example of unrelated diversification.

In this section, we begin by looking at how diversification can create value for a company and then we examine some reasons why so much diversification apparently dissipates rather than creates value. We include a consideration of the bureaucratic costs of diversification. Finally, we consider some of the factors that determine the choice between the strategies of related and unrelated diversification.

Creating Value
Through Diversification

Most companies first consider diversification when they are generating financial resources *in excess* of those necessary to maintain a competitive advantage in their original, or core, business.[14] The question they must tackle is how to invest the excess resources in order to create value. Diversification can create value in four main ways: (1) through an internal capital market, (2) by restructuring, (3) by transferring skills among businesses, and (4) by sharing functions or resources.

Establishing an internal capital market   A diversified company can create value by establishing within the company an internal capital market that takes over some of the functions of the stock market. In an internal capital market, the head office has three major roles: (1) to perform strategic planning functions concerning the composition of the corporate portfolio (decisions about acquisitions and divestments); (2) to set financial targets and monitor the subsequent performance of business units, intervening selectively in underperforming units to correct any problems; and (3) to allocate corporate capital among the competing claims of different business units. The business units themselves are set up as autonomous profit centers, subject only to financial controls from the head office.

Advocates of this strategy contend that the head office can monitor business-unit performance and allocate financial resources among units more efficiently than the stock market could do if each business unit were an independent company.[15] The reason is that the head office, as an internal investor, has access to better information about the performance of business units and is better able to use that information than could stock market investors if each business unit were independent.

For example, the head office can use its authority to demand detailed information on the efficiency of a business unit's operations, whereas stock market investors have to make judgments on the basis of whatever information a company chooses to release to them. The head office can also intervene selectively in underperforming business units and fine-tune their operations (for instance, by making relatively minor management changes), whereas the stock market can make only drastic adjustments (such as a takeover). Consequently, the stock market may fail to discipline underperforming management teams adequately and may allocate too few capital resources to some companies and too many to others. The head office of a diversified company can both discipline underperforming management teams and allocate resources much more effectively.

Since a company is more efficient than the stock market in monitoring performance and allocating capital, it should acquire potentially strong but poorly managed enterprises that are undervalued by the stock market. By exposing acquired companies to the discipline of tight financial controls and efficient capital allocation, an internal capital market encourages and rewards aggressive profit-seeking behavior by the acquired company's management. The result can be an increase in the efficiency of the value-creation process within the acquired company. Specifically, the managers of the acquired company might be motivated to look for ways to reduce the costs of value creation and to perform individual value-creation functions in a way that leads to differentiation and a premium price. Such improvements in the efficiency of value creation within the acquired company also add value to the acquiring corporation.

However, the strategy has its critics. Some contend that today's computer-drive stock market efficiently allocates resources and penalizes poorly managed companies by forcing proxy votes on key elements of corporate strategy.[16] If this is true, and it is a debatable point, the whole basis for the strategy has been destroyed. Others argue that overly tight financial controls can lead to short-run profit maximization within the business units of companies trying to create value through an internal capital market.[17] In turn, the arms-length relationship between the head office and the business units allows such behavior to go undetected until a good deal of damage has been done. The poor performance of portfolio diversifiers, such as Gulf & Western Industries, Consolidated Foods Corporation, and ITT, has lent weight to these criticisms. However, there are also some spectacular examples of how successful the strategy can be—for instance, the Anglo-American conglomerate BTR Inc.[18] More than anything else, these conflicting examples suggest that the strategy is difficult to implement.

Restructuring   A restructuring strategy has a lot in common with an internal capital market strategy. The essential differences have to do with the degree to which the head office becomes involved in business-unit operations. Companies that pursue a restructuring strategy seek out poorly managed, underperforming, or undeveloped companies. The objective is to acquire such companies and then intervene in a *proactive* fashion, frequently changing the acquired company's management team, developing new business-level strategies, and infusing the company with new financial or technological resources. If all goes well, the upshot is a dramatic improvement in the competitive position and financial health of the acquired company, creating value for the acquiring enterprise.

The diversification strategy of Hanson Trust, described in the Opening Incident, is based on restructuring. Hanson seeks out companies that are not maximizing stockholder wealth. Such companies are normally characterized by excess organizational slack. This means that they use more resources than necessary to run their business. For example, managers may be given expensive company cars as perks; corporate headquarters may be lavishly decorated and overstaffed; and the company may own a ranch to entertain its visiting executives or run a fleet of jets to fly its managers around the country.

Because of their inefficiency, companies with a high degree of organizational slack are often undervalued by the stock market. Companies such as Hanson Trust can acquire them at a reasonable price and then reorganize them to increase their efficiency. Excess staff are likely to be laid off and the executive jets, company cars, and expensive headquarters sold. Typically, unwanted subsidiary companies are also sold at this stage. Whatever remains is then subjected to central financial controls designed to instill profit discipline and efficiency awareness. The result, as in the case of the Hanson/SCM acquisition, is improved performance through lower operating costs or increased differentiation. Thus the acquiring company creates value for its stockholders by improving the efficiency of value creation in acquired companies.

Transferring skills   Companies that base their diversification strategy on transferring skills seek out new businesses related to their existing business by one or more value-creation functions (for example, manufacturing, marketing, materials management, and R&D—see Chapter 4). They may want to create value by drawing on the distinctive skills in one or more of their existing value-creation functions in order to improve the competitive position of the new business. Alternatively, they may acquire a company in a different business area in the belief that some of the skills of the acquired company might improve the efficiency of their existing value-creation activities. If successful, such skill transfers can lower the costs of value creation in one or more of a company's diversified businesses or enable one or more of a company's diversified businesses to undertake their value-creation functions in a way that leads to differentiation and a premium price.

An example is Germany's Daimler Benz, the maker of Mercedes-Benz cars. In recent years Daimler has diversified into household goods, defense electronics, automation systems, and aerospace. The strategy is based on a belief that the transfer of state-of-the-art technological know-how between the different businesses of the company will enhance the competitive position of each, enabling all of Daimler Benz's businesses to better differentiate themselves with regard to technology.

For such a strategy to work, the skills being transferred must involve activities that are important for establishing a competitive advantage. All too often, companies assume that any commonality is sufficient for creating value. General Motors' acquisition of Hughes Aircraft, made simply because autos and auto manufacturing were going electronic and Hughes was an electronics concern, demonstrates the folly of overestimating the commonalities among businesses. To date, the acquisition has failed to realize any of the anticipated gains for GM, whose competitive position has only worsened. (One may similarly raise questions about the value that Daimler Benz might create from transferring technological know-how between autos and aerospace.)

Philip Morris's transfer of marketing skills to Miller Brewing, discussed earlier, is perhaps one of the classic examples of how value *can* be created by skill transfers. Drawing on its marketing and brand-positioning skills, Philip Morris pioneered the introduction of Miller Lite, the product that redefined the brewing industry and moved Miller from number six to number two in the market. Rockwell International's diversification into factory automation with the company's 1985 acquisition of Allen-Bradley Canada Ltd. is another example of skill transfers. In this case, skill transfers were based on technological linkages between different activities. Rockwell has given Allen-Bradley strong research and development support and Rockwell's own electronics technology, and Allen-Bradley's factory automation expertise is boosting efficiency in Rockwell's commercial and defense factories.[19]

Sharing resources   Like skill transfers, diversification to share resources is possible only when there are significant commonalities between one or more of the value-creation functions of a company's existing and new activities. By *resources* we mean manufacturing, marketing, R&D, human resources, and the like. The objective of sharing resources is to create value from the realization of **economies of scope**.[20] Economies of scope arise when two or more business units share manufacturing facilities, distribution channels, advertising campaigns, R&D costs, and so on. Each business unit that shares resources has to invest less in the shared functions. For example, the costs of General Electric's advertising, sales, and service activities in major appliances are low because they are spread over a wide range of products. In addition, such a strategy can utilize the capacity of certain functions better. For example, by producing the components for the assembly operations of two distinct businesses, a component-manufacturing plant may be able to operate at a greater capacity, thereby realizing *economies of scale* in addition to economies of scope.

Thus a diversification strategy based on resource sharing can help a company attain a low-cost position in each of the businesses in which it operates. As such, diversification to share resources can be a valid way of *supporting* the generic business-level strategy of cost leadership. However, strategic managers need to be aware that the bureaucratic costs of coordination necessary to achieve resource sharing within a company often outweigh the value that can be created by such a strategy.[21] Consequently, the strategy should be pursued only when sharing is likely to generate a *significant* competitive advantage in one or more of a company's business units.

Procter & Gamble's disposable diaper and paper towel businesses offer one of the best examples of successful resource sharing. These businesses share the costs of procuring certain raw materials (such as paper) and developing the technology for new products and processes. In addition, a joint sales force sells both products to supermarket buyers, and both products are shipped by means of the same distribution system. This resource sharing has given both business units a cost advantage that has enabled them to undercut their less diversified competitors.[22]

Summary   There are four ways in which a diversified company can create value. However, as discussed early in this chapter, the *marginal value* added by each additional diversification move tends to decline as a company exploits its most profitable diversification opportunities. This suggests that there are limits to the amount of value that can be created through diversification. In addition, as also discussed early in this chapter, when considering how much diversification a company can profitably pursue, it is necessary to consider the bureaucratic costs of diversification.

The Bureaucratic Costs of Diversification

In a study that looked at the diversification of thirty-three major U.S. corporations between 1950 and 1986, Michael Porter observed that the track record of corporate diversification has been dismal.[23] Porter found that most of the companies had divested many more diversified acquisitions than they had kept. He concluded that the corporate diversification strategies of most companies have dissipated value instead of creating it. More generally, a large number of academic studies have come to the general conclusion that *extensive* diversification tends to depress rather than improve company profitability.[24] This research begs the question of why diversification so often fails.

One reason so much diversification fails is that all too often the bureaucratic costs of diversification exceed the value created by the strategy. Companies often diversify past the point at which it is profitable to do so (in terms of Figure 7.2, they diversify to the point where MVA is less than MBC). The bureaucratic costs of diversification arise from two sources: (1) the number of businesses in a company's portfolio and (2) the extent of coordination required between the different businesses of the company in order to realize value from a diversification strategy. We consider each of these sources in turn.

Number of businesses   The greater the number of businesses in a company's portfolio, the more difficult it is for corporate management to remain informed about the complexities of each business. Management simply does not have the time to process all of the information that is required to assess the strategic plan of each business unit objectively. This problem began to occur at General Electric in the 1970s. As then-CEO Reg Jones commented:

> I tried to review each plan in great detail. This effort took untold hours and placed a tremendous burden on the corporate executive office. After awhile I began to realize that no matter how hard we would work, we could not achieve the necessary in-depth understanding of the 40-odd business unit plans.[25]

One consequence of information overload in extensively diversified companies is that corporate-level management ends up making important resource allocation decisions on the basis of only the most superficial analysis of the competitive position of each business unit. Thus, for example, a promising business unit may be starved of investment funds while other business units receive far more cash than they can profitably reinvest in their operations. Another consequence is that the lack of familiarity with operating affairs on the part of corporate-level management increases the probability that business-level managers will be able to deceive corporate-level managers. For example, business-unit managers may be able to justify poor performance on the grounds that it is a consequence of difficult competitive conditions, when in reality it is the consequence of poor management.

Thus information overload can result in substantial inefficiencies within extensively diversified companies. These inefficiencies include the suboptimal allocation of cash resources within the company and a failure by corporate management to successfully encourage and reward aggressive profit-seeking behavior by business-unit managers. In other words, information overload can make it extremely difficult to create value by establishing an internal capital market within a diversified company or by pursuing a restructuring strategy.

The inefficiencies that arise from information overload can be regarded as one component of the bureaucratic costs of extensive diversification. Of course, these costs can be reduced to manageable proportions if a company limits the scope of its diversification. Indeed, a desire to reduce these costs lay behind the 1980s divestments and strategic concentration strategies of conglomerates of the 1960s and 1970s such as Esmark Corporation, General Electric, ITT, Textron, Tenneco, and United Technologies. Under the leadership of Jack Welch, for example, GE switched its emphasis from forty main business units to sixteen main business units contained within three clearly defined sectors. In terms of Figure 7.2, discussed earlier, the inefficiencies from information overload arise when a company diversifies beyond the point at which MVA equals MBC.

Coordination between businesses   A second source of bureaucratic costs arises from the coordination required to realize value from a diversification strategy based on skill transfers or resource sharing. Both transferring skills and sharing resources require close coordination between business units. The bureaucratic mechanisms necessary to achieve that coordination give rise to bureaucratic costs. (We discuss the mechanisms for achieving coordination in Chapter 11.)

More seriously, however, substantial bureaucratic costs can arise from an inability to identify the unique profit contribution of a business unit that is sharing resources with another unit. Consider a company that has two business units—one producing household products (such as liquid soap and laundry detergent) and another producing packaged food products. The products of both units are sold through supermarkets. In order to lower the costs of value creation, the parent company decides to pool the marketing and sales functions of each business unit. Pooling allows the business units to share the costs of a sales force (one sales force can sell the products of both divisions) and gain cost economies from using the same physical distribution system. The organizational structure required to achieve this might be similar to that illustrated in Figure 7.7. The company is organized into three main divisions: a household products division, a food products division, and a marketing division.

Although such an arrangement may create value, it can also give rise to substantial control problems and hence bureaucratic costs. For example, if the performance of the household products business begins to slip, identifying who is to be held accountable—the management of the household products division or the management of the marketing division—may prove difficult. Indeed, each may blame the other for poor performance: The management of the household products division might blame the marketing policies of the marketing division, and the management of the marketing division might blame the poor quality and high costs of products produced by the household products division. Although this kind of problem can be resolved if corporate management directly audits the affairs of both divisions, doing so is costly in both the time and the effort that corporate management must expend.

FIGURE 7.7   **The structure of a company sharing marketing between two business units**

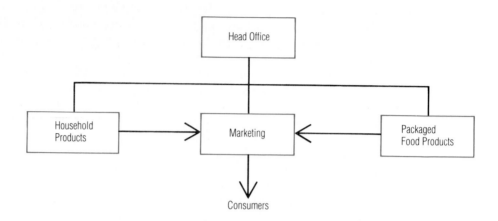

FIGURE 7.8   **Marginal-bureaucratic-cost curves and the need for coordination**

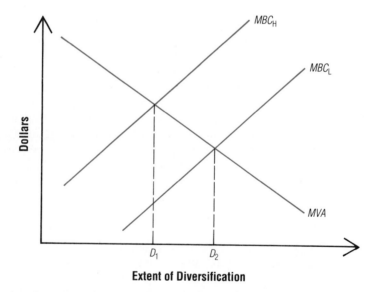

Now imagine the situation within a company that is trying to create value by sharing marketing, manufacturing, and R&D resources across ten businesses rather than just two. Clearly, the accountability problem could become far more serious in such a company. Indeed, the problem might become so serious that the effort involved in trying to tie down accountability might create a serious information overload for corporate management. When this occurs, corporate management effectively loses control of the company. The consequences of not being able to tie down accountability may include an inability by corporate management to encourage and reward aggressive profit-seeking behavior by business-unit managers, poor resource allocation decisions, and a generally high level of organizational slack. All of these inefficiencies can be considered part of the bureaucratic costs of diversification to share resources.

Summary   Although diversification can create value for a company in a number of ways, it inevitably involves bureaucratic costs. The costs tend to be greater (1) the greater the number of business units within a company and (2) the greater the need for coordination between those business units. Thus bureaucratic costs are much greater in a company that has twenty businesses, all of which are trying to share resources, than in a company that has ten businesses, none of which are trying to share resources.

The implications are illustrated in Figure 7.8. The marginal bureaucratic costs of a diversified company with a high need for coordination between business units (MBC_H) are compared with the marginal bureaucratic costs of a diversified company with a low need for coordination between business units (MBC_L). A company with a high need for coordination is one that is trying to create value through resource sharing. A company with a low need for coordination is one that is trying to create value through the operation of an internal capital market or by restructuring. As can be seen, at every level of diversification, MBC_H is greater than MBC_L. If we assume that both companies have the same marginal-value-added curve, the implication is that the company with a low need for coordination can profitably manage a greater extent of diversification than can the company with a high need for coordination. (The company with a low need for coordination can manage $0–D_2$ diversification profitably, and the company with a high need for coordination can manage only $0–D_1$ diversification profitably.) This analysis has implications for a company's choice between a strategy of related and unrelated diversification, which is discussed in a later section.

Diversification That Dissipates Value

Another reason so much diversification apparently fails to create value is that many companies diversify for the wrong reasons. As a consequence, they end up dissipating value rather than creating it. This is particularly true of diversification to "pool risks" or to "achieve greater growth," both of which are often given by company managers as reasons for diversification.

Consider *diversification to pool risks*. The benefits of risk pooling are said to come from merging imperfectly correlated income streams to create a more stable income stream. An example of risk pooling might be USX's diversification into the oil and gas industry in an attempt to offset the adverse effects of cyclical downturns in the steel industry. According to the advocates of risk pooling, the more stable income stream reduces the risk of bankruptcy and is in the best interests of the company's stockholders.

However, this argument ignores two facts. First, stockholders can easily eliminate the risks inherent in holding an individual stock by diversifying their own portfolios, and they can do so at a much lower cost than the company can. Thus, far from being in the best interests of stockholders, attempts to pool risks through diversification represent an unproductive use of resources. Second, the vast majority of research on this topic suggests that corporate diversification is not a very effective way to pool risks.[26] The business cycles of different industries are not easy to predict and in any case tend to be less important than a general economic downturn that hits all industries simultaneously. International Harvester illustrates the point. By 1979 International Harvester had diversified into three major businesses: agricultural equipment, construction equipment, and trucks. These businesses were supposed to follow different business cycles, cushioning the company against severe fluctuations. In the early 1980s, however, all these businesses suffered a downturn at the same time, cumulating a $2.9-billion loss for Harvester.

Now consider *diversification to achieve greater growth*. Such diversification is not a coherent strategy because growth on its own does not create value. Growth should be the *by-product,* not the objective, of a diversification strategy. However, companies sometimes diversify for reasons of growth alone, rather than to gain any well-thought-out strategic advantage. ITT under the leadership of Harold Geneen took this path. Geneen turned ITT from an international telecommunications company into a broadly based conglomerate consisting of more than 100 separate businesses with interests in such diverse areas as baking, car rental, defense electronics, fire hydrants, insurance, hotels, paper products, and telecommunications. The strategy seemed to have more to do with Geneen's desire to build an empire than with maximizing the company's value.[27] Since Geneen's departure in 1979, ITT's management has been trying to divest many of the businesses acquired under his leadership and to concentrate on insurance and financial services.

Related or Unrelated Diversification?

One issue that a company must resolve is whether to diversify into businesses related to its existing business by value-chain commonalities or into totally new businesses. The distinction here is between related diversification and unrelated diversification. By definition, a related company can create value by resource sharing and by transferring skills between businesses. It can also carry out some restructuring and create value by applying internal capital market concepts to the management of its diverse activities. By way of contrast, since there are no commonalities between the value chains of unrelated businesses, an unrelated company cannot create value by sharing resources or transferring skills between businesses. Unrelated diversifiers can create value only by restructuring and creating an internal capital market.

Since related diversification can create value in more ways than unrelated diversification can, one might think that related diversification should be the preferred strategy. In addition, related diversification is normally perceived as involving fewer risks because the company is moving into business areas about which top management has some knowledge. Probably because of those considerations, most diversified companies display a preference for related diversification.[28] However, research suggests that the average related company is no more profitable than the average unrelated company.[29] How can this be, if related diversification is associated with more benefits than is unrelated diversification?

The answer to this question is actually quite simple. Bureaucratic costs arise from (1) the number of businesses in a company's portfolio and (2) the extent of coordination required between the different businesses in order to realize value from a diversification strategy. An unrelated company does not have to achieve coordination between business units. Thus it has to cope only with the bureaucratic costs that arise from the number of businesses in its portfolio. In contrast, a related diversified company has to achieve coordination between business units if it is to realize the value that comes from skill transfers and resource sharing. As a consequence, it has to cope with the bureaucratic costs that arise *both* from the number of business units in its portfolio *and* from coordination between business units. Thus, although it is true that related diversified companies can create value in more ways than unrelated companies can, they have to bear higher bureaucratic costs in order to do so. These higher costs may cancel out the higher benefits, making the strategy no more profitable than one of unrelated diversification. This is summarized in Table 7.2.

How then is a company to choose between these strategies? The choice depends on a comparison of the relative value-added and bureaucratic costs associated with each strategy. In making this comparison, it is important to note that the opportunities for creating value from related diversification are a function of the extent of commonalities between the skills required to compete in the company's core business and the skills required to compete in other industrial and commercial areas. Some companies' skills are so specialized that they have few applications outside the core businesses. For example, since the commonalities

TABLE 7.2   **Comparing related and unrelated diversification**

Strategy	Ways of creating value	Source of bureaucratic costs
Related	Internal capital market	Number of businesses
	Restructuring Transferring skills Sharing resources	Coordination between businesses
Unrelated	Internal capital market Restructuring	Number of businesses

between steel making and other industrial or commercial operations are few, most steel companies have diversified into unrelated industries (LTV into defense contracting, USX into oil and gas). When companies have less specialized skills, they can find many more related diversification opportunities outside the core business. Examples include chemical companies (such as Dow Chemical and Du Pont) and electrical engineering companies (such as General Electric). Consequently, the opportunities available to them to create value from related diversification are much greater.

Thus it pays a firm to concentrate on related diversification when (1) the company's core skills are applicable to a wide variety of industrial and commercial situations and (2) the bureaucratic costs of implementation do not exceed the value that can be created through resource sharing or skill transfers. The second condition is likely to hold only for companies that are moderately diversified. At high levels of related diversification, the bureaucratic costs of additional diversification are likely to outweigh the value created by that diversification, and the strategy may become unprofitable.

By the same logic, it may pay a company to concentrate on unrelated diversification when (1) the company's core skills are highly specialized and have few applications outside the company's core business and (2) the bureaucratic costs of implementation do not exceed the value that can be created by establishing an internal capital market or pursuing a restructuring strategy. Once again, however, the second condition is unlikely to hold for companies that are highly diversified. Thus, no matter whether a company pursues a related or an unrelated diversification strategy, the existence of bureaucratic costs suggests that there are very real limits to the profitable growth of the company.

7.8 ALTERNATIVE TO DIVERSIFICATION: STRATEGIC ALLIANCES

Diversification can be unprofitable because of the bureaucratic costs associated with implementing the strategy. One way of trying to realize the value associated with diversification, without having to bear the same level of bureaucratic costs, is to enter into a strategic alliance with another company to start a new business venture.

In this context, strategic alliances are essentially agreements between two or more companies to share the costs, risks, and benefits associated with developing new business opportunities. Many strategic alliances are constituted as formal joint ventures in which each party has an equity stake. Other alliances take the form of a long-term contract between companies in which they agree to undertake some joint activity that benefits both. Agreements to work together on joint R&D projects often take this form.

Strategic alliances seem to be a particularly viable option when a company wishes to create value from transferring skills or sharing resources between diversified businesses. Alliances offer companies a framework within which to share the resources required to establish a new business. Alternatively, alliances enable companies to swap complementary skills to produce a new range of products. For example, consider the recent alliance between United Technologies and Dow Chemical to build plastic-based composite parts for the aerospace industry. United Technologies is already involved in the aerospace industry (it builds Sikorsky helicopters), and Dow Chemical has skills in the development and manufacture of plastic-based composites. The alliance calls for United Technologies to contribute its advanced aerospace skills and Dow its skills in developing and manufacturing plastic-based composites to a joint venture in which each company will have a 50 percent equity stake. The joint venture will then undertake the task of developing, manufacturing, and marketing a new line of plastic-based composite parts for the aerospace industry. Through the alliance, both companies will become involved in new activities. They will, in short, be able to realize some of the benefits associated with related diversification without having to merge activities formally or bear the costs and risks of developing the new products on their own.

Bureaucratic costs are reduced because neither Dow nor United Technologies is actually expanding its own organization, nor does either company have to coordinate internal skill transfers. Rather, after incorporation the joint venture will operate as an independent company, and both Dow and United Technologies will receive payment in the form of dividends.

Of course, there is a down side to such alliances. For one thing, profits must be split with an alliance partner, whereas with full diversification a company gets to keep all of the profits. Another problem is that when a company enters into an alliance, it always runs the risk that it might give away critical know-how to its alliance partner, who might then use that know-how to compete directly with the company in the future. Thus, for example, having gained access to Dow's expertise in plastic-based composites, United Technologies might dissolve the alliance and produce these materials on its own. However, as in the case of vertical integration, the risk can be minimized if Dow gets a *credible commitment* from United Technologies. By entering into a formal joint venture, rather than a more loosely structured alliance, United Technologies has given such a commitment because it has had to invest substantial amounts of capital. Thus, if United Technologies tried to produce plastic-based composites on its own, it would essentially be competing against itself.

7.9 RETRENCHMENT AND TURNAROUND

Vertical integration and diversification are strategies for profitable expansion. However, for many of the reasons discussed above, corporate strategies sometimes fail and corporate decline ensues. Retrenchment is not so much a corporate strategy as a strategic response to corporate decline. The objective of retrenchment is to restructure the operations of a troubled company in order to halt corporate decline and return the company to profitability. In this section, we review the causes of corporate decline and then examine the steps toward successful retrenchment and turnaround.

The Causes of Corporate Decline

Six main causes stand out in most cases of corporate decline: poor management, overexpansion, inadequate financial controls, high costs, the emergence of powerful new competition, and unforeseen shifts in demand.[30] Normally, several, if not all, of these factors are present in a decline situation. For example, Chrysler's decline toward near-bankruptcy in the 1970s was brought on by poor top management, which had failed to put adequate financial controls in place. As a result, Chrysler's cost structure got out of line, inhibiting Chrysler's ability to respond to powerful, new, low-cost Japanese competition. In addition, the unforeseen shift in demand toward compact and subcompact cars after the oil price hikes of 1974 and 1979 left Chrysler, as a manufacturer of intermediate- and full-size models, ill prepared to serve the market.

Poor management   "Poor management" covers a multitude of sins, ranging from sheer incompetence to neglect of core businesses and an insufficient number of good managers. Although not necessarily a bad thing, one-person rule often seems to be at the root of poor management. One study found that the presence of a dominant and autocratic chief executive with a passion for empire-building strategies often characterizes many failing companies.[31] Another study of eighty-one turnaround situations found that in thirty-six cases troubled companies suffered from an autocratic manager who tried to do it all and, in the face of complexity and change, could not.[32] Examples of autocratic CEOs include Bill Bricker, the former CEO of Diamond Shamrock; Harold Geneen, the former CEO of ITT; and Roy Mason, the former CEO of the one-time Fortune 500 and later bankrupt Charter Company.

In a review of the empirical studies of turnaround situations, Richard Hoffman identified a number of other management defects commonly found in declining companies.[33] These included a lack of balanced expertise at the top (for example, too many engineers), a lack of strong middle management, a failure to provide for orderly management succession by a departing CEO (which may result in an internal succession battle), and a failure by the board of directors to monitor management's strategic decisions adequately.

Overexpansion   The empire-building strategies of autocratic CEOs such as Bricker, Geneen, and Mason often involve rapid expansion and extensive diversification. Much of this diversification tends to be poorly conceived and adds little value to a company. As observed above, the consequences of too much diversification include loss of control and an inability to cope with recessionary conditions. Moreover, companies that expand rapidly tend to do so by taking on large amounts of debt financing. Adverse economic conditions can limit a company's ability to meet its debt requirements and can thus precipitate a financial crisis.

Inadequate financial controls   The most common aspect of inadequate financial controls is a failure to assign profit responsibility to key decision makers within the organization. A lack of accountability for the financial consequences of their actions can encourage middle-level managers to employ excess staff and spend resources beyond what is necessary for maximum efficiency. In such cases, bureaucracy may balloon and costs spiral out of control. This is precisely what happened at Chrysler during the 1970s. As Lee Iacocca later noted, Jerry Greenwald, whom Iacocca brought in to head the finance function in 1980, "had a hell of a time finding anybody who could be identified as having specific responsibility for anything. They would tell him, 'Well, everyone is responsible for controlling costs.' Jerry knew very well what that meant—in the final analysis nobody was."[34]

High costs   Inadequate financial controls can lead to high costs. Beyond this, the most common cause of a high-cost structure is low labor productivity. It may stem from union-imposed restrictive working practices (as in the case of the auto and steel industries), management's failure to invest in new labor-saving technologies, or, more often, a combination of both. Other common causes include high wage rates (a particularly important factor for companies competing on costs in the global marketplace) and a failure to realize economies of scale due to low market share.

New competition   For U.S. companies, powerful new competition typically comes from overseas, and many companies have been caught unprepared for its emergence. The auto majors initially ignored the Japanese threat; by the time they responded, they had already given up substantial market share. Similarly, U.S. manufacturers of microprocessors made the mistake of discounting Asian competition, only to see their market share plummet during the mid 1980s in the face of new low-cost competition.

Unforeseen demand shifts   Unforeseen, and often unforeseeable, shifts in demand can be brought about by major changes in technology, economic or political conditions, and social and cultural norms. Although such changes can open up market opportunities for new products, they also threaten the existence of many established enterprises, necessitating restructuring. The classic example is clearly the 1974 OPEC oil price increase, which, among other things, hit the demand for autos, oil-fired central heating units, and many oil-based products, such as vinyl phonographic records. Similarly, the oil price collapse of 1983–1986 devastated many oil field drilling companies and forced them into undertaking drastic restructuring.

The Main Steps of Retrenchment and Turnaround

There is no standard model of how a company should respond to a decline. Indeed, there can be no such model because every situation is unique. However, in most successful turnaround situations, a number of common features are present. They include changing the leadership, redefining the company's strategic focus, divesting or closing unwanted assets, taking steps to improve the profitability of remaining operations, and, occasionally, making acquisitions to rebuild core operations.

Changing the leadership   Since the old leadership bears the stigma of failure, new leadership is an essential element of most retrenchment and turnaround situations. At Chrysler Lee Iacocca replaced John Riccardo; at U.S. Steel David Roderick replaced the autocratic Edgar Speer; and at Apple Computer John Sculley replaced the erratic, emotional, but sometimes brilliant Steve Jobs. To resolve a crisis, the new leader should be someone who is able to make difficult decisions, motivate lower-level managers, listen to the views of others, and delegate power when appropriate.

Redefining strategic focus   For a single-business enterprise, redefining strategic focus involves a re-evaluation of the company's business-level strategy. A failed cost leader, for example, may reorient toward a more focused or differentiated strategy. For a diversified company, redefining strategic focus means identifying the businesses in the portfolio that have the best long-term profit and growth prospects and concentrating investment there. For example, in response to the profit debacle of the early 1980s, International Harvester sold its construction and agricultural equipment businesses and concentrated on heavy and medium trucks and spare parts, in which it was number one in the United States.

Asset sales and closures   Having redefined its strategic focus, a company should divest as many unwanted assets as it can find buyers for and liquidate whatever remains. It is important not to confuse unwanted assets with unprofitable assets. Assets that no longer fit in with the redefined strategic focus of the company may be very profitable. Their sale can bring the company much-needed cash, which it can invest in improving the operations that remain.

Improving profitability   Improving the profitability of the operations that remain after asset sales and closures involves a number of steps. They may include the following: (1) layoffs of white- and blue-collar employees; (2) investments in labor-saving equipment; (3) assignment of profit responsibility to individuals and subunits within the company, by a change of organizational structure if necessary; (4) tightening financial controls; and (5) cutting back on marginal products.

Kodak recently took several of these steps in an attempt to regain the market share it had lost to foreign competition. Between 1983 and 1987 Kodak cut its total work force by 20 percent; most of the job losses affected white-collar employees. The company scrapped an archaic organization based on centralized functions (manufacturing, R&D, marketing, and the like) and reorganized into twenty-four business units, each with its own profit-and-loss responsibility. In addition, a 1985 study showed that 80 or 90 percent of Kodak's products generated only 10 or 20 percent of its profits. In response, by 1987 the company had discontinued 10,000 products, reducing its total to 55,000.

Acquisitions   A somewhat surprising but quite common turnaround strategy involves making acquisitions, primarily to strengthen the competitive position of a company's remaining core operations. For example, Champion International Corporation used to be a very diversified company manufacturing a wide range of paper and wood products. After years of declining performance, in the mid 1980s Champion decided to focus on its profitable newsprint and magazine paper business. The company divested many of its other paper and wood products businesses, but at the same time it paid $1.8 billion for St. Regis Corp., one of the country's largest manufacturers of newsprint and magazine paper.

7.10 SUMMARY OF CHAPTER

The purpose of this chapter is to examine the different corporate-level strategies that companies pursue in order to maximize their value.

1. Corporate-level strategy is concerned with answering the question of how to manage a company's growth and development in order to maximize long-run profitability. The answer involves choices of both the *businesses* and the *markets* that the company is going to compete in.

2. Corporate strategies should *add value* to a corporation. To add value, a corporate strategy should enable the company, or one or more of its business units, to perform one or more of the value-creation functions at a lower cost or in a way that allows for differentiation and a premium price.

3. The advantages of concentrating on a single business include focusing the company's resources on establishing a distinctive competence within one business area and keeping top management in touch with operating realities. These benefits are particularly significant in growth industries.

4. The disadvantages of concentrating on a single business are that the company may need to integrate vertically or expand globally in order to establish a low-cost or differentiated position in its core operation. A single-business company may also miss out on opportunities to expand its market to other nations or apply its distinctive competencies to profit opportunities that arise in other industries.

5. Vertical integration allows a company to create value through production cost savings and by avoiding the costs of using the market, protecting product quality, and protecting proprietary technology.

6. The disadvantages of vertical integration include cost disadvantages if a company's internal source of supply is a high-cost one and a lack of flexibility when technology is changing fast or when demand is uncertain.

7. Taper integration is normally preferable to full integration because taper integration exposes in-house suppliers and distributors to some degree of competitive pressure, thereby keeping costs low. Taper integration also enables a company to adopt a more flexible posture toward uncertainties in demand.

8. Entering into a long-term contract can enable a company to realize many of the benefits associated with vertical integration without having to bear the same level of bureaucratic costs. However, to avoid the risks associated with becoming too dependent on its partner, when entering into a long-term contract a company needs to seek a credible commitment from its partner or establish a mutual hostage-taking situation.

9. Diversification can create value through the pursuit of a portfolio strategy, restructuring, skill transfers, and resource sharing. Diversification for other reasons is unlikely to add value.

10. The bureaucratic costs of diversification are a function of (a) the number of independent business units within the company and (b) the extent of coordination between those business units.

11. Diversification motivated by a desire to pool risks or achieve greater growth is often associated with the dissipation of value.

12. Related diversification is preferred to unrelated diversification because it enables a company to engage in more value-creation activities and is less risky. If a company's skills are not transferrable, the company may have no choice but to pursue unrelated diversification.

13. Strategic alliances can enable companies to realize many of the benefits of related diversification without having to bear the same level of bureaucratic costs. However, when entering into an alliance, a company does run the risk of giving away key technology to its partner. The risk of this occurring can be minimized if a company gets a credible commitment from its partner.

14. The causes of corporate decline include poor management, overexpansion, inadequate financial controls, high costs, the emergence of powerful new competition, and unforeseen shifts in demand.

15. Responses to corporate decline include changing the leadership, redefining the company's strategic focus, divestment or closure of unwanted assets,

taking steps to improve the profitability of the operations that remain, and occasionally, acquisitions to rebuild core operations.

Discussion Questions

1. When will a company choose related diversification and when unrelated diversification? Discuss with reference to an electronics manufacturer and an ocean shipping company.

2. Why was it profitable for General Motors and Ford to integrate backward into component-parts manufacturing in the past, and why are both companies now trying to buy more of their parts from outside?

3. Under what conditions might concentration on a single business be inconsistent with the goal of maximizing stockholder wealth? Why?

4. General Motors integrated vertically in the 1920s, diversified in the 1930s, and expanded overseas in the 1950s. Explain these developments with reference to the profitability of pursuing each strategy. Why do you think vertical integration is normally the first strategy to be pursued after concentration on a single business?

Endnotes

1. Hope Lampert, "Britons on the Prowl," *The New York Times Magazine*, November 29, 1987, pp. 22–24, 36, 38, 42. Thomas Moore, "Old Line Industry Shapes Up," *Fortune*, April 27, 1987, pp. 23–32, and "Goodbye Corporate Staff," *Fortune*, December 21, 1987, pp. 65–76. Barnaby Feder, "Hanson's Meteoric Rise," *The Wall Street Journal*, July 1989, pp. 1, 38.

2. Alfred D. Chandler, *Strategy and Structure: Chapters in the History of the Industrial Enterprise* (Cambridge, Mass.: MIT Press, 1962).

3. The argument outlined in this section is based on that of G. R. Jones and Charles W. L. Hill, "A Transaction Cost Analysis of Strategy-Structure Choice," *Strategic Management Journal*, 9 (1988), 159–172.

4. For details see Jeffrey R. Williams, Betty Lynn Paez, and Leonard Sanders, "Conglomerates Revisited," *Strategic Management Journal*, 9 (1988), 403–414.

5. Chandler, *Strategy and Structure*.

6. K. R. Harrigan, "Formulating Vertical Integration Strategies," *Academy of Management Review*, 9 (1984), 638–652.

7. This is the essence of Chandler's argument. See his *Strategy and Structure*. The same argument is also made by Jeffrey Pfeffer and Gerald R. Salancik, *The External Control of Organizations* (New York: Harper & Row, 1978). See also K. R. Harrigan, *Strategic Flexibility* (Lexington, Mass.: Lexington Books, 1985); K. R. Harrigan, "Vertical Integration and Corporate Strategy," *Academy of Management Journal*, 28 (1985), 397–425; and F. M. Scherer, *Industrial Market Structure and Economic Performance* (Chicago: Rand McNally, 1981).

8. One interpretation of the dynamics involved in this type of situation can be found in resource dependence models of organizations. See Pfeffer and Salancik, *The External Control of Organizations*, pp. 113–142. Another can be found in transaction cost analysis. See Oliver E. Williamson, *Markets and Hierarchies: Analysis and Antitrust Implications* (New York: Free Press, 1975), pp. 82–131.

9. See "IBM, Clonebuster," *Fortune,* April 27, 1987, p. 225; and "How IBM Hopes to Skin the Copycats," *Business Week,* April 6, 1987, p. 40.

10. Harrigan, *Strategic Flexibility,* pp. 67–87.

11. Standard & Poor's Industry Survey, *Autos–Auto Parts,* April 23, 1987.

12. Ibid.

13. O. E. Williamson, *The Economic Institutions of Capitalism* (New York: Free Press, 1985).

14. This resource-based view of diversification can be traced back to Edith Penrose's seminal book, *The Theory of the Growth of the Firm* (Oxford: Oxford University Press, 1959).

15. See, for example, Jones and Hill, "A Transaction Cost Analysis of Strategy-Structure Choice," pp. 159–172; and Williamson, *Markets and Hierarchies,* pp. 132–175.

16. See Michael E. Porter, "From Competitive Advantage to Corporate Strategy," *Harvard Business Review* (May–June 1987), 43–59.

17. See C. W. L. Hill, M. A. Hitt, and R. E. Hoskisson, "Declining U.S. Competitiveness: Reflections on a Crisis," *Academy of Management Executive,* 2 (February 1988), 51–59.

18. See C. W. L. Hill, "Profile of a Conglomerate Takeover: BTR and Thomas Tilling," *Journal of General Management,* 10 (1984), 34–50.

19. "Rockwell: Using Its Cash Hoard to Edge Away from Defense," *Business Week,* February 4, 1985, pp. 82–84.

20. D. J. Teece, "Economies of Scope and the Scope of the Enterprise," *Journal of Economic Behavior and Organization,* 3 (1980), 223–247.

21. For a detailed discussion, see C. W. L. Hill and R. E. Hoskisson, "Strategy and Structure in the Multiproduct Firm," *Academy of Management Review,* 12 (1987), 331–341.

22. Michael E. Porter, *Competitive Advantage: Creating and Sustaining Superior Performance* (New York: Free Press, 1985), p. 326.

23. Porter, "From Competitive Advantage to Corporate Strategy," pp. 43–59.

24. For a survey of the evidence see V. Ramanujam and P. Varadarajan, "Research on Corporate Diversification: A Synthesis," *Strategic Management Journal,* 10 (1989), 523–551.

25. C. R. Christensen et al., *Business Policy Text and Cases* (Homewood, Ill.: Irwin, 1987), p. 778.

26. For a survey of the evidence, see C. W. L. Hill, "Conglomerate Performance over the Economic Cycle," *Journal of Industrial Economics,* 32 (1983), 197–212; and D. T. C. Mueller, "The Effects of Conglomerate Mergers," *Journal of Banking and Finance,* 1 (1977), 315–347.

27. Michael Brody, "Caught in the Cash Crunch at ITT," *Fortune,* February 18, 1985, pp. 63–72.

28. For example, see C. W. L. Hill, "Diversified Growth and Competition," *Applied Economics,* 17 (1985), 827–847; and R. P. Rumelt, *Strategy, Structure and Economic Performance* (Boston: Harvard Business School Press, 1974).

29. See H. K. Christensen and C. A. Montgomery, "Corporate Economic Performance: Diversification Strategy Versus Market Structure," *Strategic Management Journal,* 2 (1981), 327–343; and Jones and Hill, "A Transaction Cost Analysis of Strategy-Structure Choice," pp. 159–172.

30. See J. Argenti, *Corporate Collapse: Causes and Symptoms* (New York: McGraw-Hill, 1976); R. C. Hoffman, "Strategies for Corporate Turnarounds: What Do We Know About Them?" *Journal of General Management,* 14 (1984), pp. 46–66; D. Schendel, G. R. Patton, and J. Riggs, "Corporate Turnaround Strategies: A Study of Profit Decline and Recovery," *Journal of General Management,* 2 (1976); and S. Siafter, *Corporate Recovery: Successful Turnaround Strategies and Their Implementation* (Harmondsworth, England: Penguin Books, 1984), pp. 25–60.

31. See Siafter, *Corporate Recovery,* pp. 25–60.

32. D. B. Bibeault, *Corporate Turnaround* (New York: McGraw-Hill, 1982).

33. Hoffman, "Strategies for Corporate Turnarounds," pp. 46–66.

34. Lee Iacocca, *Iacocca: An Autobiography* (New York: Bantam Books, 1984), p. 254.

Chapter 8

CORPORATE-LEVEL STRATEGY: THE GLOBAL DIMENSION

8.1 OPENING INCIDENT: THE MEDIA AND ENTERTAINMENT INDUSTRY

One of the biggest mergers of 1989 was between Time Inc., the largest publisher in the United States, and Warner Communications Inc., an entertainment conglomerate. The resulting company, Time Warner Inc., will generate more than $10 billion in annual revenues from a wide range of products and services, including movies, television shows, records, magazines, books, and cable television. The merger promises to make Time Warner the world's biggest media and entertainment company.

The merger was conceived by Time and Warner executives as a response to the rapid globalization of the media and entertainment industry. Many in the industry argue that we are witnessing the development of an integrated global media and entertainment network. In this vision of the future, global citizens will get their news from CNN and their music from MTV and will see worldwide best-selling novels serialized on global television networks. Enterprises that are global in scope will be able to realize significant economies in the costs of developing and running television, film, video, book, and music productions by distributing

them to global audience. Global entertainment organizations will be able to gain a competitive advantage from using the profits generated in one national market to finance expansion in other markets. And they will be better able to take products developed in one nation and sell them in another. At the forefront of globalization in the industry have been a number of foreign media conglomerates, including Germany's Bertelsmann, Britain's Maxwell Communications Corp., and Rupert Murdoch's News Corp. All of these companies have been investing heavily in the United States.

Murdoch, for example, started by building a global empire of low-priced tabloid newspapers that specialized in scandal, gossip, and contests. Then, in 1985, he turned his attention to U.S. motion pictures and television. He began his television empire in 1985, when he bought seven television stations from Metromedia Inc. for $2 billion. In 1986 he added Twentieth Century-Fox Film Corp. for $1.6 billion. As a result, Murdoch can now produce movies and television shows that he can sell or air on Sky Television, his European satellite venture, and on his Fox networks. Moreover, he can publicize his productions in *TV Guide* and *Premiere* magazines, which he also owns. During the same time period, Germany's Bertelsmann made a number of major acquisitions in the United States, including Doubleday and Co. Inc. (a book publisher), and RCA Records. Maxwell Communications Corp. purchased Macmillan Publishing Company. And Sony shocked the U.S. entertainment and media establishment with its acquisition of CBS Records and Columbia Pictures Inc.

Because of these developments, by the late 1980s both Time Inc. and Warner Communications were beginning to look like second-string competitors in their own country, and both feared being squeezed by integrated global competitors. The merger of the two was seen as a way of putting an American company back in the top league of the media industry. Time Warner Inc. promises to deliver significant synergies and have a global reach. In theory, Time Warner can now publish a book, serialize it in a magazine, turn it into a movie, sell the video rights, show the film on Home Box Office, feature the film on Time Warner's cable system, and then put the score on a compact disk. Also, Warner Communications can help Time crack the vast and fast growing overseas market—something that Time has had trouble doing. In 1988, Time generated only 6 percent of its revenues outside the United States. Strong foreign distribution systems helped Warner Communications generate 40 percent of its revenues overseas in 1988.

Whether the merger will live up to its advance billing will not be apparent for a number of years. One thing is clear, however. The merger was forced on Time and Warner Communications by the rapid globalization of the media and entertainment industry.[1]

8.2 OVERVIEW

The United States emerged from the Second World War as the most powerful industrial nation. For the next thirty-five years, U.S. enterprises had things largely their own way. U.S. companies were among the biggest in the world, and U.S. multinationals dominated a wide range of industries in countries around the globe (*multinational companies* are companies that do business in two or more countries). In 1973, for example, 126 of the world's 260 largest multinationals were U.S. enterprises, including 15 of the largest 25 multinationals.[2]

During the 1980s, things began to change rapidly. West German, French, British, Dutch, Italian, South Korean, and Japanese companies began to take an ever greater share of their own domestic markets away from U.S. multinationals. At the same time, they began to challenge U.S. companies in the North American market. Lulled into a false sense of security by years of dominance, U.S. companies all too often proved ill equipped to take on this challenge. As a result, the trade balance, one index of America's competitiveness in the global economy, steadily deteriorated. Until the late 1960s the U.S. generally ran a trade surplus with the rest of the world. Beginning in 1973, however, the trade balance began to dip into the red, and by the 1980s the problem was becoming serious, cumulating in a record $175-billion trade defect in 1986.[3]

As a result of these changes, there has been a growing awareness that a new reality is confronting American business: global competition and global competitors. The Opening Incident describes how this new reality is transforming the structure of the U.S. media and entertainment industry. Similar trends can be observed in a wide range of other industries, from autos and banking to semi-conductor chips and tire manufacturing. Consider semiconductors. In 1975 both of the key global players were U.S. companies: Motorola and Texas Instruments. Now the list of key global players also includes NEC, Fujitsu, Hitachi, and To-shiba. A similar trend has occurred in consumer electronics. In 1975, the key global players were General Electric and RCA, both U.S. enterprises. Now the list of key global players also includes Matsushita, Philips, and Sony.

This chapter describes the strategic choices that confront companies doing business in a global environment. We begin by discussing how global expansion creates value for a company. Next, we look at the different strategies that companies can pursue in the global arena and consider the factors that influence a company's choice of strategies. We consider the various options that a company has for entering a foreign market. We then discuss the motives, benefits, and costs of building global strategic alliances with competitors. The chapter closes with a look at how foreign governments' policies influence global strategy.

8.3 VALUE CREATION

Global expansion involves establishing significant operations and market interests outside a company's home country. Global expansion enables a company to add value in a number of ways not available to domestic enterprises. These arise from the ability of global enterprises to (1) transfer core skills overseas, (2) use global volume to cover product development costs, (3) realize economies of scale from global volume, and (4) configure the company's value chain so that individual value-creation functions are performed in locations where value-added is maximized.

Transferring Core Skills Overseas

The competitive advantage that many multinational companies enjoy over local competitors is based on core technological, marketing, or management skills and know-how that local competitors lack. These skills typically allow a multinational to perform one or more value-creation functions in a way that leads to differentiation and a premium price. For these multinationals, global expansion is a way of earning greater returns from their existing skills and know-how by expanding the size of their potential market. It is a way of exploiting the profit potential that their skills represent.

IBM, Xerox, and Kodak, for example, all profited from the transfer overseas of their core skills in technology and R&D. Those skills have enabled these companies to charge a premium price. Marketing skills have formed the basis of global competitive advantage for other multinationals. The overseas success of U.S. multinationals like Kellogg, Coca-Cola, H. J. Heinz, and Procter & Gamble is based more on marketing know-how than on technological know-how. Still other multinationals have based their competitive advantage over local competitors on general management skills. Such an advantage may arise from better trained or educated managers, a superior organizational structure, and more sophisticated management techniques in areas such as finance. Such factors explain the growth of international hotel chains such as Hilton International, Intercontinental, and Sheraton.

Using Global Volume to Cover Product Development Costs

Were it not for global markets, some companies would have great difficulty recouping their investment in new product development. For example, it costs pharmaceutical companies anywhere from $50 million to $150 million to put a new drug on the market. To recoup this expenditure, pharmaceutical companies need global markets; the U.S. market alone is too small. Similarly, without global markets, aircraft manufacturers like Boeing would probably be unable to cover the billions of dollars of development costs necessary to produce a new aircraft. Thus global markets may be necessary to reap the full value of investment in product development. Put another way, selling a new product to the global market allows a multinational company to spread the fixed costs of new product development over greater sales volume, thereby lowering the relative cost of investments in R&D—that is, thereby lowering the relative cost of the R&D function of the value chain.

Realizing Economies of Scale from Global Volume

By offering a standardized product to the global marketplace and by manufacturing that product in a single location or in a few choice locations, a global company can reap from its global volume scale economies that are not available to smaller domestic enterprises. By lowering the costs of value creation, these scale economies can assist a company in becoming a low-cost player in the global industry. Thus global expansion may be consistent with the generic business-level strategy of cost leadership.

For example, by using centralized manufacturing facilities and global marketing strategies, Sony was able to become the low-cost player in the global television market. Thus Sony was able to take market share in the global television market away from competitors such as Philips N.V., RCA, and Zenith, all of whom traditionally based manufacturing operations in each of their major markets and therefore lacked scale economies similar to Sony's. Similarly, Japanese manufacturers of electronic components, such as NEC Corporation, are beginning to dominate the global market, primarily because their huge global volume for a standardized product has enabled them to ride down the experience curve and gain significant cost economies over their rivals.

Configuring the Global Value Chain

The costs of factors of production, such as labor, energy, and raw material inputs, vary from country to country. The availability of certain skills, particularly skilled labor, can also vary from country to country. One way to increase value-added is to perform different value-creation functions in the locations where the mix of factor costs and skills is most favorable. By doing so, a company may be able to lower the costs of value creation and perform key value-creation functions in a way that results in greater differentiation and a premium price.

For example, consider manufacturing operations. The main factors determining the most favorable locations for global manufacturing are (1) labor costs, (2) energy costs, (3) access to a work force with appropriate skills, (4) access to the necessary infrastructure (such as roads, rail networks, and favorable political climate), and (5) proximity to important global markets (particularly when transport costs are high). After considering such issues, in the late 1980s European subsidiaries of Ford and General Motors began shifting much of their European auto production from West Germany to Great Britain because labor costs in Britain were 45 percent less than those in West Germany and productivity gains among British auto workers had been averaging 10 to 12 percent annually, against 8 percent in West Germany.[4] In short, GM and Ford were moving their operations from a high-cost, high-skill location to a low-cost, high-skill location in order to lower the costs of value creation. Similarly, Volkswagen has recently shifted production of its low-priced Polos from Wolfsburg, Germany, to Spain, where labor costs are lower. This move has enabled Volkswagen to lower the costs of manufacturing Polos. At the same time, the strategy has freed high-wage, high-skilled German labor to concentrate on the production of higher-priced Golf cars. By using high-skilled labor to produce Golf cars, Volkswagen has maintained the high quality of the Golf, which in turn allows the company to achieve greater differentiation and charge a higher price.[5]

8.4 COMPARING GLOBAL AND MULTIDOMESTIC STRATEGIES

One of the major strategic choices faced by multinational companies is whether to pursue a *global strategy* or a *multidomestic strategy*.[6] The differences between the pure versions of these two strategies are summarized in Table 8.1. A multidomestic strategy—the time-honored way in which global companies compete—is based on the assumption that national markets differ widely in consumer tastes

TABLE 8.1   **Dimensions of global and multidomestic strategies**

Dimensions	Pure multidomestic strategy	Pure global strategy
Product offering	Fully customized to each country	Fully standardized worldwide
Manufacturing	Manufacturing in each country	Manufacturing based where the factor-cost/skill mix is most favorable
Marketing	Locally determined	Centrally determined
Competitive strategy	Responsibility of national subsidiaries	Integrated across countries and centrally directed

and preferences, competitive conditions, operating conditions, and political, legal, and social structures. To deal with these differences, multidomestic companies decentralize manufacturing, marketing, and strategic decisions to national subsidiaries. Thus each national subsidiary has its own marketing function and its own manufacturing facilities. The attributes of the product vary among nations according to the tastes and preferences of local consumers, and the managers in each country decide on business-level strategy without regard for what happens in other countries.

In contrast, a pure global strategy is based on the assumption that between countries there are no tangible differences in consumer tastes and preferences. This working assumption enables a multinational company to market a standardized product to the global marketplace and to manufacture that product in a limited number of locations where the mix of factor costs and skills is most favorable so that the company can realize significant scale economies from its global volume. For example, Levi 501 blue jeans are sold as a standardized product the world over and are manufactured in a few choice locations where the mix of factor costs and skills is most advantageous. Thus Levi Strauss & Co. manufactures in Scotland most of its blue jeans sold in Western Europe, primarily because Scotland offers a relatively low-cost skilled labor force, generous government subsidies, and access to the major markets of the European Community.

In addition, companies pursuing a pure global strategy can integrate competitive moves across countries, using the profits generated in one country to support competitive attacks in another. Frequently a competitor is attacked in one country in order to drain its resources from another. For example, when Fuji Photo Film Co. began cutting deep inroads into Kodak's home market, Kodak launched powerful counterattacks in Fuji's home market, cutting the prices at which its Japanese subsidiary sold film. The result was that Kodak checked Fuji's invasion of the U.S. market by keeping Fuji busy defending its home market.

Both strategies have advantages and disadvantages, which are discussed below. The factors that determine which strategy a company should pursue are discussed in Section 8.5.

The Advantages and Disadvantages of a Pure Global Strategy

Pure global companies are able to create value in all of the ways discussed earlier. They can transfer core skills between nations to enhance value-added. They can spread the fixed costs of new product development over their global volume. They can realize scale economies by serving the global marketplace from centralized manufacturing facilities. They can site their manufacturing facilities in locations where the mix of factor costs and skills is most favorable. Above all else, the ability to realize cost economies from integrated global manufacturing suggests that a pure global strategy is most consistent with the generic business-level strategy of cost leadership. In addition, as noted above, companies pursuing a pure global strategy have the advantage of being able to coordinate competitive moves across countries. Thus they can use the profits generated in one country to support competitive attacks in another.

On the other hand, because they manufacture a standardized global product, companies pursuing a pure global strategy have to give up a certain degree of responsiveness to different national conditions. This surrender can give rise to significant disadvantages and can be very damaging. In particular, the result of attempts to lower costs through global product standardization can be a product that does not entirely satisfy anyone. For example, Procter & Gamble stumbled when it tried to introduce its Cheer laundry detergent into Japan without changing the U.S. product or marketing message (which was that the detergent was effective in water of all temperatures). In Japan, Cheer was a failure for a couple of reasons. Because the Japanese use a great deal of fabric softener, it did not make enough suds. Because the Japanese usually wash clothes in cold water, the claim that Cheer works in all temperatures was irrelevant.

Often overlooked by those who enthusiastically advocate global strategies are the organizational problems that arise from the effort to achieve coordination between national subsidiaries. A pure global strategy can give rise to significant bureaucratic costs because of the increased coordination, reporting requirements, and even the added staff that such a strategy requires. Moreover, companies pursuing a global strategy have to wrestle with the difficult issue of how to price transfers of goods and services between components of the company's value chain based in different countries. Transfer pricing problems are difficult enough to resolve within just one country. In the context of a global company, identifying the appropriate transfer price can be further complicated by volatile exchange rates.

The Advantages and Disadvantages
of a Pure Multidomestic Strategy

A pure multidomestic strategy explicitly recognizes differences among nations. That is its principal advantage. The strategy can assist a company in tailoring its products and business-level strategy to the unique conditions in each country. The central idea is to customize a product to different national requirements. Thus the extent of product differentiation may vary from country to country, depending on the tastes and preferences of consumers in each country.

Another advantage is that a pure multidomestic strategy raises far fewer difficult organizational issues than does a pure global strategy. Within multidomestic companies, the need for coordination is lower than it is within global companies. Most national subsidiaries can be managed on an arm's-length basis with relatively little input from world corporate headquarters. Also, since each national subsidiary is essentially a self-contained unit, there are few transfers of goods and services between subsidiaries. Thus the transfer pricing problem is far less complicated in multidomestic companies than in global companies. In sum, the bureaucratic costs of implementing a pure multidomestic strategy are far lower than the bureaucratic costs of implementing a pure global strategy.

A major disadvantage of a pure multidomestic strategy is that a multidomestic company has fewer ways than a global company to create value. A multidomestic company can transfer core skills between its international operations. In addition, a multidomestic company may be able to spread the fixed costs of new product development over its global volume (although the scope for doing this is limited by the need to customize a product to the unique conditions of each national market). However, by definition, a company pursuing a pure multidomestic strategy lacks the ability to realize scale economies from centralizing manufacturing facilities and offering a standardized product to the global marketplace. Moreover, because manufacturing and marketing functions are based in each country, pure multidomestic companies are unable to configure the global value chain so that different value-creation functions are performed in locations where the mix of factor costs and skills is most favorable. For these reasons, the manufacturing costs of companies pursuing a pure multidomestic strategy are likely to be significantly higher than those of a company pursuing global strategy.

In addition, because a company pursuing a pure multidomestic strategy decentralizes business-level strategy decisions to each national subsidiary, it lacks the ability to launch coordinated global attacks against subsidiaries' competitors. This can constitute a significant disadvantage for a company facing multinational competitors that have this ability.

Tradeoffs

The foregoing discussion suggests that a number of important tradeoffs are involved in the choice between a pure global and a pure multidomestic strategy.

TABLE 8.2   **Advantages and disadvantages of multidomestic and global strategies**

	Manufacturing costs	Bureaucratic costs	Strategic coordination	Consumer responsiveness
Multidomestic strategy	High	Low	Low	High
Global strategy	Low	High	High	Low

The issues are summarized in Table 8.2. As the table shows, although companies pursuing a pure global strategy have the advantage of low manufacturing costs and a high level of strategic coordination between countries, they have the disadvantages of high bureaucratic costs and a lack of responsiveness to the needs of consumers in different countries. Alternatively, although companies pursuing a pure multidomestic strategy have the advantage of low bureaucratic costs and a high level of responsiveness to the needs of consumers in different countries, they have the disadvantage of high manufacturing costs and a low level of strategic coordination between countries.

8.5 CHOOSING BETWEEN GLOBAL AND MULTIDOMESTIC STRATEGIES

Given the tradeoffs, which strategy should a multinational company choose? According to C. K. Prahalad and Yves L. Doz, the answer can be gleaned from a comparison of *pressures for global integration* and *pressures for local responsiveness*.[8] When the pressures for global integration are high and the pressures for local responsiveness are low, a company should choose a pure global strategy. When the pressures for global integration are low and the pressures for local responsiveness are high, a company should choose a pure multidomestic strategy. Of course, in practice companies often face high pressures for both global integration and local responsiveness. In such circumstances the appropriate strategic response may require a hybrid strategy that mixes elements of global and multidomestic strategies. This response is discussed later in the chapter. First, however, we discuss the factors that create pressures for global integration and local responsiveness.

Pressures for Global Integration

Pressures for global integration arise from (1) the need for cost reduction, (2) the existence of universal needs, and (3) global strategic coordination by competitors.

Need for cost reduction   The global integration of manufacturing is often a response to competitive pressures for cost reduction. Cost reduction can be of particular importance in industries producing commodity-type products where differentiation is difficult, price is the main competitive weapon, and competition is intense. Examples include hand-held calculators and semiconductor chips. Cost reduction is also important in industries where key international competitors are based in countries that have low factor costs—for example, low labor and energy costs. The need to configure the value chain in order to supply the product from low-factor-cost locations or to exploit economies of scale from global volume can drive a company toward a global strategy. This is what happened to the Dutch multinational Philips N.V. Long a multidomestic company, Philips switched to a global strategy after seeing much of its global market share in televisions being taken by Sony during the 1970s. Similarly, Britain's Imperial Chemical Industries, one of the world's largest chemical companies, switched from a multidomestic strategy to a global strategy in 1983 in direct response to cost pressures arising from a severe recession in the global chemical business. The continuing emergence of low-cost competitors based in newly industrialized countries such as South Korea is likely to make cost considerations even more important in the future.

Universal needs   The existence of universal needs creates strong pressures for a global strategy. Universal needs exist when the tastes and preferences of consumers in different countries are very similar if not identical. Products that serve universal needs require little adaptation across national markets. In such circumstances, global integration is obviously facilitated. This is clearly the case in many industrial markets. Electronic products such as capacitors, resistors, and semiconductor chips are good examples of products that meet universal needs.

Harvard Business School professor Theodore Levitt has taken this point farther than most. Levitt argues that many consumer goods markets are becoming characterized by universal needs.[9] According to Levitt, modern communications and transport technologies have created the conditions for a convergence of the tastes and preferences of consumers from different nations. The result is the emergence of enormous global markets for standardized consumer products. Levitt cites worldwide acceptance of McDonald's hamburgers, Coca-Cola, Levi Strauss blue jeans, and Sony television sets, all of which are sold as standardized products, as evidence of the increasing homogeneity of the global marketplace.

Levitt's argument, however, has been characterized as extreme by many commentators.[10] For example, Christopher Bartlett of Harvard Business School and Sumantra Ghoshal of INSEAD, a French business school, have observed that in the consumer electronics industry consumers reacted to an overdose of standardized global products by showing a renewed preference for differentiated products. They note that Amstrad, the fast-growing British computer and electronics company, got its start by recognizing and responding to local consumer need. Amstrad captured a major share of the British audio market by moving away from the standardized inexpensive music centers marketed by global companies such as Sony and Matsushita. Amstrad's product was encased in teak rather than in metal cabinets and had a control panel tailor-made to appeal to British consumers. In response, Matsushita had to reverse its bias toward standardized global design and place more emphasis on product differentiation. From fifteen models in its portable audio product range in 1980, the company increased the line to thirty in 1985.

Global strategic coordination by competitors   The presence of competitors engaged in global strategic coordination creates pressures for global integration. As noted earlier, to gain market share, global companies can use profits generated in one market to subsidize prices in other markets. This strategy enables them to move down the experience curve, realize greater cost economies, and thus increase long-run profits. This is what Canon, Hitachi, and Seiko did in order to build global market share. Reacting to such threats calls for global strategic coordination and thus creates pressures to centralize at corporate headquarters decisions about the competitive strategy of different national subsidiaries. Thus, when one multinational company in an industry adopts global strategic coordination, its competitors may be forced to respond in kind, lest they lose out.[11]

An example of this phenomenon occurred in the tire industry during the 1970s. At that time the world tire market was dominated by three multinationals: Michelin Tire Corporation, Goodyear, and Firestone Tire & Rubber. Each of these companies pursued a multidomestic strategy, thus decentralizing manufacturing, marketing, and competitive strategy to various national subsidiaries around the globe. In the early 1970s, Michelin used its strong European profits to attack Goodyear's North American home market. Goodyear could have retaliated by cutting its North American prices. However, Michelin was exposing only a small amount of its worldwide business in North America and had little to lose from a North American price war. Goodyear, in contrast, saw a major threat to profits in its largest market and struck back by cutting prices and expanding its operations in Europe. The action forced Michelin to slow its attack on Goodyear's North American market and to think again about the costs of taking market share away from Goodyear. Michelin's decision to engage in global strategic coordination forced Goodyear to respond in kind. The result was an increase in pressures for global integration in the tire industry.[12]

Pressures for Local Responsiveness

Pressures for local responsiveness arise from (1) differences in consumer tastes and preferences, (2) differences in infrastructure and in traditional practices, (3) differences in distribution channels, and (4) host-government demands.

Differences in consumer tastes and preferences   Strong pressures for local responsiveness emerge when consumer tastes and preferences differ significantly between countries. In such cases, product and marketing messages have to be customized to appeal to local consumers. Customizing typically creates pressures for the delegation of manufacturing and marketing functions to national subsidiaries. In the automobile industry, for example, there is a strong demand among individual North American consumers for pickup trucks, especially in the South and West, where many families have a pickup truck as a second or third car. In contrast, in European countries pickup trucks are seen purely as utility vehicles and are purchased primarily by companies rather than by individuals. Thus marketing messages must take into account the different nature of demand in North America and Europe.

Also in the automobile industry, Nissan has found that it has had to develop "lead country" models—products carefully tailored to the dominant and distinctive needs of individual national markets. In the United States, Nissan decided that it needed a sporty "Z" model as well as a four-wheel-drive family vehicle to serve strong consumer preferences. Neither model is in great demand in Japan and Europe. Thus Nissan sells about 5,000 "Z" cars a month in the United States but only 500 a month in Japan.[13]

Differences in infrastructure and in traditional practices   Pressures for local responsiveness emerge when there are differences in infrastructure and in traditional practices between countries. In such circumstances, a product may need to be customized to the distinctive infrastructures and practices of different nations. This customizing may necessitate the delegation of manufacturing and marketing functions to foreign subsidiaries. For example, in North America consumer electrical systems are based on 110 volts, but in some European countries 240-volt systems are standard. Thus domestic electrical appliances have to be customized to take this difference in infrastructure into account. Traditional practices often vary across nations. For example, in Britain people drive on the left-hand side of the road, thus creating a demand for right-hand-drive cars, whereas in France people drive on the right-hand side of the road, thus creating a demand for left-hand-drive cars. Automobiles have to be customized to take this difference in traditional practices into account.

Differences in distribution channels   A company's marketing strategies may have to be responsive to international differences in distribution channels. Such differences may necessitate the delegation of marketing functions to national subsidiaries. In laundry detergents, for example, five retail chains control 65 percent of the market in Germany, but no chain controls more than 2 percent of the market in neighboring Italy. Thus retail chains have considerable buying power in Germany but relatively little in Italy. Dealing with these differences requires detergent companies to use different marketing approaches. Similarly, in the pharmaceutical industry the Japanese distribution system is radically different from the U.S. system. Japanese doctors do not accept or else respond unfavorably to an American-style high-pressure sales force. Thus pharmaceutical companies have to adopt different marketing practices in Japan and the United States (soft sell versus hard sell).

Host-government demands   The term *host country* is used to signify a foreign country in which a multinational is doing business. Economic and political demands imposed by host-country governments may necessitate a degree of local responsiveness. For example, the politics of health care around the world requires that pharmaceutical companies manufacture in multiple locations. Pharmaceutical companies are subject to local clinical testing, registration procedures, and pricing restrictions, all of which require the manufacturing and marketing of a drug to meet local requirements. Moreover, since governments and government agencies control a significant proportion of the health-care budget in most countries, they are in a powerful position and can demand a high level of local responsiveness. More generally, threats of protectionism, economic nationalism, and local content rules (which require a certain percentage of a product to be manufactured locally) all dictate that multinational companies manufacture locally. Part of the motivation for Japanese auto companies setting up U.S. pro-

FIGURE 8.1   **Pressures for global integration and local responsiveness: the integration-responsiveness grid**

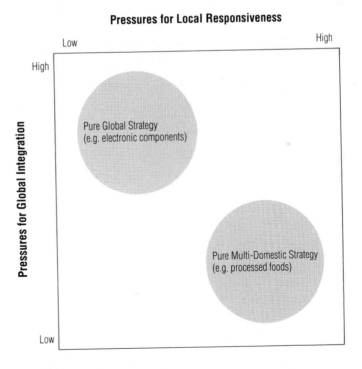

Source: Adapted by permission of The Free Press, a division of Macmillan Publishing Company, Inc. from Figure 2.1, p. 24 in *The Multinational Mission* by C.K. Prahalad and Yves L. Doz. Copyright © 1987 by The Free Press, a division of Macmillan Publishing Company, Inc.

duction operations, for example, is to counter the threat of protectionism that is being increasingly voiced by Congress.

Choosing a Strategy

What is the best strategy for a company to pursue? The answer depends on a consideration and balancing of the various factors discussed above. One way to identify which strategy is best is to plot a company's position on an integration-responsiveness grid similar to the one shown in Figure 8.1.[14] The vertical dimension of this grid measures pressures for global integration; the horizontal dimension measures pressures for local responsiveness. A pure global strategy is appropriate when the pressures for global integration are high and the pressures for local responsiveness are low. This is the case in the electronic components industry. Obviously, in such cases a company should pursue a global strategy. A pure multidomestic strategy is appropriate when the pressures for global integration are low and the pressures for local responsiveness are high. This is the case in the processed-foods and cookware industries. Obviously, in such cases a company should pursue a pure multidomestic strategy.

FIGURE 8.2a   **Pressures for global integration and local responsiveness in the television industry**

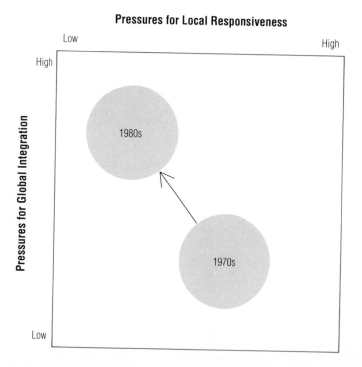

For many companies, however, the issue is not so clear-cut. Two factors complicate the picture. First, the relative importance of pressures for global integration and local responsiveness may change through time, necessitating a change in strategy. In the television industry, for example, the advent of low-cost global manufacturers such as Sony in the 1970s increased the importance of global integration for other companies in the industry (see Figure 8.2a). Thus, in order to compete on a cost basis with Sony, companies like Philips were forced to switch from a multidomestic strategy to a global strategy.

Nevertheless, despite all the talk of increasing globalization, it would be wrong to view this as the only kind of change. In some industries the need for local responsiveness has increased in recent years. As discussed earlier, in the audio market Amstrad's success in focusing on local needs increased pressures for local responsiveness in the industry (see Figure 8.2b). In particular, in an attempt to recover market share from Amstrad, competitors such as Matsushita moved away from a pure global strategy and incorporated more multidomestic elements in their strategic posture. Similarly, some researchers have reported a marked shift toward greater local responsiveness in the prepared-food industry between 1973 and 1983 (see Figure 8.2c).

FIGURE 8.2b   **Pressures for global integration and local responsiveness in the audio products industry**

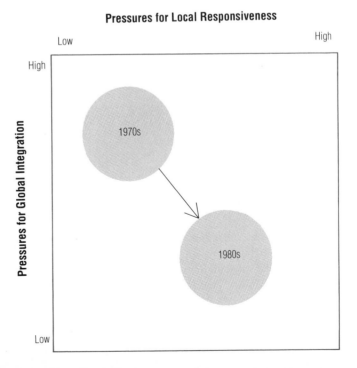

FIGURE 8.2c   Pressures for global integration and local responsiveness in the prepared foods industry

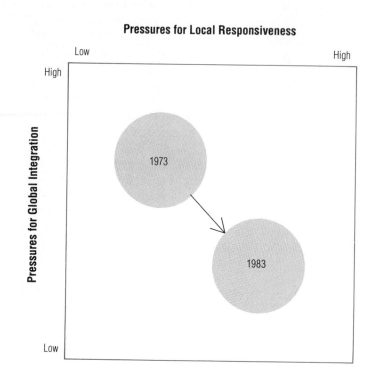

The second complicating factor is that most companies do not fall into the upper-right or lower-left corner of the integration-responsiveness grid. Indeed, it is possible for companies to be positioned anywhere on the grid. Thus some companies may have to balance conflicting demands for global integration and for local responsiveness.

8.6 THE TRANSNATIONAL COMPANY

Christopher Bartlett and Sumantra Ghoshal coined the term *transnational company* to describe companies that face pressures for both global integration and local responsiveness.[15] The strategy often adopted by such companies is neither a pure multidomestic strategy nor a pure global strategy. Rather, they combine elements of both strategies in a hybrid known as a *transnational strategy*. According to Bartlett and Ghoshal, in practice many multinational companies must simultaneously deal with demands for global integration and for local responsiveness and thus must pursue transnational strategies.

Caterpillar Tractor is a good example of a transnational company.[16] The need to compete with low-cost competitors such as Komatsu forced Caterpillar to look for greater cost economies by centralizing global production at locations where the factor-cost/skill mix was most favorable. At the same time, variations in construction practices and government regulations across countries mean that Caterpillar has to be responsive to local needs. On the integration-responsiveness grid, therefore, Caterpillar is situated toward the top right corner (see Figure 8.3).

To deal with these simultaneous demands, Caterpillar has designed its products to use many identical components and invested in a few large-scale component-manufacturing facilities to fill global demand and realize scale economies. At the same time the company augments the centralized manufacturing of components with assembly plants in each of its major global markets. At these plants, Caterpillar adds local product features, tailoring the finished product to local needs. Thus Caterpillar is able to realize many of the benefits of global manufacturing while at the same time responding to pressures for local responsiveness by differentiating its product among national markets.

Achieving a balance between the demands of global integration and local responsiveness raises difficult and complex implementation issues. Organizational

FIGURE 8.3 **Caterpillar's position on the integration-responsiveness grid**

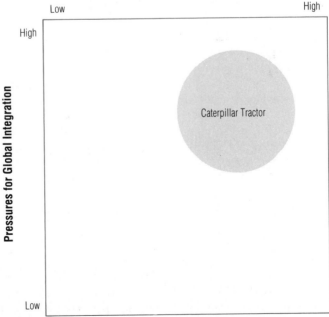

structures that are supportive of (1) collaborative information sharing and problem solving, (2) cooperative support and resource sharing, and (3) collective action among product, geographical, and functional management must be developed. To achieve this without developing a stultifying bureaucracy, companies need managers who understand the need for multiple strategic capabilities, who are able to view problems simultaneously from both local and global perspectives.

8.7 THE CHOICE OF ENTRY MODE

What is the best means of achieving global expansion? There are basically five different ways of entering an overseas market: (1) exporting, (2) licensing, (3) franchising, (4) entering into a joint venture with a host country company, and (5) setting up a wholly owned subsidiary in the host country. Each entry mode has advantages and disadvantages that strategic managers need to consider carefully.[17]

Exporting

Most manufacturing companies begin their global expansion as exporters and only later switch to one of the other modes for serving a foreign market. Exporting does have two distinct advantages. First, exporting avoids the costs of having to establish manufacturing operations in the host country. Since these costs are often substantial, this is not a trivial advantage. Second, exporting is consistent with a pure global strategy. By manufacturing the product in a centralized location and then exporting it to other national markets, a company may be able to realize substantial scale economies from its global sales volume. This is how Sony came to dominate the global television market and how many of the Japanese auto companies originally made inroads into the U.S. auto market.

On the other hand, there are a number of drawbacks to exporting. First, exporting from the company's *home* base may not be appropriate if there are lower-cost locations for manufacturing the product abroad. Thus, particularly for a company pursuing a pure global strategy, it may pay to manufacture in a location where the mix of factor costs and skills is most favorable and then export from that location to the rest of the globe in order to achieve scale economies. This, of course, is not so much an argument against exporting as an argument against exporting from a company's *home* country. Many U.S. electronics companies have moved some of their manufacturing to the Far East because of the availability of low-cost, high-skilled labor. They then export from that location to the rest of the globe, including the United States.

A second drawback to exporting is that high transport costs can make exporting uneconomical, particularly in the case of bulk products. One way of getting around this problem is to manufacture bulk products on a regional basis. This strategy enables a company to realize some economies from large-scale production while at the same time limiting the transport costs that it has to bear. Many multinational chemical companies manufacture their products on a regional basis, serving several countries in a region from one facility.

A third drawback to exporting is that tariff barriers can make the strategy uneconomical. Similarly, the threat to impose tariff barriers by the government of a host country can make the strategy very risky. Indeed, the implicit threat from Congress to impose tariff barriers on Japanese autos imported into the United States led directly to the decision by many Japanese auto companies to set up manufacturing plants in the United States. As a consequence of this trend, by 1990 almost 50 percent of all Japanese cars sold in the United States were manufactured locally, up from 0 percent in 1985.

A fourth drawback to exporting arises when a company delegates marketing activities to a local agent in each country in which it does business. This practice is common among companies that are just beginning to export. Unfortunately, there is no guarantee that a foreign agent will act in a company's best interest. Foreign agents often carry the products of competing companies and as a result have divided loyalties. Thus a foreign agent may not do as good a job as the company would do if it managed marketing itself. There are ways around this problem, however. One solution is to set up a wholly owned subsidiary in the host country to handle local marketing. By doing this, a company can reap the cost advantages that arise from manufacturing the product in a single location and simultaneously exercise tight control over marketing strategy in the host country.

Licensing

International licensing is an arrangement whereby a foreign licensee buys the rights to manufacture a company's product in the licensee's country for a negotiated fee (normally, royalty payments on the number of units sold). The licensee then puts up most of the capital necessary to get the overseas operation going. The advantage of licensing is that a company does not have to bear the development costs and risks associated with opening up a foreign market. This can make licensing a very attractive option for companies that lack the capital to develop operations overseas. In addition, licensing may be an attractive option for companies that are unwilling to commit substantial financial resources to an unfamiliar or politically volatile foreign market.

On the other hand, there are two serious drawbacks to licensing. First, licensing does not give the tight control over manufacturing, marketing, and strategic functions in foreign countries that is required if a company is going to pursue a global strategy. Typically, each licensee sets up its own manufacturing operations. This severely limits the ability of the company to realize economies of scale by manufacturing its product in a centralized location. Thus, when economies of scale are likely to be important, licensing may not be the best way of expanding overseas. In addition, pursuing a global strategy may require a company to coordinate strategic moves across countries so that the profits earned in one country can be used to respond to competitive attacks in another. Licensing, by its very nature, severely limits the ability of a company to do this. A licensee will not let a multinational company take its profits (beyond those due in the form of royalty payments) and use them to support an entirely different licensee operating in another country.

A second problem with licensing arises when a company licenses its technological know-how to foreign companies. Technological know-how constitutes the basis of the competitive advantage of many multinational companies. Most companies wish to maintain control over the use to which their technology is put. By licensing its technology, a company can quickly lose control over it. Many companies have made the mistake of thinking that they could maintain control over their know-how within the framework of a licensing agreement. Unfortunately, this has often proved not to be the case. For example, RCA once licensed its color television technology to a number of Japanese companies. The Japanese companies quickly assimilated RCA's technology and then used it to enter the U.S. market. Now the Japanese have a bigger share of the U.S. market than the RCA brand does. Similar concerns are now surfacing over the 1989 decision by Congress to allow Japanese companies to produce the advanced FSX fighter under license from McDonnell Douglas. Critics of this decision fear that the Japanese will use the FSX technology to support the development of a commercial airline industry that will compete with Boeing and McDonnell Douglas in the global marketplace.

Franchising

In many respects franchising is similar to licensing. However, whereas licensing is a strategy pursued primarily by manufacturing companies, franchising is a strategy employed primarily by service companies. Both McDonald's and Hilton International, for example, have expanded overseas by franchising. In the case of franchising, a company (the franchiser) sells limited rights to use its brand name to franchisees in return for a lump-sum payment and a share of the franchisee's profits. However, unlike the parties to most licensing agreements, the franchisee agrees to abide by strict rules defining how it does business. Thus, when McDonald's enters into a franchising agreement with a foreign company, it expects that company to run its restaurants in the same way that McDonald's restaurants elsewhere in the world are run.

The advantages of franchising as an entry mode are similar to those of licensing. Specifically, a franchiser does not have to bear the development costs and risks associated with opening up a foreign market on its own. The franchisee typically assumes those costs and risks. Thus, using a franchising strategy, a service company can build up a global presence quickly and at a low cost.

The disadvantages are less pronounced than in the case of licensing. Since franchising is a strategy used by service companies, a franchiser does not have to consider the need to coordinate manufacturing in order to achieve economies of scale. Nevertheless, franchising may inhibit the ability of a company to achieve global strategic coordination.

A more significant disadvantage of franchising concerns quality control. The foundation of franchising arrangements is the notion that a company's brand name conveys a message to consumers about the quality of the company's product. Thus a business traveler booking into a Hilton International hotel in Hong Kong can reasonably expect the same quality of room, food, and service as she or he would receive in New York. The Hilton brand name is a guarantee of the consistency of product quality. Foreign franchisees, however, may not be as concerned about quality as they should be, and the result of poor quality can go beyond lost sales in the foreign market to include a decline in a company's worldwide reputation. For example, a business traveler who has a bad experience at the Hilton in Hong Kong may never go to another Hilton hotel and urge colleagues to do likewise. The geographical distance of a franchiser from its foreign franchisees, however, makes poor quality control difficult to detect. In addition, the sheer number of individual franchisees, which in the case of McDonald's runs into the tens of thousands, can make the detection of poor quality difficult. Because of these factors, quality problems may persist.

One way around this disadvantage is to set up a subsidiary in each country or region in which a company expands. The subsidiary might be wholly owned by the company, or it might be a joint venture with a foreign company. The subsidiary assumes the rights and obligations to establish franchisees throughout that particular country or region. The combination of close proximity and the limited number of independent franchisees that have to be monitored reduces the quality-control problem. In addition, because the subsidiary is at least partly owned by the company, the company can place its own managers in the subsidiary to ensure that it does a good job of monitoring the quality of franchisees within the country or region for which it is responsible. This organizational arrangement has proved very popular in practice and is being used by McDonald's, Kentucky Fried Chicken, Hilton International, and other companies to expand international operations.

Joint Ventures

Establishing a joint venture with a foreign company has long been a popular way to enter a new market. Joint ventures have a number of advantages. First, a multinational may feel that it can benefit from a local partner's knowledge of a host country's competitive conditions, culture, language, political systems, and business systems. Thus for many U.S. companies, joint ventures have involved the American company providing technological know-how and products and the local partner providing the marketing expertise and local knowledge necessary to compete within the country. Second, when the development costs and risks of opening up a foreign market are high, a company might gain by sharing these costs and risks with a local partner. Third, in many countries political considerations make joint ventures the only feasible entry mode. For example, historically many U.S. companies found it much easier to get permission to set up operations in Japan if they went in with a Japanese partner than if they tried to enter on their own (Texas Instruments and IBM have been notable exceptions to this rule.) Furthermore, research suggests that joint ventures with local partners experience a low risk of nationalization, apparently because local equity partners, who may have some influence on host-government policy, have a vested interest in speaking out against nationalization.[18]

There are two major disadvantages to joint ventures. First, as in the case of licensing, a company that enters into a joint venture runs the risk of losing control over its technology to its venture partner. For example, the joint venture between Boeing and a consortium of Japanese companies to build the 767 commercial jetliner raised fears that Boeing was unwittingly giving away its commercial airline technology to the Japanese. (Ways of constructing joint-venture agreements to minimize this risk are discussed in Section 8.8 on global strategic alliances.)

A second disadvantage is that a joint venture does not give a company the tight control over different subsidiaries that it might need if it wishes to pursue a global strategy. Consider the entry of Texas Instruments (TI) into the Japanese semiconductor market. When TI established semiconductor facilities in Japan, it did so for the sole purpose of checking the market share of Japanese manufacturers and limiting the amount of cash available to them to invade TI's global market. In other words, TI was engaging in global strategic coordination. To implement this strategy, TI's Japanese subsidiary had to be prepared to take instructions from TI's corporate headquarters regarding competitive strategy. The strategy also required the Japanese subsidiary to be run at a loss if necessary. Clearly, a Japanese joint-venture partner would have been unlikely to accept such conditions because they would have meant a negative return on investment. Thus, in order to implement this strategy, TI set up a wholly owned subsidiary in Japan rather than entering by means of a joint venture.

Wholly Owned Subsidiaries

Establishing a wholly owned subsidiary is generally the most costly method of serving a foreign market. Companies doing this have to bear the full costs and risks associated with setting up overseas operations (in contrast with joint ventures, where the costs and risks are shared, or licensing, where the licensee bears most of the costs and risks). Despite this considerable disadvantage, however, two clear advantages are associated with setting up a wholly owned subsidiary.

First, when a company's competitive advantage is based on control over a technological competence, a wholly owned subsidiary is normally the preferred entry mode because it reduces the risk of losing control over that competence.

For this reason, many high-tech companies prefer to set up wholly owned subsidiaries overseas rather than enter into joint ventures or licensing arrangements. Thus wholly owned subsidiaries tend to be the favored entry mode in the semiconductor, electronics, and pharmaceutical industries.

Second, a wholly owned subsidiary gives a company the kind of tight control over operations in different countries that is necessary if a company is going to pursue a global strategy. When the pressures for global integration are high, it may pay a company to configure its value chain in such a way that value-added at each stage is maximized. Thus a national subsidiary may specialize in manufacturing only part of the product line or certain components of the end product, exchanging parts and products with other subsidiaries in the company's global system. Establishing such a global manufacturing system necessarily requires a high degree of *control* over the operations of national affiliates. Different national operations have to be prepared to accept centrally determined decisions about how they should produce, how much they should produce, and how their output should be priced for transfer between operations. Licensees or joint-venture partners are unlikely to accept such a subservient role.

Choosing Between Entry Modes

As the preceding discussion demonstrates, both advantages and disadvantages are associated with the different entry modes. They are summarized in Table 8.3. Inevitably, because of these advantages and disadvantages, tradeoffs affect the choice of an entry mode. For example, when considering entry into an unfamiliar country with a track record for nationalizing foreign-owned enterprises, a company might favor a joint venture with a local enterprise. Its rationale might be that the local partner will help it to establish operations in an unfamiliar environment and will speak out against nationalization if the possibility arises. However, if the company's distinctive competence is based on proprietary technology, entering into a joint venture would mean running a risk of losing control over that technology.

Given such tradeoffs, making hard and fast recommendations about what a company should do is difficult. However, a number of rough generalizations can be made. First, if a company's competitive advantage is based on control over proprietary technology, licensing and joint-venture arrangements should be avoided if possible (in order to minimize the risk of losing control over that technology). Thus, if a high-tech company is considering setting up manufacturing operations in a foreign country, it should do so through a wholly owned subsidiary.

Second, for service companies the combination of franchising and subsidiaries to control franchisees within a particular country or region seems to work well. The subsidiary may be wholly owned or a joint venture. In most cases, however, service companies have found that entering into a joint venture with a local partner in order to set up a controlling subsidiary in a country or region

TABLE 8.3   **Advantages and disadvantages of different entry modes**

Entry mode	Advantage	Disadvantage
Exporting	Ability to realize global scale economies	High transport costs
		Tariff barriers
		Problems with local marketing agents
Licensing	Low development costs and risks	Difficulties achieving global strategic coordination
		Lack of control over technology
Franchising	Low development costs and risks	Difficulties achieving global strategic coordination
		Problems of quality control
Joint ventures	Access to local partner's knowledge	Difficulties achieving global strategic coordination
	Sharing of development costs and risks	Lack of control over technology
	Political acceptability	
Wholly owned subsidiaries	Protection of technology	Assumption by company of all development costs and risk
	Establishment of tight control necessary for achieving global strategic coordination	

works best. A joint venture is often politically more acceptable to the host government and brings a degree of local knowledge to the subsidiary.

Third, the greater the pressures for global integration, the more likely it is that a company will want to pursue some combination of exporting and wholly owned subsidiaries. By manufacturing in locations where the mix of factor costs and skills is most favorable, a company may be able to realize substantial cost economies. The company might then want to export the finished product to marketing subsidiaries based in various countries. These subsidiaries are typically wholly owned and have the responsibility for overseeing distribution in a particular country. Setting up wholly owned marketing subsidiaries is preferable to a joint-venture arrangement or to using a foreign marketing agent because it gives a company the tight control over strategic decisions in the host country that might be necessary to pursue global strategic coordination.

8.8 GLOBAL STRATEGIC ALLIANCES

The term *global strategic alliances* refers to cooperative agreements between potential or actual multinational competitors. Alliances range from formal joint ventures, in which two or more multinational companies have an equity stake, to short-term contractual agreements in which two companies may agree to cooperate on a particular problem (such as developing a new product). There is no doubt that collaboration between competitors is in fashion. The 1980s saw a virtual explosion in the number of strategic alliances. For example, in the global auto industry the number of alliances between the 23 largest competitors increased from less than 10 pairwise linkages in 1978 to 52 pairwise linkages in 1988.[19] Examples in other industries include the following:

1. A cooperative arrangement between Boeing and a consortium of Japanese companies to produce the 767 wide-body commercial jet
2. An alliance between General Electric and Snecma of France to build a family of low-thrust commercial aircraft engines
3. An agreement between Siemens and Philips to develop new semiconductor technology
4. An agreement between ICL, the British computer company, and Fujitsu of Japan to develop a new generation of mainframe computers capable of competing with IBM's products
5. An alliance between Eastman Kodak and Canon of Japan under which Canon manufactures a line of medium-volume copiers for sale under Kodak's name
6. An agreement between Texas Instruments and Kobe Steel Inc. of Japan to make logic semiconductors in Japan.

The Pros and Cons of Global Strategic Alliances

Critics warn that global strategic alliances, like formal joint ventures, give competitors a low-cost route to gain new technology and market access. For example, Harvard Business School professors Robert Reich and Eric Mankin have argued that strategic alliances between U.S. and Japanese companies are part of an implicit Japanese strategy to keep higher-paying, higher-value-added jobs in Japan and to gain the project engineering and production process skills that underlie the competitive success of many U.S. companies.[20]

On the other hand, a number of commentators have argued that strategic alliances can be to the advantage of both parties.[21] Alliances can be seen as a way of sharing the high fixed costs and high risks associated with new product development or with the opening up of new markets. The alliance between Boeing and the Japanese consortium to build the 767, for example, arose because Boeing was looking for assistance to share in the increasingly heavy burden of aircraft development (development costs for a new commercial aircraft can run into billions of dollars). Similarly, strategic alliances are becoming increasingly common in the global pharmaceutical industry, where the cost of developing a new drug can amount to $150 million.

Alternatively, an alliance can be seen as a way of bringing together complementary skills and assets that neither company could easily develop on its own.

Consider the strategic alliance between France's Thompson and Japan's JVC to manufacture videocassette recorders. JVC and Thompson are trading skills; Thompson needs product technology and manufacturing skills, and JVC needs to learn how to succeed in the fragmented European market. Both sides believe that there is an equitable chance for gain. Similarly, in 1990 AT&T struck a deal with NEC Corporation of Japan to trade technological skills. AT&T will give NEC some of its computer-aided-design technology. In return, NEC will give AT&T access to the technology underlying NEC advanced logic computer chips. Such equitable skill swaps seem to underlie many of the most successful strategic alliances.

Thus, contrary to Reich and Mankin's argument, alliances need not be high-tech giveaways, and they can evolve into mutually beneficial relationships. However, in order for this to occur, alliances must be structured so that (1) a company does not unintentionally give away proprietary technology to its alliance partner and (2) a company learns important skills from its alliance partner.

Protecting Technology in Alliances

Thomas Roehl of the University of Michigan and Frederick Truitt of the University of Washington have argued that a company in an alliance can take several approaches to protecting its technology.[22] First, alliances can be designed to make it difficult or impossible to transfer technology that is not meant to be transferred. Specifically, the design, development, manufacture, and service of the alliance product are structured to *wall off* the most sensitive technologies and prevent their leakage to the other participant. In the alliance between General Electric and Snecma to build commercial aircraft engines, General Electric tried to reduce the risk of "excess transfer" by walling off certain sections of the production process. The modularization effectively cut off the transfer of what GE felt was key competitive technology while permitting Snecma access to final assembly. Similarly, in the alliance between Boeing and the Japanese to build the 767, Boeing walled off research, design, and marketing functions considered central to Boeing's competitive position but allowed the Japanese to share in production technology. Boeing also walled off new technologies not required for 767 production.

Second, the sharing of technology and information can be linked to long-term commitments that require such complex intertwining of facilities and personnel and such large expenditures on capital equipment usable only in the context of the partnership that the risk of separation and head-to-head competition is substantially reduced. The most obvious way of doing this is for both companies to enter into a formal joint venture to which they commit substantial equity. In this case, the commitment of equity by each party to the alliance is the source of protection—a kind of mutual hostage taking (as discussed in Chapter 7). However, companies often prefer not to get involved in a formal joint venture with competitors because that involvement can limit their ability to exit from the alliance when they feel it has served its purpose.

A third possibility involves linking the release of technology to an alliance partner to specific performance requirements. Motorola, for example, has taken an incremental, incentive-based approach to technology transfer in its venture with Toshiba. The agreement calls for Motorola to release its microprocessor technology incrementally as Toshiba delivers on its promise to increase Motorola's penetration of the Japanese semiconductor market. The greater Motorola's market share becomes, the greater will Toshiba's access to Motorola's technology be. This arrangement guarantees that Motorola does not give away control over its technology without first getting something in exchange.

Learning from Alliance Partners

After a five-year study of fifteen strategic alliances between major multinationals, Gary Hamel, Yves Doz, and C. K. Prahalad came to the conclusion that one of the major forces determining how much a company gains from an alliance is its ability to learn from alliance partners.[23] They focused on a number of alliances between Japanese companies and Western (European or American) partners. In every case in which a Japanese company emerged from an alliance stronger than its Western partner, the Japanese company had made a greater effort to learn. Indeed, few Western companies seemed to want to learn from their Japanese partners. They tended to regard the alliance purely as a cost-sharing or risk-sharing device rather than as an opportunity to learn about how a potential competitor does business.

Consider the alliance between General Motors and Toyota to build the Chevrolet Nova. The alliance is structured as a formal joint venture called New United Motor Manufacturing Inc. Both parties have a 50 percent equity stake. The venture owns an auto plant in Fremont, California. According to one of the Japanese managers, Toyota achieved most of its objectives from the alliance: "We learned about U.S. supply and transportation. And we got the confidence to manage U.S. workers."[24] All that knowledge was then quickly transferred to Georgetown, Kentucky, where Toyota opened a plant of its own in 1988. On the other hand, although General Motors got a new product, the Chevrolet Nova, some GM managers complain that their knowledge was never put to good use inside General Motors. They say that they should have been kept together as a team to educate GM's engineers and workers about the Japanese system. Instead they were dispersed to different GM subsidiaries.[25]

A company entering an alliance must try to learn from its alliance partner and then put that knowledge to good use within its own organization. To do this, it has been suggested, all operating employees must be well briefed on the partner's strengths and weaknesses and understand how acquiring particular skills will bolster their company's competitive position. Hamel, Doz, and Prahalad observed that this is already standard practice among Japanese companies. They made the following observation:

> We accompanied a Japanese development engineer on a tour through a partner's factory. This engineering dutifully took notes on plant layout, the

number of production stages, the rate at which the line was running, and the number of employees. He recorded all this despite the fact that he had no manufacturing responsibility in his own company, and that the alliance did not encompass joint manufacturing. Such dedication greatly enhances learning.[26]

For such learning to be of value, the knowledge acquired from an alliance must be diffused through the organization (this was not done in GM after the GM–Toyota joint venture). The managers involved in an alliance should be used specifically to educate their colleagues within the company about the skills of the alliance partner.

8.9 THE ROLE OF HOST-GOVERNMENT POLICIES

One of the major differences between a purely domestic company and a multinational company is that the multinational has to deal with host-government policies. These policies can add another dimension of difficulty to the problem of strategy formulation and implementation. The governments of independent nation-states have their own set of priorities and objectives that may conflict with the strategic objectives of a multinational. Host governments can enact all kinds of measures that limit the freedom of a multinational to pursue the strategies of its choice and alter the attractiveness of various choices. These measures include trade policies, local content requirements, tax policies, exchange controls, and price policies. In addition, host governments may require a multinational wishing to do business in their country to enter into a joint venture with a domestic enterprise.

In terms of the framework introduced earlier in this chapter, the effect of host-government policies may be to limit the ability of a multinational to pursue global integration and to increase pressures for local responsiveness. For example, as illustrated in Figure 8.4, although economic and competitive conditions may suggest a high need for integration and a low need for local responsiveness (that is, the company should pursue a pure global strategy), host-government demands may require a company to be responsive to local needs. This situation is occurring in the auto industry.

Economic and competitive conditions in the auto industry have been pushing auto companies toward global strategies. However, host-government demands for local production, coupled with the threat to raise import tariffs on autos, have forced companies to be more locally responsive than they would probably choose to be. Thus, faced with the threat of significant tariff barriers, Japanese companies have recently been setting up production plants in the United States and Western Europe—despite their previous preference for the global strategy of centralizing production in Japan and exporting.

Alternatively, a multinational may be able to establish with a host govern-

FIGURE 8.4   **The impact of host-government demands on the integration-responsiveness grid**

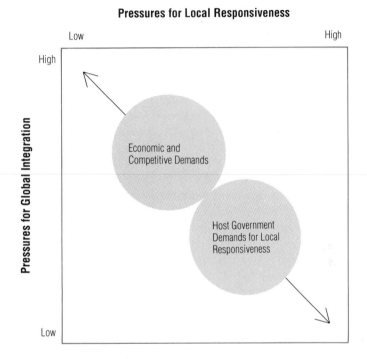

Source: Adapted by permission of The Free Press, a division of Macmillan Publishing Company, Inc. from Figure 4.1, p. 69 in *The Multinational Mission* by C.K. Prahalad and Yves L. Doz. Copyright © 1987 by The Free Press, a division of Macmillan Publishing Company, Inc.

ment a cooperative relationship that is to the benefit of both parties. Host governments often try to attract multinationals by offering generous subsidies and privileged access to their local markets. For example, economic problems and high unemployment prompted Ireland to provide large subsidies in an effort to attract multinationals that can create jobs. In spite of a relatively small domestic market, Ireland is becoming an attractive site for multinational production because it offers free access to the markets of the European Community, of which it is a member.

The Concerns of Host Governments

If a multinational company is to develop effective strategies for dealing with host governments, it must first understand their concerns about their balance of payments, transfer pricing, competitiveness, and national sovereignty.[27]

Balance of payments   The balance of payments is an important policy issue for host governments, for a balance-of-payments deficit may act as a constraint on economic growth and lead to a decline in the value of the host country's currency. When a multinational exports its production to a host country, as the Japanese auto companies used to do with regard to the United States, exporting has a negative effect on the balance of payments of the host country. Threats of protectionism and the imposition of tariffs are always possibilities in this situation, even from countries nominally committed to the preservation of "free trade." Such threats may be sufficient to force a multinational to establish production in a host country even though it would prefer to export to that country. Thus, in response to growing protectionist pressures from Congress, the Japanese auto companies rapidly increased their direct investment in the United States between 1985 and 1990. By 1990 around 20 percent of U.S.-based auto-making capacity was Japanese owned, up from 0 percent in 1985.

Even when a multinational establishes a subsidiary in a host country, however, host-government concerns about the balance of payments may not be allayed. If the subsidiary is seen as an assembly plant—that is, if most of the components are manufactured overseas and imported into the host country for final assembly—a negative balance-of-payments effect may still exist. To correct it, many host governments have enacted local content requirements specifying that a certain percentage of a multinational's output in the host country be manufactured in the host country. For example, permission from the British government for Japanese electronics companies to invest in the United Kingdom was made conditional on the use of a high proportion of British-made components.

Another issue concerns the payment of dividends, interest, royalties, or administrative charges to the parent company. The capital outflows that such payments represent can push the balance of payments into deficit and precipitate a decline in the exchange value of the host country's currency. Such concerns have prompted host governments to enact tight exchange-control regulations. These make it difficult for a multinational to send its earnings back to its home country. For example, U.S. multinationals have long considered Brazil a profitable location for direct investment. However, Brazilian exchange controls have often forbidden multinationals from taking their profits out of the country. Such policies limit a multinational's ability to use the profits generated in one country to fight competitive battles in other countries. They limit a multinational's ability to achieve global strategic coordination.

Transfer pricing   Another important issue relating to the balance of payments is transfer pricing. The *transfer price* is the price at which goods are sold between the subsidiaries of a multinational company. Multinationals can and do use transfer prices both as a means of circumventing exchange controls and as a way of consolidating profits in the most favorable locations for tax purposes (for example, tax havens such as the Bahamas). Thus a multinational may circumvent tight exchange controls by charging an artificially high price for material inputs supplied to a host-country subsidiary from one of its home-country operations. In addition to the negative impact on a host country's balance of payments, artificially high transfer prices may also result in local shareholders' losing part of their legitimate profits. The host government may also lose tax revenue because of the decline in the earnings of the multinational's host-country subsidiary implied by high transfer prices.

An investigation by the British Monopolies and Mergers Commission brought to light the excessive prices charged for drugs in the United Kingdom by Hoffmann–La Roche, a Swiss pharmaceutical company.[28] According to the company, transfer prices were determined by "what is reasonable for tax purposes." The drugs in question were purchased by the U.K. subsidiary of Hoffman–La Roche at 46 times the price at which the same goods were available on the open market. In another example, a study of transfer pricing by the Colombian government for the period 1967–1970 estimated that transfer prices within multinationals were significantly inflated. With regard to the Colombian subsidiaries of foreign multinationals, transfer prices for pharmaceuticals were 87 percent greater than the world price, 44 percent greater for rubber, 25 percent greater for chemicals, and 54 percent greater for electrical components.[29] The expansion of intracompany trade that has accompanied the growth of globally integrated manufacturing strategies has only increased host-government concerns about such transfer pricing policies.

By its nature, transfer pricing is difficult to detect, but as concern has grown in host countries, greater efforts are being made to do so. Some countries now scrutinize transfer prices and fix them directly. For example, members of the Andean Pact (Colombia, Ecuador, Peru, Bolivia, Chile, and Venezuela) have adopted a common system for attempting to control transfer prices. This involves regular screening of the transfer prices paid for technology and products within multinationals and comparing them against world prices.

Competitiveness   Host governments often fear that the subsidiaries of foreign multinationals possess greater economic power than do indigenous competitors. In particular, they worry that a multinational may be able to use its aggregate financial strength to outspend domestic competitors and drive them out of business. This fear is particularly prevalent among the governments of less-developed countries, which may be concerned that the lack of indigenous competitors creates a potential monopoly problem. To forestall this situation, host governments may require foreign multinationals to share ownership of local subsidiaries with local enterprises or with the government itself. Clearly this requirement is not always in the best interest of the multinational, for shared ownership limits its ultimate control over the operations of the subsidiary.

National sovereignty   Another fear of host governments is that if their economy becomes too dependent on foreign multinationals, their ability to pursue desired policies may be limited. For example, a multinational enterprise is less responsive than an indigenous company to monetary policy measures because it can draw on funds elsewhere. Host-government fiscal policies may be circumvented by transfer pricing. Trade policy may be determined by marketing considerations of the parent company or by political considerations imposed on the multinational by the home-country government, and so on.

Host governments in less-developed countries may also be particularly concerned that multinationals may use their dominant position in the host economy to demand tax concessions, subsidies, and expensive infrastructure investments that the host country cannot easily afford. These demands may be reinforced by threats to relocate operations elsewhere in the world, taking away jobs, unless the host government complies. Finally, host governments may be concerned about foreign domination of strategic industries—such as aircraft manufacture, shipbuilding, and steelmaking—that may be important for the country in times of war. Because of this concern, Britain, France, and many other developed countries have restricted foreign direct investment in certain industries.

All of these concerns are particularly worrying for the governments of countries whose economy is dominated by foreign multinationals—countries like Mexico, where half of the largest 300 manufacturing firms in the mid 1970s were the subsidiaries of foreign multinationals, or Brazil, where 147 of the 300 largest manufacturing enterprises and 59 of the 100 largest were foreign owned.[30] Host governments try to protect their national sovereignty vis-à-vis multinationals by pursuing policies designed to reduce the power of multinationals: nationalization of foreign-owned assets, requiring joint ventures from foreign-owned enterprises, and setting up a screening procedure that gives access only to multinationals whose investments will clearly benefit the host. For example, Kenya has an elaborate screening system to ensure that only multinationals that will be of benefit to Kenya are let in.

Strategies for Dealing with Host Governments

In some cases a multinational can do little to alleviate host-government concerns, other than accept the solutions imposed by the host government. If those solutions are not acceptable, the best thing for the multinational to do is not invest in that host country. For example, when the government of India began to demand that local investors have a majority ownership stake in the subsidiaries of all foreign-owned multinationals, a number of U.S. companies responded by shutting down their Indian operations. One such company was Coca-Cola, which felt that it might no longer be able to protect its secret formula if majority control of its Indian operation was given to local investors. Another was IBM, which feared losing control over its technology.

Generally, however, many multinationals are in a relatively strong bargaining position with host governments. In many cases, by setting up production facilities in the host country, they may be able to attenuate the demands of the host government even if they cannot fully alleviate its concerns. The fact is that many host governments need the capital investment, jobs, and technology that a multinational can provide. A multinational can use this need as a lever to gain access to a country's market on reasonably favorable terms. Thus, although a multinational may still have to agree to a degree of local ownership, it might be limited to a relatively small minority stake that offers little real local control.

The bargaining position of a multinational is further increased if it intends to use the host country as an export base to serve a regional market. Host governments can be expected to solicit such investments actively. For example, the British government offered substantial subsidies in an ultimately successful effort to persuade Nissan to base its European manufacturing operation in Britain rather than Spain.

Alternatively, it may pay a multinational to enter into a strategic alliance with an indigenous company, partly as a means of guaranteeing access to an otherwise protected market. On this point, there is little doubt that part of the motivation underlying the recent flurry of joint ventures between Japanese and U.S. auto companies (for example, General Motors and Toyota, Ford and Mazda, and Chrysler and Mitsubishi), at least from the Japanese perspective, is a belief that such alliances will moderate growing protectionist tendencies in Congress.

Perhaps most importantly, however, multinationals can further their case with host governments if they are able to stress the benefit to both parties of a long-term cooperative relationship. In particular, a tacit or explicit commitment to sharing value with the host government may alleviate concerns. IBM, for example, is willing to incur what it calls "citizenship costs" in various countries in order to be allowed to continue to operate worldwide as it sees fit. Thus IBM goes to some lengths to ensure that host-country governments are satisfied with its presence. These range from progressive labor policies, to grants for education, to efforts to manage its globally integrated manufacturing network in a way that does not have a major adverse impact on any one host country's trade balance.

8.10 SUMMARY OF CHAPTER

In this chapter we describe the strategic choices that confront companies doing business in the global environment. We see how global expansion can create value for a company, and we examine the pros and cons of the different strategies that companies can pursue in the global arena. The following points are made during the course of this discussion:

1. A new reality is confronting American business: global competition and global competitors.

2. Global expansion enables a company to add value from (a) transferring core skills overseas, (b) using global volume to cover product development costs, (c) realizing economies of scale from global volume, and (d) configuring the company's value chain so that individual value-creation functions are performed in locations where value–added is maximized.

3. One of the major strategic choices made by multinationals is whether to compete on a multidomestic or a global basis. A multidomestic strategy is based on the assumption that national markets differ. A global market is based on the assumption that a product can be standardized across national markets.

4. A tradeoff is necessary when a company chooses between a multidomestic and a global strategy. Companies pursuing a global strategy gain cost economies from the integration of manufacturing, marketing, and competitive strategy across national boundaries, but they must give up a certain degree of responsiveness to national conditions. The opposite is true of companies pursuing a multidomestic strategy.

5. Pressures for global integration arise from (a) the need for cost reduction, (b) the existence of universal needs, and (c) global strategic coordination by competitors.

6. Pressures for local responsiveness arise from (a) differences in consumer tastes and preferences, (b) differences in infrastructure and in traditional practices, (c) differences in distribution channels, and (d) host-government demands.

7. Although some companies are clearly pure global enterprises and others are pure multidomestic enterprises, most companies have to deal with competing pressures for global integration and local responsiveness.

8. Companies that attempt to deal simultaneously with pressures for global integration and local responsiveness are called *transnational companies.*

9. There are five different ways to enter an overseas market: (a) exporting, (b) licensing, (c) franchising, (d) entering into a joint venture, and (e) setting up a wholly owned subsidiary. Each mode has its advantages and disadvantages.

10. Strategic alliances are cooperative agreements between potential or actual competitors. Critics warn that strategic alliances are little more than high-tech giveaways. Proponents suggest that they are a valuable way of (a) sharing risks and costs and (b) bringing together complementary skills.

11. An alliance need not be a high-tech giveaway so long as (a) the alliance is structured to prevent the unintentional transfer of technology and (b) companies learn to learn from their alliance partners.

12. A major difference between a purely domestic enterprise and a multinational is that the multinational has to deal with host-government policies.

13. If a multinational is to develop effective strategies for dealing with host governments, it must first understand their concerns about their balance of payments, transfer pricing, competitiveness, and local sovereignty.

14. Multinationals can often further their cause with host governments if they are able to stress the benefit to both parties of a long-term cooperative relationship.

Discussion Questions

1. Pick a major diversified multinational company and attempt to plot the position of its various businesses on the integration-responsiveness grid (see Figure 8.1). Justify your choice of positioning.

2. Licensing proprietary technology to overseas competitors is the best way to give up a company's competitive advantage. Discuss.

3. What kind of companies stand to gain most from entering into a strategic alliance with potential competitors? Why?

Endnotes

1. David Lieberman, "Keeping Up with the Murdochs," *Business Week,* March 20, 1989, pp. 32–34. David Lieberman, "Will It Happen? Will It Work?" *Business Week,* March 20, 1989, p. 34. Judith H. Dobrzynski, "Giant Steps Toward the Global Village: Or an Ego Trip?" *Business Week,* March 20, 1989, p. 36.

2. Neil Hood and Stephen Young, *The Economics of the Multinational Enterprise* (London: Longman, 1979).

3. Charles W. L. Hill, Michael Hitt, and Robert Hoskisson, "Declining U.S. Competitiveness: Reflections on a Crisis," *Academy of Management Executive,* 2 (1988), 51–60.

4. "West German and British Cars: A Tale of Two Motor Industries," *The Economist,* February 13, 1988, p. 65.

5. George S. Yip, "Global Strategy in a World of Nations?" *Sloan Management Review* (Fall 1989), 29–41.

6. For example, see T. Hout, Michael E. Porter, and E. Rudden, "How Global Companies Win Out," *Harvard Business Review* (September–October 1982), 98–108; Theodore Levitt, "The Globalization of Markets," *Harvard Business Review* (May–June 1983), 92–102; and S. Ghoshal, "Global Strategy: An Organizing Framework," *Strategic Management Journal,* 8 (September–October 1987), 425–440.

7. Yip, "Global Strategy in a World of Nations?" pp. 29–41.

8. C. K. Prahalad and Yves L. Doz, *The Multinational Mission: Balancing Local Demands and Global Vision* (New York: Free Press, 1987).

9. Theodore Levitt, "The Globalization of Markets," *Harvard Business Review* (May–June 1983), 92–102.

10. Levitt's critics include Kenichi Ohmae, "Managing in a Borderless World," *Harvard Business Review* (May–June 1989), 152–161; and Christopher A. Bartlett and Sumantra Ghoshal, "Managing Across Borders: New Strategic Requirement," *Sloan Management Review* (Summer 1987), 7–17.

11. Prahalad and Doz, *The Multinational Mission.*

12. Gary Hamel and C. K. Prahalad, "Do You Really Have a Global Strategy," *Harvard Business Review* (July–August 1985), 139–148.

13. Ohmae, "Managing in a Borderless World," 152–161.

14. See Prahalad and Doz, *The Multinational Mission.*

15. Christopher A. Bartlett and Sumantra Ghoshal, *Managing Across Borders: The Transnational Solution* (Boston: Harvard Business School Press, 1989).

16. Hout, Porter, and Rudden, "How Global Companies Win Out," 98–108.

17. This section draws on the following two studies: Charles W. L. Hill, Peter Hwang, and W. Chan Kim, "An Eclectic Theory of the Choice of International Entry Mode," *Strategic Management Journal,* 11 (February 1990), 117–128; and Charles W. L. Hill and W. Chan Kim, "Searching for a Dynamic Theory of the Multinational Enterprise: A Transaction Cost Model," *Strategic Management Journal,* 9, Special Issue (1988), 93–104.

18. David G. Bradley, "Managing Against Expropriation," *Harvard Business Review* (July–August, 1977), 75–83.

19. Charles W. L. Hill and W. Chan Kim, "Cooperative Alliances in the Global Auto Industry" (Working paper, University of Washington, 1990).

20. Robert B. Reich and Eric D. Mankin, "Joint Ventures with Japan Give Away Our Future," *Harvard Business Review* (March–April 1986), 78–90.

21. See Gary Hamel, Yves L. Doz, and C. K. Prahalad, "Collaborate with Your Competitors: And Win," *Harvard Business Review* (January–February 1989), 133–139; Kenichi Ohmae, "The Global Logic of Strategic Alliances," *Harvard Business Review* (March–April 1989), 143–154; and Thomas W. Roehl and J. Frederick Truitt, "Stormy Open Marriages Are Better," *Columbia Journal of World Business* (Summer 1987), 87–95.

22. Roehl and Truitt, "Stormy Open Marriages Are Better," pp. 87–95.

23. Hamel, Doz, and Prahalad, "Collaborate with Your Competitors," pp. 133–139.

24. Bernard Wysocki, "Cross-Border Alliances Become Favorite Way to Crack New Markets," *The Wall Street Journal,* March 4, 1990, p. A1.

25. Ibid., pp. A1, A6.

26. Hamel, Doz, and Prahalad, "Collaborate with Your Competitors," pp. 138–139.

27. Hood and Young, *The Economics of the Multinational Enterprise.*

28. Monopolies Commission, *Chlordiazepoxide and Diazepan* (London: Her Majesty's Stationery Office, 1973).

29. S. Lall, "Transfer Pricing by Multinational Manufacturing Firms," *Oxford Bulletin of Economics and Statistics,* 35 (1973), 173–195.

30. Hood and Young, *The Economics of the Multinational Enterprise.*

Chapter 9

Analyzing and Changing the Corporate Portfolio

9.1 OPENING INCIDENT: ROCKWELL INTERNATIONAL

In 1974 Robert Anderson succeeded Willard Rockwell as chairman of the board of Rockwell International Corp., a broadly diversified group with activities in aerospace, automotive equipment, electronics, and consumer appliances. Anderson's task was to make some sense out of this portfolio of businesses. He focused resources on the businesses that had the best long-term growth and profit prospects and divested businesses that had poor prospects. The winner in this process was the defense-oriented aerospace business.

The focus on defense began to pay big dividends in 1981, when Congress ordered 100 B-1B bombers from Rockwell. The contract was worth $15 billion. As a consequence, in 1984 aerospace activities accounted for nearly 45 percent of Rockwell's revenues, up from around 30 percent five years earlier. However, this growth brought problems. The B-1B contract was due to end in 1988; and with few signs of congressional eagerness to order more B-1Bs, Rockwell faced the problem of how to maintain

eleven years of continuous growth. Management was also worried that Rockwell now depended too much on defense contracts. After five years of expansion, the federal defense budget would not grow indefinitely, particularly given growing political unrest over the size of the federal deficit. To make matters worse, Rockwell's nondefense activities were concentrated in the mature industrial and automotive sectors, where growth prospects were low.

In short, by the mid 1980s Rockwell International's corporate portfolio was no longer balanced. Too great a percentage of earnings came from defense contracts and mature nondefense activities. If the company was to continue growing, it had to change the mix of businesses in its portfolio. In January 1985 Rockwell took a major step toward this goal with the $1.65-billion acquisition of Allen-Bradley, a leader in computerized factory automation. Allen-Bradley gave Rockwell a fifth area that complemented its four core areas— aerospace, electronics, automotive components, and industrial products. The acquisition put Rockwell at the forefront of an expanding industry in which sales were predicted to grow from $5 billion to $20 billion between 1985 and 1990. In essence, Rockwell took the cash harvest from the B-1B bomber and invested it for the 1990s in a business with star potential.[1]

9.2 OVERVIEW

Chapter 7 reviewed the corporate-level strategies that companies pursue in order to become multibusiness enterprises. This chapter examines various techniques used by multibusiness enterprises like Rockwell to analyze their portfolio of businesses. These techniques are referred to as **portfolio techniques.** They give strategic managers an overview of the long-term prospects and competitive strengths and weaknesses of a company's various businesses, enabling them to evaluate whether a portfolio is adequate from the perspective of long-term corporate growth and profitability. For example, in the mid 1980s management's assessment was that Rockwell's portfolio provided the company with too few prospects for long-term growth and profit.

When most companies analyze their portfolios, the objective is to identify what needs to be done to construct a balanced portfolio of businesses. A **balanced portfolio** can be defined as an assortment of businesses that enables a company to achieve the growth and profit objectives associated with its corporate strategy without exposing the company to undue risks. If a company does not have the right balance of businesses in its portfolio, it needs to pursue strategies designed to correct the imbalance. Thus Rockwell acquired Allen-Bradley in an attempt to shift the balance of activities in its portfolio toward businesses with greater long-term growth and profit prospects.

In this chapter, we discuss the advantages and limitations of three different portfolio techniques: (1) a portfolio matrix developed by management consultants at the Boston Consulting Group, (2) a portfolio matrix developed originally by management consultants McKinsey & Company for use at General Electric, and (3) an industry evolution matrix developed by Charles Hofer, of the University of Georgia. We also look at the pitfalls of portfolio planning in general.[2]

After examining the different portfolio techniques, we consider the means that companies employ to change the composition of their portfolios. These means include *entry strategies* (acquisition, internal new venturing, and joint ventures) and *exit strategies* (divestment, harvest, and liquidation). Acquisition and internal new venturing and joint ventures are alternative ways of entering new business areas, and we look at the factors that influence the choice between them. Divestment, harvest, and liquidation are alternative ways of exiting from existing business areas, and we examine the factors that affect a company's choice among them.

9.3 THE BOSTON CONSULTING GROUP BUSINESS MATRIX

The main objective of the Boston Consulting Group (BCG) technique is to help strategic managers identify the cash-flow requirements of the different businesses in their portfolio. The BCG approach involves three main steps: (1) dividing a company into strategic business units (SBUs) and assessing the long-term prospects of each, (2) comparing SBUs against each other by means of a matrix that indicates the relative prospects of each, and (3) developing strategic objectives with respect to each SBU.

Defining and Evaluating Strategic Business Units

A company must create an SBU for each economically distinct business area that it competes in. When strategic managers identify **SBUs,** their objective is to divide a company into strategic entities that are relevant for planning purposes. Normally, a company defines its SBUs in terms of the product markets they are competing in. For example, Rockwell International divides itself into five SBUs—aerospace, automotive components, electronics, factory automation, and industrial products—each reflecting a particular product market. Alternatively, companies that have significant vertically integrated operations might define all the businesses involved in a single vertically integrated chain of operations as one SBU. For example, the company shown in Figure 9.1 has divided itself into three SBUs. The first contains three closely related operations in the chemical industry; the second, a business operating in the automotive components industry; and the third, three vertically integrated businesses in the industries of iron ore mining, steel refining, and steel fabricating.

Having defined SBUs, strategic managers then assess each according to two criteria: (1) the SBU's relative market share and (2) the growth rate of the SBU's industry.

Relative market share   The objective when identifying an SBU's relative market share is to establish whether that SBU's market position can be classified as a strength or a weakness. *Relative market share* is defined as the ratio of an SBU's market share to the market share held by the largest rival company in its industry. If SBU X has a market share of 10 percent and its largest rival has a market share of 30 percent, then SBU X's relative market share is 10/30, or 0.3. Only if an SBU is a market leader in its industry will it have a relative market share greater than 1.0. For example, if SBU Y has a market share of 40 percent and its largest rival has a market share of 10 percent, then SBU Y's relative market share is 40/10 = 4.0.

According to the Boston Consulting Group, market share gives a company cost advantages from economies of scale and learning effects (we discussed the

FIGURE 9.1   The division of activities into SBUs

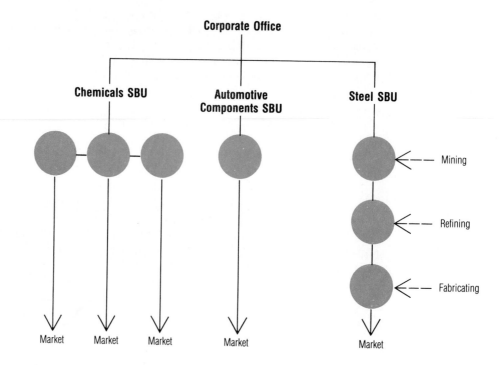

details in Chapter 4). An SBU with a relative market share greater than 1.0 is assumed to be farthest down the experience curve and therefore to have a significant cost advantage over its rivals. By similar logic, an SBU with a relative market share smaller than 1.0 is assumed to be at a competitive disadvantage because it lacks the scale economies and low-cost position of the market leader. Thus a relative market share greater than 1.0 can be characterized as a *strength*, and a relative market share smaller than 1.0 is a *weakness*. BCG characterizes SBUs with a relative market share greater than 1.0 as having a *high* relative market share and SBUs with a relative market share smaller than 1.0 as having a *low* relative market share.

Industry growth rate   The objective when assessing industry growth rates is to determine whether industry conditions offer opportunities for expansion or whether they threaten the SBU (as in a declining industry). The growth rate of an SBU's industry is assessed according to whether it is faster or slower than the growth rate of the economy as a whole. Industries with growth rates faster than the average are characterized as having *high* growth. Industries with growth rates slower than the average are characterized as having *low* growth. BCG's position is that high-growth industries offer a more favorable competitive environment and better long-term prospects than slow-growth industries. In other words, high-growth industries present an *opportunity*, low growth industries a *threat*.

Comparing Strategic Business Units

The next step of the BCG approach is comparing SBUs against each other by means of a matrix based on two dimensions: relative market share and high growth. Figure 9.2 provides an example of such a matrix. The horizontal dimension measures relative market share; the vertical dimension measures industry growth rate. Each circle represents an SBU. The center of each circle corresponds to the position of that SBU on the two dimensions of the matrix. The size of each circle is proportional to the sales revenue generated by each business in the company's portfolio. The bigger the circle, the larger is the size of an SBU relative to total corporate revenues.

The matrix is divided into four cells. SBUs in cell 1 are defined as **stars,** in cell 2 as **question marks,** in cell 3 as **cash cows,** and in cell 4 as **dogs.** BCG argues that these different types of SBUs have different long-term prospects and different implications for corporate cash flows.

Stars   The leading SBUs in a company's portfolio are the *stars*. They have a high relative market share and are based in high-growth industries. In the language of

FIGURE 9.2   **The Boston Consulting Group matrix**

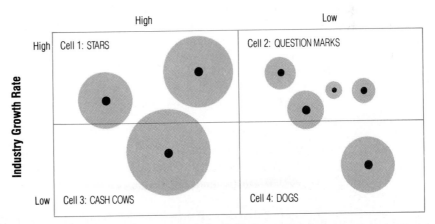

Source: Boston Consulting Group Matrix. Reprinted by permission of the Boston Consulting Group, Inc. Adapted from p. 12 in "Strategy and the Business Portfolio" by F. Hedley in *Long Range Planning,* (February 1977).

SWOT analysis, they have both competitive strengths and opportunities for expansion. Thus they offer excellent long-term profit and growth opportunities. Generally, BCG predicts that *established stars* are likely to be highly profitable and therefore can generate sufficient cash for their own investment needs. *Emerging stars,* in contrast, may require substantial cash injections to enable them to consolidate their market lead.

Question marks   SBUs that are relatively weak in competitive terms, that have low relative market shares, are *question marks.* However, they are based in high-growth industries and thus may offer opportunities for long-term profit and growth. A *question mark* can become a *star* if nurtured properly. To become a market leader, a *question mark* requires substantial net injections of cash; it is cash hungry. The corporate head office has to decide whether a particular *question mark* has the potential to become a *star* and is therefore worth the capital investment necessary to achieve stardom.

Cash cows   SBUs that have a high market share in low-growth industries and a strong competitive position in mature industries are *cash cows.* Their competitive strength comes from being farthest down the experience curve. They are the cost leaders in their industries. BCG argues that this position enables such SBUs to remain very profitable. However, low growth implies a lack of opportunities for future expansion. As a consequence, BCG argues that the capital investment requirements of *cash cows* are not substantial, and thus they are depicted as generating a strong positive cash flow.

Dogs   SBUs that are in low-growth industries but have a low market share are *dogs.* They have a weak competitive position in unattractive industries and thus are viewed as offering few benefits to a company. BCG suggests that such SBUs are unlikely to generate much in the way of a positive cash flow and indeed may become cash hogs. Though offering few prospects for future growth in returns, dogs may require substantial capital investments just to maintain their low market share.

Strategic Implications

The objective of the BCG portfolio matrix is to identify how corporate cash resources can best be used to maximize a company's future growth and profitability. BCG recommendations include the following:

1.   The cash surplus from any *cash cows* should be used to support the development of selected *question marks* and to nurture *emerging stars.* The long-term objective is to consolidate the position of *stars* and to turn favored *question marks* into *stars,* thus making the company's portfolio more attractive.

2. *Question marks* with the weakest or most uncertain long-term prospects should be divested so that demands on a company's cash resources are reduced.

3. The company should exit from any industry where the SBU is a *dog*—by divestment, harvesting market share, or liquidation (exit strategies are discussed later in this chapter).

4. If a company lacks sufficient *cash cows, stars,* or *question marks,* it should consider acquisitions and divestments to build a more balanced portfolio. A portfolio should contain enough *stars* and *question marks* to ensure a healthy growth and profit outlook for the company and enough *cash cows* to support the investment requirements of the *stars* and *question marks*

Strengths and Weaknesses of the BCG Matrix

The major strength of the BCG matrix is that it focuses attention on the cash-flow requirements of different types of businesses and points out ways of using cash flows to optimize the value of the corporate portfolio. The BCG matrix also indicates when a company needs to add another SBU to its portfolio and when it needs to remove an SBU.

However, the BCG matrix has a number of significant shortcomings. The model is simplistic. An assessment of an SBU in terms of just two dimensions, market share and industry growth, is bound to be misleading, for a host of other relevant factors should be taken into account. Although market share is undoubtedly an important determinant of an SBU's competitive position, companies can also establish a strong competitive position by differentiating their product to serve the needs of a particular segment of the market (see Chapter 5). Thus a business having a low market share can be very profitable and have a strong competitive position in certain segments of a market. The auto manufacturer Rolls-Royce is in this position, yet the BCG matrix would classify Rolls-Royce as a *dog* because it is a low-market-share business in a low-growth industry. Similarly, industry growth is not the only factor determining industry attractiveness. Many factors besides growth determine competitive intensity in an industry and thus its attractiveness (see Chapter 3).

The connection between relative market share and cost savings is not as straightforward as BCG suggests. Chapter 4 made clear that a high market share does not always give a company a cost advantage. In some industries—for example, the U.S. steel industry—low-market-share companies using a low-share technology (minimills) can have lower production costs than high-market-share companies using high-share technologies (integrated mills). The BCG matrix would classify minimill operations as the *dogs* of the American steel industry, whereas in fact their performance over the last decade has characterized them as *star* businesses.[3]

Furthermore, a high market share in a low-growth industry does not necessarily result in the large positive cash flow characteristic of *cash-cow* businesses. The BCG matrix would classify General Motors' auto operations as a *cash cow*. However, the capital investments needed to remain competitive are so substantial in the auto industry that the reverse is more likely to be true: Low-growth industries can be very competitive, and staying ahead in such an environment can require substantial cash investments.

The BCG approach, then, carries the risk of misclassifying businesses. The McKinsey matrix was developed to counter some of its weaknesses.

9.4 THE McKINSEY MATRIX

The technique developed by management consultants McKinsey & Company also divides a company into SBUs. As in the BCG matrix, each SBU is assessed along two dimensions, but the dimensions are based on many more factors. The dimensions are (1) the attractiveness of the industry in which an SBU is based and (2) an SBU's competitive position within that industry.

Assessing Industry Attractiveness

The assessment of industry attractiveness is a four-step process. Each step can be illustrated with reference to Table 9.1. The table shows how Rockwell International might assess the attractiveness of the factory automation industry, in which it now operates (see the Opening Incident). The steps are as follows:

1. Strategic managers identify a set of criteria that determine the attractiveness of an industry. The set typically includes factors acknowledged to be important determinants of industry attractiveness—factors such as growth, size, capital intensity, and competitive intensity. The competitive forces discussed in Chapter 3 are normally found in this kind of list, either individually or summarized by some aggregate criterion such as competitive intensity.

2. Strategic managers then assign a weight to each criterion in the set to indicate the relative importance of each *to the company*. To ensure consistency, the sum of the weights should add up to 1. For example, Rockwell International is shown in Table 9.1 to rank "industry growth" as the most important attractiveness criterion, assigning it a weight of 0.30. The rationale for this ranking is that Rockwell is involved in too many mature industries and needs to move into high-growth ones.

3. Next, strategic managers rate the attractiveness of each industry in the corporate portfolio according to the various attractiveness criteria. Normally, a scale of 1 to 5 is used, where 1 is unattractive and 5 is very attractive. Deci-

TABLE 9.1   Assessing industry attractiveness: factory automation industry

Industry attractiveness criteria	Weight	X	Industry rating	Weighted score
Industry size	0.10		3	0.30
Industry growth	0.30		5	1.50
Industry profitability	0.20		4	0.80
Capital intensity	0.05		5	0.25
Technological stability	0.10		5	0.50
Competitive intensity	0.20		3	0.60
Cyclicality	0.05		2	0.10
Totals	1.00			4.05

sions about the attractiveness of the criteria will reflect the company's objectives. Thus "industry growth" in Table 9.1 is rated 5 by Rockwell because factory automation is a high-growth industry and Rockwell is looking for high growth. Notice that an attractive criterion can be viewed as providing the company with an *opportunity* to realize its corporate objectives, but an unattractive criterion must be viewed as a *threat*.

4. Finally, strategic managers compute a total weighted score for each industry in the corporate portfolio. To arrive at this score, *weight* is multiplied by the *rating* for each of the attractiveness criteria, to get a *weighted score;* then the weighted scores are added. Thus in Table 9.1 Rockwell assigns to "competitive intensity" a weight of 0.20, and the factor automation industry is given a rating of 3 against this criterion. Thus the weighted score is $0.20 \times 3 = 0.60$. Adding the weighted scores together gives a *total weighted score* for each industry in the company's portfolio. The total weighted score is an index of how attractive each industry is to the company. The maximum value that this index can have is 5 and the minimum is 1; the average score is around 3. The total score of 4.05 for the factory automation industry indicates to Rockwell that the attraction of the industry is above average.

Assessing Competitive Position Within an Industry

Assessing an SBU's competitive position within its industry involves four steps similar to those followed in assessing industry attractiveness. Each step can be illustrated with reference to Table 9.2, which shows how Rockwell might assess the competitive position of its factory automation business (Allen-Bradley) within the factory automation industry.

TABLE 9.2   Assessing competitive position: factory automation SBU

Key success factors	Weight	Industry rating	Weighted score
Market share	0.15	5	0.75
Technological know-how	0.25	5	1.25
Product quality	0.15	4	0.60
After-sales service/maintenance	0.20	5	1.00
Price competitiveness	0.05	2	0.10
Low operating costs	0.10	3	0.30
Productivity	0.10	3	0.30
Totals	1.00		4.30

1. Strategic managers identify the *key success factors* in each of the industries in which the company competes. In the case of Rockwell's factory automation business, the factors are market share, technological know-how, product quality, after-sales service/maintenance, price competitiveness, low operating costs, and productivity.

2. Next, strategic managers assign a weight to each success factor, indicating its relative importance for establishing a strong competitive position within the industry being considered. As before, to ensure consistency, the weights must add up to 1. Table 9.2 shows that Rockwell views "technological know-how" as the most important success factor in the factory automation industry, followed by "after-sales service/maintenance."

3. Then strategic managers rate the competitive strengths of each SBU against relevant success factors in the various industries. As before, a scale of 1 to 5 is normally used, where 1 is very weak and 5 is very strong. Table 9.2 shows that Rockwell's factory automation SBU is in a very strong position with respect to market share, technological know-how, and after-sales service/ maintenance—all-important success factors in the factory automation industry. In other words, the *strengths* (distinctive competencies) of Rockwell's factory automation business include market share, technological know-how, and service/maintenance. Its *weaknesses* include price competitiveness, operating costs, and productivity.

4. Finally, strategic managers compute a total weighted score, which can then be used as an index of an SBU's competitive position. This score is derived by multiplying *weight* by *industry rating* to get a *weighted score* for each success factor and then adding the weighted scores to obtain the *total weighted score*. The value of the total weighted score will be between 5 (very strong com-

petitive position) and 1 (very weak competitive position), with 3 being the average. Table 9.2 shows that Rockwell's factory automation SBU is in a strong competitive position, with a total weighted score of 4.30.

Comparing Strategic Business Units

Once the foregoing analysis has been completed, the actual position of each SBU can be plotted on a matrix similar to the one shown in Figure 9.3. Industry attractiveness is plotted on the vertical dimension, competitive position on the horizontal dimension. Each circle represents an SBU. The position of the center of

FIGURE 9.3   The McKinsey matrix

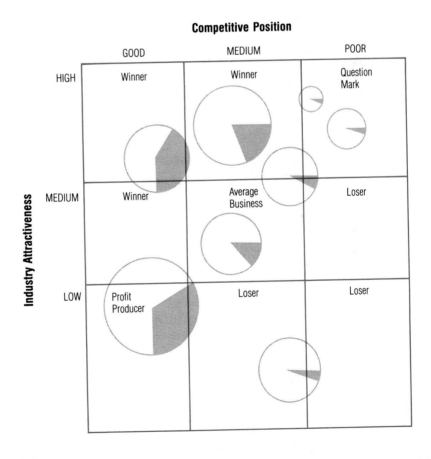

each circle is determined by the score that the SBU received on the two dimensions. The size of each circle is proportional to the size of the industry in which the SBU is based (measured total industry sales). The shaded wedge indicates an SBU's market share in that industry.

The McKinsey matrix is divided into nine cells. SBU's falling into three of the cells are characterized as **winners,** or the most desirable businesses. They are based in industries of medium to high attractiveness and have medium to strong competitive positions. Rockwell's factory automation business might be characterized as a *winner.* Three other cells are characterized as containing **losers.** These are the least desirable businesses. They have relatively weak competitive positions in unattractive industries.

One cell contains a *question mark.* As in the BCG matrix, **question marks** have an uncertain but potentially promising future. They have a weak competitive position in an attractive industry. With proper nurturing, they could become *winners;* however, they also run the risk of developing into *losers.* One cell contains **profit producers.** Analogous to the BCG matrix *cash cows,* these businesses have a strong competitive position in an unattractive industry. Finally, one cell contains **average businesses.** These businesses have no great strengths, but neither are they particularly weak.

Strategic Implications

The strategic implications of the McKinsey analysis are straightforward. *Losers* should be divested, liquidated, or told to harvest market share (a process described in detail later in the chapter). The position of *winners* and *developing winners* should be consolidated, if necessary by net injections of cash. The company should also nurture selected *question marks* in an attempt to turn them into *winners.* Since *profit producers* are based in industries whose long-term prospects are poor, these businesses should use their strong competitive position to generate profits, which can then be invested to support *winners* and selected *question marks.* The company should either try to turn *average businesses* into *winners* or consider divesting them because they are unlikely to offer the best long-term returns.

One objective of the McKinsey analysis is to identify how far out of balance a company's portfolio actually is. In this context, a **balanced portfolio** can be defined as one that contains mostly *winners* and *developing winners,* plus a few *profit producers,* to generate the cash flow necessary to support the *developing winners,* and a few small *question-mark* businesses with the potential to become *winners.*[4] Such a portfolio is balanced because it offers the company good profit and growth prospects without straining its cash-flow position.

More typically, however, a company has an unbalanced portfolio—a portfolio that places too many demands on the company's cash-flow position and offers inadequate prospects for profit and growth. Table 9.3 shows several different kinds of unbalanced portfolios, along with appropriate corrective strategies. To correct an unbalanced portfolio, strategic managers must change the compo-

TABLE 9.3   **Four basic types of unbalanced portfolios**

Problem action	Typical symptoms	Typical corrective
Too many *losers*	Inadequate cash flow Inadequate profits Inadequate growth	Divest/liquidate/harvest *losers* Acquire *profit producers* Acquire *winners*
Too many *question marks*	Inadequate cash flow Inadequate profits	Divest/harvest/liquidate selected *question marks*
Too many *profit producers*	Inadequate growth Excessive cash flow	Acquire *winners* Nurture/develop selected *question marks*
Too many *developing winners*	Excessive cash demands Excessive demands on management Unstable growth and profits	Divest selected developing winners if necessary Acquire *profit producers*

Source: Adapted from p. 52 in *Successful Strategic Management* by C. W. Hofer and M. J. Davoust. Copyright © 1977 by A. T. Kearney. Reprinted by permission.

sition of the corporate portfolio, adding or removing SBUs. For example, Rockwell International's portfolio in the early 1980s suffered from having too many *profit producers;* it was unbalanced. To correct this situation, Rockwell acquired a *developing winner,* Allen–Bradley.

Strengths and Weaknesses of the McKinsey Matrix

The McKinsey matrix is a great improvement on the BCG matrix because it is more comprehensive and avoids the simplifications and unwarranted assumptions of the BCG approach. One of its greatest strengths is its flexibility. The McKinsey matrix recognizes that different industries are characterized by different success factors, and it incorporates this fact into the analysis. Moreover, the McKinsey analysis can cover a much greater range of strategically relevant variables.

Nevertheless, the McKinsey approach is not perfect. One of the main difficulties is that it produces numbers to give strategic decisions legitimacy but does not explicitly recognize that the numbers are all subjectively derived. Strategic managers must be careful, therefore, not to let their own subjective biases enter into the analysis. Another problem is that the analysis is basically a static one. It looks at the *current* position of SBUs but does not take into account how their *future* position might change as a result of industry evolution. It does not depict the position of businesses across different stages of the industry life cycle. For example, it does not depict what might happen to a *question mark* as its industry enters the growth stage or to a *winner* as its industry enters the shakeout stage. This is where the industry evolution matrix becomes relevant.

9.5 THE INDUSTRY EVOLUTION MATRIX

To offset the shortcomings of the McKinsey matrix, Charles Hofer has suggested that companies use a portfolio matrix based on industry evolution.[5]

Evaluating and Comparing Strategic Business Units

Using the industry evolution matrix, strategic managers start by dividing business areas into SBUs. Next, using techniques similar to those of the McKinsey approach, they assess the competitive position of each SBU. The position of each SBU is plotted on a fifteen-cell matrix similar to the one shown in Figure 9.4. The horizontal dimension indicates an SBU's competitive position. The vertical dimension shows the different stages of industry evolution. Each circle represents an SBU. The size of the circle is proportional to the size of the industry in which the SBU is based (measured by total industry revenues), and the shaded wedge indicates the market share of the SBU.

The power of the industry evolution matrix lies in the story that it can tell about the distribution of a company's businesses across different stages of the industry life cycle. Using descriptive terminology similar to that of the McKinsey approach, we might characterize business A in Figure 9.4 as a *high-potential question mark*. It has a strong competitive position in the early stage of an industry's development. Thus it is well placed to capitalize on opportunities for expansion when its industry enters the growth stage. Similarly, business B is a *developing winner*. It has a strong position in a growth industry. It, too, can capitalize on opportunities for expansion. Business C, however, although also based in a growth industry, looks like a *developing loser*. Such a business is unlikely to survive the threat of the shakeout stage. The industry in which business D is based is currently undergoing a shakeout. Although this makes the industry environment a threat, business D has a strong competitive position and will probably survive and enter into maturity as a market leader or *profit producer*. Businesses E and F look to be *profit producers*, whereas business G is a definite *loser*.

Strategic Implications

The strategic implications of this analysis center on the different stages of the life cycle at which the various businesses are found. *High-potential question marks* and *developing winners*, such as businesses A and B, should be nurtured, for they may

FIGURE 9.4   **The industry evolution matrix**

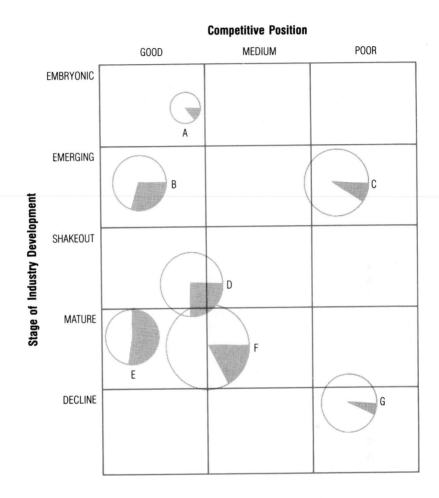

Source: Adapted from Charles W. Hofer, "Conceptual Constructs for Formulating Corporate and Business Strategies." (Dover, MA: Lord Publishing, #BP 0041, p. 3.) Copyright © 1977 by Charles W. Hofer. Reprinted by permission.

become the *established winners* and *profit producers* of the future. Potential *losers,* such as business C, should be divested as quickly as possible. Similarly, businesses such as G have few long-term prospects. The company needs to adopt an exit strategy for such operations. Business D is unlikely to be earning good returns currently, but its prospects are good. Businesses in this kind of position need to be supported. Businesses E and F should be managed in a way that consolidates and maintains their competitive strengths. Any surplus cash flows from these businesses should be used to support *developing winners* and companies going through a shakeout.

Like the McKinsey approach, the industry evolution matrix enables strategic managers to assess whether a corporate portfolio is balanced or unbalanced. A balanced portfolio should consist mainly of *established winners* and *profit producers,* such as businesses E and F; a few *developing winners,* such as business B; and a few *high-potential question marks,* such as business A. Most companies, however, find that they have unbalanced portfolios similar to those described in Table 9.3.

Unlike the McKinsey approach, the industry evolution matrix enables a company to assess how its portfolio of current operations is likely to develop over the next few years. A company with a number of *potential losers* based in currently profitable high-growth emerging industries might foresee that several years down the line it could be faced with an unbalanced portfolio containing too many *losers*. By taking corrective action now, it can avoid this situation.

Strengths and Weaknesses of the Industry Evolution Matrix

The strength of the industry evolution matrix is that it shows the distribution of a company's activities across different stages of the life cycle. As a result, a company can predict how its current portfolio might develop, and it can take immediate action to ensure that its portfolio is balanced. The industry evolution matrix has the additional advantage of focusing the attention of corporate-level personnel on potential business-level strategies. As you recall from Chapters 3 and 4, the industry life cycle is one of the most important determinants of strategic choice at the business level. For example, developing *winners,* such as business B in Figure 9.4, are at the development stage where the realization of cost economies from experience-curve effects is most important. Thus by using the industry evolution matrix, corporate-level personnel can perceive strategic requirements at the business level. No other approach has this advantage.

The drawback of the industry evolution matrix is that it does not focus on all the relevant factors of industry attractiveness. As the McKinsey matrix illustrates, the stage of industry evolution is an important but not the sole determinant of industry attractiveness. Other factors are also significant and have an impact that is independent of the stage of industry evolution.

9.6 BENEFITS AND PITFALLS OF PORTFOLIO ANALYSIS

Benefits

As a planning tool, portfolio techniques have a number of benefits. First, they enable strategic managers to analyze the diverse activities of a multibusiness company in a systematic fashion and so help make sense out of enterprise diversity. Second, they highlight the different cash-flow implications and requirements of different business activities. Such highlighting can assist the corporate head office in carrying out its resource allocation function.

Third, the concept of a balanced portfolio prods strategic managers to identify the kinds of adjustments that need to be made in the composition of the company's portfolio so that long-term growth and profitability can be optimized. Essentially, a balanced portfolio constitutes a company *strength,* an unbalanced portfolio a company *weakness.* Portfolio analysis can be used to identify gaps in the corporate portfolio that need to be filled in order to strike a balance. Thus in the early 1980s Rockwell International saw the lack of any *developing winners* as a gap in its portfolio and filled the gap with the purchase of Allen-Bradley. By the same token, portfolio analysis can indicate when there are too many businesses of a certain type in a company's portfolio. Exiting from these businesses will correct the portfolio's imbalance.

Of the three techniques discussed in this chapter, the BCG business matrix is perhaps the least useful, for it oversimplifies and makes unwarranted assumptions about the relationship between market share and performance. Both the McKinsey technique and the industry evolution matrix are more comprehensive and realistic. A strong case can be made for using them together and giving strategic managers two different but complementary perspectives of a company's portfolio. The McKinsey technique provides the company with an overview of the attractiveness of its *current* portfolio, whereas the industry evolution matrix can be used to project how the attractiveness of that portfolio might alter in the *future.*

Pitfalls

The merits of the different techniques apart, it must be recognized that the whole process of portfolio planning has its own pitfalls. Although these pitfalls do not invalidate the concept of portfolio planning, they suggest that companies should be cautious about relying too heavily on portfolio-planning techniques. Three major areas of concern can be identified.[6]

First, portfolio techniques explicitly assume that a company can be divided into a reasonable number of SBUs for the purpose of analysis. In practice, many companies are very diverse and have a large number of different business units. General Electric, for example, now has close to 300 businesses. Grouping such a large number of businesses into SBUs still results in a large number of SBUs to be managed by the head office. Large numbers of SBUs can create problems of **information overload** at the corporate office. It has been suggested that information overload starts becoming a serious problem when a company contains forty to fifty SBUs.[7] When information overload develops, the corporate office's analysis of each SBU becomes increasingly superficial. Strategic managers at the corporate office simply do not have the time to undertake the kind of thorough analysis needed to make portfolio techniques work. Thus the head office may commit large sums of money to different SBUs on the basis of insufficient knowledge of the activities involved and of the different industries that the company is active in. Poor decisions and poor performance are the inevitable results.

Second, when an SBU contains a number of different but related product divisions, as is often the case, conflicts of interest can develop between the internal cash-flow priorities of the SBU and the cash-flow priorities of the company as a whole. For example, an SBU may be defined as a *dog,* told to harvest its market share, and denied any significant capital investments. However, this SBU may contain a product division that strategic managers at the SBU level see as a *rising star.* To realize its full potential, the *rising star* needs significant capital investments, but the corporate analysis does not uncover this fact. The result can be damaging political conflict between strategic managers at the SBU level and at the corporate level over the lack of fund allocations to the *rising star.*

Third, a naive application of portfolio-planning techniques can create problems for vertically integrated companies and for companies that have pursued a strategy of related diversification. In a vertically integrated company, one SBU might be supplying inputs to another. Portfolio planning might suggest that the supplying SBU should be divested. However, divesting might be absurd if benefits in the form of lower production costs are being derived from the internal source of supply. Similarly, in a related-diversification company, two SBUs might be coordinating their activities to realize benefits from the exploitation of marketing and production synergies. Portfolio planning might suggest that one of these SBUs be divested. However, divestiture would mean the loss of the benefits derived from exploiting those synergies.

In short, a naive application of portfolio techniques can obscure important strategic relationships between SBUs. This potential limitation, however, can be overcome if strategic managers take the time to weigh the conflicting considerations of achieving a balanced portfolio against the loss of valuable strategic relationships among the SBUs.

9.7 ENTRY STRATEGIES

As noted above, correcting an imbalance in a company's corporate portfolio frequently requires entry into new business areas, adding *question marks, winners,* or *profit producers* to the portfolio. This means adding new business areas to the company through related diversification, unrelated diversification, or international expansion. In Chapter 7, we reviewed factors that influence a company's choice among these different generic corporate-level strategies. In this section, we examine the *means* of entry into a new business area (as distinct from the *type* of generic corporate-level strategy being pursued). The basic choices that strategic managers face are entry through **acquisition** and entry through **internal new venturing.** Sometimes neither is the optimal choice; in such cases, entry through a **joint venture** may prove to be the best option.

Acquisition Versus Internal New Venturing

Entry into a new business area through acquisition involves purchasing an established company, complete with all its facilities, equipment, and personnel. Entry into a new business area through internal new venturing involves starting a business from scratch: building facilities, purchasing equipment, recruiting personnel, opening up distribution outlets, and so on. Such projects are often called *greenfield projects* because the company starts with nothing but a green field.

The choice between acquisition and internal new venturing as the preferred entry strategy is influenced by a number of factors: (1) barriers to entry, (2) the relatedness of the new business to existing operations, (3) the comparative speed and development costs of the two entry modes, (4) the risks involved in the different entry modes, and (5) industry life-cycle factors.[8]

Barriers to entry   Recall from Chapter 3 that barriers to entry arise from factors associated with product differentiation (brand loyalty), absolute cost advantages, and economies of scale. When barriers are substantial, a company finds entering an industry through internal new venturing difficult. To do so, a company may have to construct an efficient-scale manufacturing plant, undertake massive advertising to break down established brand loyalties, and quickly build up distribution outlets—all hard-to-achieve goals that are likely to involve substantial expenditures. In contrast, by acquiring an established enterprise, a company can circumvent most entry barriers. It can purchase a market leader that already benefits from substantial scale economies and brand loyalty. Thus the greater the barriers to entry, the more is acquisition the favored entry mode.

Relatedness   The more related a new business is to a company's established operations, the lower are the barriers to entry and the more likely it is that the company has accumulated experience with this type of business. These factors heighten the attractiveness of new venturing. For example, IBM entered the personal computer market in 1981 by new venturing. The entry was very successful, enabling IBM to capture 35 percent of the market within two years. IBM was able to enter by this mode because of the high degree of relatedness between the personal computer market and IBM's established computer mainframe operations. IBM already had a well-established sales force and brand loyalty, and it had considerable expertise in the computer industry. Similarly, companies such as Du Pont and Dow Chemical Co. have successfully entered closely related chemical businesses through internal new venturing.

In contrast, the more unrelated a new business is, the more likely is entry to be through acquisition. By definition, unrelated diversifiers lack the specific expertise necessary to enter a new business area through greenfield development. An unrelated diversifier choosing internal new venturing has to develop its own expertise for competing in an unfamiliar industry. The learning process can be lengthy and involve costly mistakes before the company fully understands its new industry. In the case of an acquisition, however, the acquired business already has a management team with accumulated experience in competing in that particular industry. When making an acquisition, a company is also buying knowledge and experience. Thus widely diversified conglomerates such as ITT, Textron, Gulf & Western, and Hanson Trust have all expanded through acquisition.

Speed and development costs   As a rule, internal new venturing takes years to generate substantial profits. Establishing a significant market presence can be both costly and time consuming. In a study of corporate new venturing, Ralph Biggadike of the University of Virginia found that on the average it takes eight years for a new venture to reach profitability and ten to twelve years before the profitability of the average venture equals that of a mature business.[9] He also found that cash flow typically remains negative for at least the first eight years of a new venture. In contrast, acquisition is a much quicker way to establish a significant market presence and generate profitability. A company can purchase a market leader in a strong cash position overnight, rather than spend years building up a market-leadership position through internal development. Thus, when speed is important, acquisition is the favored entry mode.

Risks of entry   New venturing tends to be an uncertain process with a low probability of success. Studies by Edwin Mansfield of the University of Pennsylvania concluded that only between 12 percent and 20 percent of R&D-based new ventures actually succeed in earning an economic profit.[10] Indeed, business history is strewn with examples of large companies that lost money through internal new venturing. For example, in 1984 AT&T entered the computer market through an internal new venture. Company officials predicted that by 1990 AT&T would rank second in data processing, behind IBM. So far there are few signs of that happening. In 1985 AT&T's computer division lost $500 million, and in 1986 it lost $1.2 billion.[11]

When a company makes an acquisition, it is acquiring known profitability, known revenues, and known market share; thus it avoids uncertainty. Essentially, internal new venturing involves the establishment of a *question-mark* business, whereas acquisition allows a company to buy a *winner*. Thus many companies favor acquisition.

Industry life-cycle factors   We considered the general importance of the industry life cycle in Chapter 3. The industry life cycle has a major impact on many of the factors that influence the choice between acquisitions and internal new venturing. In embryonic and growth industries, barriers to entry are typically lower than in mature industries because established companies in the former are still going through a learning process. They do not have the same experience advantages as the established companies in a mature industry environment. Given these factors, entry by an internal new venture during the early stage of the industry life cycle means lower risks and development costs, as well as fewer penalties in terms of expansion speed, than entry into a mature industry environment. Thus internal new venturing tends to be the favored entry mode in embryonic and growth industries, whereas acquisition tends to be the favored mode in mature industries. Indeed, many of the most successful internal new ventures have been associated with entry into emerging industries—for instance, IBM's entry into the personal computer arena and John Deere Co.'s entry into the snowmobile business.

Summary   In sum, internal new venturing seems to make most sense when the following conditions exist: when the industry to be entered is in its embryonic or growth stage; when barriers to entry are low; when the industry is closely related to the company's existing operations (the company's strategy is one of related diversification); and when the company is willing to accept the attendant time frame, development costs, and risks.

In portfolio terms, internal new venturing makes most sense when a company needs more *question marks* in its portfolio or when it sees a strong possibility of establishing an *emerging winner* in an embryonic or growth industry. On the other hand, acquisition makes the most sense when a company needs more *established winners* or *profit producers* in its portfolio. Table 9.4 summarizes these situations.

In contrast, acquisition makes most sense when the following conditions exist: when the industry to be entered is mature; when the barriers to entry are high; when the industry is not closely related to the company's existing operations (the company's strategy is one of unrelated diversification); and when the company is unwilling to accept the time frame, development costs, and risks of internal new venturing.

Pitfalls of Acquisition

Despite the popularity of acquisition, it often does not bring the gains predicted.[12] For example, management consultants McKinsey & Company put fifty-eight major acquisitions undertaken between 1972 and 1983 to two tests: (1) Did the return on the total amount invested in the acquisitions exceed the cost of capital, and (2) did the acquisitions help their parent companies outperform the compe-

TABLE 9.4   **Portfolio gaps and entry strategies**

Portfolio gap	Entry strategy
Insufficient *cash cows*	Acquire companies in mature industries
Insufficient *winners*	Acquire companies in mature industries
Insufficient *question marks* or *developing winners*	Internal venture in growth or embryonic industry

tition in the stock market? Twenty-eight out of the fifty-eight clearly failed both tests, and six others failed one.[13] In terms of the generic corporate strategies discussed in Chapter 7, these test results indicate that many acquisitions fail to establish the *strategic advantages* that company's managers originally planned for. Consequently, far from acquiring an *established winner* or a *profit producer,* a company may find that it has added a *dog* to its portfolio.

Why does this happen? Why do so many acquisitions fail? There appear to be four major reasons: (1) Companies often experience difficulties when trying to integrate divergent corporate cultures. (2) Companies overestimate the potential gains from synergy. (3) Acquisitions tend to be very expensive. (4) Companies often do not adequately screen their acquisition targets.

Integration   Having made an acquisition, the acquiring company has to integrate the acquired one into its own organizational structure. Integration can entail the adoption of common management and financial control systems, the joining together of operations from the acquired and the acquiring company, or the establishment of linkages to share information and personnel. When integration is attempted, many unexpected problems can occur. Often they stem from differences in corporate cultures. After an acquisition, many acquired companies experience high management turnover because their employees do not like the acquiring company's way of doing things. The loss of management talent and expertise, to say nothing of the damage from constant tension between the businesses, can set back the realization of gains from an acquisition by several years.

For example, four years after Fluor bought St. Joe Minerals Corporation in one of the largest acquisitions of 1981, only seven of the twenty-two senior managers who had run St. Joe before the acquisition remained. Instead of reaping gains from an established *winner,* Fluor found itself struggling to transform a business that was fast becoming a *loser.* The crux of the problem was a clash in corporate cultures between Fluor, a centralized and autocratic organization, and St. Joe, a decentralized company. St. Joe's senior management resented the centralized management style at Fluor, and many managers left in protest.[14]

Overestimated synergies   Even when companies achieve integration, they often overestimate the extent of synergy between the different businesses. They overestimate the strategic advantages that can be derived from the acquisition and thus pay more for the target company than it is probably worth. For example, Coca-Cola once thought that it could use its marketing skills to dominate the U.S. wine industry. It reasoned that a beverage is a beverage. But after buying three wine companies and enduring seven years of marginal profits, Coca-Cola finally conceded that wine and soft drinks are very different products, with different kinds of appeal, pricing systems, and distribution networks. In 1983 the wine operations were sold to Joseph E. Seagram & Sons, Inc., for $210 million— the price Coca-Cola had paid for the purchases and a substantial loss when adjusted for inflation.[15]

The expense of acquisition   Acquisitions of companies whose stock is publicly traded tend to be very expensive. When a company bids to acquire the stock of another enterprise, the stock price frequently gets bid up by speculators hoping to gain from the acquisition. Thus the acquiring company often must pay a premium over the current market value of the target. In the early 1980s acquiring companies paid an average premium of 40 to 50 percent over current stock prices for an acquisition. The debt taken on to finance the acquisition can later become a noose around the acquiring company's neck, particularly if interest rates rise.

Inadequate preacquisition screening   Many companies make acquisition decisions without thoroughly analyzing the potential benefits and costs. Thus they often find that they have bought a *dog* instead of a *winner* or a *profit producer*. Philip Morris, for example, thought it could apply the same brand-management skills that it had used so successfully with cigarettes and beer to turn 7Up into another Coca-Cola. After investing eight years and hundreds of millions of dollars, Philip Morris finally faced up to something that Seven-Up Company researchers had known all along: Lemon-lime soft drinks have limited appeal. The Seven-Up Company was sold. If Philip Morris had screened Seven-Up thoroughly before acquiring the company, it could have saved itself a lot of money.

Guidelines for Successful Acquisition

To avoid pitfalls and make successful acquisitions, companies need to take a structured approach that involves three main components: (1) target identification and preacquisition screening, (2) bidding strategy, and (3) integration.[16]

Screening   Thorough preacquisition screening increases a company's knowledge about potential takeover targets, leads to a more realistic assessment of the problems involved in executing an acquisition and integrating the new business into the company's organizational structure, and lessens the risk of purchasing a *dog*. The screening should begin with a detailed assessment of the strategic rationale for making the acquisition and an identification of the kind of company that would make an ideal acquisition candidate. Hanson Trust exemplifies a company that has a very clear idea of its ideal acquisition candidate (see the Opening Incident in Chapter 7).

Next, the company should scan a target population of potential acquisition candidates, evaluating each according to a detailed set of criteria that focus on (1) financial position, (2) product market position, (3) management capabilities, and (4) corporate culture. Such an evaluation should enable the company to identify the strengths and weaknesses of each candidate, the extent of potential synergies between the acquiring and the acquired companies, potential integration problems, and the compatibility of the corporate cultures of the acquiring and the acquired companies.

The company should then reduce the list of candidates to the most-favored ones and evaluate them further. At this stage, it should sound out third parties, such as investment bankers, whose opinions may be important and who may be able to give valuable insights about the efficiency of target companies. The company that leads the list after this process should be the acquisition target.

Bidding strategy   The objective of bidding strategy is to reduce the price that a company must pay for an acquisition candidate. The essential element of a good bidding strategy is timing. Hanson Trust, for example, always looks for essentially sound businesses that are suffering from short-term problems due to cyclical industry factors or from problems localized in one division. Such companies are typically undervalued by the stock market and thus can be picked up without payment of the standard 40 or 50 percent premium over current stock prices. With good timing, a company can make a bargain purchase.

Integration   Despite good screening and bidding, an acquisition will fail unless positive steps are taken to integrate the acquired company into the organizational structure of the acquiring one. Integration should center on the source of the potential strategic advantages of the acquisition—for instance, marketing, manufacturing, procurement, R&D, financial, or management synergies. Integration should also be accompanied by steps to eliminate any duplication of facilities or functions. In addition, any unwanted activities of the acquired company should be sold. Finally, if the different business activities are closely related, they will require a high degree of integration. In the case of a company like Hanson Trust, the level of integration can be minimal, for the company's strategy is one of unrelated diversification. But a company such as Rockwell International requires greater integration because its strategy is one of related diversification.

Pitfalls of Internal New Venturing

Science-based companies that use their technology to create market opportunities in related areas tend to favor internal new venturing as an entry strategy. Du Pont, for example, has created whole new markets for the chemical industry with products such as cellophane, nylon, Freon, and Teflon—all internally generated innovations. Another company, 3M, has a near-legendary knack for shaping new markets from internally generated ideas. Internal new venturing, however, need not be based on radical innovations. Although IBM was an imitator rather than an innovator, it successfully entered the personal computer market in 1981 through a venture-based strategy rather than by acquisition. Similarly, the Gillette Company successfully diversified into the manufacture of felt-tip pens, and John Deere diversified into snowmobiles—both through internal new venturing.

As noted earlier, internal new ventures often fail, and even when they succeed, it may take years before they become profitable. In terms of portfolio techniques, new ventures are by definition *question marks*. However, management can reduce the probability of failure by avoiding three common pitfalls: (1) entering on too small a scale, (2) poor commercialization of the new venture, and (3) poor corporate management of the venture process.

Scale of entry   Research suggests that large-scale entry into a new business is the best way for an internal venture to succeed. Although in the short run large-scale entry means significant development costs and substantial losses, in the long run (that is, after eight to twelve years) it brings greater returns than small-scale entry.[17] Figure 9.5 plots the relationships among scale of entry, profitability, and cash flow over time for successful small-scale and large-scale ventures. The figure shows that successful small-scale entry involves lower losses, but in the long run large-scale entry generates greater returns. However, perhaps because of the costs of large-scale entry, many companies prefer a small-scale entry strategy. Acting on this preference can be a major mistake, for the company fails to build up the market share necessary for long-term success.

FIGURE 9.5   **The impact of large-scale versus small-scale entry on profitability and cash flow**

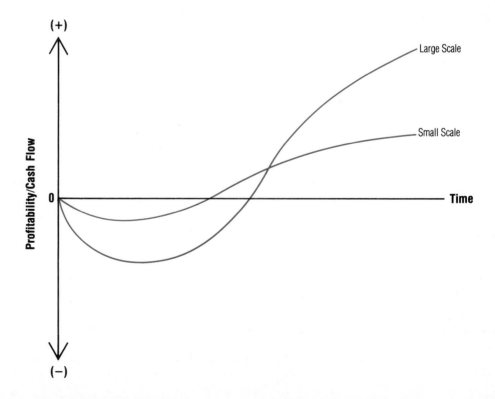

Commercialization   To be commercially successful, science-based innovations must be developed with market requirements in mind. Many internal new ventures fail when a company ignores the basic needs of the market. A company can become blinded by the technological possibilities of a new product and fail to analyze market opportunities properly. Thus a new venture may fail because of lack of commercialization, as happened when the British and French governments underwrote the development of the Concorde supersonic jet airplane.

Poor implementation   Managing the new venture process raises difficult organizational issues.[18] Although we deal with the specifics of implementation in later chapters, we must note some of the most common mistakes here. The shotgun approach of supporting many different internal new venture projects can be a major error, for it places great demands on a company's cash flow and can result in the best ventures being starved of the cash they need for success.

Another mistake involves a failure by corporate management to set the strategic context within which new venture projects should be developed. Simply taking a team of research scientists and allowing them to do research in their favorite field may produce novel results, but the results may have little strategic or commercial value.

Failure to anticipate the time and costs involved in the venture process constitutes a further mistake. Many companies have unrealistic expectations of the time frame involved. Reportedly, some companies operate with a philosophy of killing new businesses if they do not turn a profit by the end of the third year—clearly an unrealistic view, given Biggadike's evidence that it can take eight to twelve years before a venture generates substantial profits.

Guidelines for Successful Internal New Venturing

To avoid the pitfalls just discussed, a company should adopt a structured approach to managing internal new venturing. New venturing typically begins with R&D. To make effective use of its R&D capacity, a company must first spell out its strategic objectives and then communicate them to its scientists and engineers. Research, after all, makes sense only when it is undertaken in areas relevant to strategic goals.[19]

To increase the probability of commercial success, a company should foster close links between R&D and marketing personnel, for this is the best way to ensure that research projects address the needs of the market. The company should also foster close links between R&D and manufacturing personnel, to ensure that the company has the capability to manufacture any proposed new products.

Many companies achieve close integration between different functions by setting up project teams. Such teams comprise representatives of the various functional areas. The task of these teams is to oversee the development of new products. For example, Compaq's success in introducing new products in the personal computer industry has been linked to its use of project teams that oversee the development of a new product from its inception to its market introduction.

Another advantage of such teams is that they can significantly reduce the time it takes to develop a new product. Thus, while R&D personnel are working on the design, manufacturing personnel can be setting up facilities, and marketing personnel can be developing their plans. Because of such integration, Compaq needed only six months to take the first portable personal computer from an idea on a drawing board to a marketable product.

To use resources to the best effect, a company must also devise a selection process for choosing only the ventures that demonstrate the greatest probability of commercial success. Picking *future winners,* however, is a tricky business, since by definition new ventures are *question marks* with an uncertain future. A study by Edwin Mansfield and G. Beardsley found that the uncertainty surrounding new ventures was so great that a company typically took four to five years after launching the venture before it could reasonably estimate its future profitability.[20] Nevertheless, some kind of selection process is necessary if a company is to avoid spreading its resources too thinly over too many projects.

Once a project is selected, management needs to monitor the progress of the venture closely. Evidence suggests that the most important criterion for evaluating a venture during its first four to five years is market-share growth rather than cash flow or profitability. In the long run, the most successful ventures are those that increase their market share. A company should have clearly defined market-share objectives for an internal new venture and decide to retain or kill it in its early years on the basis of its ability to achieve market-share goals. Only in the medium term should profitability and cash flow begin to take on greater importance.

Finally, the association of large-scale entry with greater long-term profitability suggests that a company can increase the probability of success for an internal new venture by thinking big. Thinking big means construction of efficient-scale manufacturing facilities ahead of demand, large marketing expenditures, and a commitment by corporate management to accept initial large losses as long as market share is expanding.

Joint Ventures

In some situations a company prefers internal new venturing over acquisition as an entry strategy but is nevertheless hesitant to commit itself to an internal new venture because of the risks and costs involved in building a new operation up from the ground floor. Such a situation is most likely to occur when a company sees the possibility of establishing an *emerging winner* in an embryonic or growth industry but the risks and costs associated with the project are more than it is willing to assume on its own. In such circumstances, the company may prefer to enter into a joint venture with another company and use the joint venture as a vehicle for entering the new business area. Such an arrangement enables the company to share the substantial risks and costs involved in a new project.[21]

For example, in 1990 IBM and Motorola set up a joint venture whose purpose is to provide a service that will allow computer users to communicate over radio waves. Customers buying the service will use hand-held computers, made by Motorola, to communicate by means of a private network of radio towers that IBM had built across the United States. The venture is aimed at the potentially enormous market of people who could benefit from using computers in the field, such as people who repair equipment in offices and insurance claims adjusters. Analysts estimate that the market for such a service is currently in the tens of millions of dollars but could reach the billions over the next decade.

Because of the embryonic nature of the industry, the venture faces substantial risks. A number of competing technologies are on the horizon. For example, laptop computers are being fitted with modems that can communicate with host computers through cellular telephone networks. Although cellular networks are more crowded and less reliable than radio networks, that state of affairs could change. Thus there is no guarantee that communication between computers over radio waves is the technology of the future. Given this uncertainty, it makes sense for IBM and Motorola to combine in a joint venture and share the risks associated with building up this business.

In addition, a joint venture makes sense when a company can increase the probability of successfully establishing a new business by joining forces with another company. For a company that has some of the skills and assets necessary to establish a successful new venture, teaming up with another company that has complementary skills and assets may increase the probability of success.

Again, the joint venture between IBM and Motorola provides an example. Motorola dominates the market for mobile radios and already manufactures hand-held computers, but it lacks a nationwide radio network that users of hand-held computers might use to communicate with each other. IBM lacks radio technology, but it does have a private network of radio towers (originally built for communicating with 20,000-plus IBM service people in the field) that covers more than 90 percent of the country. Combining Motorola's skills in radio technology with IBM's radio network in a single joint venture increases significantly the probability of establishing a successful new business.

However, there are three main drawbacks with such an arrangement. First, a joint venture allows a company to share the risks and costs of developing a new business, but it also requires the profits to be shared if the new business is successful. Second, a company that enters into a joint venture always runs the risk of giving critical know-how away to its joint-venture partner, who might use that know-how to compete directly with the company in the future. As we pointed out in Section 8.8 on global strategic alliances, however, joint ventures may be structured to minimize this risk. Third, the venture partners must share control. If the partners have different business philosophies, time horizons, or investment preferences, substantial problems can arise. Conflicts over how to run the joint venture can tear it apart and result in business failure.

In sum, although joint ventures often have a distinct advantage over internal new venturing as a means of establishing a new business operation, they also have certain drawbacks. Thus when deciding whether to go it alone or to cooperate with another company in a joint venture, strategic managers need to assess carefully the pros and cons of the alternatives.

9.8 EXIT STRATEGIES

Just as building a balanced portfolio requires entry into new business areas, so it also requires exit from existing business areas. As Table 9.3 suggested, exit is normally required when a company has too many *losers* or *question marks* and sometimes when it has too many *developing winners*. (It is not unusual for a company to sell a *developing winner* if the business does not fit the basic strategic thrust of the corporation.) Exit strategies are also normally a critical component of corporate retrenchment strategies. How should a company deal with the exit problem? In essence, it has three choices: divest, harvest, or liquidate. Which strategy is best in a given situation depends on two factors: the characteristics of the relevant industry and the characteristics of the business to be divested.

Divestment, Harvest, and Liquidation

Divestment Divestment involves selling a business to another company or to the management of the business itself. As an exit option, divestment is becoming an increasingly popular strategy. In 1986 the number of divestments in the United States reached an all-time high of 1,317.[22] Divestment makes sense if the prospects for the business to be sold seem good—that is, if the business, to be divested is a *developing winner* or a particularly promising *question mark*. In these circumstances, the unit to be divested can command a high price. Divestment can be difficult to implement if the prospects for the business are poor, as in the case of a *loser*. For example, when the Bendix Corporation decided to exit from the troubled machine tool industry in 1984, it could get only $74 million for its operation. Yet five years earlier, when the machine tool industry was booming, Bendix had paid $300 million to acquire just part of the business it sold in 1984.[23]

Harvest A harvest strategy involves controlled disinvestment in a business unit to optimize cash flow as the company exits from an industry. To increase cash flow, management eliminates or severely curtails new investment, cuts maintenance of facilities, and reduces advertising and research while reaping the benefits of past good will.[24] The effects are illustrated in Figure 9.6. The business unit loses market share, but in the short run cash flow out of the business increases markedly. The cash generated by the harvest strategy can be invested elsewhere in the corporation. Once the cash flow begins to decline, liquidation is normally considered. Divestment is difficult because by this time the business is run-down and its long-term prospects are poor.

The trouble with a harvest strategy is that it can be difficult to implement. It creates motivational problems in the business being harvested and can lead to a lack of confidence on the part of customers and suppliers once they perceive what is occurring. Thus the strategy may be administratively more difficult to manage than it is worth.

Liquidation   Liquidation involves closing an operation. Liquidation is normally the exit option of last resort. It is selected only when all other options have

FIGURE 9.6   **The impact of a harvest strategy on cash flow**

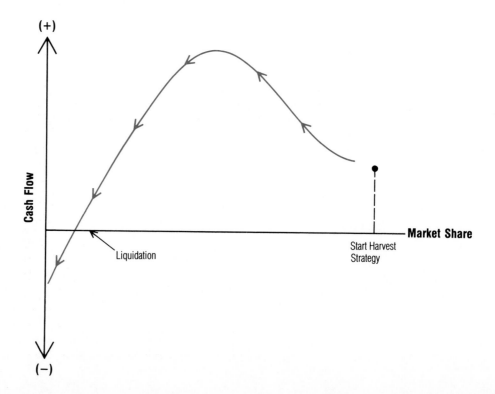

failed, because a company must take substantial write-offs on the closure of an operation and bear the fixed costs of exit, such as severance pay to employees.

Choice of Exit Strategy

The choice of exit strategy is governed by the characteristics of the business unit to be sold and the competitive intensity of the industry in which it is based. The characteristics of the business unit to be sold can be summarized by its portfolio category: *developing winner, question mark,* or *loser.* Relevant industry characteristics include factors that determine competitive intensity: barriers to entry, life-cycle factors, exit barriers, product characteristics, and so on (see Chapter 3). An industry's characteristics can be summarized by its overall competitive prospects, which are either *favorable* or *unfavorable.*

Other things being equal, a company chooses the exit strategy that maximizes the payoffs of exit. Given that liquidation normally has a negative payoff, the preferred choice is between divestment and harvest. Within this framework, the range of preferred exit strategies is illustrated in Table 9.5. By definition, *developing winners* are most likely to be found in industries with favorable prospects. Divestment makes most sense in these circumstances, since an abundance of buyers will bid up the purchase price.

Losers can be found in industries with both favorable and unfavorable prospects. The poor competitive position of *losers* makes it unlikely that they can be divested at a reasonable price. When an industry's prospects are favorable, a harvest strategy may be preferred. Even in such circumstances, however, difficulties associated with implementing a harvest strategy may prompt a company to divest *losers* at a bargain price rather than try to manage decline.

When industry prospects are unfavorable, divestment may be out of the question for *losers,* since there will be no buyers. The preferred strategy will be harvest. However, if the industry is facing rapid decline in sales, even a harvest strategy may not generate much in the way of positive cash flow. Liquidation is the only option in such circumstances.

TABLE 9.5   **Exit strategies**

Business characteristic	Favorable industry	Unfavorable industry
Developing winner	Divest	
Loser	Harvest/divest	Harvest/liquidate
Question mark	Divest	Liquidate

For *question marks* operating in a favorable industry environment, divestment is the favored option. In such cases, a company can often sell the business to its managers through a leveraged buyout. When the industry environment is unfavorable, however, few buyers are likely to be found. A harvest strategy does not work because the market share of most *question marks* is typically too low to make the strategy viable. Thus liquidation may be the only option.

9.9 SUMMARY OF CHAPTER

This chapter reviews three main techniques for analyzing the portfolio of a multibusiness company. The rationale for undertaking such an analysis is to identify what needs to be done to build a balanced portfolio. Building a balanced portfolio typically involves entry and exit strategies. The choice between different entry and exit strategies, and the pitfalls involved, are reviewed. The following points are made:

1. There are three main portfolio techniques that companies can use: the Boston Consulting Group matrix, the McKinsey matrix, and the industry evolution matrix devised by Hofer.

2. The strength of the BCG matrix is its focus on cash-flow requirements. Weaknesses include the simplistic categorization of businesses and untenable assumptions about relationships among market share, growth, and profitability.

3. The strength of the McKinsey matrix is its ability to incorporate a wide range of strategically relevant variables into the analysis. The main weakness is that the analysis is essentially static and tells little about how industry evolution might change business attractiveness.

4. The strength of the industry evolution matrix lies in what it tells about the distribution of a company's businesses across different stages of the industry life cycle. The weakness of the technique is that it ignores many strategically relevant industry factors.

5. In general, portfolio analysis helps companies conceptualize their diversity, assists in the allocation of corporate cash, and identifies the adjustments necessary to achieve a balanced portfolio. However, it has the following weaknesses: the assumption that a company can be divided into a reasonable number of strategic business units, a tendency to ignore potential conflicts of interest that might emerge between corporate cash-flow priorities and

cash-flow priorities within an SBU, and a tendency to ignore interrelation-ships among business units.

6. Correcting an imbalance in a corporate portfolio typically requires entry strategies (acquisition, internal new venturing, and joint ventures) and exit strategies (divestment, harvest, and liquidation).

7. The choice of an appropriate entry strategy is influenced by barriers to en-try, relatedness, speed and development costs of entry, risks of entry, and industry life-cycle considerations. In general, internal new venturing makes the most sense when the strategic goal is to establish *question marks* or per-haps *developing winners*. Acquisition makes the most sense when the stra-tegic goal involves establishing *profit producers* or *winners*.

8. Many acquisitions fail because of poor postacquisition integration, overes-timation of the potential gains from synergy, the high cost of acquisition, and poor preacquisition screening. Guarding against failure involves struc-tured screening, good bidding strategies, and positive attempts to integrate the acquired company into the organization of the acquiring one.

9. Many internal new ventures fail because of entry on too small a scale, poor commercialization, and poor corporate management of the internal venture process. Guarding against failure involves a structured approach toward project selection and management, integration of R&D and marketing to improve commercialization of a venture idea, and entry on a significant scale.

10. Exit strategies include divestment, harvest, and liquidation. The choice of exit strategy is governed by the characteristics of the relevant business unit and the competitive intensity of the relevant industry.

Discussion Questions

1. Why might diversified companies that use portfolio analysis techniques have an advantage over diversified companies that do not? How do you think cash flows are allocated in companies that do not use portfolio analysis techniques?

2. Under what circumstances might it be best to enter a new business area by acquisition, and under what circumstances might internal new venturing be the preferred entry mode?

3. In the face of the obvious difficulties of suc-ceeding with acquisitions, why do so many companies continue to make them?

4. What are the main pitfalls of portfolio plan-ning? How might these pitfalls be avoided?

Endnotes

1. For details, see "Rockwell: Using Its Cash Hoard to Edge Away from Defense," *Business Week,* February 4, 1985, pp. 82–84; "Bob Anderson Has New Miracles to Work at Rockwell," *Business Week,* March 31, 1986, pp. 64–65; and "Rockwell's Hard Place," *Business Week,* February 29, 1988, pp. 46–47.

2. For further details of portfolio techniques, see R. A. Bettis and W. K. Hall, "Strategic Portfolio Management in the Multibusiness Firm," *California Management Review,* 24 (1981), 23–38; P. Haspeslagh, "Portfolio Planning: Uses and Limits," *Harvard Business Review* (January–February 1983), 58–73; B. Hedley, "Strategy and the Business Portfolio," *Long Range Planning,* 10 (1977), 9–15; and Charles W. Hofer and Dan Schendel, *Strategy Formulation: Analytical Concepts* (St. Paul, Minn.: West, 1978).

3. For evidence, see D. F. Barnett and R. W. Crandall, *Up from the Ashes: The Rise of the Steel Miner* (Washington, D.C.: The Brookings Institute, 1986), pp. 1–17.

4. As defined by Hoter and Schendel, *Strategy Formulation,* p. 82.

5. Charles W. Hofer, *Conceptual Constructs for Formulating Corporate and Business Strategies* (Boston: Intercollegiate Case Clearing House, #9-378-754, 1977).

6. For details, see R. A. Bettis and W. K. Hall, "The Business Portfolio Approach: Where It Falls Down in Practice," *Long Range Planning,* 12 (1983), 95–105; and Haspeslagh, "Portfolio Planning," pp. 58–73.

7. Bettis and Hall, "The Business Portfolio Approach," pp. 95–105.

8. For further details, see H. L. Ansoff, *Corporate Strategy* (New York: McGraw-Hill, 1965); E. R. Biggadike, *Corporate Diversification: Entry, Strategy and Performance* (Cambridge, Mass.: Division of Research, Harvard Business School, 1979); M. S. Salter and W. A. Weinhold, *Diversification Through Acquisition: Strategies for Creating Economic Value* (New York: Free Press, 1979); and G. S. Yip, "Diversification Entry: Internal Development Versus Acquisition," *Strategic Management Journal,* 3 (1982), 331–345.

9. E. R. Biggadike, "The Risky Business of Diversification," *Harvard Business Review* (May–June 1979), 103–111.

10. Edwin Mansfield, "How Economists See R&D," *Harvard Business Review* (November–December 1981), 98–106.

11. Peter Petre, "AT&T's Epic Push into Computers," *Fortune,* May 25, 1987, pp. 42–50.

12. See D. C. Mueller, "The Effects of Conglomerate Mergers: A Survey of the Empirical Evidence," *Journal of Banking and Finance,* 1 (1977), 315–342, and *The Determinant and Effects of Mergers* (Cambridge, Mass.: Oelgeschlager, Gunn & Hain, 1980). See also M. H. Lubatkin, "Merger and the Performance of the Acquiring Firm," *Academy of Management Review,* 8 (1983), 218–225.

13. "Do Mergers Really Work?" *Business Week,* June 3, 1985, pp. 88–100.

14. "Fluor: Compounding Fractures from Leaping Before Looking," *Business Week,* June 3, 1985, pp. 92–93.

15. "Coca-Cola: A Sobering Lesson from Its Journey into Wine," *Business Week,* June 3, 1985, pp. 96–98.

16. For views on this issue, see L. L. Fray, D. H. Gaylin, and J. W. Down, "Successful Acquisition Planning," *Journal of Business Strategy,* 5 (1984), 46–55; C. W. L. Hill, "Profile of a Conglomerate Takeover: BTR and Thomas Tilling," *Journal of General Management,* 10 (1984), 34–50; and D. R. Willensky, "Making It Happen: How to Execute an Acquisition," *Business Horizons* (March–April 1985), 38–45.

17. Biggadike, "The Risky Business of Diversification," pp. 103–111.

18. R. A. Burgelman, "A Process Model of Internal Corporate Venturing in the Diversified Major Firm," *Administrative Science Quarterly,* 28 (1983), 223–244.

19. I. C. MacMillan and R. George, "Corporate Venturing: Challenges for Senior Managers," *Journal of Business Strategy,* 5 (1985), 34–43.

20. G. Beardsley and Edwin Mansfield, "A Note on the Accuracy of Industrial Forecasts of the Profitability of New Products and Processes," *Journal of Business,* (1978), 127–130.

21. Paul B. Carroll, "IBM, Motorola Plan Radio Link for Computers," *The Wall Street Journal,* January 29, 1990, pp. B1, B5.

22. "1986 Profile," *Mergers and Acquisitions,* 21 (1986), 57–61.

23. "Bendix: A Buy That Really Was Too Good to Be True," *Business Week,* June 3, 1985, pp. 93–94.

24. K. R. Harrigan and Michael E. Porter, "End-Game Strategies for Declining Industries," *Harvard Business Review* (July–August 1983), 111–120.

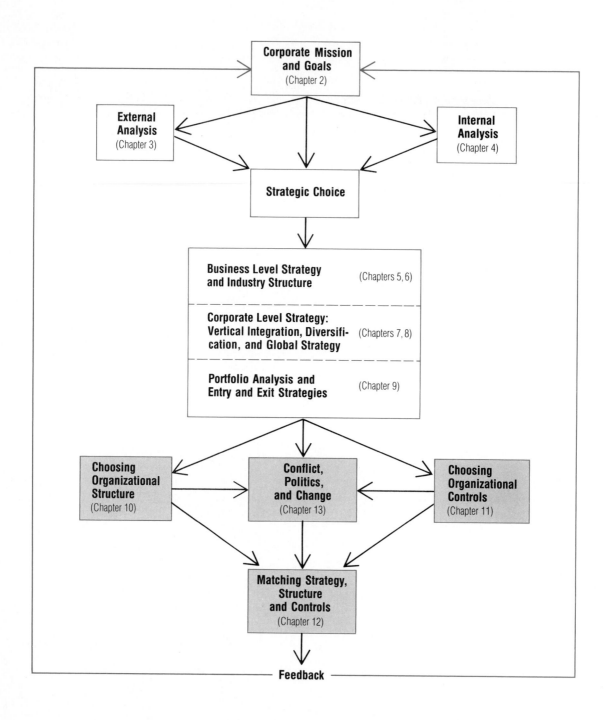

STRATEGY IMPLEMENTATION

Chapter 10

DESIGNING

ORGANIZATIONAL

STRUCTURE

10.1 OPENING INCIDENT: APPLE COMPUTER

Incorporated in 1977, Apple Computer, Inc., designs, manufactures, and markets personal computers for use in business, education, and the home.[1] Apple Computer was created in 1976, when two engineers, Steven Jobs and Steven Wozniak, collaborated to produce a computing board for personal use. As early orders for their system increased, Jobs and Wozniak realized that they needed to create an organization with a structure that could handle capital acquisitions, marketing, management and strategic planning, engineering, and production. In essence, they needed to formalize the functions necessary in any complex business. In true entrepreneurial fashion, they created a flat, decentralized structure designed to allow people to be creative, flexible, and responsive to the uncertainty in the new home computer industry. With few rules and only a vague hierarchy, the organization operated on the basis of personal contact between people in different functions through teams and task forces, many of which were chaired by Jobs and Wozniak.

By 1982 Apple's structure was taller, with more levels of management. A new chief executive, Hugh Sculley, had been hired to take control of the management side of the business. Fast growth and the introduction of a wider range of products—the Lisa and Macintosh computers—led to greater organizational differentiation. As a result, Apple moved to a divisional structure, in which each product was manufactured in a self-contained division and each division had its own set of specialist functions such as marketing, research and development, and product engineering. Problems arose with this structure, however.[2] Jobs championed the Macintosh computer against the Lisa computer for development and triggered hostile competition for resources among the divisions. Overhead costs rose dramatically because specialist functions were duplicated in each division. Furthermore, Sculley's role and the role of top managers in running the business became unclear in the organization because all direction seemed to come from the divisions and especially from Jobs. The unsettling outcome of these conditions was that IBM overtook Apple as leader in the personal computer industry.

By 1985 the recession in the computer industry had exacerbated these problems and made reorganization imperative. Sculley took total

311

control of the company and once again changed its structure.[3] He created a structure in which one set of specialist functions served the needs of all the various product lines—a product structure. The production system was also changed so that products were manufactured in one central production department, in which one management team had overall control, rather than in separate divisions by different managers. This change reduced costs massively, and centralized management control allowed the company to respond more quickly to market developments. In addition, Apple adopted company-based, rather than division-based, plans for achieving corporate objectives.

Apple Computer started out with a flat, decentralized functional structure and had moved to a second form, the divisional structure, which inhibited its development and growth. Today Apple uses a more centralized product structure and is in good financial shape. Its streamlined management team is able to address the strategic and operational needs of the business as Apple seeks to expand its market share.

10.2 OVERVIEW

As the discussion of Apple suggests, this chapter examines the creation of the right organizational structure for managing a company's strategy. In the first chapter of this book, we define strategy implementation as the way in which a company created the organizational arrangements that allow it to put its strategic plan into operation most efficiently and to achieve its objectives. Strategy is implemented through organizational design. Organizational design involves selecting the combination of organizational structure and control systems that lets a company pursue its strategy most efficiently. Different kinds of structure and control systems provide strategic planners with alternative means of pursuing different strategies because they offer the company and the people within it a variety of different ways to act.

In this chapter, the organizational structures available to strategic managers are examined. In Chapter 11, we consider the integration mechanisms that companies use to coordinate the structure, as well as the control systems through which they monitor and evaluate corporate, divisional, and functional performance. Chapter 12 traces the ways in which different strategy choices lead to the use of different kinds of structure and control systems. After reading this section of the book, you will be able to choose the right organizational design for implementing a company's strategy. You will understand why Apple Computer chose to change organizational structures as it grew and developed.

10.3 DESIGNING ORGANIZATIONAL STRUCTURES

After formulating a company's strategy, management must make designing the structure its next priority, for strategy can only be implemented through organizational structure. The activities of organizational personnel are meaningless unless some type of structure is used to assign people to tasks and connect the activities of different people or functions.[4] The terms used to describe the characteristics of organizational structure are differentiation and integration. **Differentiation** is the way in which a company allocates people and resources to organizational tasks.[5] First, management chooses how to distribute *decision-making authority* in the organization; these are **vertical differentiation** choices.[6] Second, it chooses how to divide labor in the organization and group organizational tasks; these are **horizontal differentiation** choices. **Integration** is the means by which a company seeks to coordinate people and functions to accomplish organizational tasks.[7] These means include the use of integrating mechanisms and the whole apparatus of organizational control. In short, differentiation refers to the way in which a company divides itself up into parts, and integration refers to the way in which the parts are then combined. Together the two processes determine how an organizational structure will operate and how successfully managers will be able to implement their chosen strategies.

As a comparison, consider the structure of a chemical compound such as water. It consists of different types of atoms: two of hydrogen and one of oxygen. It also comprises bonds between the atoms. The properties of the chemical—the way it functions—are a consequence both of its individual atoms (differentiation) and the way these are bonded or connected (integration). The same is true of organizational structure: The way it functions depends on what it is made up of and how it is put together—its differentiation and integration. Strategic managers must design the organization correctly if it is to be effective for a particular strategy.

10.4 VERTICAL DIFFERENTIATION

The aim of vertical differentiation is to specify the reporting relationships that link people, tasks, and functions at all levels of a company. Fundamentally, this means that management chooses the appropriate number of hierarchical levels and the correct span of control for implementing a company's strategy most effectively. The organizational hierarchy establishes the authority structure from the top to the bottom of the organization. The **span of control** is defined as the number of subordinates a manager directly manages.[8] The basic choice is whether to aim for a **flat structure,** with few hierarchical levels and thus a relatively wide span of control, or a **tall structure,** with many levels and thus a relatively narrow span of control (Figure 10.1). Tall structures have many hierarchical levels relative to size; flat structures have few levels relative to size.[9] For example, research suggests that the average number of hierarchical levels for a company employing 3,000 persons is seven. Thus an organization having nine levels would be called tall, whereas one having four would be called flat. With its 4,000 employees and four hierarchical levels, Liz Claiborne, for instance, has a relatively flat structure.

FIGURE 10.1   **Tall and flat structures**

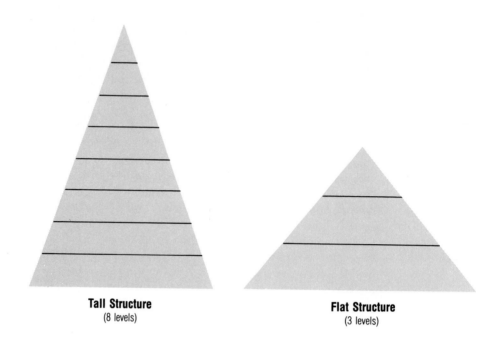

Tall Structure
(8 levels)

Flat Structure
(3 levels)

On the other hand, before reorganization, Westinghouse, with its ten hierarchical levels, had a relatively tall structure. Now it has seven levels—the average for a large organization.

Companies choose the number of levels they need on the basis of their strategy and the functional tasks necessary to achieve their strategy. For example, manufacturing companies often pursue a low-cost strategy to minimize production costs and increase operating efficiency. As a result, these companies are usually tall, with many levels in the hierarchy and prescribed areas of authority, so that managers can exert tight control over personnel and resources.[10] On the other hand, high-tech companies often pursue a strategy of differentiation based on service and quality. Consequently, these companies are usually flat, giving employees wide discretion to meet customers' demands without having to refer constantly to supervisors.[11] (We discuss this subject further in Chapter 12.) The crux of the matter is that the allocation of authority and responsibility in the organization must match the needs of corporate-, business-, and functional-level strategy.

Disadvantages of Tall Hierarchies

As a company grows and diversifies, choosing the right number of levels for managing its business becomes important because research shows that the num-

FIGURE 10.2   **Relationship between company size and number of hierarchical levels**

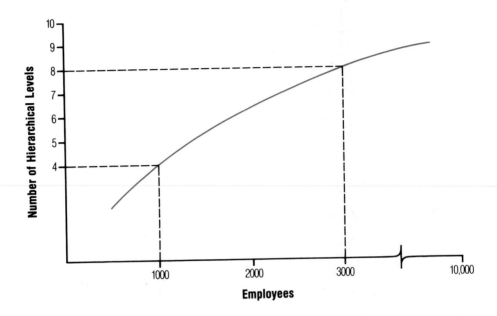

ber of hierarchical levels relative to company size is predictable as the size increases.[12] This finding demonstrates an interesting lesson in organization design concerning the correct choice of the number of hierarchical levels. The relationship between size and number of levels is presented in Figure 10.2. Companies with approximately 1,000 employees usually have four levels in the hierarchy: chief executive officer, departmental vice presidents, first-line supervisors, and shop-floor employees. By 3,000 employees, they have increased their level of vertical differentiation by raising the number of levels to eight. Beyond 3,000 employees, however, something interesting happens: Even when companies grow to 10,000 employees or more, the number of hierarchical levels rarely increases beyond nine or ten. As organizations grow, managers apparently try to limit the number of hierarchical levels. When companies become too tall, problems occur, making strategy more difficult to implement and the company less efficient in pursuing its mission.[13]

Communication problems   Too many hierarchical levels impede communication. Communication between the top and the bottom of the hierarchy takes much longer as the chain of command lengthens. This leads to inflexibility, and valuable time is lost in bringing a new product to market or in keeping up with technological developments.[14] For Federal Express, communication is vital in its business; the company therefore allows a maximum of only five layers of management between the employee and the chief executive officer to avoid communication problems.[15] On the other hand, because of its tall hierarchy, Procter & Gamble needed twice as much time as its competitors to introduce new products until it recently moved to streamline its structure.[16]

More subtle, but just as important, are the problems of information distortion that accompany the transmission of information up and down the hierarchy. Going down the hierarchy, managers at different levels (for example, divisional or corporate managers) may misinterpret information, either through accidental garbling of messages or on purpose, to suit their own interests. In either case, information from the top may not reach its destination intact. For instance, a request to share divisional knowledge among divisions to achieve gains from synergy may be overlooked or ignored by divisional managers who perceive it as a threat to their autonomy and power. This attitude among managers was one of the problems that led Iacocca to reorganize Chrysler to coordinate cost-cutting measures across divisions.

Information transmitted upward in the hierarchy may also be distorted. Subordinates may transmit to their superiors only information that improves their own standing in the organization. The greater the number of hierarchical levels, the more scope subordinates have to distort facts, so that top managers may lose control over the hierarchy. Similarly, managers may compete with each other, and, when they are free from close corporate supervision, they may hoard information to promote their own interests at the expense of the organization's.

Motivational problems   A proliferation of levels reduces the scope of managerial authority. As the number of levels in the hierarchy increases, the amount of authority possessed by managers at each hierarchical level falls. For example, consider the situation of two identically sized organizations, one of which has three levels in the hierarchy and the other seven. Managers in the flat structure have much more authority, and greater authority increases their motivation to perform effectively and take responsibility for the organization's performance. Moreover, when there are fewer managers, their performance is more visible, and therefore they can expect greater rewards when the business does well. By contrast, in the tall organization, managers' ability to exercise authority is limited, and their decisions are being constantly scrutinized by their superiors. As a result, the tendency is for managers to pass the buck and refuse to take the risks that are often necessary when pursuing new strategies. The shape of the organization's structure strongly affects the behavior of people within it and thus the way in which strategy is implemented.[17]

High costs of operation   Another problem facing tall structures is simply that many hierarchical levels imply many managers, and employing managers is expensive. Managerial salaries, benefits, offices, and secretaries are a huge expense for an organization. If the average middle manager costs a company a total of $200,000 a year, then employing 100 surplus managers will cost $20 million a year. U.S. oil companies recognized this fact when oil prices fell in 1986. When these companies made billions of dollars in profits, they had no incentive to control the number of levels in the hierarchy and the number of managers. Once they grew aware of the cost of these managers, however, companies such as ARCO and Exxon Corporation ruthlessly purged the hierarchy, reducing the number of levels, and thus of managers, to reduce costs and restore profitability.

To offer another example, when companies grow and are successful, they often hire personnel and create new positions without much regard for the effect of these actions on the organizational hierarchy. Later, when managers review that structure, it is quite common to see the number of levels reduced because of the disadvantages just discussed. Deregulation also quite often prompts a reduction in levels and personnel. In a deregulated environment, companies must respond to increased competition. After deregulation, AT&T, as well as a number of airline companies, reduced costs and streamlined their structures so that they could respond more rapidly to opportunities and threats brought about by increased competition. An examination of the nature of vertical differentiation in an organization is one means by which strategic planners are able to assess organizational strengths and weaknesses.

In sum, many problems arise when companies become too tall and the chain of command becomes too long. Strategic managers tend to lose control over the hierarchy, which means that they lose control over their strategies. Disaster often follows. One way that such problems can be partially overcome, however, is by the decentralization of authority. That is, authority is vested in lower levels in the hierarchy as well as at the top. Because this is one of the most important implementation decisions a company can make, we discuss it next in more detail.

Centralization or Decentralization?

Centralization of authority exists when managers at the upper levels of the organizational hierarchy retain the authority to make the most important decisions. When authority is decentralized, it is delegated to divisions, functional departments, and managers at lower levels in the organization. If top management delegates authority to lower levels in the hierarchy, the communication problems described earlier are avoided because information does not have to be constantly sent to the top of the organization for decisions to be made. Decentralization or delegation of authority has several other advantages. First, if strategic managers delegate *operational decision making* to lower levels, they can spend more time on *strategic decision making*. As a result, they make more effective decisions and are better at long-term planning. Second, decentralization also promotes flexibility and responsiveness because lower-level managers can make on-the-spot decisions. Thus the bottom layers in the organization can more easily adapt to local situations. As IBM has demonstrated, this can be an enormous advantage for business strategy. For example, IBM has a tall structure, but it is well-known for the amount of authority it delegates to lower levels. Operational personnel can respond quickly to customer needs and so ensure superior service, which is a major source of IBM's competitive advantage. Similarly, to revitalize its product strategy, Westinghouse has massively decentralized its operations to give divisions more autonomy and encourage risk taking and quick response to customer needs.[18]

If decentralization is so effective, why do not all companies decentralize decision making and avoid the problems of tall hierarchies? The answer is that centralization has its advantages, too. Centralized decision making allows easier coordination of the organizational activities needed to pursue a company's strategy. If managers at all levels can make their own decisions, planning becomes extremely difficult, and the company may lose control of its decision making. Centralization also means that decisions fit broad organization objectives. For example, when its branch operations were getting out of hand, Merrill Lynch & Co. increased centralization by installing more information systems to give corporate managers greater control over branch activities. Similarly, Hewlett-Packard centralized research and development responsibility at the corporate level to provide a more directed corporate strategy. Furthermore, in times of crisis, centralization of authority permits strong leadership because authority is focused on one person or group. This focus allows for speedy decision making and a concerted response by the whole organization. Perhaps Iacocca personifies the meaning of centralization in times of crisis. He provided the vision and energy for Chrysler managers to respond creatively to Chrysler's problems and designed a cohesive plan for restoring its profitability.

Summary: Vertical Differentiation

Managing the strategy-structure relationship when the number of hierarchical levels becomes too great is difficult and expensive. Depending on a firm's situation, the problems of tall hierarchies can be avoided by decentralization. As firm size increases, however, decentralization becomes less effective. How, therefore, as firms grow and diversify can they maintain control over their structures and strategies without becoming taller or more decentralized? That is, how can a firm like Exxon control 300,000 employees without becoming too tall and inflexible? There must be alternative ways to create organizational arrangements to achieve corporate objectives. The first of these ways is through the choice of form of horizontal differentiation: by deciding on the correct way to group organizational activities and tasks.

10.5 HORIZONTAL DIFFERENTIATION

Whereas vertical differentiation concerns the division of authority, horizontal differentiation focuses on the division and grouping of tasks to meet the objectives of the business.[19] Because, to a large degree, an organization's tasks are a function of its strategy, the dominant view is that companies choose a form of horizontal differentiation or structure to match their organizational strategy. Perhaps the first person to address this issue formally was the Harvard business historian Alfred D. Chandler.[20] After studying the organizational problems experienced in large U.S. corporations such as Du Pont and General Motors as they grew and diversified in the early decades of this century, Chandler reached two conclusions: (1) that in principle organizational structure follows the growth strategy of a company, or, in other words, the range and variety of tasks it chooses to pursue; and (2) that American enterprises go through stages of strategy and structure changes as they grow and diversify. In other words, a company's structure changes as its strategy changes in a predictable way.[21] The kinds of structure that companies adopt are discussed in this section.

Simple Structure

The simple structure is normally used by the small, entrepreneurial company involved in producing one or a few related products for a specific market segment. Often in this situation, one person, the entrepreneur, takes on most of the managerial tasks. No formal organization arrangements exist, and horizontal differentiation is low because employees perform multiple duties. A classic example of this structure is Apple Computer in its earliest stage. As a venture between two persons, Steven Jobs and Steven Wozniak, worked together in a garage to perform all the necessary tasks to market their personal computer. The success of their product, however, made this simple structure outdated almost as soon as it was adopted. To grow and perform all the tasks required by a rapidly expanding company, Apple needed a more complex form of horizontal differentiation.

Functional Structure

As companies grow, two things happen. First, the range of tasks that must be performed expands. For example, it suddenly becomes apparent that the services of a professional accountant or production manager are needed to take control of specialized tasks. Second, no one person can successfully perform more than one organizational task without becoming overloaded: For example, the entrepreneur can no longer simultaneously produce and sell the product. The issue arises, then, as to what grouping of activities, or what form of horizontal differentiation, can most efficiently handle the needs of the growing company. The answer for most companies is the **functional structure.** In functional structures, people are grouped on the basis of their common expertise and experience or because they use the same resources.[22] For example, engineers are grouped in a function because they perform the same tasks and use the same skills or equipment. Figure 10.3 shows a typical functional structure. Here, each of the triangles represents a different functional specialization—sales and marketing, manufacturing, research

FIGURE 10.3   Functional structure

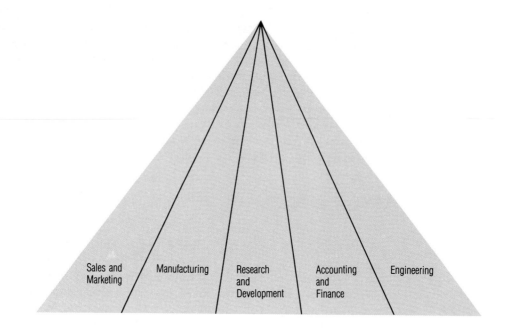

Sales and Marketing

Manufacturing

Research and Development

Accounting and Finance

Engineering

and development, and so on—and each function concentrates on its own special-ized task.

Advantages of a functional structure   The functional structure has several advantages. First, if people who perform similar tasks are grouped, they can learn from one another and become better—more specialized and productive—at what they do. Second, they can monitor one another and make sure that others are doing their tasks effectively and not shirking their responsibilities. As a result, the work process becomes more efficient, reducing costs and increasing opera-tional flexibility.

A second important advantage of the functional structure derives from its ability to give managers more control of organizational activities. As already noted, many difficulties arise when the number of levels in the hierarchy in-creases. If you group people into different functions, however, each with its own managers, then several different hierarchies are created, and the company can avoid becoming too tall. For example, there will be one hierarchy in manufac-turing and another in accounting and finance. Managing the business is much easier when different groups specialize in different organizational tasks and are managed separately.

Problems with a functional structure   In adopting a functional structure, a company increases its level of horizontal differentiation to handle more complex task requirements. The structure allows it to keep control of its activities as it grows. This structure serves the company well until it begins to grow and diversify. If the company becomes geographically diverse and begins operating in many locations or if it starts producing a wide range of products, control problems arise. Specifically, **control loss** problems develop in the functional structure, and the company is no longer able to coordinate its activities.[23]

Communications problems   As functional hierarchies evolve, functions grow more remote from one another. As a result, it becomes increasingly difficult to communicate across functions to implement strategy. This communication problem stems from **functional orientations.**[24] With increasing differentiation, the various functions develop different orientations to the problems and issues facing the organization. Different functions have different time or goal orientations. Some functions, such as manufacturing, see things in a short time framework and are concerned with achieving short-run goals, such as reducing manufacturing costs. Others, like research and development, see things from a long-term point of view, and their goals (that is, product development) may have a time horizon of several years. Moreover, different functions may have different interpersonal orientations—a further impediment to good communication. As a result of all these factors, each function may develop a different view of the strategic issues facing the company. For example, manufacturing may see a problem as the need to reduce costs, sales may see it as the need to increase responsiveness to customer needs, and research and development may see it as the need to introduce new products. In such cases, the functions find it difficult to communicate and coordinate with one another, and implementation suffers.

Measurement problems   As the number of its products proliferates, a company may find it difficult to measure the contributions of one or a group of products to its overall profitability. Consequently, the company may be turning out some unprofitable products without realizing it and may also be making poor decisions on resource allocation. In essence, the company's measurement systems are not complex enough to serve its needs.

Location problems   Location factors may also hamper coordination and control. If a company is producing or selling in many different regional areas, then the centralized system of control provided by the functional structure no longer suits it because managers in the various regions must be flexible enough to respond to the needs of these regions. Thus the functional structure is not complex enough to handle regional diversity.

Strategic problems   Sometimes the combined effect of all these factors is that long-term strategic considerations are ignored because management is preoccupied with solving communication and coordination problems. As a result, a company may lose direction and fail to take advantage of new opportunities.

Experiencing these problems is a sign that the company does not have an appropriate level of differentiation to achieve its objectives. It must change its mix of vertical and horizontal differentiation to accommodate more complex organizational tasks. To this end, many companies reorganize to a product or geographical structure.

Product or Geographical Structure

In the product or geographical structure, activities are grouped by either product lines or geographical location. In the product structure, the production function is broken down into different product lines based on the similarities and differences among the products. Figure 10.4 presents a product structure typical of a drug or pharmaceutical company. In this company, products are grouped in terms of their being wet drugs, dry drugs, or powders. Inside each product group, there may be many similar products manufactured.

FIGURE 10.4   **Product or geographical structure**

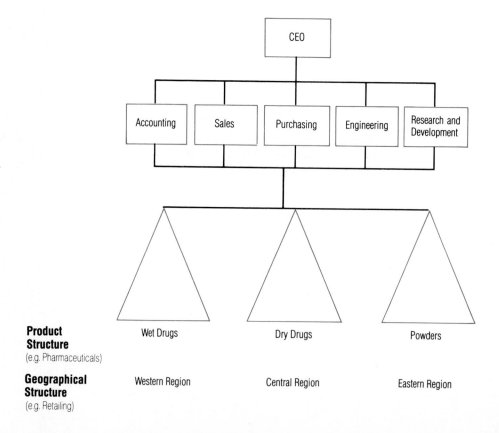

| **Product Structure** (e.g. Pharmaceuticals) | Wet Drugs | Dry Drugs | Powders |

| **Geographical Structure** (e.g. Retailing) | Western Region | Central Region | Eastern Region |

Because three different product groupings now exist, the degree of horizontal differentiation in this structure is higher than in the functional structure. The specialized support functions, such as accounting or sales, are centralized at the top of the organization, but each support function is divided in such a way that personnel tend to specialize in one of the different product categories to avoid communication problems. Thus there may be three groups of accountants, one for each of the three product categories. In sales, separate sales forces dealing with the different product lines may emerge, but because a single sales function brings economies of scale to selling and distribution, these groups will coordinate their activities. Unisys Corporation, for example, recently moved to a product structure based on serving the product needs of different customer groups: the commercial and the public sectors are two such groups. Unisys's salespeople specialize in one customer group, but all groups coordinate their sales and software activities to ensure good communication and the transfer of knowledge among product lines.

The use of a product structure, then, reduces the problems of control and communication associated with the functional structure. It pushes aside barriers among functions because the product line, rather than each individual function, becomes the focus of attention. In addition, the profit contribution of each product line can be clearly identified, and resources can be allocated more efficiently. Note also that this structure has one more level in the hierarchy than the functional structure—that of the product line manager. This increase in vertical differentiation allows managers at the level of the production line to concentrate on day-to-day operations and gives top managers more time to take a longer-term look at business opportunities.

Another example of a company that adopted a product structure to manage its product lines is Maytag. Initially, when it manufactured only washers and dryers, Maytag used a functional structure. In trying to increase its market share, however, Maytag bought two other appliance manufacturers: Jenn-Air, known for its electric ranges, and Hardwick, which produces gas ranges. To handle the new product lines, Maytag moved to the product structure presented in Figure 10.5. Each company was operated as a product line, and the major specialized support services were centralized as in the drug company shown in Figure 10.4. Maytag continued to diversify, however, and, as we discuss in the next section, it was forced to move to a multidivisional structure.

When a company operates as a geographical structure, geographical regions become the basis for the grouping of organizational activities. Thus the three parts in Figure 10.4 might be named Western Region, Central Region, and Eastern Region. The same range of products are manufactured in each region. Like a product structure, a geographical structure provides more control than a functional structure because there are several regional hierarchies carrying out the work previously performed by a single centralized hierarchy. A company like Federal Express clearly needs to operate a geographical structure to fulfill its corporate goal: next-day mail. Large merchandising organizations, such as Neiman-Marcus, also moved to a geographic structure soon after they started building

FIGURE 10.5   **Maytag's product structure**

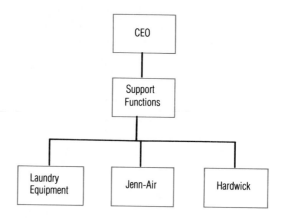

stores across the country. With a geographical structure, different regional clothing needs—sun wear in the West, down coats in the East—can be handled as required. At the same time, because the purchasing function remains centralized, one central organization can buy for all regions. Thus a company both achieves economies of scale in buying and distribution and reduces coordination and communication problems.

Once again, however, the usefulness of the product or geographical structure depends on the size of the company and its range of products and regions. If a company starts to diversity into unrelated products or to integrate vertically into new industries, the product structure would not be capable of handling the increased diversity. The reason is that it does not provide managers with enough control over organizational activities to allow them to manage the company effectively; it is not complex enough to deal with the needs of the large, multi-business company. At this point in its development, a company would normally adopt the multidivisional structure.

Multidivisional Structure

The multidivisional structure possesses two main innovations that let a company grow and diversify while overcoming control loss problems. First, each distinct product line or business unit is placed in its own self contained unit or division with all support functions. For example, Pepsi-Cola has three major divisions, soft drinks, snack foods, and restaurants, and each division has its own functions such as marketing and research and development. The result is a higher level of horizontal differentiation. Second, the office of corporate headquarters staff is created to monitor interdivisional activities and exercise financial control over each of the divisions.[25] This staff contains corporate managers who oversee all divisional and functional activities, and it constitutes an additional level in the

FIGURE 10.6   **Multidivisional structure**

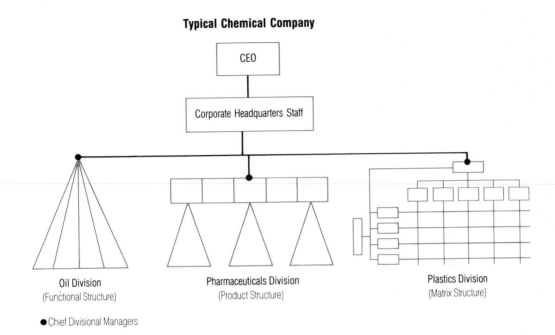

Typical Chemical Company

Oil Division
(Functional Structure)

Pharmaceuticals Division
(Product Structure)

Plastics Division
(Matrix Structure)

● Chief Divisional Managers

organizational hierarchy. Hence there is a higher level of vertical differentiation in a multidivisional structure than in a product structure. Figure 10.6 presents a typical divisional structure found in a large chemical company such as Du Pont. Although this company might easily have seventy operating divisions, only three—the oil, drugs, and plastics divisions—are represented here.

As a self contained business unit, each division possesses a full array of support services. That is, each has self-contained accounting, sales, and personnel departments, for example. Each division functions as a profit center, making it much easier for corporate headquarters staff to monitor and evaluate the activities of each.[26]

Each division is also able to adopt the structure that best suits its needs. Figure 10.6 shows that the oil division has a functional structure because its activities are standardized, the drug division has a product structure for reasons discussed earlier, and the plastics division has a matrix structure, which is discussed in detail later in this chapter. Similarly, General Motors operates the whole corporation through a multidivisional structure, but each auto division operates a product structure, in which product lines are based on the type of auto made.

In the Maytag example noted earlier, we mention that Maytag continued to diversify its operations. It purchased two more appliance manufacturers, Magic Chef Company, which produces a wide variety of air conditioners and refrigerators, and Admiral, a maker of small appliances. Management originally intended

FIGURE 10.7   **Maytag's multidivisional structure**

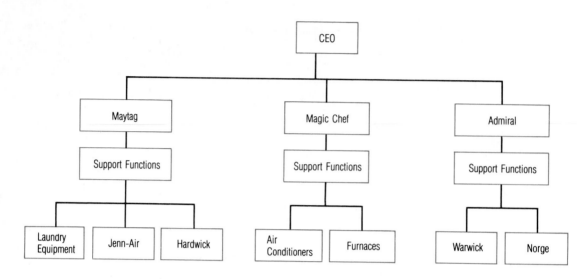

to operate the businesses as product lines through a product structure but soon realized that it would not be feasible to market several different brands in every category of the appliance industry with centralized support services.[27] The company, therefore, reorganized to a multidivisional structure with three autonomous divisions, each of which was given its own support functions. Then, within each division, a product structure was used. This change in structure proved to be very efficient and is shown in Figure 10.7.

In the multidivisional structure, day-to-day operations of a division are the responsibility of divisional management; that is, divisional management has **operating responsibility**. Corporate headquarters staff, however, which includes members of the board of directors as well as top executives, is responsible for overseeing long-term plans and providing the guidance for interdivisional projects. This staff has **strategic responsibility**. Such a combination of self-contained divisions with a centralized corporate management represents a higher level of both vertical and horizontal differentiation, as we note earlier. These two innovations provide extra control necessary to manage growth and diversification. Because this structure is now adopted by 60 percent of all large U. S. corporations, we need to consider its advantages and disadvantages in more detail.

Advantages of the Multidivisional Structure

There are several advantages that a multidivisional structure possesses when it is managed effectively by both corporate and divisional managers. Together, these advantages can raise corporate profitability to a new peak because they allow the organization to operate more complex kinds of corporate level strategy.

Enhanced corporate financial control   The profitability of different business divisions is clearly visible in the multidivisional structure.[28] Because each division is its own profit center, financial controls can be applied to each business on the basis of profit criteria. Typically, these controls involve establishing targets, monitoring performance on a regular basis, and selectively intervening when problems arise. Corporate headquarters is also in a better position to allocate corporate financial resources among competing divisions. The visibility of divisional performance also means that corporate headquarters can identify the divisions in which investment of funds would yield the greatest long-term returns. In a sense, the corporate office is in a position to act as the investor or banker in an internal capital market, channeling funds to high-yield uses.

Enhanced strategic control   The multidivisional structure frees corporate staff from operating responsibilities. The staff thus gains time for contemplating wider strategic issues and for developing responses to environmental changes. The multidivisional structure also enables headquarters to obtain the proper information to perform strategic planning functions. For example, separating individual businesses is a necessary prerequisite for the application of portfolio planning techniques.

Growth   The multidivisional structure enables the company to overcome an organizational limit to its growth. By reducing information overload at the center, headquarters personnel can handle a greater number of businesses. They can consider opportunities for further growth and diversification. Communication problems are reduced by applying accounting and financial control techniques as well as by implementing policies of "management by exception," meaning that corporate headquarters intervenes only when problems arise.

Stronger pursuit of internal efficiency   Within a functional structure, the interdependence of functional departments means that performance of functions within the company cannot be measured by objective criteria. For example, the profitability of the finance function, marketing function, or manufacturing function cannot be assessed in isolation, as they are only part of the whole. This often means that within the functional structure considerable degrees of organizational slack can go undetected. Resources might be absorbed in unproductive uses. For example, the head of the finance function might employ a larger staff than required for efficiency to reduce work pressures inside the department. Generally, a larger staff also brings a manager higher status. But because a divisional structure prescribes divisional operating autonomy, the divisions' efficiency can be directly observed and measured in terms of profit. Autonomy makes divisional managers accountable for their own performance; they can have no alibis. The general office is thus in a better position to identify inefficiencies.

A multidivisional structure then has a number of powerful advantages. No doubt that is why this structure appears to be the preferred choice of most large diversified enterprises today. Indeed, research suggests that large business companies that adopt this structure outperform those that retain the functional structure.[29]

Disadvantages of the Multidivisional Structure

A multidivisional structure has its disadvantages as well. Good management can eliminate some of them, but others are inherent in the way the structure operates and require constant attention. They are discussed next.

Establishing the divisional–corporate authority relationship   The authority relationship between corporate headquarters and the divisions must be correctly established. The multidivisional structure introduces a new level in the hierarchy—the corporate level. The problem is to decide how much authority and control to assign to the operating divisions and how much authority to retain at corporate headquarters. This problem was first noted by Alfred Sloan, the founder of General Motors. He introduced the multidivisional structure into General Motors, which became the first company to adopt it.[30] He created General Motors' familiar five-automobile divisions—Oldsmobile, Buick, Pontiac, Chevrolet, and Cadillac. The problem he noted was that when headquarters retained too much power and authority, the operating divisions lacked sufficient autonomy to develop the business strategy that might best meet the needs of the division. When too much power was delegated to the divisions, however, they pursued divisional objectives with little heed to the needs of the whole corporation. For example, all the potential gains from synergy discussed earlier would not be achieved. Thus the central issue in managing the multidivisional structure is how much authority should be centralized at corporate headquarters and how much should be decentralized to the divisions. This issue must be decided by each company in reference to the nature of its business and its corporate-level strategies. There are no easy answers, and over time, as the environment changes or the company alters its strategies, the balance between corporate and divisional control will also change.

Distortion of information   If corporate headquarters puts too much emphasis on divisional return on investment, for instance, by setting very high and stringent return on investment targets, divisional managers may choose to distort the information they supply top management and paint a rosy picture of the present situation at the expense of future profits. That is, divisions may maximize short-run profits—perhaps by cutting product development or new investments or marketing expenditures. This may cost the company dearly in the future. The problem stems from too tight financial control. General Motors has suffered from this problem in recent years, as declining performance has made managers attempt to make their divisions look good to corporate headquarters. On the other hand, if the divisional level exerts too much control, powerful divisional managers may resist attempts to use their profits to strengthen other divisions and therefore disguise their performance. Thus managing the corporate-divisional interface involves coping with subtle power issues.

Competition for resources   The third problem of managing the divisional structure is that the divisions themselves may compete for resources, and this rivalry will prevent gains from synergy from emerging. For example, the amount of money that corporate personnel has to distribute to the divisions is fixed. Generally, the divisions that can demonstrate the highest return on investment will get the lion's share of the money. But that large share strengthens them in the next time period, and so the strong divisions grow stronger. Consequently, divisions may actively compete for resources, and by doing so, reduce interdivisional coordination. For example, at Procter & Gamble, the struggle among divisions for resources has actually led to a loss in market share because resources had been inefficiently distributed as a result of competition.

Transfer pricing   Divisional competition may also lead to battles over **transfer pricing.** As we discuss in Chapter 8, one of the problems with vertical integration or related diversification is setting transfer prices between divisions. Rivalry among divisions increases the problem of setting fair prices. Each supplying division tries to set the highest price for its outputs to maximize its own return on investment. Such competition can completely undermine the corporate culture and make the corporation a battleground. Many companies have a history of competition among divisions. Some, of course, may encourage competition, if managers believe that it leads to maximum performance.

Short-term research and development focus   If extremely high return on investment targets are set by corporate headquarters, there is a danger that the divisions will cut back on research and development expenditures to improve the financial performance of the division. Although this will inflate divisional performance in the short term, however, it will reduce the ability of a division to innovate new products and lead to a fall in the stream of long-term profits. Once again, corporate headquarters personnel must carefully control their interactions with the divisions to ensure that both the short- and long-term goals of the business are being achieved.

Operations costs   Because each division possesses its own specialized functions, such as finance or research and development, these multidivisional structures are expensive to run and manage. Research and development is especially costly, and so some companies centralize such functions at the corporate level to serve all divisions, as is done in the product structure. The duplication of specialist services, however, is not a problem if the gains from having separate specialist functions outweigh the costs. Again, management must decide if duplication is financially justified. Activities are often centralized in times of downturn or recession—particularly advisory services and planning functions. Divisions, however, are retained as profit centers.

The advantages of divisional structures must be balanced against their disadvantages, but, as already noted, the disadvantages can be managed by an observant, professional management team that is aware of the issues involved. The multidivisional structure is the dominant one today, which clearly suggests its usefulness as the means of managing the multibusiness corporation.

Strategic Business Unit (SBU) Structure

As corporations have grown and developed, new variants of the multidivisional structure have emerged. The increased size of many companies has resulted in a structure with an even higher level of horizontal differentiation: the **strategic business unit (SBU)**. When a company has 200 to 300 different divisions, as does Beatrice Foods Company or General Electric, corporate management finds it almost impossible to retain control over the organization. As we note earlier, problems of information overload at the center can emerge, and with 300 divisions to control, corporate staff may not have the time to examine the operations of each division thoroughly.

To simplify this control problem, the organization may introduce yet another level in the hierarchy and split the company into groups of divisions operating in similar areas. The idea is to group divisions to realize synergies among them. Typically, these groups are referred to as strategic business units, and each SBU is controlled by an SBU headquarters staff. Each SBU, as well as each division inside each SBU, becomes a profit center, and it is the SBU headquarters staff's job to maximize the profitability of its SBU. For example, in Beatrice Foods, one SBU comprises all the divisions that produce in the food industry, and another comprises all those in the consumer products industry. Each SBU is operated independently and evaluated separately. An example of an SBU structure is shown in Figure 10.8. Each triangle represents a self-contained division, and each circle represents a collection of related divisions managed by an SBU headquarters staff. Thus one more level in the hierarchy is created.

As originally conceived, the role of the **SBU office** is to control the divisions inside the SBU and allocate resources among them. The role of corporate headquarters thus becomes to control the SBUs and allocate resources among them. As a result, the corporation becomes more manageable. Nevertheless, SBUs are not ideal solutions, and the arguments for and against their creation are similar to those for the multidivisional structure.

On the positive side, SBUs reduce the work of corporate personnel by decreasing the span of control to a manageable level and permitting the decentralization of authority. Moreover, the SBU structure can provide an effective integrating device for coordinating the needs of companies inside a group. SBU personnel are more in touch with the needs and interests of those companies than a corporate office is likely to be. They are able to promote gains from synergy between companies in their group.

On the negative side, because the corporate office is now more remote, it

FIGURE 10.8   **Strategic business unit structure**

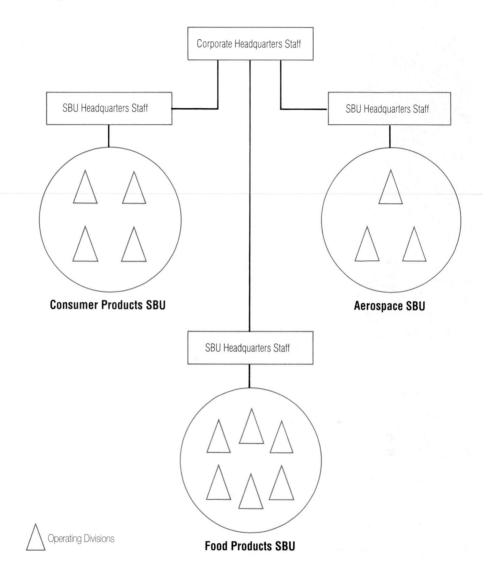

can lose touch with individual operating divisions inside an SBU because the SBU structure intervenes between it and the operating divisions. Corporate staff may not realize the seriousness of divisional problems until it is too late for counteractive measures. Besides, conflicts of interest may arise between the SBU and the corporate staff over funds for development. For example, using the Boston Consulting Group (BCG) matrix, the corporate office may define the SBU as a *dog* and limit its access to corporate capital. The SBU may also contain a *star* business, however, which would now be starved for cash. The SBU staff's challenging the authority of corporate staff would further weaken integration and accountability. Finally, the introduction of the SBU level in the organizational hierarchy may slow information transfers and communication and reduce the flexibility of the company as a whole.

On balance, then, it appears that the usefulness of this structure depends on the strategy with which the company is operating. The SBU structure is only appropriate for the companies that can group their divisions into separate, distinct categories, so that the benefits of this form of structure can be exploited. Such companies are likely to be related diversifiers.

Conglomerate Structure

The conglomerate structure is another main variant of the multidivisional form.[31] Whereas the SBU structure works best when commonalities link the various divisions or businesses in the company's portfolio, the conglomerate structure is used when there are no commonalities among divisions. The conglomerate form functions as a holding company, and each division is evaluated as a totally autonomous profit center. Textron and BAT Industries are good examples of companies that pursue unrelated diversification using a conglomerate structure.

The role of the corporate staff in a conglomerate structure is purely to perform portfolio analyses of the company's businesses. Decisions to acquire or divest businesses are linked to the goal of maximizing the profitability of the *corporate portfolio*. In contrast to the ordinary multidivisional or SBU structure, in the conglomerate structure problems of control and communication are at a minimum because the corporate staff makes no attempt to intervene in divisional strategy. This structure is therefore economical to manage because, even if the corporate staff controls as many as 300 businesses, the same portfolio matrix techniques can be applied to each business. For example, American Express Company operates its divisions loosely and treats its businesses as autonomous and self-financing fund generators. American Express believes that to attract able managers, its divisions must be given independence, and management views the divisions as "players" and the parent company as "referee." Corporate headquarters is active, however, in setting objectives, reviewing performance, and allocating capital to divisions.

Matrix Structure

A matrix structure differs from the structures discussed so far in that the matrix is based on two forms of horizontal differentiation rather than on one, as in the functional or product structure.[32] In the usual matrix design, activities on the vertical axis are grouped by *function*, so that we get a familiar differentiation of tasks into functions such as production, research and development, and engi-

FIGURE 10.9   Matrix structure

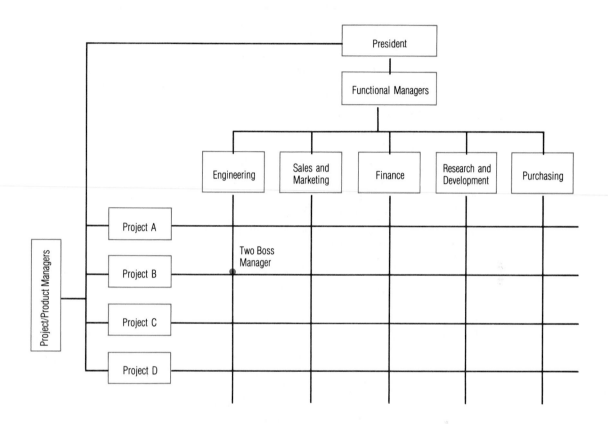

neering. In addition, superimposed on this vertical pattern is a horizontal pattern based on differentiation by *product or project*. The result is a complex network of reporting relationships among projects and functions, as depicted in Figure 10.9.

This structure also employs an unusual kind of vertical differentiation. Although matrix structures are flat, with few hierarchical levels, employees inside the matrix have two bosses: a **functional boss**, who is the head of a function, and a **project boss**, who is responsible for managing the individual projects. Employees work on a project team with specialists from other functions and report to the project boss on project matters and the functional boss on matters relating to functional issues. These employees are called **subproject managers** and are responsible for managing coordination and communication among the functions and projects.

Matrix structures were first developed by companies in high-technology industries such as aerospace and electronics—by companies such as TRW Inc. and Apple Computer. These companies are developing radically new products in uncertain, competitive environments, and speed of product development was the crucial consideration. They needed a structure that could respond to this strategy, but existing functional and product structures were too inflexible to allow the complex role and task interactions necessary to meet new product development requirements. Moreover, employees in these companies tend to be highly qualified and professional, and perform best in autonomous, flexible working conditions: The matrix structure provides such conditions. For example, this structure requires a minimum of direct hierarchical control by supervisors. Employees control their own behavior, and participation in project teams allows them to monitor other team members and learn from each other. Further, as the project goes through its different phases, different specialists from various functions are required. Thus, for example, at the first stage the services of research and development specialists may be needed, and then at the next stage engineers and marketing specialists are needed to make cost and marketing projections. As the demand for the type of specialist changes, employees can be moved to other projects that need their services. As a result, the matrix structure can make maximum use of employee skills as existing projects are completed and new ones come into existence. Finally, the freedom given by the matrix not only provides the autonomy to motivate employees, it also leaves top management free to concentrate on strategic issues because they do not have to become involved in operating matters. On all these counts, the matrix is an excellent tool for creating the flexibility necessary for quick reactions to competitive conditions.

There are disadvantages to the matrix structure, however.[33] First, it is expensive to operate compared with a functional structure. Employees tend to be highly skilled, and therefore both salaries and overheads are high. Second, the constant movement of employees around the matrix means that time and money are spent in establishing new team relationships and getting the project off the ground. Third, the subproject manager's role, balancing as it does the interests of the project with the function, is difficult to manage, and care must be taken to avoid conflict between functions and projects over resources. Over time, it is possible that project managers will take the leading role in planning and goal setting, in which case the structure works more like a product or divisional structure. If function and project relationships are left uncontrolled, they can lead to power struggles among managers, and the result is not increased flexibility, but stagnation and decline. Finally, the larger the organization, the more difficult it is to operate a matrix structure, because task and role relationships become complex. In such situations, the only option may be to change to a product or divisional structure.

Given these advantages and disadvantages, the matrix is generally used only when a company's strategy warrants it. There is no point in using a more complex structure than necessary because it will only cost more to manage. In dynamic product/market environments, the benefits of the matrix in terms of flexibility and innovation are likely to exceed the extra cost of using it, and so it becomes an appropriate choice of structure. Companies in the mature stage of the industry life cycle or those pursuing a low-cost strategy, however, would rarely choose this structure. We discuss it further in Chapter 12.

10.6 SUMMARY OF CHAPTER

This chapter introduces the issues involved in designing a structure to meet the needs of a company's strategy. The reasons that Apple Computer changed its structure over time and the problems that can arise when companies make such changes should now be clear. As the discussion in this chapter suggests, companies can adopt a large number of structures to match changes in their size and strategy over time. The structure that a company selects will be the one whose logic of grouping activities (that is, its form of horizontal differentiation) best meets the needs of its business or businesses. The company must match its form of horizontal differentiation to vertical differentiation. That is, it must choose a structure and then make choices about levels in the hierarchy and degree of centralization or decentralization. It is the combination of both kinds of differentiation that produce its internal organizational arrangements. As previously noted, however, once the company has divided itself into parts it must then integrate itself. This is discussed in the next chapter. We stress the following points:

1. Implementing a strategy successfully depends on selecting the right structure and control system to match a company's strategy.

2. The basic tool of strategy implementation is organizational design.

3. Differentiation and integration are the two design concepts that decide how a structure will work.

4. Differentiation has two aspects: (a) vertical differentiation, which refers to how a company chooses to allocate its decision-making authority; and (b) horizontal differentiation, which refers to the way that a company groups organizational activities into functions or departments or divisions.

5. The basic choice in vertical differentiation is whether to have a flat or a tall structure. Tall hierarchies have a number of disadvantages, such as problems with communication and information transfer, motivation, and cost. Decentralization or delegation of authority, however, can solve some of these problems.

6. The structures that a company can adopt as it grows and diversifies include the functional, product, and multidivisional forms. Each structure has advantages and disadvantages associated with it.

7. Other specialized kinds of structures include the matrix, conglomerate, and strategic business unit (SBU) forms. Each has a specialized use, and to be chosen, must match the needs of the organization.

Discussion Questions

1. What is the difference between vertical and horizontal differentiation? Rank the various structures discussed in this chapter along these two dimensions.

2. What kind of structure best describes the way your (a) business school and (b) university operates? Why is the structure appropriate? Would another structure fit better?

3. When would a company decide to change from a functional to a product structure? From a product to a multidivisional structure?

4. When would a company choose a matrix structure? What are the problems associated with managing this structure?

Endnotes

1. "Apple Computer, Inc.—Background History," Apple Computer, Inc., 1986.

2. "Apple Takes On Its Biggest Test Yet," *Business Week,* January 31, 1983, p. 79.

3. Bro Uttal, "Behind the Fall of Steve Jobs," *Fortune,* August 5, 1985, pp. 20–24.

4. J. R. Galbraith, *Designing Complex Organizations* (Reading, Mass.: Addison-Wesley, 1973).

5. J. Child, *Organization: A Guide for Managers and Administrators* (New York: Harper & Row, 1977), pp. 50–72.

6. R. H. Miles, *Macro Organizational Behavior* (Santa Monica, Calif.: Goodyear, 1980), pp. 19–20.

7. Galbraith, *Designing Complex Organizations.*

8. V. A. Graicunas, "Relationship in Organization," in L. Gulick and L. Urwick (eds.), *Papers on the Science of Administration* (New York: Institute of Public Administration, 1937), pp. 181—185. J. C. Worthy, "Organizational Structure and Company Morale," *American Sociological Review,* 15 (1950), 169–179.

9. Child, *Organization,* pp. 50—52.

10. G. R. Jones, "Organization-Client Transactions and Organizational Governance Structures," *Academy of Management Journal,* 30 (1987), 197–218.

11. H. Mintzberg, *The Structuring of Organizations* (Englewood Cliffs, N. J.: Prentice-Hall, 1979), p. 435.

12. Child, *Organization,* p. 51.

13. R. Carzo, Jr., and J. N. Yanousas, "Effects of Flat and Tall Organization Structure," *Administrative Science Quarterly,* 14 (1969), 178–191.

14. A. Gupta and V. Govindardan, "Business Unit Strategy, Managerial Characteristics, and Business Unit Effectiveness at Strategy Implementation," *Academy of Management Journal,* 27 (1984), 25–41. R. T. Lenz, "Determinants of Organizational Performance: An Interdisciplinary Review," *Strategic Management Journal, 2 (1981), 131–154.*

15. W. H. Wagel, "Keeping the Organization Lean at Federal Express," *Personnel* (March 1984), 4.

16. J. Koter, "For P&G Rivals, the New Game Is to Beat the Leader, Not Copy It," *Wall Street Journal,* May 6, 1985, p. 35.

17. G. R. Jones, "Task Visibility, Free Riding and Shirking; Explaining the Effect of Organization Structure on Employee Behavior," *Academy of Management Review,* 4 (1984), 684–695.

18. "Operation Turnaround—How Westinghouse's New Chairman Plans to Fire Up An Old Line Company," *Business Week,* December 14, 1983, pp. 124–133.

19. R. L. Deft, *Organizational Theory and Design,* 2nd ed. (St. Paul, Minn.: West, 1986), p. 215.

20. Alfred D. Chandler, *Strategy and Structure* (Cambridge, Mass.: MIT Press, 1962).

21. The discussion draws heavily on Chandler, *Strategy and Structure,* and B. R. Scott, "Stages of Corporate Development" (Cambridge, Mass.: Intercollegiate Clearing House, Harvard Business School, 1971).

22. J. R. Galbraith and R. K. Kazanjian, *Strategy Implementation: Structure System and Process,* 2nd ed. (St. Paul, Minn.: West, 1986). Child, *Organization.* R. Duncan, "What Is the Right Organization Structure?" *Organizational Dynamics* (Winter 1979), 59–80.

23. O. E. Williamson, *Markets and Hierarchies: Analysis and Antitrust Implications* (New York: Free Press, 1975).

24. P. R. Lawrence and J. Lorsch, *Organization and Environment* (Boston: Division of Research, Harvard Business School, 1967).

25. Chandler, *Strategy and Structure*. Williamson, *Markets and Hierarchies*. L. Wrigley, "Divisional Autonomy and Diversification" (Ph.D. diss., Harvard Business School, 1970).

26. R. P. Rumelt, *Strategy, Structure, and Economic Performance* (Boston: Division of Research, Harvard Business School, 1974); Scott, "Stages of Corporate Development." Williamson, *Markets and Hierarchies*.

27. K. Deveny, "Maytag's New Girth Will Test Its Marketing Muscle," *Business Week,* February 16, 1987, p. 68.

28. The discussion draws on each of the sources cited in endnotes 20–27, and also on G. R. Jones and C. W. L. Hill, "Transaction Cost Analysis of Strategy-Structure Choice," *Strategic Management Journal,* 9 (1988), 159–172.

29. H. O. Armour and D. J. Teece, "Organizational Structure and Economic Performance: A Test of the Multidivisional Hypothesis," *Bell Journal of Economics,* 9 (1978), 106–122.

30. Alfred Sloan, *My Years at General Motors* (New York: Doubleday, 1983), Ch. 3.

31. N. A. Berg, "Strategic Planning in Conglomerate Companies," *Harvard Business Review,* 43 (1965), 79–92. K. N. M. Dundas and R. R. Richardson, "Implementing the Unrelated Product Strategy," *Strategic Management Journal,* 3 (1982), 287–301.

32. S. M. Davis and R. R. Lawrence, *Matrix* (Reading, Mass.: Addison-Wesley, 1977). J. R. Galbraith, "Matrix Organization Designs: How to Combine Functional and Project Forms," *Business Horizons,* 14 (1971), 29–40.

33. Duncan, "What Is the Right Organizational Structure?" Davis and Lawrence, *Matrix*.

Chapter 11

CHOOSING INTEGRATION AND CONTROL SYSTEMS

11.1 OPENING INCIDENT: TRW

TRW Information Services, one of America's most successful high-tech companies, was heavily involved in the intercontinental ballistic missile (ICBM) research program and has continued to be a leader in electronics, defense, and space program development. It was one of the first companies to introduce the matrix structure as a means of coordinating and integrating its complex and constantly changing product lines. To make the matrix structure work, TRW also adopted a variety of integration and control systems to encourage high performance and increase the level of coordination between functions. First, it relied heavily on the recruitment and selection of highly skilled, professional employees with strong internal motivation to perform.[1] Second, it established project teams in which employees were able to work and integrate with employees in other functions. In addition, TRW reinforced employee commitment to high performance by avoiding employee layoffs and by developing a decentralized, freewheeling organization culture that rewarded risk taking, innovation, and creativity. Its innovative strategic organization design brought TRW huge success. It grew from a company valued at $500,000 in 1965 to one valued at more than $6 billion in 1990.[2]

With rapid growth, however, came major problems. Each project group inside its matrix structure developed into a full-fledged division within a multidivisional structure. As a result, integration among divisions dissipated, and the kind of controls that the company could use when it was small and decentralized no longer suited a high-tech giant. In fact, the company was running into the very integration problems that it had sought to avoid by developing a matrix structure. The various divisions in TRW—defense, electronics, and automotive products—were not cooperating with one another and were sharing their research and development know-how less and less. Actually, they were competing,[3] which was an enormous problem for a company that depended on technological advances for its future growth and success.

The reason for the lack of integration was that divisional managers were saying, "Why should I spend billions of dollars investing in research for my own product lines and then this other division can just come along and get the knowledge free and apply it to its own products, especially when I am evaluated on bottom-line performance?" In other words, divisions were competing rather than cooperating because the old kind of controls used by TRW were no longer appropriate, and the company had not yet developed a new set of controls to coordinate its new organizational structure. Rube Mettler, TRW's chairman, faced the problem of finding new ways to integrate divisions and new control systems that would encourage cooperation among them and prepare the corporation for future growth.

TRW attempted to improve integration by introducing new types of incentive schemes to stimulate cooperation rather than competition. For example, divisional managers' bonuses, promotions, and pay raises were linked to the results of cooperation among divisions. The company also developed a transfer pricing scheme that allowed divisions to charge a fair price for technology transferred to other divisions. In addition, to improve performance, it tried to develop a corporate culture based on cooperative corporate values rather than competitive divisional values. These efforts were just one part of TRW's overall control system, which also monitored costs, productivity, quality, and all the other indicators of organizational performance.

11.2 OVERVIEW

In Chapter 10, we discuss the various kinds of structures available to companies when they implement their strategies. As the example of TRW suggests, in this chapter we consider the various kinds of integrating mechanisms and control systems that companies use to make these structures operate efficiently. **Integrating mechanisms** coordinate the various functions and divisions of the business. More complex structures require the use of more complex kinds of integrating mechanisms. Through **control systems**, organizations can monitor, evaluate, and change their performance. These systems provide information on how well a company's strategy is working and how well the structure used to implement the strategy is working. **Strategic control** is the process of selecting the types of controls at the corporate, business, and functional levels in a company that allow strategic managers to evaluate whether the company's strategy and structure are achieving organizational objectives.

We first take up the kinds of integrating mechanisms that companies can activate. Then we outline the process of strategic control and examine in detail the types of control that companies can use. These include market control, output control, bureaucratic control, and clan control and culture. Finally, we discuss how the design of reward systems is an important element of the strategic control process. In the next chapter, we consider in detail how to match organizational structure and control to corporate-, business-, and functional-level strategy.

11.3 INTEGRATION AND INTEGRATING MECHANISMS

Matching Differentiation with Integration

As we discuss in Chapter 10, an organization must choose the appropriate form of differentiation to match its strategy. Greater diversification, for example, requires that a company move from a product structure to a divisional structure. Differentiation, however, is only one design decision to be made. Another decision concerns the level of integration necessary to make the structure work effectively. **Integration** is defined as the extent to which the organization seeks to coordinate the various activities of the organization and make them interdependent. The design issue can be summed up simply: The higher a company's level of differentiation (that is, the more complex its structure), the higher is the level of integration needed to make the structure perform effectively.[4] Thus if a company adopts a more complex form of differentiation, it requires a more complex form of integration to accomplish its goals. For example, Federal Express needs an enormous amount of integration and coordination to allow it to fulfill its promise of next-day package delivery. It is renowned for its innovative use of integrating mechanisms, such as customer-liaison personnel, to manage its transactions quickly and efficiently. Similarly, if managers adopt a multidivisional structure to manage a strategy of related diversification, they must establish means to integrate across divisions to achieve the gains from synergy. Take the problem facing Texas Air, the nation's biggest airline company. Its acquisition of Eastern Airlines, People Express, and New York Air doubled its size, and integrating these airlines with Continental caused enormous problems for the company. It was its inability to coordinate the airlines that led to its current misfortunes.

Forms of Integrating Mechanisms

Jay R. Galbraith, a prominent management theorist, has identified a series of integrating mechanisms that a company can use to increase its level of integration as its level of differentiation increases.[5] These mechanisms—on a continuum from simplest to most complex—are listed in Table 11.1 together with the examples of the individuals or groups that might perform these integrating roles.

Direct contact   The aim behind establishing direct contact among managers is to set up a context within which managers from different divisions or functional departments can work together to solve mutual problems. As TRW's experience suggests, however, several problems are associated with establishing contact among managers in different functional departments or divisions. Managers from different functional departments have different subunit orientations but equal authority and so may tend to compete rather than cooperate when conflicts arise.

TABLE 11.1   **Types and examples of integrating mechanisms**

Direct contact	Sales and production managers
Liaison roles	Assistant sales and plant managers
Task forces	Representatives from sales, production, and research and development
Teams	Organizational executive committee
Integrating roles	Assistant vice president for strategic planning or vice president without portfolio
Integrating departments	Corporate headquarters staff
Matrix	All roles are integrating roles

For example, in a typical functional structure, the heads of each of the functions have equal authority; the nearest common point of authority is the CEO. Consequently, if disputes arise, no mechanism exists to resolve the conflicts apart from the authority of the boss. In fact, one sign of conflict in organizations is the number of problems sent up the hierarchy for upper-level managers to solve. This wastes management time and effort, slows down strategic decision making, and makes it difficult to create a cooperative culture in the company. For this reason, companies choose more complex integrating mechanisms to coordinate interfunctional and divisional activities.

Interdepartmental liaison roles   A company can improve its interfunctional coordination through the interdepartmental liaison role. When the volume of contacts between two departments or functions increases, one of the ways of improving coordination is to give one person in *each* division or function the responsibility for coordinating with the other. These people may meet daily, weekly, monthly, or as needed. Figure 11.1a depicts the nature of the liaison role, the small circle representing the individual inside the functional department who has responsibility for coordinating with the other function. The responsibility for coordination is part of an individual's full-time job, but through these roles, a permanent relationship forms between the people involved, greatly easing strains between departments. Furthermore, it offers a way of transferring information across the organization, which is important in large, anonymous organizations whose employees may know no one outside their immediate department.

Temporary task forces   When more than two functions or divisions share common problems, then direct contact and liaison roles are of limited value because they do not provide enough coordination. The solution is to adopt a more complex form of integrating mechanism called a task force. The nature of the task force is represented diagrammatically in Figure 11.1b. One member of each function or division is assigned to a task force created to solve a specific problem. Essentially, task forces are *ad hoc committees,* and members are responsible for reporting back to their departments on the issues addressed and solutions recommended. Task forces are temporary because, once the problem is solved,

FIGURE 11.1   **Forms of integrating mechanisms**

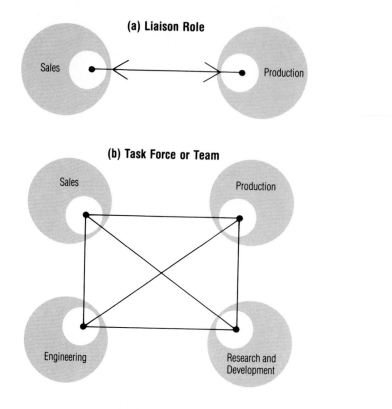

(a) Liaison Role

(b) Task Force or Team

(c) Integrating Role

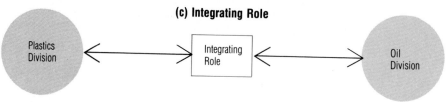

● Indicates manager with responsibility for integration

members return to their normal roles in their departments. Task force members also perform many of their normal duties while serving on the task force.

Permanent teams   In many cases, the issues addressed by a task force are recurring problems. To solve these problems effectively, an organization must establish a permanent integrating mechanism such as a permanent team. An example of a permanent team is a new product development committee, which is responsible for the choice, design, and marketing of new products. Such an activity obviously requires a great deal of integration among functions if new products are to be successfully introduced, and establishing a permanent integrating mechanism accomplishes this. Intel, for instance, emphasizes teamwork. It formed a council system based on approximately ninety cross-organizational groups, which meet regularly to set functional strategy in areas such as engineering and marketing and develop business-level strategy.

The importance of teams in the management of the organizational structure cannot be overemphasized. Essentially, permanent teams are the organization's *standing committees,* and much of the strategic direction of the organization is formulated in these meetings. Henry Mintzberg, in a study of how the managers of corporations spend their time, discovered that they spend almost 60 percent of their time in these committees.[6] The reason is not bureaucracy but rather that integration is possible only in intensive, face-to-face sessions, in which managers can understand others' viewpoints and develop a cohesive organizational strategy. The more complex the company, the more important these teams become. Westinghouse, for example, has established a whole new task force and team system to promote integration among divisions and improve corporate performance.

Integrating roles   The integrating role is a new role whose only function is to prompt integration among divisions or departments; it is a full-time job (see Figure 11.1c.). As you see, it is independent of the subunits or divisions being integrated. The role is staffed by an independent expert, who is normally a senior manager with a great deal of experience in the joint needs of the two departments. The job is to coordinate the decision process among departments or divisions to allow the synergetic gains from cooperation to be obtained. One study found that Du Pont had created 160 integrating roles to provide coordination among the different divisions of the company and improve corporate performance.[7] Once again, the more differentiated the company, the more common are these roles. Often people in these roles take the responsibility for chairing task forces and teams, and this provides additional integration.

Integrating departments   Sometimes the number of integrating roles becomes so high that a permanent integrating department is established at corporate headquarters. Normally, this occurs only in large, diversified corporations, which see the need for integration among divisions. This department consists mainly of strategic planners and may indeed be called the strategic planning department. Corporate headquarters staff in a divisional structure can also be viewed as an integrating department from the divisional perspective.

Matrix structure   Finally, when differentiation is very high and the company must be able to respond quickly to the environment, a matrix structure becomes the appropriate integrating device. The matrix contains many of the integrating mechanisms already discussed: The subproject managers integrate among functions and projects, and the matrix is built on the basis of temporary task forces.

Summary: Integration and Integrating Mechanisms

It is clear that firms have a large number of options open to them when they increase their level of differentiation as a result of increased growth or diversification. The implementation issue is for managers to match differentiation with the level of integration to meet organizational objectives. Note that while too much differentiation and not enough integration will lead to failure of implementation, the converse is also true. That is, the combination of low differentiation and high integration will lead to an overcontrolled bureaucratized organization where flexibility and speed of response is reduced and not enhanced by the level of integration. Also, integration is expensive for the company because it raises management costs. For these reasons the goal is to decide on the optimum amount of integration necessary for meeting organizational goals and objectives. It is in this connection that strategic control becomes important because it allows managers to assess whether their integration mechanisms are coordinating their structures.

11.4 STRATEGY IMPLEMENTATION AND CONTROL

In Chapter 10, we mention that implementation involves selecting the right combination of structure and control for achieving a company's strategy. Structure assigns people to tasks and roles (differentiation) and specifies how these are to be coordinated (integration). Nevertheless, it does not of itself provide the mechanism through which people can be *motivated* to make the structure work. Hence the need for control. Put another way, management can develop *on paper* an elegant organization structure with the right integrating mechanisms, but only appropriate control systems will make this structure work. For example, at TRW, top management established a complex system of teams and integrating roles to link the various divisions in the company and solve the problem of cooperation. Although this solution seemed good on paper, in practice, management found that different divisional teams were not cooperating because the company offered no rewards for cooperation. Top management had to establish a monitoring system to evaluate the divisions' attempts at cooperating with each other and also had to introduce rewards for cooperation. For a company like TRW, the right control system was vital for achieving the gains from synergy on which the company's dominance in the high-tech field depends.

TRW demonstrates that a structure will not work without the complex web of controls that allow a company to monitor, evaluate, and reward its parts—divisions, functions, and individual personnel. In the rest of this chapter, we discuss the various options open to companies in designing such a control system. First, however, we examine in more detail what a control system is.

11.5 STRATEGIC CONTROL SYSTEMS

Strategic control systems are the formal target-setting, monitoring, evaluation, and feedback systems that provide management with information about whether the organization's strategy and structure are meeting strategic performance objectives. An effective control system should have three characteristics: It should be *flexible* enough to allow managers to respond as necessary to unexpected events; it should provide *accurate information,* giving a true picture of organizational performance; and it should provide managers with the information in a *timely manner* because making decisions on the basis of outdated information is a recipe for failure.[8] As Figure 11.2 shows, designing an effective strategic control system requires four steps.[9]

1. *Establish the standards or targets against which performance is to be evaluated.* The standards or targets that managers select are the ways in which a company chooses to evaluate its performance. Generally, these targets are derived from the strategy pursued by the company. For example, if a company is pursuing a low-cost strategy, then "reducing costs by 7 percent a year" might be a target. If the company is a service organization like McDonald's, its standards might include time targets for serving customers or guidelines for food quality.

2. *Create the measuring or monitoring systems that indicate whether the targets are being achieved.* The company establishes procedures for assessing whether work goals at all levels in the organization are being achieved. In many cases, measuring performance is a difficult task because the organization is engaged in many complex activities. For example, managers can measure quite easily

FIGURE 11.2   **Steps in designing an effective control system**

Establish Standards and Targets

↓

Create Measuring and Monitoring Systems

↓

Compare Actual Performance Against
the Established Targets

↓

Evaluate Result and Take Action if Necessary

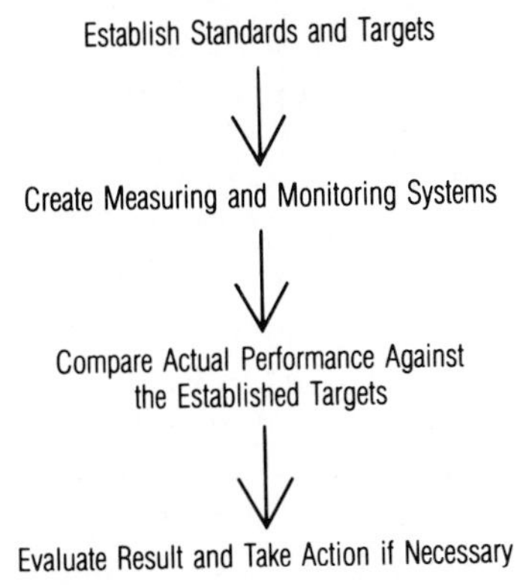

how many customers their employees serve: they can count the number of receipts from the cash register. Yet how can they judge how well their research and development department is doing when it may take five years for products to be developed? Or how can they measure the company's performance when the company is entering new markets and serving new customers? Or how can they evaluate how well divisions are integrating? The answer is that they need to use various types of control, which we discuss later in this chapter.

3. *Compare actual performance against the established targets.* Managers evaluate whether—and to what extent—performance deviates from the targets developed in step 1. If performance is higher, management may decide that it had set the standards too low and may raise them from the next time period. The Japanese are renowned for the way they use targets on the production line to control costs. They are constantly trying to raise performance, and they constantly raise the standards to provide a goal for managers to work toward. On the other hand, if performance is too low, managers must decide whether to take remedial action. This decision is easy when the reasons for poor performance can be identified—for instance, high labor costs. More often, however, the reasons for poor performance are hard to uncover. They may involve external factors, such as a recession. Or the cause may be internal. For instance, the research and development laboratory may have underestimated the problems it would encounter or the extra costs of doing unforeseen research. For any form of action, however, step 4 is necessary.

4. *Evaluate the result and initiate corrective action when it is decided that the target is not being achieved.* If managers decide to begin corrective action, they have two choices. They can *alter the control systems* being used to measure and monitor the performance of divisions, departments, or individuals—they may change budgets or replace rules for example. In adopting this response, managers are acting on the work system itself to correct the deviation, and they may push for more creative decision making or try to increase productivity by offering better bonuses. The other option available to managers is to *act on the target itself.* Perhaps a target was incorrectly set—for example, a sales target was too optimistic or too high. In this situation, the objective would be to change the target rather than the type of control being used to achieve it. Essentially, then, managers can act on the *means,* that is, the actual types of controls used, or the *ends,* that is, the standards or targets.

The simplest example of a control system is the thermostat in a home. By setting the thermostat, you establish the standard with which actual temperature is to be compared. The thermostat contains a sensing or monitoring device, which measures the actual temperature against the desired temperature. Whenever there is a difference between them, the furnace or air-conditioning unit is activated, to bring the temperature back to the standard: in other words, corrective action is initiated. Note that this is a simple control system for it is entirely self-contained and the target (temperature) is easy to measure.

Obviously, establishing targets and designing measurement systems is much more difficult in the strategic arena because there are many different targets or standards to choose from. We turn to this issue next.

11.6 SELECTING PERFORMANCE STANDARDS

In selecting performance standards, managers are deciding what criteria they will use to evaluate the organization's performance. Standards or measures of a company's performance fall into four basic categories.[10] These are summarized in Table 11.2, along with the individual kinds of measures within each category.

Performance Standards

The first category contains standards that measure a company's ability *to meet efficiency goals*. Thus standards relating to productivity, cost, or quality of production are set up and used as the base line measures for evaluating performance. The second category consists of standards that measure *human resources* in an organization. A company creates targets concerning the level of absenteeism, turnover, or job satisfaction that is acceptable in the organization. Much more difficult to formulate are standards pertaining to the *internal functioning and responsiveness* of the organization, which make up the third category. Here managers are concerned with factors such as creativity, flexibility, decision making, and organizational communication. In the fourth, and last, category standards relate to an organization's ability to *exploit the environment and obtain scarce resources*. Hence such measures as ability to respond to changes in the environment or to manage external constituencies, such as stockholders, customers, or the government, are important. These standards are also difficult to devise.

Generally, performance is measured at four levels in the organization: the corporate, divisional, functional, and individual levels. Managers at the corporate level are most concerned with overall and abstract measures of organizational

TABLE 11.2   **Types and examples of performance targets**

Efficiency targets	Productivity, profit, quality, output, costs
Human resource targets	Absenteeism, turnover, job satisfaction, morale, commitment, cooperation
Internal functioning targets	Flexibility, planning, goal-setting, communication, conflict management
Environmental targets	External constituency building, political legitimacy, control of scarce inputs and outputs

FIGURE 11.3   Levels of organizational control

performance such as profit, return on investment, or total labor force turnover. The aim is to choose performance standards that measure overall corporate performance. Similarly, managers at the other levels are most concerned with developing a set of standards to evaluate business- or functional-level performance. These measures should be tied as closely as possible to the work activities needed to meet strategic objectives at each level. Care must be taken, however, to ensure that the standards used at each level do not cause problems at the other levels— for example, that divisions' attempts to improve their performance do not conflict with corporate performance. Furthermore, controls at each level should provide the basis on which managers at the levels below can select their control systems. Figure 11.3 illustrates these links.

Problems with Selecting Standards

Selecting the appropriate standards for evaluating performance is one of the most important decisions that strategic managers can make because these standards determine what the company should be doing—that is, its strategic mission. But managers must watch out for some problems.

First, because so many different kinds of standards are available, assessments of a company's performance can vary according to the measure selected. If managers choose measures that emphasize productivity but ignore those concerning the environment, they may end up with conflicting impressions of a company's performance. A classic case is that of the large American car makers at the time of high oil prices. Although car makers were very efficient—they could produce large cars at low cost—they were hardly effective because nobody wanted to buy large cars. Thus they were not satisfying their outside constituencies—customers or shareholders. Thus through the measures they select and try to control, managers can create a misleading impression of a company's performance. It is vital, therefore, that they measure the right things.

Second, the four categories of standards are not always consistent and may be incompatible—that is, pursuing one type of standard may stop a company from achieving another. For example, a company's attempts to minimize cost and maximize productivity often lead to higher employee absenteeism and turnover because employees must work under more intense pressure. As another example, companies often like to maintain large inventories of spare parts or components to ride out shortages in stocks of finished goods and respond properly to customer needs. Nevertheless, maintaining buffer stocks and inventory is expensive and therefore raises costs. In such a situation, a company is trading off efficiency against its internal flexibility.

An important tradeoff at the heart of this second problem is that between short-run efficiency and long-term effectiveness. For example, the competitive advantage that the Japanese have over U.S. manufacturers is often attributed to their long-term planning, large investments of funds in research and development, and expectation of a slower payoff (or return on investment). U.S. corporations, on the other hand, are so concerned with maximizing short-run returns that they limit investment in research and development and, in general, try to reduce costs in the short run. As a result, they suffer in the long run because they have not made the investment for the future. The kind of measures management adopts to evaluate its performance can strongly influence whether this will occur, and large companies such as General Motors are now building long-term quality standards into their control system. For example, in its attempt to catch up with the Japanese, General Motors has increased its research and development budgets. In the last five years, it has spent so much on improving its product quality that it could have easily bought Toyota on the stock exchange and still have had money to spare. A company must design a control system that can evaluate whether it is meeting all the objectives necessary to accomplish its strategic mission.

The third problem is that the measures chosen to evaluate performance may depend on whose interests are at stake. You see in Chapter 2 that a company's primary function is to maximize stockholder wealth, but what path should be pursued to achieve this? Suppose some stockholders prefer short-term dividends whereas others prefer long-term capital appreciation. Which measure of performance should management adopt? Furthermore, if it adopts the standard of maximizing long-term wealth, how should it move toward this goal? Should it reduce costs, maximize its ability to deal with the environment, maximize employee welfare to encourage productivity, or maximize research and development spending? Although these are all possible targets, no easy rules determine which of them are best. Some companies are more successful than others simply because they adopt the right kind of measures.

Management needs to use all four categories of standards to create the mix of standards necessary to pursue a successful long-term strategy. Specifically, management must minimally satisfy all the constituencies that have an interest in the company.[11] As we identify in Chapter 1, these constituencies include shareholders, customers, and the company's employees. In satisfying their interests, management will be balancing the needs of short-run operating efficiency against long-run strategic effectiveness.

11.7 TYPES OF CONTROL SYSTEMS

The control systems that managers can use range from those measuring **organizational outputs** to those measuring and controlling **organizational behaviors**.[12] In general, outputs are much easier to measure than behaviors because outputs are relatively tangible or objective. Hence output controls tend to be the first type that a company employs. In many situations, however, organizational outputs cannot be easily measured or evaluated. For example, measuring organizational creativity or flexibility objectively is difficult. In addition, the more complex the organizational tasks, the harder it is to use output control because evaluating the work of people such as research and development personnel or strategic planners is both difficult and expensive. Similarly, the higher the interdependence among functions or divisions—for instance, when a company is seeking to achieve gains from synergy—the tougher it is for a company to pinpoint divisional contributions to performance.

In these situations, a company usually adopts control systems that shape the behaviors necessary to reach its targets.[13] Although such behavior control systems are generally more expensive to employ, they are often the only means a company has to monitor and evaluate performance when organizational activities are complex. Table 11.3 shows the various types of control systems along this output-to-behavior control continuum. We discuss each of these types in turn and also consider the use of different kinds of control mechanisms at the various organizational levels—corporate, divisional, functional, and individual.

TABLE 11.3   **Types of control systems**

Market control	Output control	Bureaucratic control	Clan control
Stock price	Divisional goals	Rules and procedures	Norms
ROI	Functional goals	Budgets	Values
Transfer pricing	Individual goals	Standardization	Socialization

Market Control

Market control is the most objective kind of output control and is achieved by setting a *system of prices* to monitor and evaluate performance. Market control can therefore be used only when an organization is able to establish objective financial measures of performance. In practice, this means that there must be competition of some kind, because only through a competitive market mechanism can a fair price be established.

Types of market control systems   There are three common forms of market control: stock market price, return on investment, and transfer pricing.

Stock market price   Stock price is a useful measure of a company's perform-ance primarily because the price of the stock is determined competitively by the number of buyers and sellers in the market. Movements in the price of a stock provide top management with feedback on its performance. They act as a pow-erful means of control because managers tend to be sensitive to falls in the stock market prices, since their compensation is often related to stock price. Falls in stock price may also stimulate takeover attempts, and this factor also serves to control managerial action. Finally, because stock price reflects the long-term fu-ture return from the stock, it can be regarded as an indicator of the company's long-run potential.

Return on investment   Return on investment (ROI), determined by dividing net income by invested capital, is another form of market control. At the cor-porate level, the performance of the whole company can be evaluated *against* other companies, and it is in this sense that ROI acts as a market control. ROI can also be used *inside* the company, however, at the divisional level, to evaluate the relative performance of one operating division either against similar free-standing businesses or against other internal divisions. For example, one reason for selecting the multidivisional structure is that each division can be evaluated as a self-contained profit center. Consequently, management can directly measure the performance of one division against another. The ability to use this standard was one of the reasons for General Motors' original move to a divisional struc-ture. ROI is a powerful form of market control at the divisional level when man-agers are concerned with the performance of the whole corporation.

Transfer pricing   Transfer pricing involves establishing the price at which one division will transfer outputs (goods or services) to another—for example, the price at which the oil division will transfer petroleum products to the chemical division, as in Conoco Inc., or the price at which the aerospace division at TRW will transfer research and development knowledge to the vehicle division. There are two basic methods of setting transfer prices. The **market-based method** is the more objective one because the price charged in the external market is the gauge. Competitors' prices are commonly used to set the internal price. In the

cost-based method, on the other hand, prices are set relative to some standard-cost or full-cost method, but the problem lies in determining the markup to be charged to the buying division.

Both methods are used equally, and each has its drawbacks.[14] With the cost-based method, the issue is determining how much profit the supplying division should earn. Internal transfer prices between divisions can be difficult to set, and sometimes divisions fight over prices to be charged, creating additional problems for corporate managers. When the market-based method is used, the price may be set too high because the supplying division may have a cost advantage over its competitors. This doubly penalizes the buying divisions: Not only are they paying more to the selling division than is really necessary, but, as a result, they may have to charge a price in the market for their product that would rob them of sales. The conflicts stemming from transfer price decisions are among the hardest problems that a vertically integrated and related company must face. Unrelated companies, obviously, are spared these difficulties because there are no transactions between divisions.[15]

Problems with market controls   The use of market controls such as ROI and transfer pricing are two prime ways in which strategic managers can evaluate corporate and divisional performance. As this section suggests, however, market control is appropriate only under one condition: when some form of comparison system exists. In comparisons with other companies, market controls such as ROI or stock market price function well. But whether market control can work at the divisional level depends on the skills of managers and their willingness to reach equitable solutions over transfer prices for products. Finally, failure to meet stock price or ROI targets also indicates that corrective action is necessary. It signals the need for corporate reorganization to meet corporate objectives, and such reorganization could involve a change in structure or liquidation and divestiture of businesses.

Output Control

The next most objective method of organizational control is **output control**. When no market system can be devised to allocate and price organizational resources because no system of comparison (between companies or divisions) exists, companies must turn to alternative methods of control. The easiest and cheapest kind of control available it output control. To apply output control, a company must be able to estimate or forecast appropriate targets for its various divisions, departments, or personnel.

Common forms of output controls   We next discuss the most common forms of output controls.

Divisional goals   In creating divisional goals, corporate management is setting the standards against which divisional performance will be judged. Such standards include sales, productivity, growth, and market share goals. Divisional managers use the standards as the basis for designing the organizational structure to meet the objectives. Generally, corporate managers try to raise these standards over time to force divisions to adopt more efficient forms of structure. Goal setting is also used to evaluate divisions' attempts to cooperate for the sake of achieving synergies or to measure the efficiency of scheduling resources among divisions. Thus divisional goals are a way of assessing the alignment of structure with strategy.

Functional goals   Output control at the functional level is achieved by setting goals for each function. For example, sales goals are the typical means through which managers control the sales function. Sales targets are established for the whole function, and then individual personnel are given specific goals, which they in turn are required to achieve. Functions and individuals are then evaluated on the basis of achieving or not achieving their goals, and, of course, compensation is pegged to achievement. As at the divisional level, functional goals are established to encourage development of functional competencies that provide the company with a competitive advantage at the business level. The achievement of these goals is a sign that the company's strategy is working and meeting organizational objectives.

Individual goals   Output control at the individual level is also common. You have already seen how sales compensation is normally based on individual performance. In general, whenever employee performance can be easily monitored and evaluated, output controls are usually appropriate. Thus, for example, piece-rate systems, in which individuals are paid according to exactly how much they produce, are characteristic output control systems. For many jobs, output control is impossible because individuals' performance cannot be evaluated. For example, if individuals work in teams, it is impossible or very expensive to measure their individual outputs. Similarly, if their work is extremely complex, such as research and development, it makes little sense to control people on the basis of how much they produce. In general, to prevent problems, individual goals must be set with the functional strategy in mind.

Problems with output control   The inappropriate use of output control at all levels of the organization can lead to unintended and unfortunate consequences. For instance, the wrong goals may be used to evaluate divisions, functions, or individuals. If short-term measures of performance, such as quantity produced, are used, they can conflict with quality goals. In a classic example of the unintended consequence of output control, an employment placement agency rewarded its workers on the basis of how many people they placed weekly in new jobs. The result was that they directed prospective applicants to job positions for which they were totally unsuited—for instance, they sent accountants to production line jobs. Realizing its mistake, the agency changed the reward system to emphasize how long new employees stayed in their positions after placement.

The moral of the story is clear: Monitoring, evaluating, and rewarding employee behavior requires the right set of controls.

The same is true at the functional and divisional levels. The use of the wrong reward system can have the unintended effect of producing conflict among departments, which start to compete for resources, as happened at TRW. To give another example, F. W. Whyte, a famous researcher, was studying the effect of reward systems on the relation between the production function and packaging and distribution in a manufacturing organization. Management introduced a new output control system for production personnel. Performance rose sharply, and employee salaries increased proportionately. These unskilled workers were now making more than semiskilled workers in packaging and distribution, however. Chaos ensued when the other workers insisted that their salaries be raised above the production people's salaries. Because such raises would have led to high salary levels, management responded by removing the output control system, and all the gains from productivity were forfeited as production workers reverted to their previous performance levels.

We note earlier that clashes over transfer prices may occur at the divisional level. In general, setting across-the-board output targets, such as ROI targets, for divisions can lead to destructive results if divisions single-mindedly try to maximize divisional profits at the expense of the corporate objectives. Moreover, to reach output targets, divisions may start to distort the numbers and engage in strategic manipulation of the figures to make their divisions look good.[16] Thus strategic managers need to design output controls that stimulate divisions to pursue long-run profitability goals at the divisional and corporate levels. In practice, output or market controls must be used in conjunction with bureaucratic (and clan) controls if the right strategic behaviors are to be achieved.

Bureaucratic Control

Market and output controls require that relatively objective, measurable standards exist for monitoring and evaluating performance. When measurable standards are difficult or expensive to develop, and when they are not sufficient to fulfill corporate objectives, managers must turn to bureaucratic control. **Bureaucratic control** is control through the establishment of a comprehensive system of rules and procedures to direct the actions or behavior of divisions, functions, and individuals.[17] In using bureaucratic control, the intention is not to specify the goals, but the best *means* to reach the goals.

Types of bureaucratic control   Types of bureaucratic control include not only impersonal rules and procedures, but also budgets and the standardization of activities. The specific types of bureaucratic controls chosen by an organization to direct employee behavior will be the ones best matched to its particular strategy. Each of the various types of bureaucratic control available to strategic planners is discussed next.

Rules and procedures   Rules and procedures are important sources of control in most organizations. The power of the rule is that it standardizes behavior. If employees follow the rules, then actions or decisions are performed the same way time and time again. The result is predictability and accuracy, which are the goals of all control systems. Rules are essentially guides to action that can be followed in all routine situations. The more unusual the situation, however, the less useful are the rules, for if frequent exceptions have to be made, the rules cease to serve the purpose of a simple guide to action. Nevertheless, much routine business is done through written rules, which specify how different functions are to coordinate their behavior and how people are to perform their tasks and roles. As strategy changes over time, the kinds of rules and procedures a company uses also change. The point is to devise a system of rules and procedures that will accomplish the activities necessary to pursue a particular strategy.

Budgets   Budgets are a second source of bureaucratic control. **Budgets** are essentially collections of rules for allocating resources, principally financial resources.[18] Organizations establish budgets for divisions, functions, and individuals. Then they organize their behavior around the rules the budget establishes.[19] For example, the research and development department normally has a budget for new product development. Managers know that if they spend too much on one project, they will have less to spend on other projects. Hence they modify their behavior to suit the budget. Similarly, sales personnel have budgets that indicate how much money they can spend on advertising or distributing their products. These rules control the behavior of salespeople and lead to decisions about the best way to use scarce resources to meet the company's strategy. The main types of budgets are (1) operating budgets, which specify what the company intends to produce and the resources needed to produce it; (2) sales budgets, which focus on the revenue the company expects to earn from sales per time period; and (3) expense budgets, which specify the resources that managers in various functions have to conduct activities and meet their goals.[20] Merck, the chemical company, is well known for its innovative design and use of budgets in manufacturing to squeeze out costs; by these means it has gained a major cost advantage over competitors.

As with the other means of control, care must be taken to design the budget so that it does not lead to conflict or competition among functions. Such feuding frequently occurs in sales/production relationships. For example, production is often evaluated on its ability to reduce production costs and come in under budget. Therefore production managers try to reduce costs by lengthening production runs, which lowers costs, because less time is spent on changing the production line specifications to turn out other products. Although such action allows production managers to beat their budgets (and get appropriately rewarded), it often hurts the sales function because sales can reduce its costs only by selling more and can sell more only by being able to respond quickly to customer demands. Production personnel will not respond to sales' needs, however, because rescheduling production to satisfy sales customers will increase production costs. The result is that the two functions frequently clash because each follows the needs of its own budget, and the company as a whole suffers.

The budget thus becomes the *goal* to be strived for rather than remains a set of rules that simply guide decision making. Managers are driven into short-term behavior paths to meet the budget, and the performance of the whole organization suffers. Changes in the environment can worsen this problem if management cannot respond creatively to changing circumstances because an inflexible budget has put it in a straightjacket. An advantage of budgets, however, is that they provide the guidelines that let managers monitor their own behavior effectively and enable superiors to measure functional activities accurately. They also provide a natural means through which the company can link functional and divisional activities to the corporate mission. The goals of the organization—for instance, high-quality products or customer service—can be built into the size of the budgets allocated to each function, and such action aligns employee behavior with the company's strategy.

Standardization   Standardization is a potent weapon that organizations can use to influence behaviors.[21] Indeed, to a large degree, bureaucratic control is based on standardization. Rules are a part of the standardization process, but only one part of it. In practice, there are three things that an organization can standardize: its *inputs*, its *throughput activities*, and its *outputs*.

1. *Standardization of inputs.* One way in which an organization can control the behavior of both people and resources is by standardizing the inputs into the organization. This means that the organization screens inputs and allows only those that meet its standards to enter. For example, if employees are the input in question, then one way of standardizing them is to recruit and select only those people who possess the qualities or skills needed by the organization. Arthur Andersen & Company, the accounting firm, is very selective in the way it recruits people into the organization, and so are most prestigious organizations. If the inputs in question are raw materials or component parts, then the same considerations apply. The Japanese are renowned for high quality and precise tolerances they demand from component parts to minimize problems with the product at manufacturing stage.

2. *Standardization of throughput activities.* The aim of standardization of throughputs is to program work activities so that they are done the same way time and time again. The goal is predictability. As already noted, the use of bureaucratic controls such as rules and procedures in one main way in which organizations can standardize throughputs. Another way is to organize production tasks to facilitate the movement of semifinished goods from one stage to the next and to reduce the time and resources needed to produce outputs. The goal is to improve the efficiency with which goods are produced and to find improved ways to control and standardize production. Output controls are important because they provide the means by which management monitors and evaluates the success of its efforts.

3. *Standardization of outputs.* The goal of standardizing outputs is to specify what the performance characteristics of the final product or service should be— what the dimensions or tolerances of the product should conform to, for example. To ensure that their products are standardized companies apply quality control and use various criteria to measure this standardization. One criterion might be the number of goods returned from customers or the number of customer complaints. On production lines, periodic sampling of products can indicate whether they are meeting performance characteristics. Given the intensity of foreign competition, companies are devoting extra resources to standardizing outputs, not just to reduce costs but to retain customers, because companies will retain their customers' business if the product's performance satisfies the customers. For example, if you buy a Japanese car and have no problems with its performance, which car are you most likely to buy next time? That is why companies such as U.S. car makers have been emphasizing the quality dimension of their products. They know how important standardizing outputs is in a competitive market.

McDonald's is an excellent example of a company that uses all three types of standardization. First, the quality of its inputs is standardized through controlling food supplies and franchise holders. Then, at the throughput phase, its food operations are totally standardized, and so, at the output phase, we get uniform burgers and strict output control over employee behavior. In general, fast-food restaurants, convenience stores, and all types of service-oriented chain stores use standardization as a main means of control.

Problems with bureaucratic control   As with other kinds of controls, the use of bureaucratic control is accompanied by problems, and they must be managed if the organization is to avoid unforeseen difficulties. Because bureaucratic control is central to the operation of all large organization structures, these problems are considered in more detail.

First, management must be careful to monitor and evaluate the usefulness of bureaucratic controls over time. Rules lead to standardized, predictable behavior and constrain people's behaviors. Rules are always easier to establish than to get rid of, however, and over time the number of rules an organization uses tends to increase. As new developments lead to additional rules, often the old rules are not discarded, and the company becomes overly bureaucratized. Consequently, the organization and the people in it become inflexible and therefore unable to deal effectively with changing or unusual circumstances. Such inflexibility hampers strategy implementation and makes the company slow to react. Managers must therefore continually be on the alert for reducing the number of rules and procedures necessary to manage the business and should always prefer to discard a rule rather than use a new one.

The second major problem is the cost of using bureaucratic controls. Just as structure is expensive, so is bureaucratic control. To give a dramatic example, according to a recent estimate, 20 percent of the cost of health care is spent on managing the paperwork necessary to satisfy organizational and government health care rules and procedures. This amount runs to billions of dollars a year. Hence reducing the number of rules and procedures to the essential minimum is important. Management frequently neglects this task, however, and often only a change in strategic leadership brings the company back on course.

Because outputs are relatively easy to evaluate but behaviors are not, bureaucratic control costs much more than market or output control. For this reason, output controls are selected first and bureaucratic controls second. They are most useful when combined: For example, in a divisional structure, market controls may be used to monitor divisional performance, and inside the division, bureaucratic controls such as budgets or standardization become appropriate. To prevent short-term profit-seeking behaviors from emerging because of the sole emphasis on output control, it is necessary to apply bureaucratic controls to evaluate other aspects of a division's or function's performance.

When rules are used, authority is delegated to lower levels in the hierarchy. If subordinates are not monitored closely, however, functions or divisions may develop their own goals at the expense of organizational goals. This is the control loss phenomenon, which we discuss in Chapter 10. Care must be taken that the rules corporate headquarters devises minimize control loss problems; otherwise the structure will not work, as managers may start to distort information or even compete with other divisions for resources.

Managers must realize that much of the decision making and work that gets done in the organization gets done not formally through prescribed bureaucratic controls, but through managers themselves meeting and communicating informally. Indeed, in many cases a fourth form of control is being used in the organization—a very subtle form, often taken for granted by people who fail to realize the important effect it has on their behavior. This is control through the development of common norms and values.

Clan Control and Culture

Clan control is control through the establishment of an internal system of organizational norms and values.[22] The goal of clan control is self-control: Individuals feel responsible for working to the best of their ability in the interests of the organization. With clan control, employees are not controlled by some external system of constraint, such as direct supervision, outputs, or rules and procedures. Rather, employees are said to internalize the norms and values of the organization and make them part of their own value system.[23] Just as we internalize the values of society—for instance, "thou shalt not steal"—so in organizations employees internalize the expectations of the organization and act in terms of them. The value of clan control for an organization is its ability to specify the beliefs, norms, and values that govern employee behavior.[24] Wal-Mart is a good example of a company that actively promotes organizational norms and values. Its employees are called "associates" and are encouraged to take initiative as partners in the organization.

Clan control is initially expensive to use because it requires a great amount of time and resources to generate norms and values strong enough to control employee behavior. Consequently, clan control is used particularly in small companies or in departments staffed by professional employees, who, through their training, have already developed a professional orientation toward their job. In fact, clan control is used more often in conjunction with standardization of inputs. In other words, the first company recruits experts or professionals, and then it allows them to develop their own codes of behavior to guide their work activities. That is why in professional contexts, such as research and development teams, you find a common code of dress or language in the group. For example, clan control is most likely to thrive in a matrix structure or in an organization such as Apple Computer, in which employees were guided by the common vision of creating a desk-top computer, or in IBM, where a commitment to service is a major value.

Much of the most recent research, however, does not talk about clan control, but rather about the development of an organizational culture for managing a company's strategy. The terms *clan control* and *culture* are similar and are used interchangeably in the following discussion.

Culture refers to that specific collection of norms, standards, and values that are shared by members of an organization and affect the way an organization does business.[25] The principal difference between the way this concept controls behavior and, say, the organization's mission statement, is that culture is implicit in the way people act in the organization; it does not need to be written to be understood. Socialization is the term used to describe how people learn organizational culture. Through socialization, people internalize the norms and values of the culture and learn to act like existing personnel.[26] Control through culture is so powerful because, once these values are internalized, they become a part of the individual, and the individual follows organizational values without thinking about them. As shown in Figure 11.4, culture may be transmitted in the organization by several means.

FIGURE 11.4   **Ways of transmitting culture**

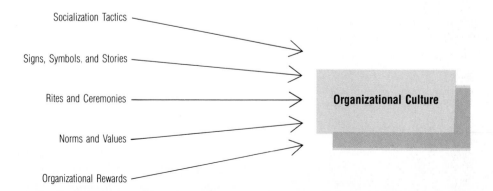

Socialization Tactics

Signs, Symbols, and Stories

Rites and Ceremonies — **Organizational Culture**

Norms and Values

Organizational Rewards

Traits of strong corporate cultures   Several scholars in the field have tried to uncover the common traits that strong corporate cultures share and to find out whether there is a particular set of values that dominates strong cultures but is missing from the weak. Perhaps the best-known attempt is T. J. Peters and R. H. Waterman's account of the norms and values characteristic of successful organizations and their cultures.[27] They argue that successful organizations show three common value sets. First, successful companies have values promoting a *bias for action*. The emphasis is on autonomy and entrepreneurship, and employees are encouraged to take risks—for example, to create new products, even though there is no assurance that these products will be winners. Managers are closely involved in the day-to-day operations of the company and do not simply make strategic decisions isolated in some "ivory tower," and employees have a "hands-on, value-driven approach."

The second set of values stems from the *nature of the organization's mission*. The company must stick with what it does best and maintain control over its core activities. A company can easily get side-tracked into pursuing activities outside its area of expertise just because they seem to promise a quick return. Management should cultivate values so that a company "sticks to the knitting," which means staying with the businesses it knows best. A company must also establish close relations with the customer as a way of improving its competitive position. After all, who knows better about a company's performance than those who use its products or services? By emphasizing customer-oriented values, organizations are able to learn customer needs and improve their ability to develop products and services customers desire. All these management values are strongly represented in companies such as IBM, Hewlett-Packard, and Toyota that are sure of their mission and take constant steps to maintain it.

The third set of values bear on *how to operate the organization*. A company should try to establish an organizational design that will motivate employees to do their best. Inherent in this is the belief that productivity is obtained through people and that respect for the individual is the primary means by which a company can create the right atmosphere for productive behavior. As William Ouchi has noted, a similar philosophy pervades the culture of Japanese companies.[28] Many U.S. companies pay this kind of attention to their employees—for instance, Kodak, Procter & Gamble, and Levi Strauss. An emphasis on entrepreneurship and respect for the employee leads to establishing a structure that gives employees the latitude to make decisions and motivates them to succeed. Because a simple structure and a lean staff best fit this situation, the organization should be designed with only the number of managers and hierarchical levels that are necessary to get the job done. The organization should also be sufficiently decentralized to permit employee participation but centralized enough for management to make sure that the company pursues its strategic mission and that cultural values are followed.

These three main sets of values are at the heart of an organization's culture, and management transmits and maintains them through stories, myths, symbols, and socialization. Pursuing these values is not enough to ensure organizational success, however, and over time cultural values should change to suit the environment in which the company is operating. A company needs to establish the values that are good for it and base its organizational structure and control system on them. When that is accomplished, only those people who fit the values are recruited into the organization, and, through training, they become a part of the organization's culture. Thus the types of control systems chosen should reinforce and build on one another in a cohesive way. Although, as we note earlier, culture is difficult and expensive to develop, it is a powerful form of control. Nevertheless, it is not free of problems, and we now consider its debit side.

Problems with clan control   The development of unique systems of norms and values at the divisional and functional levels can lead to communications problems across divisions and functions. Thus when clan control is used, care must be taken that integration does not suffer because of such failures in communication. Moreover, clan control is not suitable where rapid growth or changes in the environment do not provide a context within which stable norms and values can develop. A classic case of the failure of clan control under these conditions is People Express, which started off with a system based on a team structure, where clan control was used as the main means of getting the work done. As the company grew quickly through its takeover of other airlines and rapid increase in flights, it could not maintain control of its operations, and its costs rose dramatically.

Clan control is also not appropriate when employee turnover is high because there is no time to develop a stable system of values and the costs rise dramatically with increased turnover. Consequently, it is of little use in most production line systems. The Japanese, however, can use clan control in their factories because turnover there is typically low, and if lifetime employment exists, turnover is negligible.

Finally, organizational culture cannot by itself control organizational performance and make structure work. It must be backed by output and bureaucratic controls and matched to a reward system so that employees will in fact cultivate organizational norms and values and modify their behavior to organizational objectives. Because of the expense involved, many companies abandon culture in favor of tight objective control and close supervision of behavior.

Summary: Types of Control Systems

Choosing a control system to match the firm's strategy and structure offers management a number of important challenges. Management must select controls that provide a framework to accurately monitor, measure, and evaluate the standards or targets organizations choose to achieve their strategic objectives at step 1 in the control process. Market and output controls are the cheapest and easiest to use, but they must be backed up with bureaucratic and clan control to ensure that the firm is achieving its goals in the most efficient way possible. In general, these controls should reinforce one another, and care must be taken to ensure that they do not result in unforeseen consequences such as competition between functions, divisions, and individuals.

11.8 STRATEGIC REWARD SYSTEMS

A final way in which organizations attempt to control employee behavior is by linking reward systems to their control systems.[29] An organization must decide which behaviors it wishes to reward, adopt a control system to measure these behaviors, and then link the reward structure to them. How to relate rewards to performance is a crucial strategic decision because it affects the way managers and employees at all levels in the organization behave. For example, in designing a pay system for salespeople, the choice would be whether to employ salespeople on the basis of straight salary or salary plus a bonus based on how much is sold. Neiman-Marcus, the luxury retailer, pays employees a straight salary because it wants to encourage high-quality service but discourage hard sell. Thus there are no incentives based on quantity sold. On the other hand, the pay system for rewarding car salespeople typically contains a high bonus for the number of cars sold.

What behaviors to reward is therefore an important decision, tied closely to a company's business-level strategy, as we discuss in Chapter 12. Next we consider the types of reward systems available to strategic managers.[30] Generally, reward systems are found at the individual and group or total organizational levels. Often these systems are used in combination; for example, merit raises at the individual level may be accompanied by a bonus based on divisional or plant performance. Within each type, several forms of reward systems are available.

Individual Reward Systems

Piecework plans   Piecework plans are used when outputs can be objectively measured. Essentially, employees are paid on the basis of some set amount for each unit of output produced. Piecework plans are most commonly used for employees working on production lines, where individuals work alone and their performance can be directly measured. Because this system encourages quantity rather than quality, the company normally applies stringent quality controls to ensure that the quality is acceptable.

Commission systems   Commission systems resemble piecework systems, except that they are normally tied not to what is produced but to how much is sold. Thus they are most commonly found in sales situations. Often the salaries of salespeople are based principally on commission to encourage superior performance. Thus first-rate salespeople can earn more than $1 million per year.

Bonus plans   Bonus plans at the individual level generally reward the performance of a company's key individuals, such as the CEO or senior vice presidents. The performance of these people is visible to the organization as a whole and to stakeholders such as shareholders. Consequently, there is a strong rationale for paying these individuals according to some measure of functional or divisional performance. A company must proceed carefully, however, if it is to avoid problems such as emphasis on short-run rather than long-term objectives. For example, paying bonuses based on quarterly or yearly ROI rather than on five-year growth can have a markedly different effect on the way strategic managers behave.

Group and Organizational Reward Systems

Group and organizational reward systems provide additional ways in which companies can relate pay to performance. In general, the problem with these systems is that the relationship is less direct and more difficult to measure than in the case of individually based systems. Consequently, they are viewed as less motivating. The most common reward systems at these levels involve group bonuses, profit sharing, employee stock options, and organization bonuses.

Group-based bonus systems   Sometimes a company can establish project teams, or work groups, that perform all the operations needed to turn out a product or provide a service. This arrangement makes it possible to measure group performance and offer rewards on the basis of group productivity. The system can be highly motivating because employees are allowed to develop the best work procedures for doing the job and are responsible for improving their own productivity. For example, Wal-Mart supports a group bonus plan based on controlling shrinkage (i.e., employee theft).

Profit-sharing systems   Profit-sharing plans are designed to reward employees on the basis of the profit a company earns in any one time period. Such plans encourage employees to take a broad view of their activities and feel connected with the company as a whole. Wal-Mart uses this method as well to develop its organizational culture.

Employee stock option systems   Rather than reward employees on the basis of short-term profits, a company sometimes allows them to buy its shares at below-market prices, heightening employee motivation. As shareholders, the employees will focus not only on short-term profits, but also on long-term capital appreciation, for they are now the company's owners. Over time, if enough employees participate, they can control a substantial stock holding, as did the employees of Eastern Airlines, and thus become vitally interested in the company's performance.

Organization bonus systems   Profit is not the only basis on which a company can reward organization-wide performance. Rewards are also commonly based on cost savings, quality increases, or production increases obtained in the last time period. Because these systems usually require that outputs be measured accurately, they are most common in production line organizations or in service companies, where it is possible to cost out the price of the services of personnel. The systems are mainly a back-up to other forms of pay systems. In rare situations, however, such as at The Lincoln Electric Company, a company renowned for the success of its cost-savings group plan, they become the principal means of control.

Control through organizational reward systems complements all the other forms of control we discuss in this chapter. The reward systems help determine how output or clan control, for example, will work. Rewards act as the oil for making a control system function effectively. To ensure that the right strategic behaviors are being rewarded, rewards should be closely linked to an organization's strategy. Moreover, they should be so designed that they do not lead to conflicts among divisions, functions, or individuals.

11.9 SUMMARY OF CHAPTER

The purpose of this chapter is to discuss the types of integrating mechanisms and control systems available to strategic planners to influence organizational performance. Companies must use more complex integrating mechanisms when they adopt more complex structures. They must also select the combination of controls that will make the structure work and meet the company's strategic objectives. Companies may use a variety of controls because different types of controls may suit different divisions or functions or different types of employees.

The essential task for companies is to select controls that are consistent with one another and also match the organizational structure. Companies with a high level of differentiation and integration require a more complex set of controls than those with a low degree of differentiation and integration. For example, as we discuss in the opening incident about TRW, controls should spur divisions to cooperate rather than compete. The control system has to provide rewards for both cooperation based on establishing a fair price for each division's technological know-how and sharing knowledge (such as group bonus plans). In the case of simple functional structures, on the other hand, output controls can monitor each function's performance separately from the others, making control much easier to achieve. In the next chapter, we consider in detail how structure and control should be jointly matched to the company's corporate- and business-level strategies.

This chapter makes the following main points:

1.   The more complex the company and the higher its level of differentiation, the higher is the level of integration needed to manage its structure.

2. The kinds of integrating mechanisms available to a company range from direct contact to matrix structure. The more complex the mechanism, the greater are the costs of using it. A company should take care to match these mechanisms to its strategic needs.

3. Strategic control is the process of setting targets, monitoring, evaluating, and rewarding organizational performance.

4. Control takes place at all levels in the organization: corporate, divisional, functional, and individual.

5. Effective control systems are flexible, accurate, and able to provide quick feedback to strategic planners.

6. There are four steps to designing an effective control system: establishing performance standards, creating measuring systems, comparing performance against targets, and evaluating the result taking corrective action.

7. Many kinds of performance standards are available for strategy implementation. The kinds of measures managers choose affect the way a company operates.

8. Control systems range from those directed at measuring outputs or productivity to those measuring behaviors or actions.

9. The three main forms of market control are stock market price, return on investment, and transfer pricing.

10. Output control establishes goals for divisions, functions, and individuals. It can be used only when outputs can be objectively measured.

11. Bureaucratic control is used to control behaviors when it is impossible to measure outputs. The main forms of bureaucratic control are rules and procedures, budgets, and standardization.

12. When neither outputs nor behaviors can be monitored and evaluated, organizations turn to clan control. Clan control is control through a system of norms and values that individuals internalize as they are socialized into the organization. Organizational culture is a collection of the norms and values that govern the way in which people act and behave inside the organization.

13. An organization's reward systems constitute the final form of control. A company links its reward systems to organizational goals and objectives to provide an incentive for employees to perform well.

14. Organizations use all these forms of controls simultaneously. Management must select and combine those that are consistent with each other and with the strategy and structure of the organization.

Discussion Questions

1. What are the relationships among differentiation, integration, and strategic control systems? Why are these relationships important?

2. For each of the structures we discuss in Chapter 10, outline the integrating mechanisms and control systems most suitable for matching them.

3. What kinds of integration and control systems does your (a) business school and (b) university use to operate its structure and control personnel?

4. List the kinds of integration and control systems you would be likely to find in (a) a small manufacturing company, (b) a chain store, (c) a gourmet restaurant, and (d) a big five accounting firm.

Endnotes

1. Robert Sheehan, "Thompson Ramo Wooldridge: Two Wings in Space," *Fortune,* February 1963, p. 95.

2. TRW Inc. Annual Report, 1990.

3. "TRW Leads a Revolution in Managing Technology," *Business Week,* November 15, 1982, p. 124.

4. P. R. Lawrence and J. Lorsch, *Organization and Environment* (Homewood, Ill.: Irwin, 1967), pp. 50–55.

5. J. R. Galbraith, *Designing Complex Organizations* (Reading, Mass.: Addison-Wesley, 1977), Ch. 1. J. R. Galbraith and R. K. Kazanjian, *Strategy Implementation: Structure, System, and Process* (St. Paul, Minn.: West, 1986), Ch. 7.

6. Henry Mintzberg, *The Nature of Managerial Work* (Englewood Cliffs, N.J.: Prentice-Hall, 1973), Ch. 10.

7. Lawrence and Lorsch, *Organization and Environment,* p. 55.

8. W. G. Ouchi, "The Transmission of Control Through Organizational Hierarchy," *Academy of Management Journal,* 21 (1978), 173–192. W. H. Newman, *Constructive Control* (Englewood Cliffs, N.J.: Prentice-Hall, 1975.

9. K. A. Merchant, *Control in Business Organizations* (Marshfield, Mass.: Pitman, 1985). E. E. Lawler III and J. G. Rhodes, *Information and Control in Organizations* (Pacific Palisades, Calif.: Goodyear, 1976).

10. J. P. Campbell, "On the Nature of Organizational Effectiveness," in R. S. Goodman and J. M. Pennings (eds.) *New Perspectives on Organizational Effectiveness* (San Francisco: Jossey-Bass, 1977), pp. 13–55.

11. T. Connolly, E. J. Conlon, and S. J. Deutsch, "Organizational Effectiveness: A Multiple-Constituency Approach," *Academy of Management Review,* 5 (1980), 211–217: R. E. Quinn and J. Rohrbaugh, "A Spatial Model of Effectiveness Criteria: Towards a Competing Values Approach to Organizational Analysis," *Management Science,* 29 (1983), 33–51.

12. W. G. Ouchi, "The Relationship Between Organizational Structure and Organizational Control," *Administrative Science Quarterly,* 22 (1977), 95–113.

13. J. D. Thompson, *Organizations in Action* (New York: McGraw-Hill, 1967), Ch. 10. W. G. Ouchi, "A Conceptual Framework for the Design of Organizational Control Systems," *Management Science,* 25 (1979), 833–848.

14. R. F. Vancil, *Decentralization: Managerial Ambiguity by Design* (Homewood, Ill.: Dow-Jones Irwin, 1978).

15. R. G. Eccles, *The Transfer Pacing Problem* (Lexington, Mass.: Lexington Books, 1985), Ch. 2.

16. E. Flamholtz, "Organizational Control Systems as a Managerial Tool," *California Management Review* (Winter 1979), 50–58.

17. O. E. Williamson, *Markets and Hierarchies* (New York: Free Press, 1975). W. G. Ouchi, "Markets, Bureaucracies, and Clans," *Administrative Science Quarterly,* 25 (1980), 129–141.

18. P. Lorange, *Corporate Planning* (Englewood Cliffs, N. J.: Prentice-Hall, 1980). G. A. Welsch, *Budgeting: Profit Planning and Control,* 4th ed. (Englewood Cliffs, N.J.: Prentice-Hall, 1976).

19. C. S. Trapani, "Six Critical Areas in the Budgeting Process," *Management Accounting,* 64 (1982), 52–58.

20. Trapani, "Six Critical Areas," p. 54.

21. H. Mintzberg, *The Structuring of Organizations* (Englewood Cliffs, N.J.: Prentice-Hall, 1979), pp. 5–9.

22. Ouchi, "Markets, Bureaucracies, and Clans," p. 130.

23. G. R. Jones, "Socialization Tactics, Self-Efficacy, and Newcomers' Adjustments to Organizations," *Academy of Management Journal,* 29 (1986), 262–279.

24. M. R. Louis, "Surprise and Sensemaking: What Newcomers Experience in Entering Unfamiliar Settings," *Administrative Science Quarterly,* 25 (1980), 226–251.

25. L. Smircich, "Concepts of Culture and Organizational Analysis," *Administrative Science Quarterly,* 28 (1983), 339–358.

26. J. Van Maanen and E. H. Schein, "Towards a Theory of Organizational Socialization," in B. M. Staw (ed.), *Research in Organizational Behavior* (Greenwich, Conn.: JAI Press, 1979), pp. 1, 209–264.

27. T. J. Peters and R. H. Waterman, *In Search of Excellence: Lessons from America's Best-Run Companies* (New York: Harper & Row, 1982).

28. W. G. Ouchi, *Theory Z. How American Business Can Meet the Japanese Challenge* (Reading, Mass.: Addison-Wesley, 1981).

29. E. E. Lawler III, *Motivation in Work Organizations* (Monterey, Calif.: Brooks/Cole, 1973). Galbraith and Kazanjian, *Strategy Implementation,* Ch. 6.

30. E. E. Lawler III, "The Design of Effective Reward Systems," in J. W. Lorsch (ed.), *Handbook of Organizational Behavior* (Englewood Cliffs, N.J.: Prentice-Hall, 1987), pp. 386–422. R. Mathis and J. Jackson, *Personnel,* 2nd ed. (St. Paul, Minn.: West, 1979), p. 456.

Chapter 12

MATCHING STRUCTURE AND CONTROL TO STRATEGY

12.1 OPENING INCIDENT: TEXAS INSTRUMENTS

Texas Instruments (TI) was started by two entrepreneurs, Clarence Karcher and Eugene McDermott, who invented the technique of using sound waves to map underground strata. This technique became the dominant way for oil companies to prospect for oil, and its applications for sonar and radar in the military became evident. The real breakthrough for TI, however, came in the 1950s, when it pioneered transistors small enough for use in radios and developed silicon transistors for use in military operations. Miniaturization of electronic circuits became TI's chief competitive advantage and allowed the company to grow rapidly, even when companies such as General Electric and RCA entered the market. It solidified its competitive advantage by emphasizing efficiency, and it emerged as the lowest-cost producer of these circuits.[1]

To maintain its technological edge, TI adopted a decentralized matrix structure, so that product and technological knowledge could be shared across its many divisions. Divisional sharing gave TI a leading edge in two fast-growing and highly profitable businesses: computers and consumer electronics. In controlling the matrix, the president of TI at this time, Patrick E. Haggerty, decentralized decision making to the divisional level. He made little attempt to interfere in the various divisions' business-level strategies. He saw the role of the corporate center as one of managing a portfolio of investments and instituted a strict set of financial controls to evaluate divisional performance. Under his leadership, and then under J. Fred Bucy's, the company prospered and grew.[2] By 1983, however, the company was experiencing problems.

TI faced substantial competition from Japanese companies that had imitated many of TI's products and technical innovations, while usurping its cost-leadership position. In addition, the company received a major blow to its morale when its consumer products business reported record losses and plunged TI into its first quarterly loss ever. Bucy, in a statement to stockholders, explained the company's downturn: "TI is suffering from the problems of the company's success. As it passes through phases of corporate life, it must accommodate its organization and structures to these phases as it grows. This failure to adjust affected operating and strategic structures."[3]

TI realized that it had to alter its structure and control system as its competitive position changed over time. To restore profitability, TI abandoned its matrix structure because it had begun to fragment both people and resources, making it almost impossible for management to exert effective control over divisional operations. TI moved to a more centralized, divisional structure, where control could be exercised more easily. In the new structure, divisional managers were evaluated on their division's performance as a profit center. In addition, corporate-level personnel designed new control systems to promote the sharing of information and knowledge across divisions more efficiently and to promote synergies. In essence, TI went to a strategic business unit (SBU) structure, which, when coupled with the right mix of integrating mechanisms and divisional controls, put the company back on track.

TI realized that its structure had to match its business- and corporate-level strategy. It recognized, too, that as changes in the competitive environment caused changes in its strategy, management would have to keep moving quickly to implement the structure and control system best suited to its objectives.

12.2 OVERVIEW

At Texas Instruments, strategic managers moved to implement the right mix of structure and control systems to allow the company to deal with changes in its strategy and the competitive environment. In this chapter, we discuss how strategic choice at the corporate, business, and functional levels affects the choice of structure and control systems—in other words, how to match different forms of structure and control to strategy. As we emphasize in Chapter 1, the issue facing strategic managers is to match strategy formulation with strategy implementation. All the tools of strategy formulation and implementation are discussed in previous chapters. Now we put the two sides of the equation together and examine the issues involved in greater detail.

First, we consider how functional-level strategy affects structure and control and then how a company's choice of generic business-level strategy affects the choice of structure and control for implementing the strategy. Next, we take up the special problems that different kinds of corporate-level strategy pose for strategic managers in designing a structure and note how changes in corporate-level strategy over time affect the form of structure and control systems adopted by a company, paying particular attention to ways of implementing international strategy. Finally, we examine the problems relating to the two entry strategies we discussed in Chapter 9: managing mergers and acquisitions and providing the setting that encourages internal venturing. By the end of this chapter, you will understand why Texas Instruments and all companies go through a series of transitions in structure and control as they attempt to deal with the changing nature of their strategy and environment.

12.3 STRUCTURE AND CONTROL AT THE FUNCTIONAL LEVEL

In Chapter 4, in our discussion of strategy formulation at the functional level, we emphasize that a company must develop distinctive competencies to give it a competitive advantage. We discuss how different competencies could be developed in each function and then, in Chapter 5, we note that at the business level different generic competitive strategies require the development of different types of distinctive competencies. In this section, we consider how a company can create a structure and control system that permit the development of various distinctive functional competencies or skills.

Decisions at the functional level fall into two categories: choices about the level of vertical differentiation and choices about monitoring and evaluation systems. (Choices about horizontal differentiation are not relevant here because we are considering each function individually.) The choices made depend on the distinctive competence that a company is pursuing.

Manufacturing

In manufacturing, functional strategy usually centers on reducing production costs. A company must create an organizational setting in which managers can learn from experience curve effects how to economize on costs. To move down the experience curve quickly, the company must exercise tight control over work activities and employees, so that it can squeeze out costs wherever possible. This is why manufacturing generally has the tallest structure of all the functions.

Besides supervision from the hierarchy, however, manufacturing also relies on bureaucratic and output controls to reduce costs. Standardization is frequently used to squeeze out costs. For example, human inputs are standardized through the recruitment and training of personnel, the work process is standardized or programmed to reduce costs, and quality control is used to make sure that outputs are being produced correctly. In addition, managers are closely monitored and controlled through output control and production budgets.

Finally, in some manufacturing settings, especially those run on Japanese-style principles, companies attempt to develop a production culture. Employees are given benefits that normally only management receives, quality control circles are created to exchange information and suggestions about problems and work procedures, and workers share in the increases in output through some form of bonus system. The aim is to match structure and control so that they jointly create a low-cost competence and the function achieves its strategy.

Research and Development

In contrast, the functional strategy for a research and development department is to develop a technological distinctive competence. Consequently, the structure should produce a setting in which personnel can develop innovative products or processes. In practice, research and development departments have flatter structures than any other function in an organization (that is, they usually have the fewest number of hierarchical levels relative to their size). Flatter structures give research and development personnel the freedom and autonomy to be innovative. Furthermore, because evaluating research and development personnel is difficult, adding layers of hierarchy would waste resources.[4]

Controlling the research and development function is somewhat problematical because it is difficult to monitor employee behavior. Using output controls for the purpose is difficult and expensive. The solution, therefore, is to use input control and recruit only highly trained employees. Research and development departments also rely heavily on small teams and clan control to reinforce innovation, and a professional culture emerges to control employee behavior.

Sales

Like research and development, the sales function usually has a flat structure. Most commonly, three hierarchical levels—sales director, regional or product sales managers, and individual salespeople—can accommodate even large sales forces. Flat structures are possible because the organization does not depend on direct supervision for control. Salespeople's activities are often complex; moreover, because they are dispersed in the field, these employees are difficult to monitor. Rather than depend on the hierarchy, the sales function usually implements output and behavioral controls. These controls take the form of specific sales goals as well as detailed reports that salespeople must file describing their interactions with customers.[5] Supervisors can then review salespeoples's performance easily.

Similar considerations apply to the other functions, such as accounting, finance, engineering, or personnel. Managers must select the right combination of structure and control mechanisms to achieve functional objectives. Table 12.1 lists the appropriate choices of structure and control for all the principal organizational functions.

TABLE 12.1   **Structure and control at the functional level**

Function	Type of structure	Main type of control
Production	Tall/centralized	Output control (e.g., cost targets)
Materials management	Flat/centralized	Output control (e.g., inventory and purchasing targets)
Research and development	Flat/decentralized	Clan control (e.g., norms, values, and culture)
Sales	Flat/decentralized	Output control (e.g., sales targets)
Accounting/finance	Tall/decentralized	Bureaucratic control (e.g., budgets)
Human resources	Flat/centralized	Bureaucratic control (e.g., standardization)

12.4 STRUCTURE AND CONTROL AT THE BUSINESS LEVEL

Generic Business-Level Strategies

Designing the right mix of structure and control at the business level is a continuation of designing a company's functional departments. Having implemented the right structure and control system for each individual function, the company must then implement the organizational arrangements so that all the functions can be managed together to achieve business-level strategy objectives. Because the focus is on managing interfunctional relationships, the choice of *horizontal differentiation* (division of organizational activities) and *integration* for achieving business-level strategies becomes very important.[6] Control systems must also be selected with the monitoring and evaluating of interfunctional activities in mind. Table 12.2 summarizes the appropriate organizational structure and control systems that companies can use when following a low-cost, differentiation, or focused strategy.

Cost-leadership strategy and structure   The aim of the cost-leadership strategy is to make the company pursuing it the lowest-cost producer in the market.[7] At the business level, this means reducing costs not just in production, but across all functions in the organization—including research and development and sales and marketing.

If a company is following a cost-leadership strategy, its research and development efforts probably focus on process engineering rather than on the more expensive product research, which carries no guarantee of success. In other words, the company stresses research that lowers the cost of making existing

TABLE 12.2   Generic strategy, structure, and control

	Strategy		
	Cost leadership	Differentiation	Focus
Appropriate structure	Functional or product	Product or matrix	Functional
Integrating mechanisms	Center on manufacturing	Center on R&D or marketing	Center on product or customer
Output control	Great use (e.g., cost control)	Some use (e.g., quality goals)	Some use (e.g., cost and quality)
Bureaucratic control	Some use (e.g., budgets, standardization)	Great use (e.g., rules, budgets)	Some use (e.g., budgets)
Clan control	Little use (e.g., quality control circles)	Great use (e.g., norms and culture)	Great use (e.g., norms and culture)

products. Similarly, the company tries to decrease the cost of sales and marketing by offering a standard product to a mass market rather than by offering different products aimed at different market segments.[8]

To implement such a strategy, the cost leader chooses the simplest structure—the one with the lowest level of differentiation that can meet the needs of the strategy. Simple structures are the least expensive to operate and thus match the needs of the low-cost strategy. In practice, the structure chosen is normally a functional or perhaps a product structure. Each of these structures allows manufacturing activities to be programmed or standardized, a major source of cost saving.[9] The two structures are also relatively easy to manage because they require a low degree of integration. The company does not need to coordinate as many new products or innovations and so avoids the expense of creating task forces or teams. Seagate Technology, producer of hard disks, is an example of a cost leader that continually streamlines its structure to maintain a competitive advantage. It periodically reduces levels in the hierarchy and institutes strict production controls to minimize costs. This process puts it substantially ahead of its Japanese competitors.

To reduce costs, cost-leadership companies want to use the cheapest and easiest forms of control available—output controls. For each function, a company adopts output controls that allow it to monitor and evaluate functional performance closely, so that waste is curtailed and cost savings maximized. In the production function, for example, the company imposes tight controls and stresses meeting budgets based on production or cost targets.[10] In research and development, too, the emphasis falls on the bottom line. Research and development personnel concerned with demonstrating their contribution to saving costs may focus their efforts on improving process technology, where actual savings are calculable. Heinz Foods clearly illustrates such efforts. In following a cost-leadership strategy, it places enormous emphasis on production improvements that can reduce the cost of a can of beans. Like manufacturing and research and development, the sales function is closely monitored, and sales targets are usually challenging. Cost-leadership companies, however, are likely to reward employees by generous incentive and bonus schemes to encourage high performance. Often their culture is based on values that emphasize the bottom line, such as in Heinz, Lincoln Electric, and PepsiCo.

In short, pursuing a successful cost-leadership strategy requires close attention to the design of structure and control to economize on costs. Managers, rules, and organizational control mechanisms cost money, and low-cost companies must try to economize when implementing their structures. When a company's competitive advantage depends on achieving and maintaining a low-cost advantage, adopting the right organizational arrangements is vital.

Differentiation strategy and structure   To pursue a differentiation strategy, a company must develop a distinctive competence in a function such as research and development or marketing and sales. To make its product unique in the eyes of the customer, the differentiated company must design its structure and control systems around the *particular source* of its competitive advantage.[11] As a result, the differentiated company usually employs a more complex structure—that is, a structure with a higher level of differentiation and integration than the cost leader.

For example, suppose the differentiator's strength lies in technological competence; the company has the cutting-edge technology. In this case, the company's structure and control systems should be designed around the research and development function. Implementing a *matrix structure,* as Texas Instruments and TRW have done, helps develop technological innovations, for it allows for the cross-fertilization of ideas among functions. Integrating mechanisms, such as tasks forces and teams, help transfer knowledge among functions and are designed around the research and development function. For example, sales, marketing, and production targets are geared to research and development goals, marketing devises advertising programs that focus on technological possibilities, and salespeople are evaluated on their understanding of new product characteristics and their ability to inform potential customers about them. Stringent sales targets are unlikely to be set in this situation because the goal is quality of service.

When the source of the differentiator's advantage is in the breadth of its product range or the number of different market segments it serves, a different structure is required. In such cases, companies design a structure around their products, and thus a *product* or *geographical* structure fits best. Consequently, if a company manufactures a distinctive range of products, research and development or sales are organized by product, and task forces and teams have a product, not a research orientation. If designed around types of customers, the company may have a structure based on regional needs or even on different types of customers such as businesses, individual consumers, or the government. For example, both Compaq and Rockwell have recently reorganized their structures to concentrate on the needs of specific customers or regions to gain a competitive advantage.

The control systems used to match the structure can also be geared to the company's distinctive competence. For the differentiator, it is important that the various functions do not pull in different directions; indeed, cooperation among the various functions is vital. But when functions work together, output controls become much harder to use. In general, it is much more difficult to measure the performance of people in different functions when they are engaged in cooperative efforts. As a result, a company must rely more on behavior controls and clan control when pursuing a strategy of differentiation. That is why companies pursuing a differentiation strategy often have a markedly different kind of culture than those pursuing a low-cost strategy. Because the quality of human resources is often the source of differentiation—good scientists, designers, or marketing people—these organizations have a culture based on professionalism or collegiality, a culture that emphasizes the distinctiveness of the human resource rather than the high pressure of the bottom line.[12] Hewlett-Packard, IBM, and Frito-Lay, Inc., all of which emphasize some kind of distinctive competence, exemplify firms with professional cultures.

The structure and control system of the differentiator are more expensive than the cost leader's, but the benefits are also greater if companies reap the rewards of a premium price.

Focus strategy and structure   In Chapter 5, we define a focus strategy as one that was directed at a particular customer segment. A company focuses on a product or range of products directed at one sort of customer or region. This strategy tends to have higher production costs than the other two strategies because output levels are lower, making it harder to obtain substantial economies of scale. As a result, a focused company must exercise cost control. On the other hand, because some attribute of its product usually gives the focused company its unique advantage—possibly its ability to provide customers with high-quality, personalized service—a focused company has to develop a unique competence. For both these reasons, the structure and control system adopted by the focused company have to be inexpensive to operate but flexible enough to allow a distinctive competence to emerge.

The focused company normally adopts a functional structure to meet these needs. This structure is appropriate because it is complex enough to manage the activities necessary to service the needs of the market segment or produce a narrow range of products. At the same time, a functional structure is also relatively easy to control, and there is less need for complex, expensive integrating mechanisms. This structure permits more personal control and flexibility than the other two, and so reduces the costs of control while fostering the development of a distinctive competence.[13] Given its small size, a focused company can rely less on bureaucratic control and more on clan control and culture, which is vital to the development of a service competence. Although output controls need to be used in production and sales, this form of control, as with clan control, is inexpensive in a small organization.

The combination of functional structure and low cost of control help offset the higher costs of production while still allowing the firm to develop unique strengths. It is little wonder, then, that there are so many focused companies. Additionally, because a focused company's competitive advantage is often based on personalized service, the flexibility of this kind of structure allows it to respond quickly to customer needs and change its products in response to customer requests. The structure, then, backs up the strategy and helps the firm develop and maintain its distinctive competence.

Au Bon Pain Company, Inc., a fast-food chain specializing in fancy coffees and baked goods such as croissants, is a good example of a company that recognized the need to design a structure and control system to match a focused strategy aimed at an upscale customer group. To encourage franchises to perform highly and satisfy customer needs, it decentralized control to each franchise, making each a self-contained functional unit. Then, through a profit-sharing plan that rewarded cost cutting and quality, it gave each franchise manager the incentive to create a set of control arrangements that minimized costs but maximized quality of service. The result was a strategy-structure fit that led to a massive increase in franchise profits.

Although research corroborates that these are appropriate forms of structure and control associated with different kinds of strategies, these forms are ideals. Many companies do *not* use the right forms. Quite likely, they are not as successful or may not survive as long as those that do match their strategy, structure, and control systems.[14] In Chapter 13, we discuss some of the problems that companies may encounter when they attempt to change their structures or strategies, and we also examine the reasons that their structures do not match their strategies.

Business Strategies and the Industry Life Cycle

Although the choice of generic strategy is at the heart of a company's business-level strategy, the stage of the industry life cycle that the company is in also influences its business strategy. Table 12.3 shows the relationship between industry life cycle strategy and form of organizational structure and control.

TABLE 12.3   Life cycle strategy and structure and control

Life cycle strategy	Appropriate structure	Integrating mechanisms	Type of control: Output	Type of control: Bureaucratic	Type of control: Clan
Embryonic	Simple	Personal and group meetings	Little use	Little use (e.g., sales targets)	Great use (e.g., entrepreneurial culture)
Growth	Functional, product, or matrix	Liaison roles task forces and teams (e.g., product innovation committee)	Little use	Little use	Little use
Shakeout	Product or matrix (depends on generic strategy)	Fully developed teams and task forces (e.g., product development committee)	Some to great use	Some to great use (depends on generic strategy)	Some to great use
Maturity	Product/functional	Teams and task forces (e.g., process development committee)	Some to great use	Some to great use (depends on generic strategy)	Some to great use
Decline	Move to simplify structure (e.g., product to functional)	Streamline integrating mechanisms	Great use	Great use	Some use

Embryonic stage strategy and structure   In the embryonic industry stage, the principal problem facing companies at the business level is to perfect the product and educate the customer about the product. The computer industry in the early 1970s is a good example of an industry in the embryonic stage. At this stage, a *share-building strategy* is the appropriate choice because the company's objective is to establish a reputation and market share. Generally, because the company is small at this stage, it has a flat structure, and its founder probably exercises a great deal of centralized control.

In terms of horizontal differentiation, a functional structure is likely to emerge as a firm establishes its goals and objectives and begins to group activities by function. Developing market share depends primarily on product development; hence the research and development and the marketing functions take precedence in the new structure. Integration, in turn, will be organized around that function providing the distinctive competence that the company is trying to develop.

Companies in embryonic industries are likely to be entrepreneurial, with a fast-moving culture that stems mainly from a technological or marketing orientation. Clan control, like that used by Apple Computer in its early years, is the main type of control because the company is essentially discovering how to do things right. These companies settle for loose control because output controls or stringent rules and procedures do not suit a company that does not know as yet what targets it can achieve. In fact, establishing targets can hurt the company by lowering aspirations and stifling creativity. Thus structure and control are best kept simple and fluid.

Growth-stage strategy and structure   By the time it reaches the growth stage of the life cycle, an organization has learned how to do the right things in the right way. It therefore adopts a *growth strategy* to retain its share of the rapidly expanding market.[15] By now, it has established a relatively stable grouping of functional activities, and functional managers have emerged to take control of the functions, lessening the burden on the founding entrepreneur. Consequently, the company is also taller, with a higher level of vertical differentiation. More managerial control results as well. These changes mean that the company is operating with a fully developed functional structure that gives it a firm foundation on which to build. The boundaries among functions are still likely to be fluid, however, and cross-functional communication that integrates the organization persists. As the company grows and becomes more complex, it increasingly uses teams and task forces. At this stage, the company's goal should be to perfect its manufacturing operations to ride down the experience curve, and to design its structure to suit its distinctive competence.

Nevertheless, problems can occur at this stage when companies do not change their structure and controls to suit future contingencies. Because of the large increase in market growth, many companies neglect their costs because they can still sell all they can produce. As there is no pressure to cut costs, a company has a lot of slack, and it has little incentive to exert tight control over itself. Often companies develop complex structures with little concern for their costs. You saw earlier in the Opening Incidents to this chapter and Chapter 10 how lax control was at Texas Instruments and Apple Computer during their period of unprecedented growth. Apple thought it had the luxury to develop the expensive divisional structure that duplicated design, research and development, and marketing activities for each product line. When the next stage of the life cycle, the shakeout stage, arrived, Apple scrambled to restructure itself more efficiently. Similarly, at Texas Instruments, managers recognized the consequences of using an expensive matrix structure in a maturing market. Organizational design during growth almost inevitably determines a company's success in future stages.

Shakeout strategy and structure   In the shakeout stage, a *share-maintaining* or *share-increasing* strategy is the appropriate choice. In a shakeout, the market is increasing, but at a decreasing rate: excess capacity develops throughout the industry as demand growth slows. To survive, a company must hold onto its share of the market. The companies that have perfected their manufacturing systems and streamlined their structures are in the best position because they have accumulated more experience and lowered costs faster than the others. Companies that paid close attention to adopting the right organizational structure and controls in the growth stage now find themselves in the best position to develop their generic business-level strategy and to sustain their competitive advantage in the shakeout. Such companies control their structures and can choose the right organizational arrangements to capitalize on generic strategy. As discussed earlier, companies at this stage are forced to decide what kind of structure they need because cost leadership and differentiation have different kinds of structure and control requirements.

To increase market share and reduce costs, both low-cost and differentiated companies usually adopt a product structure based on product lines or market segments. This structure allows a low-cost company to control its production system efficiently. For a differentiator, such a structure helps increase market share because the company can group its activities to mirror its market segments and different kinds of customers. The company's integration mechanisms can be closely tied to its product lines, which also makes coordination easier. Apple's reorganization to a product structure as it went after the school market, home market, and so on, illustrates this point. Similarly, Hewlett-Packard, faced with increasing competition from the Japanese, reorganized its structure around six product/market segments to achieve a fit between its strategy and structure.

A company's controls also change. Managers quite likely are more attentive to the bottom line and develop tough performance standards for the various functions. Standardization of inputs, throughputs, and outputs is the chief concern. Bonuses for key employees in the management team and for salespeople are usually linked to increases in market share. The culture of the organization probably changes as well, to reflect the more competitive and uncertain industry environment. Management must become less freewheeling and more efficiency oriented, and rewards are tied to cost effectiveness. Marketing, not just selling, is emphasized. If the company is a differentiator, customers have to be convinced of its dedication to product quality, reliability, or after-sales service.[16] Thus a marked shift in the kind of controls companies use occurs at this stage in the industry life cycle. Dealing with the new reality of the competitive environment is hard on strategic managers, and consequently many organizations go into decline and fail. Companies undergo major changes in competitive position and advantage as they are forced to readjust their structure and control system to the new competitive conditions.

Maturity strategies and structure   In the maturity stage, *hold-and-maintain* market share and *profit strategies* are most likely. Companies try to exploit the benefits of having made the right strategy-structure choices at the previous stages and enjoy their competitive advantage. At this stage, the goals of the research and development and production functions are to keep up with incremental product and process innovations. Products have been standardized, and a company's principal concern is to increase the product range to suit different kinds of customers and iron out any distribution difficulties to maximize sales. Its competitive strategy determines how the company strives to hold and maintain its position at this stage and to reap profits.

With a strategy of differentiation, a hold-and-maintain position means concentrating resources on developing the customer base. Companies use resources to improve marketing, distribution, and after-sales service. Decentralization occurs, and autonomy is granted to lower-level employees so that they can respond creatively and flexibly to customer needs. A high level of interfunctional communication is emphasized. The sales force feeds information to research and product development personnel so that they can refine products to enhance customer satisfaction, and research and development coordinates with manufacturing to bring new products on line. Because it needs as much integration as possible, the company frequently relies on task forces to trade and share information. Structure is buttressed by a culture that stresses service and customer satisfaction. IBM is renowned for its cultural values that allow it to respond effectively to customer needs.

Although a company may be following a differentiation strategy, costs are still a concern, especially if a profit strategy is being pursued. In production, strict cost control is likely to be stringently enforced, and in fact, production may be contracted out to Third World countries with lower labor costs.

If the company is following a low-cost strategy, both the hold-and-maintain and profit positions require continuing attention to materials management and the regulation of procurement, production, and distribution to control costs. Thus control is likely to become increasingly stringent. These companies also develop tall structures, with rigid rules and procedures that standardize organizational activities. Output controls increase and include strict accounting procedures and quantitative and qualitative measures of performance.[17] The culture of a company pursuing a profit strategy will combine a rigid cost-cutting mentality with a heavy managerial emphasis on the bottom line. Bonus systems linked directly to cost reduction or sales targets tied to increases in the customer base dominate the reward system and reinforce the production culture.[18] The combined result of all these measures is an organization that is a far cry from the decentralized and flexible differentiating company. It reaps profits from its meticulous attention to cost cutting. Crown Cork & Seal Company, Inc., is the epitome of a company in the mature stage and has remained the cost leader in the bottling and capping market for many years because of its innovative cost-cutting methods.

Decline strategies and structure   As all the decline strategies we discuss in Chapter 5—harvest, asset reduction, divestiture, and others—suggest, companies choosing to remain in the industry must shift to a structure and control system that reduces their total costs of production. Otherwise they cannot respond to the inevitable fall in demand in a declining industry. Because the industry has excess capacity, companies must change their structure and move rapidly to remove excess capacity by closing down plants. If they operate with a product structure, product lines should be trimmed and consolidated. General Motors did so, though very belatedly, when the demand for its vehicles declined. It shut down plants across the country, streamlined its structure, and cut costs by reducing its numbers of white-collar employees. Similarly, Kodak responded to increasing competition and a stagnating market by reducing capacity and combining many of its operating facilities both at home and abroad.

The move to streamline structure is often accompanied by a centralization of authority at the top levels in the organization.[19] That is, management moves to reassert tight personal control over lower levels in the hierarchy. Increased control is often attended by a reduction in the number of hierarchical levels as the company streamlines its structure. After deregulation, AT&T eliminated two levels in the hierarchy and recentralized control.

Obviously, decline is difficult for companies to manage. Employees, accustomed to prosperity, find that promotion opportunities and bonuses have dried up and that layoffs may ensue. Layoffs threaten morale and exacerbate the problems that the company is trying to deal with. Corporate culture deteriorates. Large oil companies suffered these consequences when they terminated thousands of employees during the oil price slump. During decline, top management continually tightens control, autonomy at lower levels is reduced, and any function or activity that cannot demonstrate bottom-line results is in danger. Output controls work in a punitive fashion and are reinforced by strict accounting procedures and bureaucratic control.

The resulting structure is far less costly to operate, and the company is in a better position to survive. If the company is pursuing a low-cost strategy, its only option is to move quickly to reduce costs even further. The cost leader may be able to survive comfortably for many years as other, less efficient, companies are driven out of the market. For the differentiator in a declining situation, cost cutting will mean reducing distribution costs. Although it must protect its distinctive competence, the differentiator may have room to reduce its product range or trim marginal customer segments to reduce costs without hurting revenues too much. In essence, it pursues a strategy of market concentration, which lowers costs but permits the company to retain its differentiated appeal. Many companies may also decide to specialize in one niche and essentially move to a focused strategy, serving one customer segment. These companies can streamline and simplify their structure because they have simplified their strategies. They can reduce the costs of coordination and control by selecting a simplified structure that has a lower level of differentiation and integration.

Summary: Structure and Control at the Business Level

Companies must match their structures and control systems to their business level strategies if they are to survive and prosper in competitive environments. Not only does the basic choice between a low cost and a differentiation strategy require the company to make a different set of choices, but choices of structure and control must be continually changed and modified to suit the nature of the industry life cycle. This is a complex job for strategic managers and one that many companies do not do well. The evidence suggests that strategy, structure, and performance are strongly linked at the business level: Companies that do not alter their structures do not perform as well as those that do.

12.5 STRUCTURE AND CONTROL AT THE CORPORATE LEVEL

At the corporate level, a company needs to choose the organizational structure that will enable it to operate efficiently in a number of different businesses. Although product structures are sometimes used to manage the multibusiness company, the structure normally chosen at the corporate level is the multidivisional structure or one of its variants (discussed in Chapter 10). The larger and more diverse the businesses in the corporate portfolio, the more likely is the company to have a multidivisional structure. The reason is that each division requires the services of full-scale specialist support functions and that a headquarters corporate staff is needed to oversee and evaluate divisional operations. Once it selects a divisional structure, a company must make two more choices: the right mix of integrating mechanisms to match the particular divisional structure and the right control systems to make the divisional structure work.

In Chapters 7 and 8, we discuss the various types of corporate strategy that a company can pursue. For the first of these types—concentration on a single business—the corporate- and business-level strategies are identical. Thus the previous discussion of structure and business-level strategy covers the issue of choice of structure and control for the single-business firm. We next discuss how the corporate-level strategies of vertical integration, related diversification, and unrelated diversification affect the choice of structure and control systems. Then we consider how to implement international strategy.

As we discuss in Chapter 7, the main reason a company pursues vertical integration is to achieve *economies of integration* among divisions.[20] For example, the company can coordinate resource scheduling decisions among divisions to reduce costs. For instance, locating a rolling mill next to a steel furnace saves the costs of reheating steel ingots. Similarly, the chief gains from related diversification come from obtaining *synergies* among divisions: Divisions benefit by sharing distribution and sales networks or research and development knowledge. With both of these strategies, the benefits to the company come from some transfer of resources among divisions. To secure these benefits, the company must coordinate activities between divisions. Consequently, structure and control must be designed to handle the transfer of resources among divisions.

In the case of unrelated diversification, however, the benefits to the company come from the possibility of achieving an *internal capital market,* which allows corporate personnel to make better allocations of capital than the external capital market. With this strategy, there are no transactions or exchanges among divisions; each operates separately. Structure and control must therefore be designed to allow each division to operate independently.

A company's choice of structure and control mechanisms thus depends on the degree to which the company must control the interactions among divisions. The more interdependent the division—that is, the more they depend on each other for resources—the more complex are the structure and control mechanisms required to make the strategy work.[21]

Table 12.4 indicates what forms of structure and control companies should

TABLE 12.4   Corporate strategy and structure and control

			Type of control		
	Appropriate structure	**Need for Integration**	Market	Bureaucratic	Clan
Unrelated diversification	Conglomerate	Low (no exchanges between divisions)	Great use (e.g., ROI)	Some use (e.g., budgets)	Little use
Vertical integration	Multidivisional	Medium (scheduling resource transfers)	Great use (e.g., ROI, transfer pricing)	Great use (e.g., standardization, budgets)	Some use (e.g., shared norms and values)
Related diversification	Multidivisional SBU	High (achieve synergies between divisions by integrating roles)	Little use	Great use (e.g., rules, budgets)	Great use (e.g., develop corporate culture)

Corporate strategy

adopt to manage the three corporate strategies. We examine them in detail in the next sections.

Unrelated Diversification

Because there are *no linkages* among divisions, unrelated diversification is the easiest and cheapest strategy to manage. The main requirement of the structure and control system is that it lets corporate personnel easily and accurately evaluate divisional performance. Thus the *conglomerate structure,* discussed earlier, is the appropriate choice, and market and bureaucratic controls are used with it. Each division is evaluated by strict return on investment criteria, and each division is given a budget in relation to its return on investment. The company also applies sophisticated accounting controls to obtain information quickly from the divisions so that corporate managers can readily compare divisions on several dimensions. Textron is a good example of a company that operates a conglomerate structure through the use of sophisticated computer networks and accounting controls, which allow it almost daily access to divisional performance.

Divisions in the conglomerate structure usually have considerable autonomy unless they fail to reach their return on investment objectives. Generally, corporate headquarters is not interested in the types of business-level strategy pursued by each division unless there are problems. If problems arise, corporate headquarters may step in to take corrective action, perhaps replacing managers or providing additional financial resources, depending on the reason for the problem. If they see no possibility of a turnaround, however, corporate personnel may just as easily decide to divest the division. This structure therefore allows the unrelated company to operate its businesses as a portfolio of investments, which can be bought and sold as business conditions change. Usually, managers in the various divisions do not know one another, and they may not know what companies are in the corporate portfolio.

The use of market controls to manage a company means that no integration among divisions is necessary. Thus the costs of managing an unrelated company are low. The biggest problem facing corporate personnel is to decide on capital allocations to the various divisions to maximize the overall profitability of the portfolio. They also have to oversee divisional management and make sure that divisions are achieving return on investment targets.

Vertical Integration

Vertical integration is an expensive strategy to manage because *sequential resource flows* from one division to the next must be coordinated. The multidivisional structure effects such coordination. This structure provides the centralized control necessary for the vertically integrated company to achieve benefits from the control of resource transfers. Corporate personnel assume the responsibility for devising market and bureaucratic controls to promote the efficient transfer of resources among divisions. Complex rules and procedures are instituted to manage interdivisional relationships and specify how exchanges are to be made. In addition, an internal transfer pricing system is created to allow one division to sell its products to the next. As we previously note, these complex links can lead to ill will among divisions, and so corporate personnel must try to minimize divisional conflicts.

Centralizing authority at corporate headquarters must be done with care in vertically related companies. It carries the risk of involving corporate personnel in operating issues at the business level to the point where the divisions lose their autonomy and motivation. As we note in Chapter 10, the company must strike the right balance of centralized control at corporate headquarters and decentralized control at the divisional level if it is to implement this strategy successfully.

Because their interests are at stake, divisions need to have input into scheduling and resource transfer decisions. For example, the plastics division in a chemical company has a vital interest in the activities of the oil division, for the quality of the products it gets from the oil division determines the quality of its own products. Divisional integrating mechanisms can bring about direct coordination and information transfers among divisions.[22] To handle communication among divisions, the company can set up task forces or teams for the purpose. At the very least, it should establish liaison roles; in high-tech and chemical companies, integrating roles among divisions are common. Thus a strategy of vertical integration is managed through a combination of corporate and divisional controls. Although the organizational arrangements for managing this strategy cost more than those for operating unrelated diversification, the benefits derived from vertical integration often outweigh its costs.

Related Diversification

In the case of related diversification, divisions share research and development knowledge, information, customer bases, and goodwill to obtain gains from synergy. The process is difficult to manage, and so a multidivisional structure is used to facilitate the transfer of resources to obtain synergies. Even with this structure, however, high levels of resource sharing and joint production by divisions make it hard for corporate managers to measure the performance of each individual division. Besides, as you read in the Opening Incident in Chapter 11 about TRW, the divisions themselves may not want to exchange products or knowledge because transfer prices—inherently difficult to set—are perceived as unfair. If a related company is to obtain gains from synergy, it has to adopt complicated forms of integration and control at the divisional level to make the structure work efficiently.

First, market control is impossible because resources are shared, so the company needs to develop a corporate culture that stresses cooperation among divisions and to set corporate, rather than divisional, goals. Second, corporate managers must establish sophisticated integrating devices to ensure coordination among divisions. Integrating roles and teams are crucial because they provide the context in which managers from different divisions can meet and develop a common vision of corporate goals. Hewlett-Packard, for example, created three new high-level integrating teams to make certain that the new products developed by its technology group made their way quickly to its product divisions.

An organization with a multidivisional structure must have the right mix of incentives and rewards for cooperation if it is to achieve gains from synergy. With unrelated diversification, divisions operate autonomously, and the company can quite easily reward managers on their division's individual performance. With related diversification, however, rewarding divisions is more difficult because they are engaged in joint production, and strategic managers must be sensitive and alert to achieve equity in rewards among divisions.

In this situation, the strategic business unit (SBU) structure, discussed in earlier chapters, can prove useful. If the company designs its structure around the basic commonalities among divisions, it can evaluate divisional performance more easily. Thus, for example, one SBU could be operated around a customer group, such as chain stores, whereas another SBU could be operated around technological similarities. SBUs make it easier to integrate and control the performance of the company and allow management to sense opportunities and threats as well as develop the company's distinctive competencies. The aim always is to design the structure so that it can maximize the benefits from the strategy at the lowest management cost.

Managing a strategy of related diversification also raises the issue of how much authority to centralize and how much to decentralize. Corporate managers need to take a close look at how their controls affect divisional performance and autonomy. If corporate managers get too involved in the day-to-day operations of the divisions, they can endanger divisional autonomy and undercut divisional managers' decision making. Corporate managers, after all, see everything from a corporate, rather than a divisional, perspective. For example, in the Heinz case previously mentioned, management attempted to develop one form of competitive advantage, low-cost advantage, in every division.[23] Although this approach may work well for Heinz, it may be markedly inappropriate for a company that is operating a totally diverse set of businesses, each of which needs to develop its own unique competence. Too much corporate control can put divisional managers in a straightjacket, and performance suffers.

Global Expansion

In Chapter 8, we note how most large companies have an international, or global, dimension to their strategy because they produce and sell their products in international markets. For example, Procter & Gamble and food companies such as Heinz, Kellogg Co., and Nestlé Enterprises, Inc. have production operations throughout the world, as do the large auto companies and computer makers. In this section, we examine how the need to manage foreign operations affects a company's choice of structure and control and how a company changes its structure as it expands internationally.

In general, the choice of structure and control systems for managing an international business is a function of three factors. The first is the need to choose a level of vertical differentiation that provides effective supervision of foreign operations. Companies operating in international markets must create a hierarchy of authority that clarifies the responsibilities of domestic managers for handling the sale of products abroad and also allocates responsibility for foreign operations between domestic and foreign managers. Second, such companies must choose a level of horizontal differentiation that groups foreign operation tasks with domestic operations in a way that allows the company to market its products abroad and serve the needs of foreign customers in the most effective way. In practice, a company's choice of structure is a function of the complexity and the extent of its foreign operations. Third, the company must choose the right kinds of market, bureaucratic, and clan controls to make the structure function effectively.

When a company sells only domestically made products in foreign markets, problems of coordinating foreign and domestic operations are minimal. Companies like Mercedes-Benz or Jaguar, for example, make no attempt to produce in the foreign market; rather they sell or distribute their domestic products internationally. Such companies usually just add a **foreign operations department** to their existing structure and continue to use the same control system. If a company is using a functional structure, this department has the responsibility for coordinating manufacturing, sales, and research and development activities according to the needs of the foreign market. In the foreign country, the company usually establishes a subsidiary to handle sales and distribution. For example, Mercedes-Benz's foreign subsidiaries have the responsibility for allocating dealerships, organizing supplies of spare parts, and, of course, selling cars. A system of bureaucratic controls is then established to keep the home office informed of changes in sales, spare parts requirements, and so on, in the foreign countries.

A company with many different products or businesses operating from a multidivisional structure has a more serious coordination problem: to coordinate the flow of different products across different countries. To manage these transfers, many companies create an **international division**, which they add to their existing divisional structure.[24] International operations are managed as a separate divisional business whose managers are given the authority and responsibility for coordinating domestic product divisions and foreign markets. The international division also controls the foreign subsidiaries that market the products and decides how much authority to delegate to foreign management. This arrangement permits the company to engage in more complex foreign operations.

The next level of complexity arises when companies establish **foreign subsidiaries** to produce goods and services abroad. In terms of vertical differentiation, the problem for the company is how to allocate responsibility for foreign operations between management in the United States and management in the foreign country. Clearly, the lines of communication and chain of command lengthen in managing foreign production operations making control more difficult. The company has to maintain control of the strategy of the foreign subsidiary while giving the management of the foreign branch the flexibility it needs to deal with its own unique situation. Because strategic managers are much farther away from the scene of operations, it makes sense to decentralize control and grant decision-making authority to managers in the foreign operations while using market and bureaucratic controls to keep abreast of foreign developments. Many companies adopt the policy of creating autonomous foreign operating divisions, which, like home divisions, are evaluated on the basis of their rate of return, growth in market share, or operations costs. Chrysler and General Motors both did just that when they moved into Europe and began developing, producing, and marketing cars to suit Europeans' particular needs. In this situation, developing the right mix of controls that give foreign managers sufficient autonomy but keep home management informed of the current situation is critical.

When synergies can be obtained from cooperation between a company's home divisions and its autonomous foreign subsidiaries, an organization must choose a structure and control system to exploit these synergies. One solution lies in grouping foreign subsidiaries into world regions; the domestic divisions then coordinate with world regions rather than with individual subsidiaries. For example, when a company makes and sells the same products in many different markets, it often groups its foreign subsidiaries into world regions to simplify the coordination of products across countries; Europe might be one region, the Pacific Basin another, and the Middle East a third. This sort of grouping across world markets results in an **international SBU structure** in which subsidiaries inside each SBU are grouped on the basis of geographical region and the same set of market and bureaucratic controls can be applied to all subsidiaries. This allows companies to obtain synergies from dealing with broadly similar cultures because information can be transmitted more easily. For example, consumer preferences regarding product design and marketing are likely to be more similar among countries in one world region than among countries in different world regions.

Sometimes the potential gains from sharing product, marketing, or research and development knowledge between home and foreign operations are so great that companies adopt **an international matrix structure** for organizing their international activities. Such a structure appears in Figure 12.1. The figure represents the structure adopted by a large chemical company such as Du Pont. On the vertical axis, instead of functions, are the company's *product divisions,* which provide product and marketing information to the foreign subsidiaries. For example, these might be the petroleum, plastics, drug, or fertilizer divisions. On the horizontal axis are the company's foreign subsidiaries in the various *countries or world regions* in which it operates. Managers in the foreign subsidiary control foreign operations and through a system of bureaucratic controls report to divisional personnel back in the United States. They are also responsible, together with U.S. divisional personnel, for developing control and reward systems that permit marketing or research and development information to be shared to

FIGURE 12.1   **An international matrix structure**

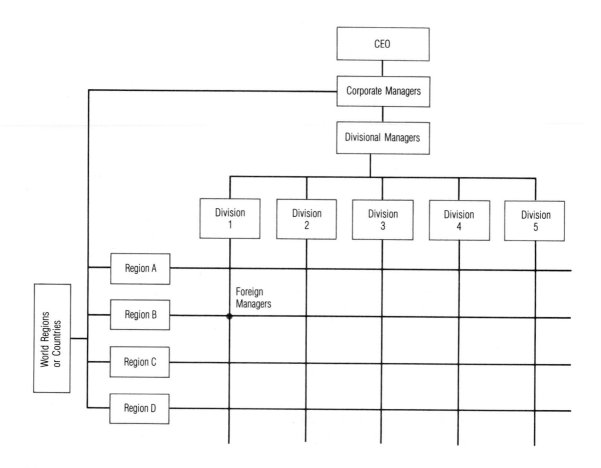

achieve gains from synergies. This structure therefore both provides a great deal of local flexibility and gives divisional personnel in the United States considerable access to information about local affairs. Additionally, the matrix form allows knowledge and experience to be transferred among geographical regions and among divisions and regions. The matrix structure, providing as it does a great deal of opportunity for face-to-face contact between domestic and foreign managers, makes the transmission of company norms and values easier so that it facilitates the development of clan control. This is especially important for an international company in which lines of communication are longer and information is subject to distortion. Club Med Inc. fully exploits these synergies in the way it manages its holiday resorts. The matrix also allows each home division to rationalize (that is, balance) production so that, for example, a lack of demand in one world region can be compensated by increased demand in another. Philip

Morris does this with cigarettes. Slumping demand in the United States is countered by supplying regions where cigarette sales are expanding. Similarly, Japanese car manufacturers plan their international strategy to compensate for import restrictions or currency changes in the world market.

Most large companies have an international component in their organizational structures. The issue with multinational companies, as with all others, is to adopt the structure and control system that best meets the needs of their strategy. The need to implement international strategy successfully has put an increasing burden on corporate managers to design the company's structure and controls to respond to the challenges of the world market.

12.6 CHANGES IN CONTROLS AND STRUCTURE

As we discuss in Chapter 10, the main growth path for U.S. corporations is from vertical integration to related diversification. Given the previous discussion, this means that, to succeed, a company has to alter its structure and control systems as it changes from one strategy to another. It must change the controls that were appropriate when it was pursuing a strategy of vertical integration to those that suit a strategy of related diversification. In practice, this means moving from transfer prices and output controls to bureaucratic and clan control.

But often corporate and divisional managers do not understand that the benefits from related diversification cannot be achieved using the old market controls. Managers do not foresee the new pattern of relationships successfully and do not choose controls matched to the new strategy.[25] As a result, companies fail to realize the benefits from their new strategy. The Greyhound Corporation is an example of a company that is experiencing problems in managing its new acquisition strategy because it seems to be unable to decide if it is pursuing related or unrelated diversification.

Mixing two strategies leads to similar problems. For example, companies pursuing a strategy of related diversification often buy unrelated businesses and pursue both related and unrelated diversification simultaneously. What often happens is that managers tend to apply the same types of controls across all divisions. Thus if they control their unrelated companies using controls appropriate for related ones their new unrelated businesses perform badly. That is the situation at Greyhound. Strategic managers have not put the right controls in place to achieve internal capital market gains.

Switching strategies in midstream thus creates some serious implementation problems. Managers must be sensitive to the need to readjust their controls and form of divisional structure to achieve their objectives. Mixed structural forms such as the strategic business unit (SBU) structure are useful for this purpose because this structure can be designed to allow companies to pursue different strategies together. For example, an SBU structure permits companies to manage the strategies of vertical integration, related diversification, and unrelated diversification simultaneously because divisions can be grouped into business units based on the similarities or differences among their businesses. When companies are grouped according to the types of benefit expected from the strategy, the costs of managing them are reduced and many of the problems just outlined are avoided. In the next sections, we look in more detail at the strategy implementation problems that emerge when companies acquire new businesses, develop new businesses through internal corporate venturing, or both.

12.7 MERGERS, ACQUISITIONS, AND STRUCTURE

In Chapter 9, we note that mergers and acquisitions are principal vehicles by which companies enter new product markets and expand the size of their operations.[26] We discuss earlier the strategic advantages and disadvantages of mergers. We now consider how to design structure and control systems to manage the new acquisitions. This issue is important because, as we note elsewhere, many acquisitions are unsuccessful, and one of the main reasons is that many companies do a very poor job of integrating the new divisions into their corporate structure.[27]

The first factor that makes managing new acquisitions difficult is the nature of the businesses that a company acquires. If a company acquires businesses related to its existing businesses, it should find it fairly easy to integrate these businesses into its corporate structure. The controls already being used in the related company can be adapted to the new divisions. To achieve gains from synergies, the company can expand its task forces or increase the number of integrating roles, so that the new divisions are drawn into the existing divisional structure.

If managers do not understand how to develop connections among divisions to permit gains from synergy, the new businesses will perform poorly. Some authors have recently argued that that is why the quality of management is so important. A company must employ managers who have the ability to recognize synergies among apparently different businesses and so derive benefits from acquisitions and mergers.[28] For instance, Porter cites the example of Philip Morris, the tobacco maker, which took over Miller Brewing Company.[29] On the surface these seem to be very different businesses. When their products are viewed as consumer products that are often bought and consumed together, however, the possibility of sales, distribution, and marketing synergies becomes clearer. Because both businesses require the same kind of managerial skills, even management synergies are feasible. Because it is usually easier to see the potential synergies between very similar businesses, companies should take over only related businesses, where they have the knowledge and expertise to manage the new acquisitions and make them profitable.

If companies acquire businesses for the sake of capital market gains alone, however, strategy implementation is easier. If companies acquire unrelated businesses and seek to operate them only as a portfolio of investments, they should have no trouble managing the acquisitions. Implementation problems are likely to arise only when corporate managers try to interfere in businesses that they know little about or when they use inappropriate structure and controls to manage the new business and attempt to achieve the wrong kind of benefits from the acquisition. For example, if managers try to integrate unrelated companies with related ones, apply the wrong kinds of controls at the divisional level, or interfere in business-level strategy, corporate performance suffers. These mistakes explain why related acquisitions are sometimes more successful than unrelated ones.[30]

Strategic managers therefore need to be very sensitive to the problems involved in taking over new businesses through mergers and acquisitions. Like other managers, they rarely appreciate the real issues inherent in managing the new business until they have to deal with these issues personally. Even in the case of acquiring closely related businesses, new managers must realize that each business has a unique culture or way of doing things. Such idiosyncrasies must be understood to manage the new organization. Over time new management can change the culture and alter the internal workings of the company, but this is a difficult implementation task, as we discuss in the next chapter, when politics and strategic change are considered.

12.8 INTERNAL NEW VENTURES AND STRUCTURE

The main alternative to growth through acquisition and merger is for a company to develop new businesses internally. In Chapter 9, we call this strategy the *new venturing process,* and we discuss its advantages for growth and diversification. Now we consider the design of the appropriate internal arrangements for encouraging the development of new ventures. At the heart of this design process must be the realization by corporate managers that internal new venturing is a form of entrepreneurship. The design should encourage creativity and give new venture managers the opportunity and resources to develop new products or markets. Hewlett-Packard, for example, gives managers a great deal of latitude in this respect. To encourage innovation, it allows them to work on informal projects while they carry out their assigned tasks.[31] More generally, management must choose the appropriate structure and controls for operating new ventures.[32]

One of the main design choices is the creation of **new venture divisions**. To provide new venture managers with the autonomy to experiment and take risks, the company sets up a new venture division separate from other divisions and makes it a center for new product or project development. Away from the day-to-day scrutiny of top management, divisional personnel pursue the creation of new business as though they were external entrepreneurs. The division is operated by controls that reinforce the entrepreneurial spirit. Thus market and output controls are inappropriate because they can inhibit risk taking. Instead, the company uses clan control and develops a culture for entrepreneurship in this division to provide a climate for innovation. Care must be taken, however, to institute bureaucratic controls that put some limits on freedom of action. Otherwise costly mistakes may be made and resources wasted on frivolous ideas.

In managing the new venture division, it is important to use integrating mechanisms such as task forces and teams to screen new ideas. Managers from research and development, sales and marketing, and product development are heavily involved in this screening process. Generally, the champions of new products must defend their projects before a formal evaluation committee, consisting of proven entrepreneurs and experienced managers from the other divisions, to secure the resources for developing them. Companies such as 3M, IBM, and Texas Instruments are examples of successful companies that use this method for creating opportunities internally.

Care must be taken to preserve the autonomy of the new venture division. As mentioned earlier, the costs of research and development are high and the rewards uncertain. After spending millions of dollars, corporate managers often become concerned about the division's performance and introduce tight output controls or strong budgets to increase accountability. These measures hurt the entrepreneurial culture.

Sometimes, however, after creating a new invention, the new venture division wants to reap the benefits by producing and marketing it. If this happens, then the division becomes an ordinary operating division and entrepreneurship declines.[33] Strategic managers must take steps to provide a structure that can sustain the entrepreneurial spirit.[34] Hewlett-Packard has a novel way of dealing with new venturing. In the operating divisions, as soon as a new, self-supporting product is developed, a new division is formed to produce and market the product. By spinning off the product in this fashion, the company keeps all its divisions small and entrepreneurial. The arrangement also provides a good climate for innovation. In the last few years, however, Hewlett-Packard found that having many new venture divisions was too expensive and so has merged some of them. The company appears to be moving toward the creation of a single new venture division.

Internal new venturing is an important means by which large, established companies can maintain their momentum and grow from within.[35] The alternative is to acquire small businesses that have already developed some technological competence and to pump resources into them. This approach can also succeed, and it obviously lessens management's burden if the company operates the new business as an independent entity. In recent years Kodak has taken this path to diversification, buying a share in many small companies. In practice, companies are likely to operate in both ways, acquiring some new businesses and developing others internally. Recently, many companies have made acquisitions when increasing competition from abroad has threatened their dominance in existing businesses and has forced them to evaluate opportunities for maximizing long-term growth in new businesses.

12.9 SUMMARY OF CHAPTER

This chapter brings together strategy formulation and strategy implementation and examines how a company's choice of strategy affects the form of its structure and control systems. The cause of Texas Instrument's problems with its structure should now be clear: Its structure no longer fit the strategy that the company had to pursue to regain its competitive advantage. The following are the main points of the chapter:

1. At the functional level, each function requires a different kind of structure and control system to achieve its functional objectives.

2. At the business level, the structure and control system must be designed to achieve business-level objectives, which involves managing the relationships among all the functions to permit the company to develop a distinctive competence.

3. Cost-leadership and differentiation strategies each require different structures and control systems if the company is to develop a competitive advantage.

4. The form of the company's structure and control systems varies at different stages of the industry life cycle.

5. At the corporate level, the company must choose the structure and control system that will allow it to operate a collection of businesses.

6. Unrelated diversification, vertical integration, and related diversification require different forms of structure and control if the benefits of pursuing the strategy are to be realized.

7. As companies grow and enter foreign markets, international considerations affect their choice of structure and control. Consequently, companies develop foreign divisions to operate in these markets. When there are gains to be derived from synergy, companies often adopt an international matrix form to trade knowledge and expertise.

8. As companies change their corporate strategies over time, they must change their structures because different strategies are managed in different ways.

9. The profitability of mergers and acquisitions depends on the structure and control systems that companies adopt to manage them and the way a company integrates them into its existing businesses.

10. To encourage internal new venturing, companies must design a structure that gives the new venture division the autonomy it needs in order to develop new products and protect it from excessive interference by corporate managers.

Discussion Questions

1. How should (a) a high-tech company, (b) a fast-food franchise, and (c) a small manufacturing company design their functional structures and control systems to implement a generic strategy?

2. How should (a) a differentiated company and (b) a low-cost company alter their structures and control systems over the industry life cycle?

3. If a related company begins to buy unrelated businesses, in what ways should it change its structure or control mechanisms to manage the acquisitions?

4. How would you design a structure and control system to encourage entrepreneurship in a large, established corporation?

Endnotes

1. "Texas Instruments Inc.," *Moody's Industrial Manual, 2* (1986), 6120.

2. "TI: Shot Full of Holes and Trying to Recover," *Business Week,* March 6, 1984, pp. 82–84.

3. "Texas Instruments Cleans Up Its Act," *Business Week,* September 19, 1983, p. 56.

4. W. G. Ouchi, "The Relationship Between Organizational Structure and Organizational Control," *Administrative Science Quarterly,* 22 (1977), 95–113.

5. K. M. Eisenhardt, "Control: Organizational and Economic Approaches," *Management Science,* 16 (1985), 134–148.

6. J. R. Galbraith, *Designing Complex Organizations* (Reading, Mass.: Addison-Wesley, 1973). P. R. Lawrence and J. W. Lorsch, *Organization and Environment* (Cambridge, Mass.: Harvard University Press, 1967). D. Miller, "Strategy Making and Structure: Analysis and Implications for Performance," *Academy of Management Journal,* 30 (1987), 7–32.

7. Michael E. Porter, *Competitive Strategy: Techniques for Analyzing Industries and Competitors* (New York: Free Press, 1980). D. Miller, "Configurations of Strategy and Structure," *Strategic Management Journal,* 7 (1986), 233–249.

8. D. Miller and P. H. Freisen, *Organizations: A Quantum View* (Englewood Cliffs, N.J.: Prentice-Hall, 1984).

9. J. Woodward, *Industrial Organization: Theory and Practice* (London: Oxford University Press, 1965). Lawrence and Lorsch, *Organization and Environment.*

10. R. E. White, "Generic Business Strategies, Organizational Context and Performance: An Empirical Investigation," *Strategic Management Journal,* 7 (1986), 217–231.

11. Porter, *Competitive Strategy.* Miller, "Configurations of Strategy and Structure."

12. E. Deal and A. A. Kennedy, *Corporate Cultures* (Reading, Mass.: Addison-Wesley, 1985). "Corporate Culture," *Business Week,* October 27, 1980, pp. 148–160.

13. Miller, "Configurations of Strategy and Structure." R. E. Miles and C. C. Snow, *Organizational Strategy, Structure, and Process* (New York: McGraw-Hill, 1978).

14. Lawrence and Lorsch, *Organization and Environment.*

15. C. W. Hofer and D. Schendel, *Strategy Formulation: Analytical Concepts* (St. Paul, Minn.: West, 1978).

16. Porter, *Competitive Strategy.*

17. T. Burns and G. M. Stalker, *The Management of Innovation* (London: The Tavistock Institute, 1961). Lawrence and Lorsch, *Organization and Environment.*

18. G. R. Jones, "Transaction Costs, Property Rights, and Organizational Culture: An Exchange Perspective," *Administrative Science Quarterly,* 28 (1983), 454–467.

19. D. A. Whetten, "Sources, Responses, and Effects of Organizational Design," in J. R. Kimberly and R. H. Miles (eds.), *The Organizational Life Cycle* (San Francisco: Jossey Bass, 1980).

20. G. R. Jones and C. W. L. Hill, "Transaction Cost Analysis of Strategy-Structure Choice," *Strategic Management Journal,* 9 (1988), 159–172.

21. Jones and Hill, "Transaction Cost Analysis of Strategy-Structure Choice."

22. Lawrence and Lorsch, *Organization and Environment.* Galbraith, *Designing Complex Organizations.* Porter, *Competitive Advantage: Creating and Sustaining Superior Performance.*

23. Porter, *Competitive Strategy.*

24. J. Stopford and L. Wells, *Managing the Multinational Enterprise* (London: Longman, 1972).

25. C. K. Prahalad and R. A. Bettis, "The Dominant Logic: A New Linkage Between Diversity and Performance," *Strategic Management Journal,* 7 (1986), 485–501.

26. M. S. Salter and W. A. Weinhold, *Diversification Through Acquisition* (New York: Free Press, 1979).

27. F. T. Paine and D. J. Power, "Merger Strategy: An Examination of Drucker's Five Rules for Successful Acquisitions," *Strategic Management Journal,* 5 (1984), 99–110.

28. Prahalad and Bettis, "The Dominant Logic." Porter, *Competitive Strategy.*

29. Ibid.

30. H. Singh and C. A. Montgomery, "Corporate Acquisitions and Economic Performance," unpublished manuscript, 1984.

31. T. J. Peters and R. H. Waterman Jr., *In Search of Excellence* (New York: Harper & Row, 1982).

32. R. A. Burgelman, "Managing the New Venture Division: Research Findings and the Implications for Strategic Management," *Strategic Management Journal,* 6 (1985), 39–54.

33. N. D. Fast, "The Future of Industrial New Venture Departments," *Industrial Marketing Management,* 8 (1979), 264–279.

34. Burgelman, "Managing the New Venture Division."

35. R. A. Burgelman, "Corporate Entrepreneurship and Strategic Management: Insights from a Process Study," *Management Science,* 29 (1983), 1349–1364.

Chapter 13

CONFLICT, POLITICS AND CHANGE IN STRATEGY-STRUCTURE CHOICE

13.1 OPENING INCIDENT: CBS INC.

CBS Inc. is a diversified entertainment and information company engaged in the principal businesses of broadcasting, recorded music, and publishing. One of America's most prestigious organizations, CBS experienced much turmoil in recent years. Its troubles began when outside investors, deciding that the company's profitability and return on assets were under par, led several takeover attempts against it. In successive attacks, Jesse Helms, a senator from North Carolina, Ivan Boesky, an arbitrager, and finally Ted Turner, the founder of Turner Broadcasting System, Inc., announced takeover attempts.[1] CBS realized that it had to take these takeover attempts seriously if it wanted to remain independent.

First, Thomas Wyman, the chairman of CBS at the time, authorized a repurchase of CBS stock for $150 a share (Turner's offer was only $130). This increased CBS's debt from $510 million to $1.4 billion. Next, CBS searched for a white knight who would buy a major portion of CBS stock in the event that a hostile bid seemed likely to succeed. Laurence Tisch of Loew's Companies, Inc. agreed to play this role. By 1986, however, Tisch had purchased 25 percent of CBS stock, making him the largest stockholder, and board members, including Wyman, began to fear that he would take over CBS. Tisch did nothing to stop these rumors.[2]

Tisch began to take a more active role in CBS to question or disagree with Wyman's policies. Wyman himself was now suffering on two fronts. Although he had been brought in by the legendary founder of CBS, William Paley, Paley had become increasingly disturbed that Wyman was not consulting him on CBS policy, particularly because CBS was going through bad times. Tensions increased, and at a board meeting at the end of 1986 Wyman revealed that he had been secretly negotiating with Coca-Cola for the sale of CBS to the soft drink company. Board members were shocked and withdrew their support. Wyman resigned, Paley became acting chairman, and Tisch became acting CEO.

After this power struggle, the pressing issue facing the company became to change CBS's strategy and structure to increase its ratings. The CBS news division posed a problem. It had been CBS's most prestigious operation since the golden days of Edward Murrow and Walter Cronkite, but the recruitment of a new president for the division, Van Gordon Sauter, had led to conflict between management and staff. Sauter believed that to earn the highest ratings, the news should be entertaining, whereas the news staff believed that the news should remain free of entertainment value, as in the past. In the ensuing conflict, Dan Rather, Bill Moyers, and Don Hewitt, executive producer of "60 Minutes," all offered to buy the news division and take it out of CBS. The offer was refused, but Tisch decided to remove Sauter to restore stability to the division.[3]

The next problem was reorganizing CBS's structure and control systems. The trend in the three main networks was to increase efficiency by downsizing and reducing staff and costs. Tisch, as the chief executive officer of CBS, began this change process by laying off staff. He eliminated more than 1,500 employees, about 9 percent of the CBS work force; this number included 150 people from the news division. He also severely cut expense accounts and reduced the slack that CBS personnel had previously enjoyed. Tisch's goal was to change CBS so that it functioned like a company in the maturity stage of the industry life cycle and to attain a 12 percent return on investment goal.[4] This change process caused more conflict and further hurt morale at CBS, however, particularly in the news division.

13.2 OVERVIEW

As the example of CBS suggests, this chapter is about organizational politics, conflict, and the problems that occur when companies attempt to change their strategy and structure. Until now in our study of strategic management, we have treated strategy formulation and implementation from an impersonal, rational perspective, where decisions are made coldly and logically. In reality, this picture of how companies make decisions is incomplete because politics and conflict influence the decision-making process and the selection of organizational objectives. CBS most likely would not have made the tough choices it did if Tisch, an outsider with concern for the bottom line, had not approached the problems facing CBS's broadcasting division with a fresh perspective—one that was not colored by years spent in a CBS culture, where this division's dominance was taken for granted and the bottom line got scant attention.

The power struggle at CBS for control of the corporation indicates the importance of politics at the company. Wyman's failure to share power with Tisch and Paley and their subsequent removal of him is an example of the use of power in organizations to change organizational objectives. The problems in the news division underscore not only the issue of power, but also that of conflict between different interests—between a manager who wanted high ratings by being entertaining and a news staff that wanted ratings based on the quality of the news broadcasts. The time it took to recognize the need for organizational change and the difficulties CBS had in pushing changes through exemplify the problems of implementing strategic change.

In this chapter, we look at each of these issues. We probe the sources of organizational politics and discuss how individuals, departments, and divisions seek to increase their power so that they can influence organizational decision making. Then we examine the nature of organizational conflict and note how managers must deal with conflict to make better strategy-structure choices. Finally, we consider why it is difficult to change organizations, and we outline ways in which managers can direct organizational change so that their company's strategy and structure matches new competitive environments.

13.3 ORGANIZATIONAL POLITICS AND POWER

So far, we have assumed that in formulating the corporate mission and setting policies and goals strategic managers strive to maximize corporate wealth. This picture of strategic decision making is known as the **rational view**. It suggests that managers achieve corporate goals by following a calculated, rational plan, in which only shareholders' interests are considered. In reality, strategic decision making is quite different. Often, strategic managers' decisions further their personal, functional, or divisional interests. In this **political view** of decision making, goals and objectives are set through compromise, bargaining, and negotiation.[5] Top-level managers constantly clash over what the correct policy decisions should be, and, as at CBS, power struggles and coalition building are a major part of strategic management. As in the public sphere, politics is the name given to the process in which different individuals or groups in the organization try to influence the strategic management process to further their own interests.

In this section, we examine the nature of organizational politics and the process of political decision making. **Organizational politics** is defined as the process by which self-interested but interdependent individuals and groups seek to obtain and use power to influence the goals and objectives of the organization to further their own interests.[6] First, we consider the sources of politics and why politics is a necessary part of the strategic management process. Second, we look at how managers or divisions can increase their power so that they can influence the company's strategic direction. Third, we explore the ways in which the organization can manage politics to help it fulfill its strategic mission.

Sources of Organizational Politics

According to the political view of organizational decision making, several factors foster politics in corporate life. Figure 13.1 contrasts these factors with those underlying the rational view of organizational decision making.

The rational view assumes that complete information is available and no uncertainty exists about outcomes, but the political view suggests that strategic managers can never be sure that they are making the best decisions.[7] From a

FIGURE 13.1   **Rational and political views of decision making**

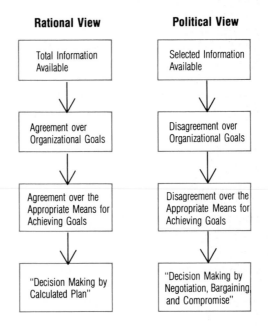

Rational View	Political View
Total Information Available	Selected Information Available
Agreement over Organizational Goals	Disagreement over Organizational Goals
Agreement over the Appropriate Means for Achieving Goals	Disagreement over the Appropriate Means for Achieving Goals
"Decision Making by Calculated Plan"	"Decision Making by Negotiation, Bargaining, and Compromise"

political perspective, decision making always takes place in uncertainty, where the outcomes of actions are difficult to predict. According to the rational view, moreover, managers lack consensus about appropriate organizational *goals* and the appropriate *means,* or strategies, for achieving these goals. According to the political view, on the other hand, the choice of goals and means is linked to each individual's, function's, or division's pursuit of self-interest. Disagreement over the best course of action is inevitable in the political view because the strategic decisions made by the organization necessarily help some individuals or divisions more than others. For example, if managers decide to invest in resources to promote and develop one product, other products will not be created. Some managers win, and others lose.

Given this point of view, strategy choices are never right or wrong; they are simply better or worse. As a result, managers have to promote their ideas and try to lobby support from other managers so that they can build up backing for a course of action. Thus coalition building is vital in strategic decision making.[8] Managers join coalitions to lobby for their interests, because in doing so they increase their political muscle in relation to their organizational opponents.

Managers also engage in politics for personal reasons. Because organizations are shaped like pyramids, individual managers realize that the higher they rise the more difficult it is to climb the next position.[9] If their views prevail and the organization follows their lead, however, *and* if their decisions bear results, they reap rewards and promotions. Thus by being successful at politics, they increase their visibility in the organization and make themselves contenders for high organizational office.

The assumption that personal, rather than shareholder or organizational, interest governs corporate actions is what gives the word *politics* bad connotations in many people's minds. But because no one knows for certain what decision is truly best, letting people pursue their own interest may in the long run mean that the organization's interests are being followed. Competition among managers stemming from self-interest may improve strategic decision making, with successful managers moving to the top of the organization over time. If a company can maintain checks and balances in its top management circles, politics can be a healthy influence, for it can prevent managers from becoming complacent about the status quo and thus avert organizational decline.

If politics grows rampant and if powerful managers gain such dominance that they can suppress the views of managers who oppose their interests, however, major problems may arise. Checks and balances fade, debate is restricted, and performance suffers. For example, at Gulf & Western, as soon as its founder died, the company sold off fifty businesses that the new top management considered pet projects (and therefore his political preferences) and not suited to the company's portfolio. Ultimately, companies that let politics get so out of hand that shareholder interests suffer are taken over by aggressive new management teams, as happened at Diamond Shamrock.

If kept in check, politics can be a useful management tool in making strategic decisions. The best chief executive officers recognize this fact and create a strategic context in which managers can fight for their ideas and reap the rewards from their lobbying efforts. For example, 3M is well known for its top management committee structure, in which divisional managers who request new funds and new venture managers who champion new products must present their projects to the entire top management team and lobby for support for their ideas. All top managers in 3M experienced this learning process, and presumably the ones in the top management team are those who succeeded best at mobilizing support and commitment for their concepts.

To play politics, managers must have power. **Power** can be defined as the ability of one individual, function, or division to cause another individual, function, or division to do something that it would not otherwise have done.[10] Power differs from authority, which stems from holding a formal position in the hierarchy. Power comes from the ability to informally influence the way other parties behave. Perhaps the simplest way to understand power is to look at its sources.

Sources of Power

To a large degree, the relative power of organizational functions and divisions derives from a company's corporate- and business-level strategies. Different strat-

FIGURE 13.2   **Sources of power**

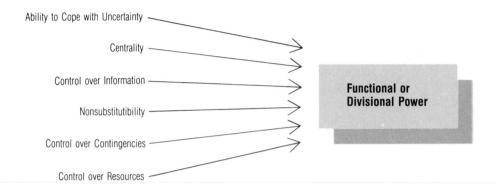

egies make some functions or divisions more important than others in achieving the corporate mission. We consider sources of power at the *functional or divisional level,* rather than at the individual level, because we are primarily interested in the links between politics and power and business- and corporate-level strategy. Figure 13.2 lists the sources of power that we discuss next.

Ability to cope with uncertainty   A function or division gains power if it can reduce uncertainty on behalf of another function or division.[11] Let us suppose that a company is pursuing a strategy of vertical integration. A division that controls the supply and quality of inputs to another division has power over it because it controls the uncertainty facing the second division. At the business level, in a company pursing a low-cost strategy, sales has power over production because sales provide information about customer needs necessary to minimize production costs. In a company pursuing a differentiation strategy, research and development have power over marketing at the early stages in the product life cycle because it controls product innovations. But once innovation problems are solved, marketing is likely to be the most powerful function because it supplies research and development with information on customer needs. Thus a function's power depends on the degree to which other functions rely on it.

Centrality   Power also derives from the **centrality** of a division or function.[12] Centrality refers to the extent to which a division or function is at the center of resource transfers among divisions. For example, in a chemical company, the division supplying specialized chemicals is likely to be central because its activities are critical to both the petroleum division, which supplies its inputs, and the end-using divisions such as plastics or pharmaceuticals, which depend on its outputs. Its activities are central to the production process of all the company's businesses.

Therefore it can exert pressure on corporate headquarters to pursue policies in its own interest.

At the functional level, the function that has the most centrality and therefore power is the one that provides the distinctive competence on which a company's business-level strategy is based. For example, at Apple Computer the function with the greatest centrality is research and development because the company's competitive advantage rests on a technical competence. On the other hand, at Wal-Mart the purchasing and distribution function is the most central because Wal-Mart's competitive advantage depends on its ability to provide a low-cost product.

Control over information   Functions and divisions are also central if they are at the heart of the information flow—that is, if they can control the flow of information to other functions or divisions (or both).[13] Information is a power resource, because by giving or withholding information, one function or division can cause others to behave in certain ways. For example, sales can control the way production operates. If sales manipulates information to satisfy its own goals—for instance, responsiveness to customers—production costs will rise, but production may be unaware that costs could be lowered with a different sales strategy. Similarly, research and development can shape managers' attitudes to the competitive prospects of different kinds of products by supplying favorable information on the attributes of the products it prefers and by downplaying others.

In a very real sense, managers in organizations are playing a subtle information game when they form policies and set objectives. We discuss in Chapter 10 how divisions can disguise their performance by providing only positive information to corporate managers. The more powerful a division, the easier it can do this. In both strategy formulation and implementation, by using information to develop a power base, divisions and functions can strongly influence policy in their own interests.

Nonsubstitutability   A function or division can accrue power proportionately to the degree to which its activities are **nonsubstitutable**—that is, cannot be duplicated.[14] For example, if a company is vertically integrated, supplying divisions are nonsubstitutable to the extent that the company cannot buy what they produce in the marketplace. Thus the petroleum products division is not very powerful if a large supply of oil is available from other suppliers. In an oil crisis, the opposite would be true. On the other hand, the activities of a new venture division—a division in which new products are developed—are nonsubstitutable to the extent that a company cannot buy another company that possesses similar knowledge or expertise. If knowledge or information can be bought, the division is substitutable.

The same holds true at the functional level. A function and the managers inside that function are powerful to the extent that no other function can perform their task. As in the case of centrality, which function is nonsubstitutable depends on the nature of a company's business-level strategy. If the company is pursuing a low-cost strategy, then production is likely to be the key function, and research and development or marketing has less power. But if the company is pursuing a strategy of differentiation then the opposite is likely to be the case.

Thus the power that a function or division gains by virtue of its centrality or nonsubstitutability derives from the company's strategy. Eventually, as a company's strategy changes, the relative power of the functions and divisions also changes. This is the next source of power that we discuss.

Control over contingencies   Over time, the nature of the contingencies—that is, the opportunities and threats—facing a company from the competitive environment will change as the environment changes.[15] The functions or divisions that can deal with the problems confronting the company and allow it to achieve its objectives gain power. Conversely, the functions that can no longer manage the contingency lose power. To give an example, if you look at which functional executives rose to top management positions during the last fifty years, you find that generally the executives who reached the highest posts did so from functions or divisions that were able to deal with the opportunities and threats facing the company.[16]

In the 1950s, for example, the main contingency problem a company confronted was to produce goods and services. Pent-up demand from the years of World War II led to a huge increase in consumer spending for automobiles, homes, and durable goods. Goods needed to be produced quickly and cheaply to meet demand, and during this period the managers who rose to the top were from the *manufacturing* function or consumer products divisions. In the 1960s, the problem changed: Most companies had increased their productive capacity, and the market was saturated. Producing goods was not as difficult as selling them. Hence, *marketing and sales* functions rose to prominence. The rise of executives in companies reflected this critical contingency, for greater numbers of them emerged from the sales function and from marketing-oriented divisions than from any other groups. In the 1970s companies began to realize that competitive conditions were permanent. They had to streamline their strategies and structures to survive in an increasingly hostile environment. As a result, *accounting and finance* became the function that supplied most of the additions to the top management team. Today a company's business- and corporate-level strategy determines which group gains preeminence.

Control over resources   The final source of power that we examine is the ability to control and allocate scarce resources.[17] This source gives corporate-level managers their clout. Obviously, the power of corporate managers depends to a large extent on their ability to allocate capital to the operating divisions and to allot cash to or take it from a division on the basis of their expectations of its future success.

But power from this source is not just a function of the ability to allocate resources immediately; it also comes from the ability to *generate resources in the future*. Thus individual divisions that can generate resources will have power in the corporation. For example, if the Boston Consulting Group matrix is used to categorize divisions, rising stars have power because of the future resources they are expected to generate, whereas cash cows have power because of their ability to generate resources right away. This balance of power between the stars and cash cows explains why corporate management must intervene to allocate resources. Left to themselves, the divisions would never agree on the correct price to charge for capital or on the most efficient way to allocate capital among divisions. Obviously, from a resource perspective, dogs have no power at all, and question marks are in a very weak position, unless they have a strong corporate champion. At the functional level, the same kinds of considerations apply. The ability of sales and marketing to increase customer demand and generate revenues explains their power in the organization. In general, the function that can generate the most resources has the most power.

The most powerful division or function in the organization, then, is the one that can reduce uncertainty for others, is most central and nonsubstitutable, has control over resources and can generate them, and is able to deal with the critical external strategic contingency facing the company. In practice, each division in the corporation has power from one or more of these sources, and so there is a distribution of power among divisions. This condition gives rise to organizational politics, for managers form coalitions to try to get other power holders on their side and thus gain control over the balance of power in the organization.

Effects of Power and Politics on Strategy–Structure Choice

Power and politics strongly influence a company's choice of strategy and structure because the company has to maintain an organizational context that is responsive both to the aspirations of the various divisions, functions, and managers and to changes in the external environment. The problem companies face is that the internal structure of power always lags behind changes in the environment because, in general, the environment changes faster than companies can respond. Those in power never voluntarily give it up, but excessive politicking and power struggles reduce a company's flexibility and may erode its competitive advantage.

For example, if power struggles proceed unchecked, divisions start to compete and to hoard information or knowledge to maximize their own returns. As we note in the Opening Incident to Chapter 11, this condition prevailed at TRW. It also occurred at Digital Equipment Corp. when its product groups became self-contained units that cared more about protecting their interests than about achieving organizational goals. In such situations, exchanging resources among divisions becomes expensive, and gains from synergy are difficult to obtain. These factors in turn lower a company's profitability and reduce organizational growth. Similar problems arise at the functional level: If one function starts to exercise its political muscle, the other functions are likely to retaliate by decreasing their cooperation with the function in question and not responding to its demands. For example, in a company pursuing a low-cost strategy, if the manufacturing function starts to exploit its position and ignores the need of sales to be responsive to customers, over the long run sales can hurt manufacturing by accepting bigger orders but at lower prices or even by seeking many small customer accounts to deliberately elevate production costs and so squeeze profits for the manufacturing function.

Managing Organizational Politics

To manage its politics, a company must devise organizational arrangements that create a **power balance** among the various divisions or functions so that no single one dominates the whole enterprise. In the divisional structure, the corporate headquarters staff plays the balancing role because they can exert power even over strong divisions and force them to share resources for the good of the whole corporation. In a single-business company, a strong chief executive officer is important because he or she must replace the corporate center and balance the power of the strong functions against the weak. The forceful CEO takes the responsibility for giving the weak functions an opportunity to air their concerns and interests and tries to avoid being railroaded into decisions by the strong function pursuing its own interests.

The CEO of a large divisional corporation also has great potential for exerting power. Here the CEO plays another important role, however, that of arbiter of acceptable political decision making. Politics pervade all companies, but the chief executive officer and top-level managers can shape its character. In some organizations, power plays are the norm because chief executive officers themselves garnered power in that way. However, other companies—especially those founded by entrepreneurs who believed in democracy or in decentralized decision making—may not tolerate power struggles, and a different kind of political behavior becomes acceptable. It is based on a function or division manager's competence or expertise rather than on her or his ability to form powerful coalitions. At PepsiCo, politics is of the cutthroat power-play variety, and there is a rapid turnover of managers who fail to meet organizational aspirations. At Coca-Cola, however, ideas and expertise are much more important in politics than power plays directed at maximizing functional or divisional self-interest. Similarly, Intel Corporation does not tolerate politicking or lobbying for personal gain; instead, it rewards risk taking and makes promotion contingent on performance, not seniority.

To design an organizational structure that creates a power balance, strategic managers can use the tools of implementation that we discuss in Chapters 10 and 11. First, they must create the right mix of integrating mechanisms to allow functions or divisions to share information and ideas. A multidivisional structure offers one means of balancing power among divisions, and the matrix structure among functions. A company can then develop norms, values, and a common culture that emphasize corporate, rather than divisional, interests and that stress the company's mission. In companies such as IBM or 3M, for instance, culture serves to harmonize divisional interests with the achievement of corporate goals. Finally, as we note earlier, strong hierarchical control by a gifted chief executive officer can also create the organizational context in which politics can be put to good use and its destructive consequences avoided. When chief executive officers use their expert knowledge as their power, they provide the strong leadership that allows a company to achieve its corporate mission. Indeed, it should be part of the strategic manager's job to learn how to manage politics and power to further corporate interests because politics is an essential part of efficiently allocating scarce organizational resources.

13.4 ORGANIZATIONAL CONFLICT

Politics implies an attempt by one party to influence the goals and decision making of the organization to further its own interests. Sometimes, however, the attempt of one group to further its interests thwarts another group's ability to attain its goals. The result is conflict within the organization. **Conflict** can be defined as a situation that arises when the goal-directed behavior of one organizational group blocks the goal-directed behavior of another.[18] In the discussion that follows, we examine (1) the effect of conflict on organizational performance, (2) the sources of conflict, (3) the ways in which the conflict process operates in the organization, and (4) the ways in which strategic managers can regulate the conflict process using effective conflict resolution practices so that—just as in the case of politics—it yields benefits rather than costs.

Conflict: Good or Bad?

The effect of conflict on organizational performance is continually debated. In the past, conflict was viewed as always bad, or dysfunctional, because it leads to lower organizational performance.[19] According to that view, conflict occurs because managers have not implemented strategy correctly and have not designed the appropriate structure that would make functions or divisions cooperate to achieve corporate objectives. Without doubt, bad implementation can cause conflict and good design can prevent it. If carefully managed, however, conflict can increase organizational performance.[20] The graph in Figure 13.3 indicates the effect of organizational conflict on performance.

The graph shows that to a point conflict increases organizational performance. The reason is that conflict leads to needed organizational change because it exposes weaknesses in organizational design. Managers can respond by changing structure and control systems, thus realigning the power structure of the organ-

FIGURE 13.3   **Effect of conflict on performance**

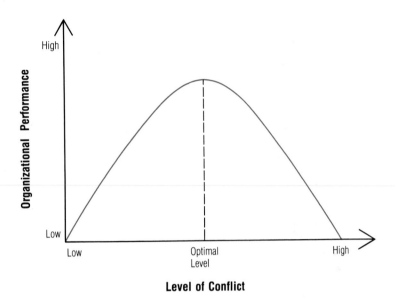

ization and shifting the balance of power in favor of the group that can best meet the organization's needs. Conflict signals the need for change. After the optimum point, however, a rise in conflict leads to a decline in performance, for conflict gets out of control and the organization fragments into competing interest groups. Astute managers prevent conflict from passing the optimum point and therefore can use it to increase organizational performance. Managing conflict, then, like managing politics, is a means of improving organizational decision making and of allocating resources and responsibilities. Politics, however, does not necessarily cause conflict, and effective management of the political process is a way of avoiding destructive clashes among groups. Conflict in organizations has many sources, and strategic managers need to be aware of them, so that when conflict does occur it can be quickly controlled or resolved.

Sources of Conflict

As we note elsewhere, conflict arises when the goals of one organizational group thwart those of another. Many factors inherent in the way organizations operate can produce conflict among functions, divisions, and individuals.[21] We focus on three main sources of organizational conflict, and they are summarized in Figure 13.4 on the following page.

FIGURE 13.4   **Sources of organizational conflict**

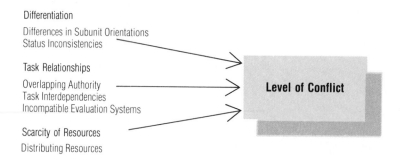

Differentiation

Differences in Subunit Orientations
Status Inconsistencies

Task Relationships

Overlapping Authority
Task Interdependencies
Incompatible Evaluation Systems

Scarcity of Resources

Distributing Resources

Level of Conflict

Differentiation   In Chapter 10, we define differentiation as the way in which a company divides authority and task responsibilities. The process of splitting the organization into hierarchical levels and functions or divisions may produce conflict because it brings to the surface the differences in the goals and interests of groups inside the organization. This kind of conflict has two main causes.

Differences in subunit orientations   As differentiation leads to the emergence of different functions or subunits in a company, each group develops a unique orientation toward the organization's major priorities, as well as its own view of what needs to be done to increase organizational performance. Goals of the various functions naturally differ. For example, production generally has a short-term, cost-directed efficiency orientation. Research and development is oriented toward long-term, technical goals, and sales is oriented toward satisfying customer needs. Thus production may see the solution to a problem as one of reducing costs, sales as one of increasing demand, and research and development as product innovation. Differences in subunit orientation make strategy hard to formulate and implement because they slow a company's response to changes in the competitive environment and reduce its level of integration.

Differences in orientation are also a major problem at the divisional level. For example, cash cow divisions emphasize marketing goals, whereas stars promote technological possibilities. Consequently, it is extremely difficult for divisions such as these to find a common way of viewing the problem. In large corporations, such disagreements can do considerable harm because they reduce the level of cohesion and integration among divisions, hamper cooperation and synergy, and thus lower corporate performance. Many large companies, such as DEC International, Inc., Westinghouse, and Procter & Gamble, have had to cope with this handicap; they responded by reorganizing their structure and improving integration.

Status inconsistencies   In a differentiated company, over time some functions or divisions come to see themselves as more vital to its operations than others.

As a result, they make little attempt to adapt their behaviors to the needs of other functions, thus blocking the goals of the latter. For example, at the functional level, production usually sees itself as the linchpin in the organization and the other functions as mere support services. This leads to line and staff conflict, where production, or line, personnel thwart the goals of staff, or support, personnel.[22] The kind of business-level strategy that a company adopts may intensify line and staff conflict because it increases the status of some functions relative to others. In low-cost companies, production is particularly important, and in differentiators, marketing or research and development is most important.

At the divisional level, the divisions that are more central to the company's operations—for example, those that supply resources to the end-using divisions—may come to see themselves as the system's linchpins. They also may pay little attention to the needs of the end users (for example, developing new products). The end users may retaliate by buying in the marketplace or, more typically, by fighting over transfer prices, which, as we discuss earlier, is a major sign of conflict among divisions. Thus the relationships among divisions must be handled carefully by corporate headquarters to prevent conflicts from flaring up and damaging interdivisional relationships.

Task relationships   As we discuss in Chapter 10, several features of task relationships may generate conflict among functions and divisions.[23]

Overlapping authority   If two different functions or divisions claim authority and responsibility for the same task, then conflict may develop in the organization. This often happens when the organization is growing, and thus functional or divisional relationships are not yet fully worked out. Likewise, when changes occur in task relationships, for instance, as when divisions start to share sales and distribution facilities to reduce costs, disputes over who controls what emerge. As a result, divisions may fight for control of the resource and thus spawn conflict.

Task interdependencies   To develop or produce goods and services, the work of one function flows horizontally to the next so that each function can build on the contributions of the others.[24] If one function does not do its job well, then the function next in line is seriously hampered in its work, and this too, generates conflict. For example, the ability of manufacturing to reduce costs on the production line depends on how well research and development has designed the product for cheap manufacture and how well sales has attracted large, stable customer accounts. At the divisional level, when divisions are trading resources, the quality of the products supplied by one division to the next affects the quality of the next division's products.

The potential for conflict is great when functions or divisions are markedly interdependent. In fact, the higher the level of interdependence, the higher is the potential for conflict among functions or divisions.[25] Interdependence among functions, along with the consequent need to prevent conflict from arising, is the reason that managing a matrix structure is so expensive. Similarly, managing a strategy of related diversification is expensive because conflicts over resource transfers arise and have to be continually dealt with. Conversely, with unrelated diversification, the potential for interdivisional conflict is minimal because divisions do not trade resources.

The merger between Burroughs Corporation and Sperry Corporation to create Unisys Corporation created the types of problems that must be managed to prevent conflict from task interdependence. The CEO of Burroughs, W. M. Blumenthal, has taken enormous pains to manage new task interdependences to avoid major conflicts among divisions and has used a variety of integrating mechanisms to bring the two companies together. The problem is so severe because each company has the same set of functions, which, in the long run, must be merged.

Incompatible evaluation systems   We mention in Chapter 11 that a company has to design its evaluation and reward systems so that they do not interfere with task relationships among functions and divisions. Inequitable performance evaluation systems stir up conflict.[26] Typical problems include finding a way of jointly rewarding sales and production to avoid scheduling conflicts and setting budgets and transfer prices so that they do not lead to competition among divisions. Again, the more complex the task relationships, the harder it is to evaluate each function's or division's contribution to revenue, and the more likely is conflict to arise.

Scarcity of resources   Competition over scarce resources also produces conflict.[27] This kind of conflict most often occurs among divisions and between divisions and corporate management over the allocation of capital, although budget fights among functions can also be fierce when resources are scarce. As we discuss in other chapters, divisions resist attempts to transfer their profits to other divisions and may distort information to retain their resources. Other organizational stakeholders also have an interest in the way a company allocates scarce resources. For example, shareholders care about the size of the dividends, and unions and employees want to maximize their salaries and benefits.

Given so many potential sources of conflict in organizations, conflict of one kind or another is always present in strategic decision making. We need to consider how a typical conflict process works itself out in the organization and whether there are any guidelines that corporate managers can use to try to direct conflict and turn its destructive potential to good strategic use. A model developed by Lou R. Pondy, a famous management theorist, helps show how the conflict process operates in organizations.[28] We discuss this in the next section.

The Organizational Conflict Process

Conflict is so hard to manage strategically because it is usually unexpected. The sources of conflict that we have just discussed are often inherent in a company's

FIGURE 13.5   **Stages in the conflict process**

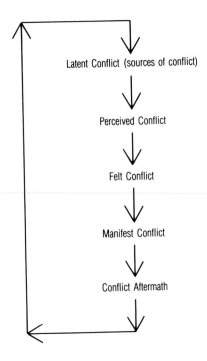

mode of operation. The first stage in the conflict process, then, is *latent conflict—* potential conflict that can flare up when the right conditions arise. (The stages in the conflict process appear in Figure 13.5.) Latent conflicts are frequently activated by changes in an organization's strategy or structure that affect the relationship among functions or divisions. For example, if a company has been pursuing a dominant product strategy using a functional structure to implement the strategy, it might decide to widen its product range. To overcome problems of co-ordinating a range of specialist services over many products, the company may adopt a product structure. The new structure changes task relationships among product managers, and this in turn changes the relative status and areas of authority of the different functional and product managers. Conflict between functional and product managers or among product managers is likely to ensue.

Because every change in a company's strategy and structure alters the organizational context, conflict can easily arise unless the situation is carefully managed to avoid it. But avoidance is not always possible, and consequently the latent stage of the conflict process quickly leads to the next stage: *perceived conflict.*

Perceived conflict means that managers become aware of the clashes. After a change in strategy and structure, managers discover that the actions of another function or group are obstructing the operations of their group. Managers start to react to the situation, and from the perceived stage, they go quickly to the *felt conflict* stage. Here managers start to personalize the conflict. Opinions polarize, as one function or division starts to blame the others for causing the conflict. Production might blame the inefficiency of sales for a fall in orders, while sales might blame production for a fall in product quality. Typically, there is a marked lack of cooperation at this stage, and integration among functions or divisions breaks down as the groups start to polarize and develop an "us versus them" mentality. If not managed, this stage in the conflict process leads quickly to the next stage, *manifest conflict*.

At this point, the conflict among functions or divisions comes into the open, and each group strives to thwart the goals of the other. Groups compete to protect their own interests and block the interests of other groups. Manifest conflict can take many forms. The most obvious is open aggression among top managers as they start to blame other functions or divisions for causing the problem. Other forms of manifest conflict are transfer pricing battles and knowledge hoarding. Defamatory information about other divisions is also likely to be circulated at this stage in the conflict process. These actions are much worse than political maneuvering because divisions are trying not simply to promote their interests but also to damage the performance of the other divisions. As a result, the company cannot achieve any gains from scheduling resource transfers or from developing synergy between divisions.

At the functional level, the effects of conflict can be equally devastating. A company cannot pursue a low-cost strategy if the functions are competing. If sales makes no attempt to keep manufacturing informed about customer demands, manufacturing cannot maximize the length of production runs. Similarly, a company cannot successfully differentiate if marketing does not inform research and development about changes in consumer preferences or if product engineering and research and development are competing over product specifications. Companies have experienced each of these conflicts at one time or another and suffered a loss in performance and competitive advantage because of them.

The long-term effects of manifest conflict emerge in the last stage of the conflict process, the *conflict aftermath*. Suppose that in one company a change in strategy leads to conflict over transfer prices. Then divisional managers, with the help of corporate personnel, resolve the problem to everyone's satisfaction and re-establish good working relationships. In another company, however, the conflict between divisions over transfer prices is resolved only by the intervention of corporate managers, who *impose* a solution on divisional managers. A year later, a change in the environment occurs that makes the transfer pricing system in both companies no longer equitable, and prices must be renegotiated. How will the two companies react to this situation? The managers in the company in which the conflict was settled amicably will approach this new round of negotiations with a cooperative, and not an adversarial, attitude. In the company in which divisions never really established an agreement, however, a new round of intense clashes is likely, with a resulting fall in organizational performance.

The conflict aftermath in each company was different because in one company conflict was resolved successfully but in the other it was not. The conflict aftermath sets the scene for the next round of conflict that will certainly occur because conflict is inherent in the ways companies operate and the environment is constantly changing. The reason that some companies have a long history of bad relations among functions or divisions is that their conflict has never been managed successfully. In companies in which strategic managers have resolved the conflict, a cohesive organizational culture obtains. In those companies, managers adopt a cooperative, not a competitive, attitude when conflict occurs. The question we need to tackle, however, is how best to manage the conflict process strategically to avoid its bad effects and make transitions in strategy-structure choice as smooth as possible.

Managing Conflict Strategically

Given the way the conflict process operates, the goal of strategic managers should be to intervene as early as possible so that conflict does not reach the felt, and particularly the manifest, stage. At the manifest stage, conflict is difficult to resolve successfully and is much more likely to lead to a bad conflict aftermath. At what point, then, should managers intervene?

Ideally, managers should intervene at the latent stage and act on the sources of conflict.[29] Good strategic planning early can prevent many of the problems that occur later. For example, when managers are changing a company's strategy, they should be consciously thinking about the effects of these changes on future group relationships. Similarly, when changing organizational structure, strategic managers should anticipate the effects the changes will have on functional and divisional relationships. Many large organizations do act in this way and require that the potential effect of strategy-structure changes on the organization be included in the strategic planning process to prevent conflict from arising later on.

Nevertheless, often it is impossible to foresee the ramifications of changes in strategy. Organizations are complex, and many unexpected things can happen as managers implement organizational change. Consequently, managers cannot always intervene at the latent stage to prevent conflict from arising. Thus changes in strategy or structure may lead to failure, as when Apple Computer went to a divisional structure or when Kodak's instant camera proved a financial disaster.

Frequently, intervention is only possible between the felt and the manifest stage. It is here that managers may have the best chance to find a solution to the problem. Managers can adopt a number of different solutions, or conflict resolution strategies, and we consider them next.

Conflict Resolution Strategies

Using authority   As we discuss in Chapter 11, integration among functions and divisions is a major problem because they have equal authority and thus cannot control each other. When functions cannot solve their problems, these problems are often passed on to corporate managers or to the chief executive officer, who has the authority to impose a solution on parties. In general, there are two ways of using authority to manage conflict. First, the chief executive officer or corporate managers can play the role of arbiters and impose a solution on the parties in conflict. Second, they can act as mediators and try to open up the situation so that the parties in conflict can find their own solution. Research shows that the latter approach works better because it leads to a good conflict aftermath.

Change task relationships In this approach, the aim is to change the interdependence among functions or divisions so that the source of the conflict is removed. Task relationships can be altered in two ways: First, strategic managers can *reduce* the degree of dependence among the parties. For example, they can develop a structure in which integration among groups is easier to accomplish. Thus a shift from a functional to a divisional structure can reduce the potential for conflict. Similarly, establishing a strategic business unit structure can lessen the chances of conflict among divisions.

Alternatively, conflict may arise because the correct integrating mechanisms for managing task interdependence have not been adopted. In this case, managing the conflict means *increasing* integration among divisions and functions. Thus in high-tech companies, in which functions are very highly task interdependent, managers can use a matrix structure to provide the integration necessary to resolve conflict. In a divisional structure, managers can use integrating roles and establish integrating departments to allow divisions to price and transfer resources. At Hewlett-Packard, corporate staff created three integrating committees to allow divisions to share resources and minimize conflict over product development. Increased integration prevents conflicts from emerging. Managers also use structure through the process of strategy implementation to solve conflicts.

Changing controls Conflict can also be managed by altering the organization's control and evaluation systems. For example, in some organizations it may be possible to develop joint goals among functions and divisions and to create a reward system based on the achievement of these joint goals, as when sales and production are jointly rewarded on the basis of how much revenue they generate. Similarly, corporate evaluation systems can be created to measure the degree to which divisions cooperate with one another. We discuss in an earlier chapter how TRW attempted to develop such evaluation systems so that divisions could share information and knowledge while being appropriately rewarded for it. Finally, to some degree, conflict is the result of managers in one function not appreciating the position of those in another. To give managers a broader perspective and to overcome differences in subunit orientations, managers can be rotated among divisions and given assignments at the corporate level to show them the problems faced by managers elsewhere in the company.

Summary: Organizational Conflict

Conflict is an ever present organizational phenomenon that must be managed if the firm is to achieve its objectives. The whole process of strategy-structure choice creates the potential for conflict, and in a rapidly changing environment conflict is increasingly likely. It is a part of the strategic manager's job to develop the personal skills and abilities needed to solve conflict problems. These skills involve the ability to analyze the organizational context to pinpoint the source of the problem and handling managers who are in conflict. It is possible now to consider the process of managing organizational change.

13.5 MANAGING CHANGES IN STRATEGY-STRUCTURE CHOICE: STEPS IN THE CHANGE PROCESS

In the modern corporation, change rather than stability is the order of the day. Rapid changes in technology, the competitive environment, and customer demands have increased the rate at which companies have to alter their strategies to survive in the marketplace.[30] Consequently, companies have to go through rapid structural reorganizations as they outgrow their structures. E. F. Hutton, for example, estimates that more than half of the top 800 major corporations have undergone major restructuring in recent years.[31] In this section, we discuss the problems associated with managing such changes in strategy and structure.

The management of strategic change involves a series of distinct steps that managers must follow if the change process is to succeed. These steps are listed in Figure 13.6.

FIGURE 13.6   Stages in the change process

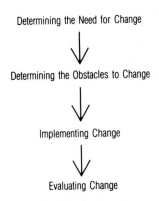

Determining the Need for Change

Determining the Obstacles to Change

Implementing Change

Evaluating Change

Determining the Need for Change

The first step in the change process involves strategic managers' determining the need for change. Sometimes this change is obvious, as when divisions are fighting or competitors introduce a product that is clearly superior to anything that the company has in production. More often, however, managers have trouble determining that something is going wrong in the organization. Problems may develop gradually, and organizational performance may be slipping for a number of years before it becomes obvious. At CBS, for example, profitability fell, but because it was a reputable stock, the fall caused little stir. After a lapse of time, however, investors realized that the stock had been undervalued and that CBS could be made to perform better. In other words, outside investors realized sooner than inside management did that there was a need for change.

Thus the first step in the change process occurs when the company's strategic managers or others in a position to take action recognize that there is a gap between desired company performance and actual performance.[32] Using measures such as falls in stock price or market share as indicators that change is needed, managers can start looking for the source of the problem. To discover it, they conduct a SWOT analysis. First, they examine the company's strengths and weaknesses. For example, management conducts a strategic audit of the functions and divisions and looks at their contribution to profitability over time. Perhaps some divisions have become dogs without management's realizing it or the company has too many rising stars. Management also analyzes the company's level of differentiation and integration to make sure that it is appropriate for its strategy. Perhaps a company does not have the integrating mechanisms in place to achieve gains from synergy. Management then examines environmental opportunities and threats that might explain the problem. For instance, the company may have had intense competition from substitute products without being aware of it, or a shift in consumer tastes or technology may have caught it unawares.

Once the source of the problem has been identified, management must determine the ideal future state of the company—that is, how it should change its strategy and structure. A company may decide, like CBS, to lower its costs by streamlining its operation. Or, like General Motors, it may increase its research and development budget or diversify into new products to increase its future profitability. Essentially, strategic managers apply the conceptual tools that this book has described to work out the best choice of strategy and structure to maximize profitability. The choice they make is specific to each individual company, and, as noted earlier, there is no way that managers can determine its correctness in advance. This is the adventure of strategic management.

Thus the first step in the change process involves determining the need for change, analyzing the organization's current position, and determining the ideal future state that strategic managers would like it to attain. This process is diagrammed in Figure 13.7.

FIGURE 13.7   A model of change

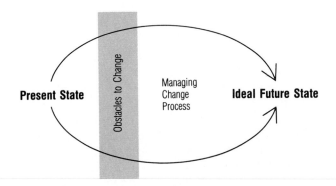

Determining the Obstacles to Change

The second step in the change process involves determining the obstacles to change.[33] Strategic managers must analyze the factors that may prevent the company from reaching its ideal future state. Obstacles to change are found at four levels in the organization: corporate, divisional, functional, and individual levels.

At the corporate level, there are several potential obstacles to consider. First, changing strategy or structure even in seemingly trivial ways may significantly affect a company's behavior. For example, suppose that to reduce costs the company decides to centralize all divisional purchasing and sales activities at the corporate level. Such consolidation could severely damage each division's ability to develop a unique strategy for its own individual markets. Or suppose that in response to low-cost foreign competition the company decides to pursue a policy of differentiation. This action would change the balance of power among functions and lead to politicking and even conflict as functions start fighting to retain their status in the organization. A *company's present structure and strategy* are powerful obstacles to change. They produce a massive amount of inertia that has to be overcome before change can take place. This is why change is usually such a slow process.

The *type of structure* a company uses can also impede change. For example, it is much easier to change strategy if a company is using a matrix, rather than a functional, structure, or if it is decentralized rather than centralized, or if it has a high, rather than a low, level of integration. Decentralized, matrix structures are more flexible than highly controlled functional structures. It is easier to change subunit orientations, and thus there is a lower potential for conflict.

Some *corporate cultures* are easier to change than others. For example, change is notoriously difficult in the military because everything is sacred to obedience and the following of orders. Some cultures, however, such as Hewlett-Packard's, are based on values that emphasize flexibility or change itself. Consequently, they are much easier to change when change becomes necessary.

Similar factors operate at the divisional level. Change is difficult at the divisional level if divisions are *highly interrelated and trade resources,* because a shift in one division's operations will affect other divisions. Consequently, it is more difficult to manage change if a company is pursuing a strategy of related, rather than unrelated, diversification. Furthermore, changes in strategy affect divisions in different ways because change generally favors the interests of some divisions over those of others. Divisions may thus have different attitudes to change, and some will not support the changes in strategy that the company makes. Existing divisions may resist establishing new product divisions because they will lose resources and their status inside the organization may fall.

The same obstacles to change exist at the functional level as well. Like divisions, different functions have different strategic orientations and react differently to the changes management proposes. For example, in a decline situation, sales will resist attempts to cut back on sales expenditures to reduce costs if it believes the problem stems from inefficiency in manufacturing. At the individual level, too, people are notoriously resistant to change because change implies uncertainty, which breeds insecurity and the fear of the unknown.[34] Because managers are people, this individual resistance reinforces the tendency of each function and division to oppose changes that may have uncertain effects on them.

All these obstacles make it difficult to change organizational strategy or structure quickly. That is why American car manufacturers took so long to respond to the Japanese challenge. They were accustomed to a situation of complete dominance and had developed inflexible, centralized structures that inhibited risk taking and quick reaction. Paradoxically, companies that experience the greatest uncertainty may become best able to respond to it. When they have been forced to change often, they develop the ability to handle change easily.[35] Strategic managers must understand all these potential obstacles to change as they design a company's new strategy and structure. All these factors are potential sources of conflict and politics that can dramatically affect a company's ability to move quickly to exploit new strategic opportunities. Obstacles to change must be recognized and incorporated into the strategic plan. The larger and more complex the organization, the harder it is to implement change.

Implementing Change

Implementing—that is, introducing and managing—change raises several questions. For instance, who should actually carry out the change: internal managers or external consultants? Although internal managers may have the most experience or knowledge about a company's operations, they may lack perspective because they are too much a part of the organization's culture. They also run the risk of appearing to be politically motivated and of having a personal stake in the changes they recommend. Companies therefore often turn to external consultants who can view the situation more objectively. Outside consultants, however, must spend a lot of time learning about the company and its problems before they can propose a plan of action. Thus the issue of who should manage the change is complex, and most companies create a task force consisting of both internal managers and external consultants. In this way, companies can get the benefits of inside information and the external perspective.

Generally, a company can take two main approaches to change: top-down change or bottom-up change.[36] With **top-down change**, the change task force analyzes how to alter strategy and structure, recommends a course of action, and then moves quickly to implement change in the organization. The emphasis is on speed of response and management of problems as they occur. **Bottom-up change** is much more gradual. The change task force consults with managers at all levels in the organization. Then, over time, it develops a detailed plan for change, with a timetable of events and stages that the company will go through. The emphasis in bottom-up change is on participation and keeping people informed about the situation, so that uncertainty is minimized.

The advantage of bottom-up change is that it removes some of the obstacles to change by incorporating them into the strategic plan. In addition, the aim of consulting with managers at all levels is to reveal potential problems. The disadvantage of bottom-up change is its slowness. On the other hand, in the case of the much speedier top-down change, the problems may emerge later and may be difficult to resolve. In general, the type of change that companies adopt depends on the nature of their situation. Flexible companies that are used to change risk fewer problems with top-down change. For corporate lumbering giants, bottom-up change may be the only way of getting anything done because managers are so unaccustomed to and threatened by change.

Evaluating Change

The last step in the change process is to evaluate the effects of the changes in strategy and structure on organizational performance. A company must compare the way it operates after implementing change with the way it operated before. Managers use indices such as changes in stock market price or market share to assess the effects of change in strategy. It is much more difficult, however, to assess the effects of changes in structure on company performance because they are so much more difficult to measure. Whereas companies can easily measure the increased revenue from increased product differentiation, they do not have any sure means of evaluating the effects that moving from a product to a divisional structure has had on performance. Managers can be surveyed, however, and over time it may become obvious that organizational flexibility and the company's ability to manage its strategy have increased. Managers can also assess whether the change has decreased the level of politicking and conflict and strengthened cooperation among the divisions and functions.

Organizational change is a complex and difficult process for companies to manage successfully. The problem starts from the beginning in getting managers to realize that change is necessary and to admit that there is a problem. Once the need for change is recognized managers can go about the process of recommending a course of action and analyze potential obstacles to change. Depending on the organization and the nature of the problem the company is dealing with, either bottom-up or top-down change is appropriate. However, in both cases it is best to use a mix of internal managers and external consultants to implement the change. After implementing change, managers assess its effects on organizational performance and then the whole process is repeated as companies strive to increase their level of performance. This is why companies in which change is a regular occurrence find it much easier to manage than do companies in which complacent managers only start a change effort when the company is already in trouble.

13.6 SUMMARY OF CHAPTER

This chapter has examined the political side of strategy formulation and implementation and discussed the problems that can arise in managing changes in strategy and structure. It should now be apparent that organizations are not just rational decision-making systems in which managers coldly calculate the potential returns from their investments. Organizations are arenas of power, in which individuals and groups fight for prestige and possession of scarce resources. In the pursuit of their interests, managers compete and engage in conflict. The very nature of the organization makes this inevitable. Managers have to deal with politics and conflict creatively to achieve organizational benefits from them. They also have to manage the process of organizational change so that the company can maximize its ability to exploit the environment. The most successful companies are those in which change is regarded as the norm and managers are constantly seeking to improve organizational strengths and eliminate weaknesses so that they can maximize future profitability. This chapter makes the following main points:

1. Organizational decision making is a combination of both rational and political processes. Formation of coalitions, compromise, and bargaining are integral parts of the strategic management process.

2. Organizational politics occurs because different groups have different interests and different perceptions of the appropriate means to further their interests.

3. To play politics, managers must have power. Power is the ability of one party to cause another party to act in the first party's interest.

4. The sources of power available to strategic managers include coping with uncertainty, centrality, control over information, nonsubstitutability, and control over contingencies and resources.

5. Politics must be managed if the company is to obtain benefits from the process, and one of the best ways of doing so is to create a power balance in the organization. A strong chief executive officer or a well-designed structure can create a power balance.

6. Organizational conflict exists when divisions, functions, or individuals go beyond competition and strive to thwart each other's goals. Conflict can be defined as a situation that occurs when the goal-directed behavior of one group blocks the goal-directed behavior of another.

7. Whether conflict is good or bad for the organization depends on the way it is managed. In general, conflict is useful in exposing organizational weaknesses, but it must be managed quickly, before it gets out of hand.

8. Conflict is inherent in the nature of an organization's design. The sources of conflict include differentiation, task relationships, and scarcity of resources.

9. Conflict can be regarded as a process with a series of stages. These stages are latent conflict, perceived conflict, felt conflict, manifest conflict, and conflict aftermath.

10. Organizational change is the process by which companies alter their strategy and structure to improve performance.

11. Organizational change is managed through a series of stages. First, the need for change must be recognized, and the company must decide on its ideal future state. Then the obstacles to change must be analyzed and incorporated into the change plan, and change must be implemented. Finally, the change process must be evaluated to assess its effects on organizational performance.

12. Well-run organizations are constantly aware of the need to monitor their performance, and they institutionalize change so that they can realign their structures to suit the competitive environment.

Discussion Questions

1. How can managing (a) politics and (b) conflict in organizations lead to improved organizational decision making? How might a company create a system of checks and balances in the organization through the design of its structure and control systems?

2. How might conflict and politics affect the formulation and implementation of (a) generic competitive strategies and (b) corporate-level strategies?

3. What are some of the political problems a company might encounter if it takes over a related business and tries to integrate it into its organizational structure? (Hint: Use the sources of power to frame your answer.)

4. Discuss how you would set up a plan for change for an unrelated company that is starting to pursue a strategy of related diversification. What problems will the company encounter? How should it deal with them?

Endnotes

1. "Corporate Shoot-Out at Black Rock," *Time,* September 22, 1986, pp. 68–72.

2. "Civil War at CBS," *Newsweek,* September 15, 1986, pp. 46–54.

3. P. W. Barnes, "Tisch Wins Praise for Fast Action at CBS," *The Wall Street Journal,* October 28, 1986, p. 5.

4. P. J. Boyers, "Three New Bosses are Slashing Operations and Putting Nearly Everyone's Job on the Line," *The New York Times,* November 2, 1986, p. 26.

5. A. M. Pettigrew, *The Politics of Organizational Decision Making* (London: Tavistock, 1973).

6. R. H. Miles, *Macro Organizational Behavior* (Santa Monica, Calif.: Goodyear, 1980).

7. J. G. March and H. A. Simon, *Organizations* (New York: Wiley, 1958).

8. J. G. March, "The Business Firm as a Coalition," *The Journal of Politics,* 24 (1962), 662–678. D. J. Vredenburgh and J. G. Maurer, "A Process Framework of Organizational Politics," *Human Relations,* 37 (1984), 47–66.

9. T. Burns, "Micropolitics: Mechanism of Institutional Change," *Administrative Science Quarterly,* 6 (1961), 257–281.

10. R. A. Dahl, "The Concept of Power," *Behavioral Science,* 2 (1957), 201–215. G. A. Astley and P. S. Sachdeva, "Structural Sources of Intraorganizational Power," *Academy of Management Review,* 9 (1984), 104–113.

11. This section draws heavily on D. J. Hickson, C. R. Hinings, C. A. Lee, R. E. Schneck, and D. J. Pennings, "A Strategic Contingencies Theory of Intraorganizational Power," *Ad-

ministrative Science Quarterly,* 16 (1971), 216–227; and C. R. Hinings, D. J. Hickson, J. M. Pennings, and R. E. Schneck, "Structural Conditions of Interorganizational Power," *Administrative Science Quarterly,* 19 (1974), 22–44.

12. Hickson et al., "A Strategic Contingencies Theory."

13. Pettigrew, *The Politics of Organizational Decision Making.*

14. Hickson et al., "A Strategic Contingencies Theory." Pettigrew, *The Politics of Organizational Decision Making.*

15. Hickson et al., "A Strategic Contingencies Theory."

16. H. A. Landsberger, "The Horizontal Dimension in Bureaucracy," *Administrative Science Quarterly,* 6 (1961), 299–232.

17. G. R. Salancik and J. Pfeffer, "The Bases and Use of Power in Organizational Decision Making: The Case of a University," *Administrative Science Quarterly,* 19 (1974), 453–473.

18. J. A. Litterer, "Conflict in Organizations: A Reexamination," *Academy of Management Journal,* 9 (1966), 178–186. S. M. Schmidt and T. A. Kochan, "Conflict: Towards Conceptual Clarity," *Administrative Science Quarterly,* 13 (1972), 359–370. Miles, *Macro Organizational Behavior.*

19. Miles, *Macro Organizational Behavior.*

20. S. P. Robbins, *Managing Organizational Conflict: A Nontraditional Approach* (Englewood Cliffs, N.J.: Prentice-Hall, 1974). L. Coser, *The Functions of Social Conflict* (New York: Free Press, 1956).

21. This discussion owes much to the seminal work of the following authors: Lou R. Pondy, "Organizational Conflict:

Concepts and Models," *Administrative Science Quarterly*, 2 (1967), 296–320; and R. E. Walton and J. M. Dutton, "The Management of Interdepartmental Conflict: A Model and Review," *Administrative Science Quarterly*, 14 (1969), 62–73.

22. M. Dalton, *Men Who Manage* (New York: Wiley, 1959). Walton and Dutton, "The Management of Interdepartmental Conflict."

23. Walton and Dutton, "The Management of Interdepartmental Conflict." J. McCann and J. R. Galbraith, "Interdepartmental Relationships," in P. C. Nystrom and W. H. Starbuck (eds.), *Handbook of Organizational Design* (New York: Oxford University Press, 1981).

24. J. D. Thompson, *Organizations in Action* (New York: McGraw-Hill, 1967).

25. Walton and Dutton, "The Management of Interdepartmental Conflict," p. 65.

26. Ibid., p. 68.

27. Pondy, "Organizational Conflict," p. 300.

28. Ibid., p. 310.

29. Ibid., p. 316.

30. T. J. Peters and R. H. Waterman Jr., *In Search of Excellence* (New York: Harper & Row, 1982).

31. J. Thackray, "Restructuring Is the Name of the Hurricane," *Euromoney* (February 1987), 106–108.

32. R. Beckhard, *Organizational Development* (Reading, Mass.: Addison-Wesley, 1969). W. L. French and C. H. Bell Jr., *Organization Development*, 2nd ed. (Englewood Cliffs, N.J.: Prentice-Hall, 1978).

33. L. C. Coch and R. P. French Jr., "Overcoming Resistance to Change," *Human Relations* (August 1948), 512–532. P. R. Lawrence, "How to Deal with Resistance to Change," *Harvard Business Review* (January–February 1969), 4–12.

34. P. Kotter and L. A. Schlesinger, "Choosing Strategies for Change," *Harvard Business Review* (March–April 1979), 106–114.

35. J. R. Galbraith, "Designing the Innovative Organization," *Organization Dynamics* (Winter 1982), 5–25.

36. M. Beer, *Organizational Change and Development* (Santa Monica, Calif.: Goodyear, 1980). L. E. Greiner, "Patterns of Organizational Change," *Harvard Business Review* (May–June 1967), 3–5.

P A R T

IV

CASE STUDY
ANALYSIS

Chapter 14

ANALYZING AND
WRITING A
CASE STUDY

14.1 WHAT IS CASE STUDY ANALYSIS?

Case study analysis is an integral part of a course in strategic management. The purpose of a case study is to provide students with experience of the strategic management problems faced by actual organizations. A case study presents an account of what happened to a business or industry over a number of years. It chronicles the events that managers had to deal with, such as changes in the competitive environment, and charts the managers' response, which usually involved changing the business- or corporate-level strategy. The cases in Part IV of this book cover a wide range of issues and problems that managers have had to confront. Some cases are about finding the right business-level strategy to compete in changing industry conditions. Some are about companies that grew by acquisition, with little concern for the rationale behind their growth, and how this affected their future profitability. Each case is different because each organization is different. The underlying thread in all the cases, however, is the use of strategic management techniques to solve business problems.

Cases prove valuable in a strategic management course for several reasons. First, cases provide you, the student, with experience of organizational problems that you probably have not had the opportunity to experience firsthand. In a relatively short period of time, a semester, you will have the chance to appreciate and analyze the problems faced by many different companies and to understand how managers tried to deal with them.

Second, cases illustrate the theory and content of strategic management—that is, all the information that we have presented to you in the previous thirteen chapters of this book. This information has been collected, discovered, and distilled from the observations, research, and experience of managers and academics. The meaning and implication of this information are made clearer when they are applied to case studies. The theory and concepts help reveal what is going on in the companies studied and allow you to evaluate the solutions that specific companies adopted to deal with their problems. Consequently, when you analyze cases, you will be like a detective who, with a set of conceptual tools, probes what happened and what or who was responsible, and then marshals the evidence that provides the solution. Top managers enjoy the thrill of testing their problem-solving abilities in the real world. After all, it is important to remember that no one knows what the right answer is. All that managers can do is to make the best guess. In fact, managers say repeatedly that they are happy if they are right only half the time in solving strategic problems. Strategic management is an uncertain game, and using cases to see how theory can be put to practice is one way of improving your skills in diagnostic investigation.

The third advantage of case studies is that they provide you with the opportunity to participate in class and gain experience in presenting your ideas. Sometimes the instructor will call on students as a group to identify what was going on in a case, and through classroom discussion the issue and solutions to the problem in the case will reveal themselves. In this situation, you will have to organize your views and conclusions so that you can present them to the class. Be prepared for a discussion of your ideas. Because your classmates may have analyzed the issues differently from you, they will want you to argue your points before you can convince them, and so be prepared for debate. This mode of discussion is an example of the dialectical approach to decision making that you may recall from Chapter 1. This is how decisions are made in the actual business world. Sometimes instructors will assign an individual, or more commonly a group, to analyze the case before the whole class. The individual or group will probably be responsible for a thirty- to forty-minute presentation of the case to the class, and in that presentation must cover the issues involved, the problems facing the company, and a series of recommendations for resolving those problems. Then the discussion will be thrown open to the class, and you will have to defend your ideas. Through such discussions and presentations, you will experience how to convey your ideas effectively to others. Remember that a great deal of managers' time is spent in these kinds of situations, presenting their ideas and engaging in discussion with other managers, who have their own views about what is going on. Thus you will experience in the classroom the actual process of strategic management, and this will serve you well in your future career.

If you work in groups to analyze case studies, you will also learn about the group process involved in joint work. When people work in groups, it is often difficult to schedule time and allocate responsibility for the case analysis. There will always be group members who shirk or who are so sure of their own ideas that they try to dominate the group's analysis. Most of strategic management takes place in groups, however, and it is best if you learn about these problems now.

14.2 ANALYZING A CASE STUDY

As just mentioned, the purpose of the case study is to let you apply the concepts of strategic management when you analyze the issues facing a specific company. Thus to analyze a case study, it is necessary to closely examine the issues with which the company is involved. This will often take several readings of the case: a first reading, to grasp the overall picture of what is happening to a company, and then subsequent readings, to discover and grasp the specific problems.

Generally, detailed analysis of a case study should include eight areas:

1. The history, development and growth of the company over time
2. The identification of the company's internal strengths and weaknesses
3. The nature of the external environment surrounding the company
4. A SWOT analysis
5. The kind of corporate-level strategy pursued by a company
6. The nature of the company's business-level strategy
7. The company's structure and control systems and how they match its strategy
8. Recommendations

To analyze a case, you need to apply the course concepts to each of these areas. Which concepts to use is obvious from the chapter titles. For example, to analyze the company's environment, you would use Chapter 3, on environmental analysis. To help you further, we next offer a brief guide to some of the main strategic management concepts that can be used to analyze the case material for each of the points we have just noted.

1. *Analyzing the company's history, development and growth.* A convenient way to investigate how a company's past strategy and structure affect it in the present is to chart the critical incidents in its history—that is, the events that were the most unusual or the most essential for its development into the company it is today. Some of the events have to do with its founding, its initial products, how it made new product market decisions, and how it developed and chose functional competencies to pursue. Its entry into new businesses and shifts in its main lines of business are also important milestones to consider.

2. *Identification of the company's internal strengths and weaknesses.* Once the historical profile is completed, you can begin the SWOT analysis. Take all the incidents you have charted and use them to develop an account of the company's strengths and weaknesses as they have emerged historically. Examine each of the value creation functions of the company, and identify the functions in which the company is currently strong and currently weak. Some companies might be weak in marketing, and some strong in research and development. Make lists of these strengths and weaknesses. Table 14.1 gives examples of what might go in these lists.

3. *Environmental analysis.* The next step is to identify environmental opportunities and threats. Here you should apply all the concepts from Chapter 3, on industry and macroenvironments, to analyze the environment the company is confronting. Of particular importance at the industry level is Porter's five forces model and the stage of the life cycle model. Which factors in the macroenvironment will appear salient depends on the specific company being analyzed. However, use each concept in turn—for instance, demographic factors—to see if it is relevant for the company in question.

TABLE 14.1   **A SWOT checklist**

Potential internal strengths	Potential internal weaknesses
Many product lines?	Obsolete, narrow product lines?
Broad market coverage?	Rising manufacturing costs?
Manufacturing competence?	Decline in R&D innovations?
Good marketing skills?	Poor marketing plan?
Good materials management systems?	Poor materials management systems?
R&D skills and leadership?	Loss of customer good will?
Information system competencies?	Indequate information systems?
Human resource competencies?	Inadequate human resources?
Brand name reputation?	Loss of brand name capital?
Portfolio management skills?	Growth without direction?
Cost or differentiation advantage?	Bad portfolio management?
New-venture management expertise?	Loss of corporate direction?
Appropriate management style?	Infighting among divisions?
Appropriate organizational structure?	Loss of corporate control?
Appropriate control systems?	Inappropriate organizational structure and control systems?
Ability to manage strategic change?	High conflict and politics?
Well-developed corporate strategy?	Poor financial management?
Good financial management?	Others?
Others?	
Potential environmental opportunities	**Potential environmental threats**
Expand core business(es)?	Attacks on core business(es)?
Exploit new market segments?	Increases in domestic competition?
Widen product range?	Increase in foreign competition?
Extend cost or differentiation advantage?	Change in consumer tastes?
Diversify into new growth businesses?	Fall in barriers to entry?
Expand into foreign markets?	Rise in new or substitute products?
Apply R&D skills in new areas?	Increase in industry rivalry?
Enter new related businesses?	New forms of industry competition?
Vertically integrate forward?	Potential for takeover?
Vertically integrate backward?	Existence of corporate raiders?
Enlarge corporate portfolio?	Increase in regional competition?
Overcome barriers to entry?	Changes in demographic factors?
Reduce rivalry among competitors?	Changes in economic factors?
Make profitable new acquisitions?	Downturn in economy?
Apply brand name capital in new areas?	Rising labor costs?
Seek fast market growth?	Slower market growth?
Others?	Others?

Having done this analysis, you will have generated both an analysis of the company's environment and a list of opportunities and threats. Table 14.1 also lists some common environmental opportunities and threats that you might look for, but the list you generate will be specific to your company.

4.   *The SWOT analysis.* Having identified the company's external opportunities and threats, as well as its internal strengths and weaknesses, you need to consider what your findings mean. In other words, you need to balance strengths and weaknesses against opportunities and threats. Is the company in an overall strong competitive position? Can it continue to pursue its current business- or corporate-level strategy profitably? What can the company do to turn weaknesses into strengths and threats into opportunities? Can it develop new functional, business, or corporate strategies to accomplish this change? *Never merely generate the SWOT analysis and then put it aside.* Because it provides a succinct summary of the company's condition, a good SWOT analysis is the key to all the analyses that follow.

5. *Analyzing corporate-level strategy.* To analyze a company's corporate-level strategy, you first need to define the company's mission and goals. Sometimes the mission and goals will be stated explicitly in the case; at other times you will have to infer them from available information. The information you need to collect to find out the company's corporate strategy includes such factors as its line(s) of business and the nature of its subsidiaries and acquisitions. It is important to analyze the relationship among the company's businesses. Do they trade or exchange resources? Are there gains to be achieved from synergy? Or is the company just running a portfolio of investments? This analysis should enable you to define the corporate strategy that the company is pursuing (for example, related or unrelated diversification, or a combination of both) and also to conclude whether the company operates in just one core business. Then take your SWOT analysis and debate the merits of this strategy. Is it appropriate, given the environment the company is in? Could a change in corporate strategy provide the company with new opportunities or transform a weakness into a strength? For example, should the company diversify from its core business into new businesses?

There are other issues to be considered as well. How has the company's strategy changed over time? Why? What is the claimed rationale for the change? Often it is a good idea to apply a *portfolio matrix technique* to the company's businesses or products to analyze its situation and identify which divisions are stars or dogs. It is also useful to explore how the company has built its portfolio over time. Did it acquire new businesses or did it internally venture its own? All these factors provide clues about the company and indicate ways of improving its future performance.

6. *Analyzing business-level strategy.* Once you know the company's corporate-level strategy and have done the SWOT analysis, the next step is to identify the company's business-level strategy. If the company is a single-business company, then its business-level strategy is identical to its corporate-level strategy. If the company is in many businesses, then each business will have its own business-level strategy. You will need to identify the company's generic competitive strategy—differentiation, low cost, or focus—and its investment strategy, given the company's relative competitive position and the stage of the life cycle. The company may also market different products using different business-level strategies: For example, it may offer a low-cost prod-

uct range and a line of differentiated products. You should be sure to give a full account of a company's business-level strategy to show how it competes.

Identifying the functional strategies that a company pursues to achieve its business-level strategy is very important. The SWOT analysis will have provided you with information on the company's functional competencies. You should further investigate production, marketing, or research and development strategy to gain a picture of where the company is going. For example, pursuing a low-cost or a differentiation strategy successfully requires a very different set of competencies. Has the company developed the right ones? If it has, how can it exploit them further?

The SWOT analysis is especially important at this point if the industry analysis, particularly Porter's model, has revealed the threats to the company from the environment. Can the company deal with these threats? How should it change its business-level strategy to counter them? To evaluate the potential of a company's business-level strategy, you must first perform a thorough SWOT analysis that captures the essence of its problems.

Once you complete this analysis, you will have a full picture of the way the company is operating and be in a position to evaluate the potential of its strategy. Thus you will be able to make recommendations concerning the pattern of its future actions. But first you need to consider strategy implementation, or the way the company tries to achieve its strategy.

7. *Analyzing structure and control systems.* The aim of the analysis here is to identify what structure and control systems the company is using to implement its strategy and to evaluate whether that structure is the appropriate one for the company. As we discuss in Chapter 12, different corporate and business strategies require different structures. The chapter, and particularly Tables 12.2, 12.3, and 12.4, provide you with the conceptual tools to determine *the degree of fit between the company's strategy and structure.* For example, you need to assess whether the company has the right level of vertical differentiation (for instance, does it have the appropriate number of levels in the hierarchy or decentralized control?), or horizontal differentiation (does it use a functional structure when it should be using a product structure?). Similarly, is the company using the right integration or control systems to manage its operations? Are managers being appropriately rewarded? Are the right rewards in place for encouraging cooperation among divisions? These are all issues that should be considered.

In some cases, there will be little information on these issues, whereas in others there will be a lot. Obviously, in writing each case, you should gear the analysis toward its most salient issues.

In some cases, organizational conflict, power, and politics will be important issues. Try and analyze why these problems are occurring. Is it because of bad strategy formulation or bad strategy implementation? Organizational change is an issue in most of the cases because companies in the cases are attempting to alter their strategies or structures to solve strategic problems. Thus as a part of the analysis, you might suggest an action plan that the company in question could use to achieve its goals. For example, you might list the steps it would need to go through to alter its business-level strategy from differentiation to focus in a logical sequence.

8. *Making recommendations.* The last part of the case analysis process involves making recommendations based on your analysis of the case. Obviously, the quality of your recommendations is a direct result of the thoroughness with which you prepared the case analysis. The work you put into the case analysis is obvious to the professor from the nature of your recommendations. Recommendations are directed at solving whatever strategic problem the company is facing and at increasing its future profitability. Your recommendations should be in line with your analysis, that is, should follow logically from the previous discussion. For example, your recommendations will generally center on the specific ways of changing functional, business, and corporate strategy and organizational structure and control to improve business performance. The set of recommendations will be specific to each case, and so it is difficult to discuss these recommendations here. Such recommendations might include an increase in spending on specific research and development projects, the divesting of certain businesses, a change from a strategy of unrelated to related diversification, an increase in the level of integration among divisions by using task forces and teams, or a move to a different kind of structure to implement a new business-level strategy. Again, make sure your recommendations are mutually consistent and are written in the form of an action plan. The plan might contain a timetable that sequences the actions for changing the company's strategy and a description of how changes at the corporate level will necessitate changes at the business level and subsequently at the functional level.

After following all these stages, you will have performed a thorough analysis of the case and will be in a position to join in class discussion or present your ideas to the class, depending on the format used by your professor. Remember that you must tailor your analysis to suit the specific issue discussed in your case. In some cases, you might omit completely one of the stages of the analysis because it is not relevant to the situation you are considering. You must be sensitive to the needs of the case and not apply the framework we have discussed in this section blindly. The framework is meant only as a guide, and not as an outline that you must use to do a successful analysis.

14.3 WRITING A CASE STUDY

Often, as part of your course requirements, you will need to write up one or more of the cases and present your instructor with a written case analysis. This may be an individual or a group report. Whatever the situation, there are certain guidelines to follow in writing a case that will improve the evaluation that your analysis will receive from your teacher. Before we discuss these guidelines, and before you use them, make sure that they do not conflict with any instructions your teacher has given you.

The main point is how to structure the writing of a case study. Generally, if you follow the stages of analysis just discussed, *you will already have a good structure for your written discussion.* All reports begin with an *introduction* to the case. In it, you outline briefly what the company does, how it developed historically, what problems it is experiencing, and how you are going to approach the issues in the case write-up. Do this sequentially, saying, "First, we discuss the environment of Company X . . . third, we discuss Company X's business-level strategy . . . Last, we provide recommendations for turning around Company X's business."

In the second part of the case, the strategic analysis section, do the SWOT analysis, analyze and discuss the nature and problems of the company's business-level and corporate strategy, and then analyze its structure and control systems. Make sure you use plenty of headings and subheadings to structure your analysis. For example, have separate sections on any important conceptual tool you use. Thus you might have a section on Porter's five forces model as part of your analysis of the environment. Or you might offer a separate section on portfolio techniques when analyzing a company's corporate strategy. Tailor the sections and subsections to the specific issue of importance in the case.

In the third part of the case write-up, present your solutions and recommendations. Be comprehensive, do this in line with the previous analysis so that the recommendations fit together, and move logically from one to the next. The recommendations section is very revealing because, as we mentioned earlier, your teacher will have a good idea of how much work you put into the case from the quality of your recommendations.

Following this framework will provide a good structure for most written reports, though obviously it must be shaped to fit the individual case being considered. Some cases are about excellent companies experiencing no problems. In such instances, it is hard to write recommendations. Instead, you can focus on analyzing why the company is doing so well and using that analysis to structure the discussion. There are some minor points to note that can also affect the evaluation you receive.

1. Do not repeat in summary form large pieces of factual information from the case and feed them back to the instructor in the report. The instructor has also read the case and knows what is going on. Rather, use the information in the case to illustrate your statements, to defend your arguments, or to make salient points. Beyond the brief introduction to the company, you must avoid being *descriptive;* instead, you must be *analytical.*

2. Make sure the sections and subsections of your discussion flow logically and smoothly from one to the next. That is, try to build on what has gone before so that the case study builds to a climax. This is particularly important for

group cases. With group cases there is a tendency for people to split up the work and say, "I'll do the beginning, you take the middle, and I'll do the end." The result is bad because the parts of the analysis do not flow from one to the next, and it is obvious to the instructor that no real group work has been done.

3. Avoid grammatical and spelling errors. They make the paper seem sloppy.

4. Some cases dealing with well known companies end in 1986 or 1987 because no later information was available when the case was written. If possible, do a library search for more information on what has happened to the company since then. Following are sources of information for performing this search:

    Datext is a service on compact disk that gives an amazing amount of good information.
    F&S Predicasts provide a listing on a yearly basis of all the articles written about a particular company. Simply reading the titles gives an indication of what has been happening in the company.
    10K annual reports often provide an organizational chart.
    Write to the company for information.
    Fortune and *Business Week* have many articles on companies featured in the cases in this book.
    Standard & Poor's industry reports provide detailed information about the competitive conditions facing the company's industry.

5. Sometimes the instructor will hand out questions for each case to help you in your analysis. Use these as a guide for analyzing and writing the case because they often illuminate the important issues that have to be covered in the discussion.

If you follow the guidelines in this section, you should be able to write a thorough and effective evaluation.

14.4 THE ROLE OF FINANCIAL ANALYSIS IN CASE STUDY ANALYSIS

Another important aspect of analyzing and writing a case study is the role and use of financial information. A careful analysis of the company's financial condition immensely improves a case write-up. After all, these figures represent the concrete results of the company's strategy and structure. Many useful financial performance ratios can be derived from a company's balance sheet and profit and loss accounts. These can be broken down into four different subgroups: profit ratios, liquidity ratios, leverage ratios, and shareholder-return ratios. In addition to these performance ratios, a company's *cash flow* position is of critical importance and should be assessed.

Profit Ratios

Profit ratios measure the efficiency with which the company uses its resources. The more efficient the company, the greater is its profitability. It is useful to compare a company's profitability against that of its major competitors in its industry. Such a comparison will tell you whether the company is operating more or less efficiently than its rivals. In addition, the change in a company's profit ratios over time will tell you whether its performance is improving or declining.

A number of different profit ratios can be used, and each of them measure a different aspect of a company's performance. The most commonly used profit ratios are as follows:

1. *Gross profit margin.* The gross profit margin gives an indication of the total margin available to cover operating expenses and yield a profit. It is a measure of the value a company creates net of the cost of performing value creation activities. It is defined as follows:

$$\text{Gross Profit Margin} = \frac{\text{Sales Revenue} - \text{Cost of Goods Sold}}{\text{Sales Revenue}}$$

2. *Return on total assets.* This measures the return earned on the total investment in a company. It is defined as follows:

$$\text{Return on Total Assets} = \frac{\text{Profits After Tax} + \text{Interest}}{\text{Total Assets}}$$

Total assets refer to fixed assets, plus current assets. Interest payments are added back to after-tax profits to account for the financing of current assets by creditors.

3. *Return on stockholders' equity.* Often referred to as return on net worth, this measures the rate of return on stockholders' investment in the company. In theory, a company attempting to maximize the wealth of its stockholders should be trying to maximize this ratio. It is defined as follows:

$$\text{Return on Stockholders' Equity} = \frac{\text{Profit After Tax and Interest}}{\text{Total Stockholders' Equity}}$$

Liquidity Ratios

A company's liquidity is a measure of its ability to meet unexpected contingencies such as a prolonged strike or price war. An asset is termed "liquid" if it can be quickly converted into cash. A company's current assets are liquid assets. Liquidity can be in the form of idle working capital, marketable securities, or funding in reserve, such as unused lines of credit. A company that lacks liquidity is in a weak financial position. For example, if a company whose sales revenues are hurt by a strike lacks liquidity, it might not be able to generate the cash necessary to meet the claims of short-term creditors, such as banks. Bankruptcy could ultimately result from such a scenario. Companies with major investment in fixed assets, such as steel mills or auto plants, tend to be less liquid than companies with a lower level of fixed assets. This is because fixed assets cannot be easily translated into cash and because they often necessitate major fixed costs, which place heavy demands on a company's cash reserves in times of trouble.

Two commonly used liquidity ratios are as follows:

1. *Current ratio.* The current ratio measures the extent to which the claims of short-term creditors are covered by assets that can be quickly converted into cash. If a company's current ratio declines to less than 1, the company could be in serious trouble should an unexpected contingency arise. The ratio is defined as follows:

$$\text{Current Ratio} = \frac{\text{Current Assets}}{\text{Current Liabilities}}$$

2. *Quick ratio.* The quick ratio measures a company's ability to pay off the claims of short-term creditors without relying on the sale of its inventories. This is a valuable measure since in practice the sale of inventories is often difficult. It is defined as follows:

$$\text{Quick Ratio} = \frac{\text{Current Assets} - \text{Inventories}}{\text{Current Liabilities}}$$

Leverage Ratios

A company is said to be highly leveraged when it relies on external sources of funds rather than internally generated funds to finance its investments. In some situations, it may make good sense for a company to be highly leveraged. For example, many successful high-tech start-ups have relied almost entirely on external sources of funds to finance their initial investments. On the other hand, high leverage can become a terminal weakness, particularly when rising interest rates increase the cost of debt beyond a company's ability to service that debt. Generally, a highly leveraged company is more vulnerable to changes in the cost of finance than a company that funds its investments from internally generated cash.

Three commonly used leverage ratios are as follows:

1. *Debt-to-assets ratio.* The debt-to-assets ratio is the most direct measure of the extent to which borrowed funds have been used to finance a company's investments. It is defined as follows:

$$\text{Debt-to-Assets} = \frac{\text{Total Debt}}{\text{Total Assets}}$$

Total debt is the sum of a company's current liabilities and its long-term debt, and total assets are the sum of fixed assets and current assets.

2. *Long-term debt-to-equity ratio.* The long-term debt-to-equity measure indicates the balance between debt and equity in a company's long-term capital structure. This is perhaps the most widely used measure of a company's leverage. It is defined as follows:

$$\text{Debt-to-Equity} = \frac{\text{Long-term Debt}}{\text{Total Stockholders' Equity}}$$

3. *Times-covered ratio.* The times-covered ratio measures the extent to which a company's gross profit covers its annual interest payments. If the times-covered ratio declines to less than 1, then the company is unable to meet its interest costs and is technically insolvent. The ratio is defined as follows:

$$\text{Times-covered Ratio} = \frac{\text{Profits Before Interest and Tax}}{\text{Total Interest Charges}}$$

Shareholder-Return Ratios

Shareholder-return ratios measure the return earned by shareholders from holding stock in the company. Given the goal of maximizing stockholder wealth, providing their shareholders with an adequate rate of return is a primary objective of most companies. As with profit ratios, it can be helpful to compare a company's shareholder returns against those of similar companies. This will give you a yardstick for determining how well the company is satisfying the demands of this particularly important group of organizational constituents. Two commonly used ratios are given below.

1. *Total shareholder returns.* Total shareholder returns measure the returns earned by time $t + 1$ on an investment in a company's stock made at time t. (*Time t* is the time at which the initial investment is made.) Total shareholder

returns include both dividend payments and appreciation in the value of the stock (adjusted for stock splits) and are defined as follows:

$$\text{Total Shareholder Returns} = \text{Stock Price}(t + 1) - \text{Stock Price}(t)$$

$$+ \frac{\text{Sum of Annual Dividends per Share}}{\text{Stock Price}(t)}$$

Thus if a shareholder invests $2 at time t, and at time $t + 1$ the share is worth $3, while the sum of annual dividends for the period t to $t + 1$ has amounted to $0.2, total shareholder returns are equal to $(3 - 2 + 0.2)/2 = 0.6$, that is a 60-percent return on an initial investment of $2 made at time t.

2. *Dividend yield.* The dividend yield measures the return to shareholders received in the form of dividends. It is defined as follows:

$$\text{Dividend Yield} = \frac{\text{Dividends per Share}}{\text{Market Price per Share}}$$

Market price per share can be calculated for the first of the year, in which case the dividend yield refers to the return on an investment made at the beginning of the year. Alternatively, the average share price over the year may be used. A word of caution: a company that pays out high annual dividends may leave itself with too few cash reserves to meet its investment needs and may have to borrow more than it would choose to do from external sources of finance. In turn, the subsequent high level of debt may depress the market value of a company's stock. Thus a high dividend yield is not always a good thing.

Cash Flow

A company's cash flow position is an important indicator of its financial status. Cash flow refers to the surplus of internally generated funds over expenditure. Some businesses are cash hungry, whereas others are net generators of cash. Cash flow is important for what it tells us about a company's financing needs. A strong positive cash flow enables a company to fund future investments without having to borrow money from bankers or investors. This is desirable because the company avoids the need to pay out interest or dividends. A weak or negative cash flow means that a company has to turn to external sources to fund future investments. Generally, companies in high-growth industries often find themselves in a poor cash flow position (because their investment needs are substantial), whereas successful companies based in mature industries find themselves in a strong cash flow position.

A company's internally generated cash flow is calculated by adding back its depreciation provision to profits after interest, taxes, and dividend payments. If this figure is insufficient to cover proposed new investment expenditures, the company has little choice but to borrow funds to make up the shortfall—or curtail investments. If this figure exceeds proposed new investments, the company can use the excess to build up its liquidity (that is, through investments in financial assets) or to repay existing loans ahead of schedule.

14.5 CONCLUSION

When evaluating a case, it is important to be *systematic*. Analyze the case in a logical fashion, beginning with the identification of operating and financial strengths and weaknesses and environmental opportunities and threats. Move on to assess the value of a company's current strategies only when you are fully conversant with the SWOT of the company. Ask yourself whether the company's current strategies make sense, given its SWOT. If they do not, what changes need to be made? What are your recommendations? Above all, link any strategic recommendations you may make to the SWOT analysis. State explicitly how the strategies you identify take advantage of company strengths to exploit environmental opportunities, how they rectify company weaknesses, and how they counter environmental threats. And do not forget to outline what needs to be done to implement your recommendations.

Index